TASTING GOOD

TASTING GOOD

The International Salt-Free Diet Cookbook

by MERLE SCHELL

The Bobbs-Merrill Company, Inc.
Indianapolis New York

Library of Congress Cataloging in Publication Data

Schell, Merle.
  Tasting good.

  Includes index.
  1. Salt-free diet—Recipes.   I. Title.   II. Title:
International salt-free diet.
RM237.8.S33   613.2′8   80-2729
ISBN 0-672-52623-9

Designed by J. Tschantre Graphic Services, Ltd.
Manufactured in the United States of America

First printing

*To all who will, I hope, find this book helpful
and to those whose thoughtful,
generous guidance and kind encouragement
enabled me to write it.*

CONTENTS

PREFACE

The importance of sodium as a contributing factor in the development of high blood pressure has been demonstrated in a large number of studies both in man and in animal experiments. There is general agreement that while sodium chloride is essential for the maintenance of normal blood pressure and circulatory function, most Americans eat much more sodium chloride than is necessary or desirable. Sodium is widely distributed as a food preservative and consumers may be unaware of its presence in food. It is also generally believed that in the absence of great physical activity or extremely hot climates, dietary sodium intake should be reduced to approximately 2 grams of sodium chloride per day. In the presence of hypertension and certain forms of heart and kidney disease, salt intake may have to be reduced substantially.

It is in this context of frequently life-long excessive salt intake in most adult Americans and the common occurrence of high blood pressure which, as noted earlier, is aggravated by high salt diets, that this book by Merle Schell is particularly timely. Miss Schell has written a practical guide to maintaining a low sodium diet. The reader will find a list of low sodium foods and manufacturers and a great deal of encouragement for continuing low sodium dietary habits.

Food labelling for sodium content is one important method of educating consumers and helping them to avoid high sodium foods. The Federal Register of December 21, 1979, contains "a summary of food labelling guides" prepared by three Federal agencies: the Food and Drug Administration, the U.S. Department of Agriculture, and the Federal Trade Commission. This document contains recommendations for future legislative action to require sodium labelling in the interest of public health. Regulations will also be developed for defining low sodium and reduced sodium foods. These regulations, together with greater public understanding of the role of sodium in the development of cardiovascular disorders, may ultimately lead to a reduction in the incidence of hypertension in the United States. Miss Schell's recipes will help in this continued effort for public education in the benefits of reduced sodium chloride intake.

Leslie Baer, M.D.

Dr. Leslie Baer is a research and hypertension specialist, affiliated with the Columbia-Presbyterian Hospital in New York City. Dr. Baer identified the author's own medical problem, thus encouraging her to write this book.

ACKNOWLEDGMENTS

Anyone who has ever written a book gratefully appreciates the love and patience of family and friends who love you in spite of yourself, even when the going gets rough. I'd like to thank mine.

And there are other special people who helped and encouraged me to put it all together. To them, my sincere and heartfelt thanks:

- Dr. Leslie Baer, my doctor, Hypertension and Kidney Reseach Specialist, The Columbia Presbyterian Hospital, New York City, for his care and wonderful advice.
- Dr. Frank Pappalardo, Nephrologist, associated with Northern Westchester Hospital, New York. Dr. Pappalardo, who also specializes in renal disorders, guided me to pertinent research material and checked the fundamental medical data presented here. For his constant and sincere support, my grateful thanks.
- Ms. Almeda Dickson, Research Dietician with the Department of Medicine at Columbia University, New York City. Ms. Dixon has a special interest in the clinical application of nutrition. She not only provided source material in this area but personally reviewed the diet master plan and all other nutritional information provided in this book. To her, my special thanks for her invaluable contributions and her patient willingness to answer my innumerable questions.
- Mary Corey, Andrea Feinberg, William McGuire and Michael Young who spent week after week making order out of the chaotic scribble of my recipes.
- Ms. Carol Wilson whose total professionalism and unflagging good humor produced the finished, beautifully typed manuscript.
- Ms. Pam Rabin for her professional care and knowledge in preparing this book for publication. Her skill has made the recipes easy to understand and follow.
- Mr. Peter Ginsberg and Ms. Lynne Spaulding, my agent and editor, respectively. Their belief and enthusiasm made this book a reality.

INTRODUCTION

The purpose of this book is to reverse the belief that saltless food is bland, boring, and tasteless, and that people on salt restricted diets are thereby automatically denied the pleasure of eating. It isn't true.

Herbs, wine, vinegar, garlic, lemon juice, low sodium condiments and foods, and other wonderful and versatile flavorings—when used with imagination, creative flair, and a sense of humor—can create the taste of salt or overcome the need for it. And *Tasting Good* will show you how to use them all to create a varied and plentiful selection of international dishes so delicious you'll swear they contain salt. But they'll only taste that way.

With *Tasting Good,* you can continue to eat all the foods you like, drink if you want to, yet stay easily within your salt limits. Do you enjoy a cocktail before dinner? Wine with your meal? Be my guest. Do you like butter or gravy on your potatoes? Relish it. Do you love Chinese food? Italian food? Mexican, French, and German food? Have them all. With the recipes in this book, you won't even have to give up the salty taste —just the salt!

I know because I'm on a 250 mgs. sodium diet and have been for the last six years. My problem is unusual. It's a combination of hypokalemia (low potassium) and a high tendency to retain fluid which, in the past, caused chronic weight fluctuations. I'm 5' 3", and my normal weight is 102 pounds. But I used to ride up and down the scales like the proverbial yo-yo. Doctor after doctor placed me on every conceivable diet and prescribed numerous diuretics. Nothing worked. Temporary weight loss was followed by abnormal weight gains—up to 5 pounds per day.

I was caught in a vicious Catch-22. The diets all allowed salt. The diuretics washed it away, along with potassium and so much fluid I became dehydrated. So my body craved fluid which the salt obligingly retained. What's more, I was scared because I knew how toxic diuretics can be. I suffered from all the side effects: extremely low blood pressure, nausea, dizziness, general weakness, double vision, shortness of breath, severe cramps in my legs and hands. I was thin, but the penalty was severe.

This went on for 10 years. Finally, a doctor I knew urged me to see Dr. Leslie Baer

1

who had done extensive research in salt-related illnesses. Dr. Baer had me check into the hospital where he ran extensive tests, told me what was wrong, and planned a program for me. Two weeks later, I walked out of the hospital, pill-free yet two pounds lighter than the day I walked in, feeling in complete control of my body, my physical energy on a par with my mental spirit.

Normal. Healthy. With peace of mind for the first time I could remember. And my weight and I have stayed that way on a low sodium diet. The pleasure and relief I felt from knowing what was wrong and how to control it were and are extraordinary. But when I left the hospital, I was also resentful that I'd never again be able to enjoy Chinese food, Italian food, French food, or any of the other ethnic delights that call for generous amounts of salt.

I refused to accept this. The sacrifice was too great. Simply eliminating salt (soy sauce in Chinese cuisine) from recipes was not the answer if the food was to taste authentically good. So I decided to find ways to provide a salt flavor for these foods.

Tasting Good is the result. Experimenting, learning how to cook for people used to tasting salt, as well as for myself, is exciting. It's an art to be constantly mastered. And when I have dinner guests, and no one asks for the salt shaker, I feel positively victorious. So will you.

I want to share these recipes so that you, too, can discover that salt-free foods can be prepared with a minimum of fuss and time and taste so wonderful everyone will enjoy them. Salt-free living is an easy and tasty way to stay healthy. You need only adjust your outlook and replace a few ingredients. Your taste buds will never notice the difference, but your body will.

What's more, if—like me—water retention is part of your weight problem, a well-balanced program that controls sodium and calories can be your means to a permanent happy end. Salt is a sponge for water, which comprises 70% of our body weight. To facilitate weight loss, many doctors are advocating the avoidance of "hidden" salt. For example, hidden salt can be found in ketchup, mayonnaise, pickles, canned fish, and vegetables. The list goes on. But all these foods and more are available in a low sodium version.

So don't count yourself among the 95% of those who lose weight on one fad diet or another only to regain it in a matter of months. Don't torture yourself on starvation diets, banana diets, high protein, low cholesterol, high acid and low fat diets. Just use common sense: don't take in more calories than your body can burn; and hold the salt.

Whatever your reason for living salt-free, know that you are not alone. Millions of people, in the United States alone, are on salt restricted diets. They may suffer from hypertension, gout, heart disease, severe edema, or an assortment of other illnesses.

In general, Americans consume far more salt than is healthy for them. We eat more salt than any other people in the world. And there is a growing awareness of its potential harm.

So why bother with salt when the alternatives can be so tasty? Savor your life as well as your food. A healthful menu and restricted salt will be more naturally tasteful, more beneficial for all of us. Because eating good, feeling good, and looking good go hand in hand in hand.

One final word: You should check with your doctor before using this or any other diet book and its tips.

YOUR DAILY SALT REQUIREMENT

The consensus among medical and health professionals in the United States is that food in its natural state easily supplies enough sodium for our daily needs. But through added or hidden salt (found in processed foods), the average American consumes ten times the amount required. In other words, we overdose on salt and thereby jeopardize our health.

In 1979 a popular woman's magazine interviewed Dr. D. Mark Hegsted who is both Administrator of the Human Nutrition Center of the Department of Agriculture and a member of the Department of Nutrition at Harvard's School of Public Health. On the subject of diet basics, Dr. Hegsted stated, "There is no doubt that we should cut down on our salt intake. The amount anyone needs is probably less than one gram (1000 mgs.) a day—and it is virtually impossible not to get that." Moreover, Dr. Hegsted noted the potential health hazard of salt by expressing, "If salt were a new additive, it is doubtful it would be classified as safe—certainly not at the level at which most consume it."

His opinion echoes the majority. Plainly, there is no need for a minimum daily salt requirement. Foods naturally supply the proper level. However, it is in our best interests to establish and publicize the safe, maximum consumption. So serious is this issue, so widespread the concern, members of Congress have endorsed a petition urging the labelling and limiting of sodium content of commercially prepared foods. Those who actively supported the petition include former Senator George McGovern, as Chairman of the Nutrition Subcommittee of the Senate Agricultural Committee; Representative Claude Pepper, as Chairman of the House Select Committee on Aging; Representative Fred Richmond, for Consumer Relations and Nutrition; and Representative Shirley Chisholm, representing the Black National Caucus.

In 1980, the Food and Drug Administration published that they favor "development of guidelines for restricting the amount of salt in processed foods." Further regulations are being pursued by the sponsors of the original petition—namely, the Center for Science in the Public Interest, a non-profit organization of medical and health professionals.

Such legislation will benefit all of us. Once we consumers are informed, we can act to protect our health. Those on self-imposed salt-restricted diets or those perhaps medically instructed to decrease their salt intake will find it easier to follow their doctor's advice. The rest of us will be able to judge not how much salt we do need, but just how much we don't.

SALT: YOUR SECRET HEALTH ENEMY

Salt is a secret killer. It affects all of us—those with medical problems, those with none. Salt can cause gout, adrenal problems, premature hardening of the arteries, and hypertension. Indeed, it has been traced as the single leading factor of teenage hypertension. It aggravates the condition of people suffering from heart disease, emphysema, and diabetes. It can promote these diseases in people who are presently healthy.

The National Center of Health Statistics reports the number of Americans suffering from salt-related illnesses:

	Approximate No. of Americans
Angina	4,000,000
Arteriosclerosis	680,000
Arthritis	23,000,000
Cardiovascular Disease	40,000,000
Congestive Heart Failure	N/A*
Diabetes	4,000,000
Emphysema	2,000,000
Gout	N/A*
Hypertension	35,000,000**
Kidney Malfunction	6,000,000

Rheumatic Heart Failure	2,000,000
Rheumatism	800,000

*Statistics not available
**There are 25,000,000 people in the U.S. with borderline hypertension.

In other words, millions of people suffer from salt-related illnesses in the United States.

Salt is our enemy—potentially a deadly one. But one we can conquer. All of these diseases can be relieved, to some extent, through salt restriction. In fact, once diagnosed, most doctors prescribe low salt diets as part of a patient's treatment. Yet we can help prevent the onslaught of such illnesses by curbing our salt intake now—especially those of us with family histories of the above cited conditions.

We drink Perrier because it's pure mineral water. We jog to keep our bodies in shape. We cream our skin to help prevent wrinkles. We use fluoride toothpaste to help prevent cavities. But what do we do to help thwart high blood pressure, clogging and hardening of the arteries? In a country where the commitment to looking good and feeling good is almost a constitutional amendment, we do everything but the most important thing to keep our bodies healthy, vigorous, graceful, and slim. We do not eat properly, healthily. Instead we overdose and poison our bodies with salt.

The potential risk of abusive salt consumption is more firmly confirmed each year. In 1977, the Senate Select Committee on Nutrition and Human Needs, headed by Senator George McGovern, advocated dietary goals that urged Americans to reduce their intake of fats, cholesterol, sugar, and sodium and increase consumption of starches and fiber to protect their health.

In a June, 1978, article, Dr. Lot B. Page, professor of medicine at Tufts University School of Medicine, stated that salt, in the present quantities consumed, "constitutes a real health hazard."

In July, 1979, the Surgeon General's Report on Health Promotion and Disease Prevention advised modifying one's lifestyle to "substantially reduce risk for several diseases," including the reduction of salt in the diet. As recently as February, 1980, further efforts to improve health and help prevent disease resulted in dietary guidelines issued jointly by the Departments of Agriculture and Health, Education and Welfare, including the advice to avoid too much sodium.

And again in May, 1980, still another warning came from the Food and Nutrition Board of the National Research Council cautioning that American salt consumption is for many "excessive, averaging about 10 grams a day . . . 20 times more sodium than is needed for good nutritional health."

Other health professionals and consumer organizations are also sounding the alarm. They include: the American College of Preventive Medicine, the American College of Cardiology, the National Urban Coalition, the National Consumers League,

5

and the Consumer Federation of America. Their purpose is to make us aware of salt's dangerous impact on our health, our very lives. We can help ourselves simply by practicing a little preventive medicine.

DIFFERENT WAYS TO CREATE SALTY TASTE

If you crave the taste of salt, don't despair. There are so many food helpers just waiting for you to discover them.

Let's start with herbs and spices. They can distinguish the simplest dish and make it deliciously enjoyable, with no need to pass the salt, thank you. In truth, these particles of plant magic bring out and enhance the natural good flavor of foods and add a sparkle you just might think is salt.

Specifically, black pepper and garlic and onion powders are among the most common seasonings that should be up front on your spice rack. Stir mustard powder or paprika into your favorite dish and *voilà*—a zing you'll want to repeat. Dill, parsley, oregano, sage, tarragon, and thyme—even sweeter spices like cinnamon, cloves, and nutmeg—all add such lovely flavors you'll never miss the salt. In fact, any herbs or spices you choose will give you the same happy surprise with few calories and just as little sodium.

So experiment. Buy in small quantities for spices lose flavor over time. You'll also save money while you decide which ones you rely on most often.

Just remember, a little dash will do you. So for your own creations, start with ¼ teaspoon (less for hot spices like cayenne pepper). You can always add more to taste. And the trick is not to let the spices dominate the food, only celebrate it. Ground spices release their fragrance right away and should be added a half hour or so before a slow-cooked dish is done. But for uncooked foods, like salad dressings, let the herbs and spices permeate the food several hours before serving to allow their full flavors to develop. Otherwise, use spices to season whenever you would have used salt.

In addition to spices, lemon juice and vinegar add a tangy, yes, even salty, flavor to foods. So do wines in a more delicate way. But don't use cooking wines which do contain salt. Inexpensive table wines are better tasting and no higher in price. Fruits and fruit juices are equally wonderful ways to spark foods to new taste pleasures.

And low sodium products are truly a boon. They're easy to find. Most health food stores offer every available low sodium product. More and more supermarkets and cheese shops carry these foods to satisfy customer demand. For openers, stock up on low sodium beef and chicken bouillons. They'll be your best friends because they are instant salt taste-alikes whether you add them to cooked foods or sprinkle them on at the table. They're also high in potassium so you get a double benefit. Make your favorite Russian dressing with low sodium ketchup, mayonnaise, and pickles. Absolutely terrific. Low sodium mustard comes in salad and Dijon style. There are also many low sodium cheeses to choose from. So whenever you feel like mayonnaise, ketchup, or other condiments containing high quantities of hidden salt, opt for their low sodium counterparts. They taste better and you'll be better for it.

One final word about salt taste-alikes. There are many salt substitutes on the market, and some are quite good. But don't latch onto them as the easy answer. First of all, they may not be good for you. You see, salt substitutes usually replace sodium chloride with potassium chloride at high levels which could throw your body off balance. So check with your doctor before you indiscriminately start to shake the container. Second, you could miss out on all the marvelous ways of creating salt taste that we've been discussing.

Whatever you use, you're sure to experience new delights in ways you may not have thought of. Rice steamed in wine; potatoes stuffed with herbs; fish, meat, chicken melting in one of the many low sodium sauces. There are so many ways to create salty taste, you can enjoy the health and weight loss benefits of a salt-free diet with pleasure. And the recipes in this book will enable you to create meals so delicious you'll wish you had made them sooner.

COOKING TIPS

Stock up on herbs, spices, and low sodium foods. Make your own special spice mixes in advance and store them in tightly closed jars in your spice cabinet.

Note: All herbs in this book are dried unless otherwise specified. If you prefer using fresh herbs, substitute three times the amount of dried herbs called for.

Reduce the oils or other fats (and their high calorie content) in recipes as follows:

- *Frying.* For meat or poultry, sear in an ungreased pan over high heat to cook in its own fat. For other foods, use one tablespoon of oil or unsalted butter and cook over very low heat. The foods will release their own juices and continue cooking in them. To keep your pan from burning, add a small amount of broth or wine. Foods will be crispy, ''fried,'' and a lot less fattening.

- *Roasting.* If your favorite recipe calls for frying the meat, fish, or poultry, roast in a very hot oven (425° to 450°) instead. The food will brown quickly and have the same crunchy texture outside and moist, juicy succulence inside.
- *Broiling.* For that delectable contrast of crispiness outside and melting tenderness inside, broil close to the flame.
- *Salad Dressings.* Use half the amount of oil called for plus an equal amount of warm water, shaking thoroughly to blend.
- *Sauces.* A touch of butter or cream, usually added last, will provide all the flavor of more generous quantities.
- *Meats.* Trim meat of fat and you'll also cut away calories. Flank steak (London broil) and round steak have fewer calories (by as much as half) than other cuts of beef.
- *Fish.* Whole fish are sweeter if cooked with head and tail intact.
- *Chicken.* Deduct the weight of skin and carcass to determine how much food you're actually eating. Rule of thumb: 60% of total weight is edible meat. By the way, in recipes calling for chicken legs, you may use both the leg and thigh of a small fryer; the leg or the thigh if the bird is roaster size.
- Whether it's meat, fish, or poultry, slicing, boning, and skinning are always easier, faster, and more precise when you start with slightly frozen food. You can slice to the exact thickness required with no fuss or mess of slippery foods, and skinning becomes a simple task. Just slip a sharp knife under the fibrous membrane connecting the skin to the flesh. Continue cutting as you pull the skin back and off. Slice the meat off the bone, and you've boned it. That's all there is to it.
- Consider the following buying tips for meat, fish, and poultry:

  Without Bone: Figure 4 ounces per serving.
  With bone: Figure 5 ounces per serving.
  Remember, shrinkage during cooking will yield approximately 3 to 3½ ounces per serving. You shouldn't have more than 6 ounces of cooked meat per day.

- Canned fruit packed in water, juice, or light syrup has fewer calories than fruit packed in heavy syrup.
- Vinegar is a great tenderizer. Apply directly to meat or poultry before cooking. Or add to marinade or cooking broth and see tougher meats

emerge plump and tender. (The longer the vinegar has time to work, the more tender the meat or poultry will be.)

- Use your options. If you don't like a recipe ingredient, choose your own replacement. The dish will be just as good—maybe better—and you'll have created your own specialty.
- Use leftovers. You can turn them into a new meal the next day—a quick salad, a nourishing soup, hash patties—or freeze them for use later on.
- Final word: The recipes in this book are not necessarily authentic. They are adaptations faithful to the style, spirit, and flavor of the cultures and countries selected. Suggested accompaniments to a main dish, unless listed as ingredients, are not included in the calorie and sodium counts of the recipes.

DO'S AND DON'TS

- Do read labels. If salt or any sodium compound is listed, do not buy the item. For example:

      sodium bicarbonate (bicarbonate of soda)
      sodium benzoate
      sodium citrate

You get the idea. Other compounds that signal the presence of salt include:

      sodium chloride (salt–2300 mgs. sodium per tsp.)
      sodium alginate
      sodium hydroxide
      sodium propianate
      sodium sulfite
      baking powder (370 mgs. sodium per tsp.)
      baking soda (1000 mgs. sodium per tsp.)
      soda
      brine
      di-sodium phosphate

sodium saccharin
monosodium glutamate (750 mgs. sodium per tsp.)

Do not confuse the last ingredient with monammonium or monopotassium glutamate which are used to flavor low sodium foods.
Do read the label. I cannot stress enough the importance of this simple task. Apparently innocent things—low calorie sodas, upset-stomach remedies, mouthwashes, some mineral waters, some dried fruits, even toothpaste—things you don't think of as salty contain salt or one of its compounds. Read before you buy.

- Do be suspicious of foods marked "No preservatives or artificial ingredients." The fine print on the back will usually reveal the presence of salt.
- Do travel—whether for business, pleasure, or even to a party—with your own personal Care Package. For example, a bottle of your favorite spice mix will slip into your purse and brighten a simple salad or main dish. Other items—available in low sodium varieties—that travel well include: canned goods, potato chips, nuts, mustard, peanut butter. Pack them along with other necessities, and don't forget the can opener. They'll be worth their weight in pleasure when you want to snack or find yourself in a salty environment. But leave behind such perishables as mayonnaise, ketchup, pickles, bread, and cheese unless you'll have access to a refrigerator.
- Do plan in advance. Many railroads and airlines supply special dietary meals. Be sure to ask for salt-free meals and make your request at least 48 hours in advance since such meals are not automatically included.
- Do be careful when eating out. Remember, keep it *simple* to be safest, healthiest, and thinnest. Some tips:

  Request broiled meat, fish, or poultry with no butter, seasoning, sauce, or marinade of any kind. (And remember, portions are usually double what you'd have at home.)
  Order raw vegetables only with your salad, plus oil, vinegar, and a wedge of lemon on the side. Pass on all cooked vegetables since they are prepared in salted water.

- Say "No, thank you" to soups, salad dressings, and sauces. They are salty. Likewise to breads, baked desserts, rice, pasta, and all except baked potatoes. Ask that your potato be served unopened and with no sour cream or butter. (Restaurants usually serve the salted kind.)
- Stick to fresh fruits for dessert.

Following these precautions will keep you healthy and thin. What's more, you can still dine sumptuously and enjoy the best part of eating out— being with friends and not having to clean up afterward.

- Do *ask,* whatever the place or occasion. In stores, if you can't find something you want, speak to the manager. Many stores are just becoming aware of the need for and the variety of low sodium foods. Most—particularly health food stores—will be happy to add your request to their order. If you can supply the manufacturer's name and address (see list in this book), you'll help insure stocking. And remember, the more of us who ask for these foods, the greater the chance they'll be kept in stock. Supply generally meets the demand. In restaurants, be very specific about your requirements. Don't hesitate. Don't be embarrassed or afraid. And don't settle. If the food isn't suitable send it back. Friends will understand. Strangers will have to. Your body and health are of utmost importance to you. They're what counts. No apologies necessary.
- Do check with your doctor before taking salt substitutes, artificial sweeteners, antibiotics, cough medicines, laxatives, pain relievers, and sedatives. Many contain sodium, sometimes in quantities high enough to interfere with your diet.
- Do eat something of everything. Not only will you enjoy the different flavors and textures, but your body will look and feel better, healthier, for the variety and nutritional balance.
- Don't buy foods that have no ingredient listing. (Frozen vegetables are the exception and will be discussed below.) They may be all right, but chances are they're not. So why take chances?
- Don't buy canned vegetables, except those marked low sodium. Don't buy frozen vegetables that carry the phrase "contains a small amount of salt" or something similar. Frozen peas and lima beans, for example. Otherwise, if prepared without a sauce, all other frozen vegetables are packaged without salt. By the way, you can chop fresh vegetables and freeze your own in a tightly closed plastic bag.
- Don't waste your sodium allotment on vegetables high in that element. (See list on Pages 20–21.)
- Don't think the word dietetic means low sodium. It doesn't. Dietetic refers to a lower calorie count due to sugar or fat reduction. Such foods, diet sodas and artificial sweeteners, for example, often contain sodium. Check the ingredients listing.
- Don't use cooking wines or frozen juices. They contain sodium or salt.
- Don't drink carbonated sodas unless you check with your doctor first. Depending on the water source, such drinks may be high in sodium. Two that have been tested and recommended to me are Canada Dry ginger

ale and Coca-Cola, each containing approximately 1 mg. sodium per ounce.

- Don't think all mineral waters are healthy for you. Some may have too much sodium. See list below:

Brand	Sodium Rating	Sodium Mgs. Per 8 oz. Glass
Apollinaris	Very High	127.1 mgs.
Badoit	Almost Sodium Free	N/A
Bru	Moderate	N/A
Caddo Valley	Very Low	N/A
Contrexeville	Low	N/A
Deer Park	Low	N/A
Ephrata Diamond	Very Low	5.3 mgs.
Evian	Almost Sodium Free	1.5 mgs.
Fachingen	Very High	146.28 mgs.
Ferrarelle	Moderate	10.69 mgs.
Fiuggi	Almost Sodium Free	N/A
Gerolsteiner Sprudel	High	30.8 mgs.
Mattoni	High	N/A
Montclair	N/A	N/A
Mountain Valley	Almost Sodium free	.72 mgs.
Perrier	Almost Sodium Free	2.8 mgs.
Poland Water	Almost Sodium Free	.66 mgs.
Ramlosa	N/A	N/A
San Pellegrino	Moderate	9.29 mgs.
Saratoga Vichy	Moderate	16 mgs.
Spa Reine	Almost Sodium Free	2.3 mgs.
Vichy Celestins	Almost Sodium Free	.625 mgs.
Vittelloise	Low	N/A

- If you're on a strict low sodium diet, don't drink the water unless you know what's in it. The table below should be part of your travel guide. When in doubt, call the local Board of Health or drink bottled water.

Public Water Supplies
Mgs. Sodium In 1 Cup (8 Ozs.)*

Aberdeen, S.D.	48.0	Albuquerque, N.M.	12.0
Albany, N.Y.	0.4	Annapolis, Md.	0.4

*Reprinted with permission from Mead Johnson Research Laboratory.

Ann Arbor, Mich.	4.8	Houston, Tex.	38.4
Atlanta, Ga.	0.4	Huntington, W. Va.	7.2
Augusta, Me.	0.4	Indianapolis, Ind.	2.3
Austin, Tex.	7.2	Iowa City, Iowa	1.1
Baltimore, Md.	0.7	Jackson, Miss.	0.9
Baton Rouge, La.	21.6	Jacksonville, Fla.	2.3
Beloit, Wis.	1.1	Jefferson City, Mo.	7.2
Biloxi, Miss.	55.2	Jersey City, N.J.	0.7
Birmingham, Ala.	4.8	Kansas City, Kans.	9.4
Bismarck, N.D.	14.4	Kansas City, Mo.	23.6
Boise, Ida.	4.8	Lansing, Mich.	2.3
Boston, Mass.	0.7	Lincoln, Neb.	7.2
Brownsville, Tex.	14.4	Little Rock, Ark.	0.2
Buffalo, N.Y.	1.6	Los Angeles, Cal.	
Burlington, Vt.	0.4	Aqueduct source	14.1
Carson City, Nev.	0.9	Metro source	40.1
Charleston, N.C.	2.3	River source	12.0
Charleston, W. Va.	0.7	Louisville, Ky.	4.8
Charlotte, N.C.	0.7	Madison, Wis.	0.9
Charlottesville, Va.	0.4	Manchester, N.H.	0.4
Cheyenne, Wyo.	0.7	Marion, Ohio	40.8
Chicago, Ill.	0.7	Memphis, Tenn.	4.8
Cincinnati, Ohio	1.6	Miami, Fla.	4.8
Cleveland, Ohio	2.3	Milwaukee, Wis.	0.7
Columbia, S.C.	0.9	Minneapolis, Minn.	1.1
Columbus, Ohio	12.0	Minot, N.D.	60.0
Concord, N.H.	0.4	Montgomery, Ala.	1.8
Crandall, Tex.	408.0	Montpelier, Vt.	0.2
Dallas, Tex.	7.2	Nashville, Tenn.	0.7
Denver, Colo.	7.2	Nevada, Mo.	77.8
Des Moines, Iowa	2.3	Newark, N.J.	0.4
Detroit, Mich.	0.7	New Haven, Conn.	0.7
Dover, Ill.	4.8	New Orleans, La.	2.3
Durham, N.C.	0.9	New York, N.Y.	0.7
El Paso, Tex.	16.8	Oakland, Cal.	0.7
Evansville, Ind.	4.8	Oklahoma City, Okla.	23.6
Fargo, N.D.	12.0	Olympia, Wash.	1.1
Frankfort, Ky.	0.7	Omaha, Neb.	18.8
Galesburg, Ill.	72.0	Philadelphia, Pa.	4.8
Galveston, Tex.	81.6	Phoenix, Ariz.	25.9
Harrisburg, Pa.	0.4	Pierre, S.D.	21.6
Hartford, Conn.	0.4	Pittsburgh, Pa.	14.1
Helena, Mont.	0.7	Portland, Me.	0.4

Portland, Ore.	0.2	Rochester, Minn.	1.6
Providence, R.I.	0.4	Rochester, N.Y.	0.7
Raleigh, N.C.	0.9	Sacramento, Cal.	0.7
Reno, Nev.	1.1	Santa Fe, N.M.	0.9
Richmond, Va.	1.6	St. Louis, Mo.	12.0
St. Paul, Minn.	1.1	Syracuse, N.Y.	0.4
Salem, Ore.	0.4	Tallahassee, Fla.	0.7
Salt Lake City, Utah	1.8	Topeka, Kans.	2.3
San Diego, Cal.	12.0	Trenton, N.J.	0.2
San Francisco, Cal.	2.3	Tucson, Ariz.	7.2
Seattle, Wash.	0.4	Washington, D.C.	0.7
Sioux Falls, S.D.	2.3	Wichita, Kans.	12.0
Springfield, Ill.	1.8	Wilmington, Del.	1.8

The moral: when in doubt, drink distilled, bottled water, if possible, or check the local Board of Health.

- Don't use stomach remedies or alkalizers. They all contain sodium, usually sodium bicarbonate. You won't even need them if you eat properly. If you're really sick, old-fashioned, homemade chicken soup is still a great remedy.
- Don't use salt substitutes before checking with your doctor. Many contain some salt; others, high levels of potassium which could upset the important sodium-potassium balance your body should maintain.
- Don't use half-and-half or light cream without checking ingredients. Many contain sodium preservatives. Stick to heavy cream, or skim milk.
- Don't lick stamps and envelopes if you're really watching the salt. They don't taste good, and a wet sponge or Scotch tape will do the trick.
- Don't swallow toothpaste and mouthwashes. They contain sodium.
- Don't ever be afraid to do what's best for you.

FOOD SUMMARY GUIDE*

In general, avoid all foods which list any of the following in the ingredients: salt, sodium compounds, baking soda, baking powder. However, some foods labelled low sodium do use small amounts of sodium compounds. In those cases, check the sodium milligrams per serving to see if the amount is acceptable in your dish.

If no sodium level is indicated, do not use except as indicated in this book. Tables of food nutritive values for calories, potassium, and sodium begin on page 368.

Baked Goods
and Other Wheat Products

The following should be avoided:

- Commercially prepared breads, rolls, cakes, pies, and pastries. For example, 1 slice of regular bread (or 1 regular roll) contains 200 mgs. sodium.
- Quick cooking and enriched cereals which contain sodium. Check label.
- Dry cereals which contain sodium. Check label. Exceptions are noted below.
- Self-rising flour and corn meal.
- Commercially prepared crackers, cookies, popcorn, potato chips, or pretzels, except those labelled low sodium.

You are allowed the following:

- Low sodium breads, rolls, cakes, pies, and pastries.
- Low sodium bread and cake mixes.
- Quick cooking cereals, as follows:
  Farina (Cream of Wheat)
  Grits
  Oatmeal
  Rolled Wheat
  Wheat Meal
- Dry Cereals, as follows:
  Puffed Rice
  Puffed Wheat
  Shredded Wheat
  Those labelled low sodium
- Flour and cornmeal, except self-rising.
- Low sodium crackers, cookies, potato chips, and pretzels. Unsalted popcorn. Unsalted matzo.
- Any form of pasta, except those to which sodium has been added.

*With special thanks to The American Heart Association. Note: This guide is based on requirements for a 500 mg. sodium diet. If you are allowed a higher level of sodium, you may add foods up to your allotment by referring to the tables of Nutritional Values that begin on page 368.

- Rice, white or brown, except those with seasonings added.
- Barley

Dairy

The following should be avoided:

- Butter or margarine, salted
- Buttermilk, salted
- Cheeses, commercially prepared
- Condensed milk
- Milk products, commercially prepared (see Page 374)
- Skim milk
- Whole milk

You are allowed the following:

- Butter or margarine, unsalted
- Buttermilk (if it doesn't contain salt or sodium)
- Cheeses (low sodium)
- Cream (if it doesn't contain sodium)
- Eggs (if doctor allows)
- Milk products, all forms (low sodium)
- Skim milk (if doctor allows)
- Whole milk (if doctor allows)

Fats

The following should be avoided:

- Salted butter or margarine
- Bacon or bacon fat. For example, 2 thin slices of bacon, crisp and drained, contain 200 mgs. of sodium.
- Salt pork
- Sausage casings
- Commercial salad dressings, including dietetic, except low sodium
- Commercial mayonnaise or peanut butter, except low sodium
- Salted nuts

You are allowed the following:

- Unsalted butter or margarine
- Salad or cooking oils
- Low sodium salad dressings
- Low sodium mayonnaise or peanut butter
- Unsalted nuts

Fruits

The following should be avoided:

- Crystallized or glazed fruit
- Maraschino cherries
- Canned or frozen fruit to which salt has been added.
- Dried fruit to which sodium has been added

You are allowed the following, all of which contain approximately 2 mgs. sodium per piece or serving:

- All fresh fruit
- All canned fruit, except as noted above
- All frozen fruit, except those to which salt or sodium has been added. Check label.
- All dried fruit, except those to which salt or sodium has been added. Check label.

Meat, Fish and Poultry

The following should be avoided:

- Beef liver
- Brains
- Canned, cured, salted, smoked, or koshered meats. For example, bacon, bologna, corned beef, ham, hot dogs, pastrami, salt pork, sausage, etc.
- Canned, cured, dried, salted, smoked, pickled, or brined fish. For example, anchovies, caviar, herring, lox, etc.
- Canned, smoked, or barbequed poultry
- Frozen, packaged meats, fish, and poultry containing salt or sodium. This includes self-basting turkeys.

17

- Kidneys
- Shellfish

You are allowed the following:

- All canned meats (low sodium)
- All canned fish (low sodium)
- All canned poultry (low sodium)
- All fresh meats, fish, and poultry (except those noted above)
- All frozen meats, fish, and poultry prepared without sodium compounds

Spices and Seasonings

The following should be avoided, unless they are low sodium:

- Barbeque sauce
- Bouillon cubes
- Celery flakes
- Chili ketchup
- Chili powder
- Cooking wine
- Garlic salt
- Horseradish
- Ketchup
- Meat extracts
- Meat sauces
- Meat tenderizers
- Mint sauce
- Monosodium glutamate
- Mustard, prepared
- Onion salt
- Pickles
- Relishes
- Salt
- Salt substitutes (unless your doctor approves)
- Sodium cyclamate (artificial sweetener)
- Soy sauce
- Worcestershire sauce
- Any spice or condiment containing salt or a sodium compound

You are allowed the following:

	Mgs. Per Tsp.*
• Allspice	1.4
• Almond extract	N/A
• Aniseed	N/A
• Basil	0.4
• Bay leaves	0.3
• Bouillon (low sodium)	
Beef	10.0
Chicken	5.0
• Calcium cyclamate (artificial sweetener)	N/A
• Caraway seed	0.4
• Cardamom seed	0.2
• Celery seed	4.1
• Chili con carne powder (check label)	1.0
• Chili ketchup (low sodium)	6.2
• Chives	N/A
• Cinnamon	0.2
• Cloves	4.2
• Coconut	N/A
• Coriander seed	0.3
• Cumin seed	2.6
• Curry powder (check label)	1.0
• Dill	0.2
• Fennel seed	1.9
• Garlic powder	0.1
• Ginger	0.5
• Horseradish (low sodium)	1.0
• Juniper berries	N/A
• Ketchup (low sodium)	2.0
• Lemon juice	0.3
• Lime juice	0.3
• Mace	1.3
• Maple syrup	N/A
• Marjoram	1.3
• Molasses	
Light	4.3
Medium	10.3
• Meat extract (low sodium)	N/A

*The American Spice Trade Association provided the sodium mgs. per tsp. for this spice list. To them, our special thanks.

•	Meat tenderizers (low sodium)	N/A
•	Mint	N/A
•	Mustard, powder or prepared (low sodium)	2.0
•	Nutmeg	0.2
•	Onion powder	0.8
•	Orange extract	N/A
•	Oregano	0.3
•	Paprika	0.4
•	Parsley flakes	5.9
•	Pepper, black or white	0.2
•	Pepper, chili or red	0.2
•	Peppermint extract	N/A
•	Pickles (low sodium)	2.0
•	Poppy seed	0.2
•	Poultry seasoning (check label)	N/A
•	Relishes (low sodium)	2.0
•	Rosemary	0.5
•	Saccharin*	N/A
•	Saffron	N/A
•	Sage	0.1
•	Salt substitutes (if doctor permits)	N/A
•	Savory	0.3
•	Sesame seed	0.6
•	Tarragon	1.0
•	Thyme	1.2
•	Turmeric	0.2
•	Vanilla extract	N/A
•	Walnut extract	N/A
•	Wine (if doctor permits)	1.4

*Calcium saccharin; not sodium saccharin

Vegetables

Certain vegetables should not be eaten in any form. These are listed below:

- Artichokes*
- Beets and beet greens*
- Carrots*
- Celery*
- Chard

- Dandelion greens
- Hominy
- Kale
- Mustard greens
- Olives
- Sauerkraut**
- Spinach*
- Turnips, white

*Only forbidden to those on diets restricted to 500 mgs. sodium or less.

**Permitted if low sodium

You are allowed the following.

- All fresh vegetables except those just listed
- Canned, low sodium vegetables
- Frozen vegetables, except those processed with salt. Check label.
- Vegetable juices, except those processed with salt. Check label. Many —tomato juice, for example—are available in low sodium form.

Miscellaneous

The following should be avoided:

- Baking powder and baking soda, commercially prepared (except low sodium)
- Beer
- Blackstrap molasses
- Candy and chocolate, commercially prepared (except low sodium)
- Carbonated beverages, including dietetic ones (except low sodium)
- Cocoa mixes
- Commercial milk products, including: ice cream, sherbet, milk shakes, malted milk, chocolate milk, condensed milk, non-dairy creamers, milk mixes (except low sodium)
- Fruit flavored beverages, powdered (check labels on frozen)
- Fruit flavored gelatin mixes (except low sodium)
- Pudding mixes
- Rennet tablets
- Tapioca desserts

You are allowed the following:

- Alcoholic beverages (if doctor allows, except beer and cooking wines)
- Baking chocolate (if it doesn't contain sodium)
- Baking powder (low sodium)
- Candy and chocolate (low sodium)
- Carbonated beverages (low sodium)
- Carob powder
- Coffee, instant or regular
- Cornstarch
- Cream of tartar
- Gelatin, unflavored and fruit flavored (low sodium)
- Honey
- Jams and jellies preserved without pectin or sodium
- Milk, whole and skim (if doctor allows) plus low sodium
- Molasses, light and medium extracts
- Rennet powder
- Sugar
- Tapioca, plain dry form
- Tea
- Yeast

Just a word about fats and cholesterol. Although it's a well-known fact that polyunsaturated fats are better for all of us than saturated fats, this is often particularly true for those of us who have to cut back on sodium as well. For us, a final list:

The following should be avoided:

- bacon and salt pork
- butter
- chicken fat
- coconut oil
- meat fat
- palm kernel oil
- suet and lard
- vegetable fat and shortening

You are allowed the following:

- corn oil
- cottonseed oil
- low sodium mayonnaise

- low sodium salad dressing
- olive oil (occasionally)
- peanut oil (occasionally)
- polyunsaturated margarine
- safflower oil
- sesame seed oil
- soybean oil
- sunflower seed oil

HORS D'OEUVRES

Party snacks, appetizers. Both translate hors d'oeuvres—frilly and fancy, light and fun. But going to a cocktail party is like going out to gain five pounds. Per square inch, these tiny, innocent-looking finger foods probably contain more salt, more fattening anguish than anything else you could eat.

But just remember what hors d'oeuvres munching is all about. It's an opportunity to gather with family, friends, associates and relax, flirt, share experiences and ideas, have some fun. The drink in one hand and canapé in the other enhance the setting the way props do a play.

When you think of them that way, you can have hors d'oeuvres, but of a different order.

Cocktail hour in restaurants is hard whether you're watching your salt, your weight, or both. What do you do when everyone is nibbling on barbequed ribs or Swedish meatballs? You decide which is more important: tummy gratification or ego satisfaction when a good looking man or woman stares appreciatively. Tummy bulge or bathing suit form. It's that simple.

But cheer up. In restaurants, while your friends are gorging themselves on fried chicken wings and miniature hot dogs, order a plate of fresh tomatoes to have with your drink. You'll feel refreshed, light, and a wee bit smug for being so beautifully disciplined.

At a party, there's usually no problem. Most hosts provide a heaping bowl of crudités. And no one will mind if you bring your own. Sometimes I even bring my own peanuts and potato chips, salt-free, of course.

There's no reason not to be part of the crowd because of self- or medically-imposed eating habits. You'll have more fun than anyone because you won't have to regret it later.

In your own home, dig right in. Eat with gusto and joy. Sample everything without guilt or fear. You'll know what's in it, how good it tastes, how good it is for you. Cheese stuffed mushrooms, fried eggplant, deviled eggs, minced oysters, chopped liver, salmon mousse—all the blissfully delicious morsels you can dream of and concoct are yours for the eating.

So turn the page and plan a party—a beautiful, flattering, unfattening party.

American

The French invented the word, but it is the Americans who have given hors d'oeuvres their ultimate meaning. For nowhere else is the cocktail hour so much a part of everyday life. And where there are cocktails, there are always hors d'oeuvres.

CHICKEN LIVER KEBABS

Makes 24 Hors d'oeuvres

½ cup Vinaigrette (See Page 299)
3 Tbs. lemon juice
3 Tbs. honey
1 lb. chicken livers

24 small mushrooms, stems reserved for later use
2 green peppers, cut into 1½" chunks

Combine Vinaigrette, lemon juice, and honey.
Cut vein on each liver to make 2 pieces.
With toothpicks, sandwich each liver between a mushroom and a pepper chunk.
Arrange in shallow baking pan. Pour vinaigrette mixture over all. Marinate 10 minutes, turning once.
Preheat oven to broil.
Broil 6" from heat 5 minutes.
Turn. Baste with pan juices and broil 7 to 10 minutes longer, or till liver is cooked.

Calories per serving: 50   Sodium per serving: 17 mgs.

CHICKEN STUFFED EGGS

Makes 24 Hors d'oeuvres

12 hard boiled eggs
3½ ozs. leftover chicken, minced
3 Tbs. low sodium mayonnaise
2 tsps. dill
1 tsp. parsley
1 tsp. tarragon

½ medium-size onion, minced
1 Tbs. cider vinegar
2 Tbs. lemon juice
2 tsps. low sodium chicken bouillon
2 Tbs. paprika

Cut eggs in half lengthwise. Being careful not to break whites, scoop out egg yolks and mash thoroughly.
Combine remaining ingredients except paprika. Blend well.

25

Add egg yolks and mix to blend well.
Fill pastry bag with egg mixture and pipe into egg hollows. Chill.
Garnish with paprika.
Note: The same amount of leftover fish or meat may be substituted for the chicken.

Calories per serving: 45   Sodium per serving: 40 mgs.

CORN RELISH

Makes 2 Cups

½ cup water
¼ cup cider vinegar
6 Tbs. sugar
2 cans (8 ozs. each) low sodium corn
    niblets, drained
½ green pepper, chopped

1 small onion, minced
3 Tbs. sweet pepper flakes
Black pepper to taste
½ tsp. mustard seed
Dash of hot pepper flakes
3 low sodium cucumber pickles, minced

In saucepan, combine first 3 ingredients. Bring to a boil, stirring constantly. Transfer to bowl.
Stir in remaining ingredients. Let stand 20 minutes. Spoon into pint jar. Cover tightly and refrigerate overnight.
Keeps in refrigerator 1 week.

Calories per recipe: 533   Sodium per recipe: 54 mgs.
Calories per Tbs.: 33   Sodium per Tbs.: 3 mgs.

CREAMY HERB DIP

Makes 2 Cups

2 Tbs. unsalted butter or margarine
1 small onion, minced
1 lb. low sodium cottage cheese
¼ cup low sodium mayonnaise

1 Tbs. low sodium beef bouillon
1 Tbs. dill
1 tsp. Curry Powder (See Page 288)

In skillet, melt butter. Sauté onion till golden.
In bowl, combine remaining ingredients. Purée in blender till smooth.
Stir in onion and chill 1 hour.
Serve with raw vegetables or low sodium crackers.

Calories per recipe: 1279   Sodium per recipe: 239 mgs.
Calories per Tbs.: 40   Sodium per Tbs.: 8 mgs.

MARINATED MUSHROOMS

Serves 20

½ cup oil
½ cup warm water
¾ cup red wine vinegar
Black pepper to taste
½ tsp. basil
½ tsp. thyme

1 tsp. mustard powder
1 tsp. tarragon
6 cloves garlic, minced
1 small onion, minced
2 lbs. small mushrooms

In large bowl, beat together oil and water.
Beat in vinegar, spices, and herbs.
Stir in garlic and onion.
Stir in mushrooms. Cover and refrigerate overnight, stirring occasionally.
Drain mushrooms before serving. Reserve marinade as a vinaigrette dressing.

Calories per serving: 64   Sodium per serving: 9 mgs.

MINCED FISH

Makes 1 Cup

2 Tbs. sesame oil, unsalted butter, or
   margarine
6 ozs. pollack fillets, chopped
1 small onion, minced

4 scallions, minced, including greens
1 tsp. low sodium chicken bouillon
Black pepper to taste
1 Tbs. lemon juice

In skillet, heat oil. Add fish and onion. Cook over low heat 10 minutes, stirring often.
Stir in remaining ingredients. Raise heat to medium and cook 2 minutes, stirring often.
Cover and chill 1 hour.
Serve on low sodium crackers.

Calories per recipe: 494   Sodium per recipe: 106 mgs.
Calories per Tbs.: 31   Sodium per Tbs.: 7 mgs.

STUFFED CUCUMBERS

Makes 16 Canapes

½ lb. leftover chicken, chopped
2 scallions, minced, including greens
3 Tbs. low sodium mayonnaise
3 Tbs. dry white wine

2 tsps. tarragon
2 tsps. low sodium Dijon mustard
2 cucumbers, halved lengthwise and
   seeded

In bowl, combine all ingredients except cucumbers. Blend thoroughly.
Stuff each cucumber half with a quarter of the chicken mixture. Cut each half into 4 pieces.

Calories per serving: 44   Sodium per serving: 13 mgs.

Chinese

Almost any Chinese dish can be served as an appetizer before the main event. But other specialties are classic hors d'oeuvres. Indeed, it is commonplace for a party to descend on a dim sum parlor and make a meal of pork dumplings, paper fried shrimp, egg rolls, and miniature barbequed spare ribs. For no cuisine lends itself to nibbling pleasure as much as Chinese.

EGG ROLLS

Makes 12 Egg Rolls, 24 Hors d'oeuvres

2½ cups all-purpose flour
1 egg
1¾ cups water

3 tsps. cider vinegar
1½ Tbs. low sodium chicken bouillon
Oil

In bowl, combine all ingredients except oil. Stir till batter is smooth.
Lightly oil a small skillet and heat. Pour a stream of batter into skillet, just covering the bottom. Cook over low heat till set and starting to curl around edges. Turn onto dish towel.
Repeat till all batter is used.
Place 1 Tbs. Egg Roll Filling (See Page 29) in center of each pancake. Fold in sides.
Fry in small amount of oil, seam side down.
Cut each Egg Roll in half. Serve with Sweet and Sour Sauce (See Page 286)

Calories per serving: 68*   Sodium per serving: 6 mgs.*
*Does not include filling

EGG ROLL FILLING

Makes 2 Cups (Enough for 12 Egg Rolls or 18 Won Tons)

½ lb. leftover pork, beef, or chicken,
   minced
4 water chestnuts, minced
2 cups fresh bean sprouts, chopped
6 scallions, chopped, including greens

1 tsp. sugar
1½ tsps. cider vinegar
1 Tbs. sesame oil
1 cup boiling water
5 tsps. low sodium beef bouillon

    In large bowl, combine all ingredients. Stir to blend well. Cover and refrigerate 1 hour.
   Drain off liquid and use mixture to fill 12 Egg Rolls (Page 28) or 18 Won Tons (See Page 66).

Pork: Calories per recipe: 1051	Sodium per recipe: 203 mgs.
Beef: Calories per recipe: 961	Sodium per recipe: 192 mgs.
Chicken: Calories per recipe: 913	Sodium per recipe: 203 mgs.

For Egg Rolls

Pork: Calories per serving: 88	Sodium per serving: 17 mgs.
Beef: Calories per serving: 80	Sodium per serving: 16 mgs.
Chicken: Calories per serving: 76	Sodium per serving: 16 mgs.

For Won Tons

Pork: Calories per serving: 58	Sodium per serving: 11 mgs.
Beef: Calories per serving: 53	Sodium per serving: 11 mgs.
Chicken: Calories per serving: 51	Sodium per serving: 11 mgs.

PORK BALLS

Makes 18 Hors d'oeuvres

1 lb. ground pork
1 Tbs. all-purpose flour
4 cloves garlic, minced
2 tsps. low sodium beef bouillon
2 tsps. low sodium chicken bouillon
½ tsp. sugar

Coarse black pepper to taste
¼ tsp. cinnamon
4 tsps. dry sherry
2 scallions, minced, including greens
2 Tbs. oil
3 Tbs. cider vinegar

    In bowl, combine all ingredients except oil and vinegar. Blend thoroughly. Form into 1″ balls.
    In large skillet, heat oil. Cook balls over low heat till browned all over, about 15 minutes.

Turn heat to high. Add vinegar and stir balls till vinegar is absorbed. Skewer balls with toothpicks and serve hot.

Calories per serving: 83   Sodium per serving: 19 mgs.

SWEET AND SOUR RADISHES

Serves 8

1 lb. radishes, trimmed, sliced in half
1 medium-size onion, minced
2 tsps. low sodium beef bouillon
1 carrot, grated

2 Tbs. sugar
2 Tbs. water
2 Tbs. honey
¼ cup cider vinegar

In bowl, combine first 3 ingredients.
In saucepan, combine remaining ingredients. Bring to a boil, stirring constantly.
Pour vinegar sauce over radish mixture. Cover and refrigerate overnight.

Calories per serving: 40   Sodium per serving: 17 mgs.

French

In France, mastering the art of hors d'oeuvres preparation is a special course required of all apprentice chefs. The appearance of these delicacies is as important as the taste, as is true of all French foods. These tiny wonders are not reserved for cocktail parties. They are, rather, a relaxing prelude to the serious immersion in the main meal. In short, the French enjoy hors d'oeuvres as a first course, carefully planned to complement, but never conflict with, the main course.

CHILI CHICKEN CANAPES

Makes 12 Hors d'oeuvres

12 chicken wings
¼ cup lemon juice

4 tsps. oregano
12 Tbs. low sodium chili ketchup

Preheat oven to broil.

Place chicken wings on shallow baking sheet. Pour on lemon juice. Sprinkle with oregano. Broil 4 minutes per side.

Spoon chili ketchup over wings. Broil 30 seconds longer.

Calories per serving: 84	Sodium per serving: 36 mgs.

STUFFED MUSHROOMS

Makes 8 Hors d'oeuvres

8 large mushrooms, stems removed, and minced
2 cloves garlic, minced
1 small onion, minced
Black pepper to taste
⅛ tsp. marjoram

1 slice low sodium bread, toasted and crumbed, or 8 low sodium crackers, crumbed
8 tsps. lemon juice
1 Tbs. unsalted butter or margarine

Preheat oven to 450°.

Combine mushroom stems, garlic, onion, pepper, marjoram, and bread crumbs. Spoon mixture into mushroom caps.

Sprinkle lemon juice on mushrooms. Dot with butter.

Place mushrooms on baking sheet and bake 6 minutes.

Calories per serving: 40	Sodium per serving: 5 mgs.

German

In Germany, hors d'oeuvres are really between-meal snacks rather than party delights. The Germans often create complete buffet spreads from a sumptuous variety of delicatessen-type foods—truly delicate eating.

DILLED HERRING

Makes 24 Canapes

⅓ cup oil
⅓ cup hot water
¼ cup low sodium Dijon mustard

6 Tbs. cider vinegar
6 Tbs. lemon juice
4 Tbs. dry sherry

12 black peppercorns, crushed
1 tsp. thyme
½ cup fresh dill, chopped, or 2 Tbs. dried
1 tsp. allspice

2 scallions, minced, including greens
6 fresh herrings, boned and cut into
  1″ chunks
1 orange, cut into thin wedges

In bowl, beat together oil, hot water, and mustard.
Beat in vinegar, lemon juice, and sherry.
Stir in all remaining ingredients except herrings and orange wedges.
In 9″ square casserole, place herrings and orange wedges. Pour marinade on top.
Cover and marinate in refrigerator 2 days, stirring occasionally.
Discard orange wedges.
Serve fish chunks, skewered with toothpicks, in marinade.

Calories per serving: 57

Sodium per serving: 12 mgs.

SALMON CREAM

Makes 3 Cups

1 Tbs. unflavored gelatin
2 Tbs. cold water
¼ cup boiling water
1 tsp. sugar
½ cup heavy cream
2 Tbs. White Horseradish (See Page 290)
1 Tbs. dill

½ Tbs. green peppercorns,* crushed
1 cucumber, peeled and minced
1 tsp. low sodium mustard
2 cans (7¾ ozs. each) low sodium
  salmon
4 tsps. low sodium beef bouillon
Black pepper to taste

Natural green peppercorns, packed in water or vinegar
In small bowl, combine gelatin and cold water. Stir to dissolve. Stir in boiling water and sugar. Chill 10 minutes.
In second bowl, beat cream till stiff. Fold in Horseradish. Stir into gelatin mixture.
Stir in remaining ingredients, blending thoroughly. Cover and chill at least 2 hours.
Serve with raw vegetables or low sodium crackers.

Calories per recipe: 1208
Calories per Tbs.: 25

Sodium per recipe: 350 mgs.
Sodium per Tbs.: 7 mgs.

Greek

The Greeks are closely akin to Americans in their fondness for hors d'oeuvres, with one difference. In Greece, hors d'oeuvres are accompanied by cocktails, rather than vice versa.

TUNA AND AVOCADO SPREAD

Makes 36 Canapes

1 Tbs. low sodium chicken bouillon
¼ cup boiling water, divided
2 Tbs. sweet pepper flakes
½ cup low sodium mayonnaise
2 hard boiled eggs, chopped
2 tsps. low sodium mustard

½ tsp. caraway seed (optional)
⅛ tsp. ground coriander
1 can (6½ ozs.) low sodium tuna,
   including liquid
1 avocado, peeled and pitted
36 low sodium crackers

In bowl, combine bouillon and 2 Tbs. boiling water, stirring to dissolve.
In second bowl, combine pepper flakes and remaining water. Let stand 10 minutes. Drain. Stir into bouillon mixture.
In large bowl, blend bouillon mixture, mayonnaise, and eggs. Mash thoroughly.
Stir in mustard, caraway, coriander, tuna, and liquid. Blend thoroughly.
Mash in avocado. Cover mixture and chill 1 hour.
Serve on low sodium crackers.

Calories per serving: 22   Sodium per serving: 10 mgs.

Indian

Hors d'oeuvres are not hors d'oeuvres per se in India. They are cocktail accompaniments, between meal snacks, or any excuse for a tasty treat.

BATTER FRIED CAULIFLOWER

Makes 30 Canapes

1 cup oil
1 cup all-purpose flour
⅔ cup water

1 Tbs. low sodium chicken bouillon
2 tsps. turmeric
4 Tbs. lemon juice

33

⅛ tsp. nutmeg
Dash of cayenne pepper
¼ tsp. ground cumin

1 head cauliflower, separated into flowerets

In wok or medium-size skillet, heat oil over low heat till bubbly.
In bowl, combine all remaining ingredients except cauliflower. Stir to blend well.
Dip flowerets in batter. Drop into oil. Fry over medium heat 5 minutes or till brown, turning once. Drain on paper towels.

Calories per serving: 52

Sodium per serving: 3 mgs.

CURRIED CHICKEN SPREAD

Makes 36 Canapes

1 lb. leftover chicken, chopped fine
¼ cup golden raisins*
¼ cup unsalted peanuts, chopped
8 scallions, chopped, including greens
½ cup low sodium mayonnaise

½ tsp. Curry Powder (See Page 288)
½ tsp. mustard powder
½ tsp. savory
2 chili peppers, chopped
36 low sodium crackers

*Preserved in non-sodium ingredient
  Combine all ingredients except crackers. Chill at least 1 hour.
  Serve on crackers.

Calories per serving: 75

Sodium per serving: 20 mgs.

OYSTERS IN SPICY TOMATO SAUCE

Makes about 12 Hors d'oeuvres

½ tsp. minced ginger root or dash of
  ginger powder
4 cloves garlic, chopped
2 Tbs. water
1 pt. oysters, drained, liquid reserved for
  other use

Black pepper to taste
1½ tsps. mustard powder
2 Tbs. lemon juice
1½ tsps. turmeric
1 can (6 ozs.) low sodium tomato paste

In blender, combine ginger, garlic, and water. Purée. Set aside.
In ungreased skillet, cook oysters, seasoned with pepper and mustard, 30 seconds over low heat. Transfer to platter.
Add ginger mixture and lemon juice to skillet. Stir fry over medium heat 1 minute.

Stir in turmeric and tomato paste. Stir fry 1 minute more.
Return oysters to skillet. Coat thoroughly with sauce and heat 30 seconds more.
Place oysters and sauce on platter. Serve with toothpicks stuck in each oyster.

Calories per serving: 41   Sodium per serving: 20 mgs.

Italian

In Italian, the word is "antipasto," and it is literally translated as "before the pasta." Practically speaking, an antipasto is a warm-up for the main course. It may be hot or cold, but always comprises a selection of seafood, cheeses, meats, and vegetables to be tasted and enjoyed independent of the main meal.

BAKED OYSTERS

Makes about 24 Hors d'oeuvres

2 pts. oysters, shells reserved, liquid
  reserved for other use.
½ cup low sodium Bread Crumbs (See
  Page 291)
2 ozs. low sodium Gouda cheese,
  shredded
1 Tbs. parsley

1 Tbs. oregano
1 Tbs. olive oil
2 cloves garlic, minced
2 tsps. low sodium chicken bouillon
3 Tbs. lemon juice
Coarse black pepper to taste

Preheat oven to 400°.
Chop oysters and place in bowl.
Add remaining ingredients. Blend thoroughly.
Spoon mixture into oyster shells and place on baking sheet. Bake 10 minutes, or till lightly browned.

Calories per serving: 32   Sodium per serving: 17 mgs.

MEAT STUFFED ZUCCHINI

Makes 16 Canapes

2 large zucchini, halved lengthwise
2 Tbs. olive oil
1 medium-size onion, chopped

½ lb. ground beef, pork, or veal
½ cup low sodium Seasoned Bread
  Crumbs (See Page 291)

Black pepper to taste
2 tsps. low sodium beef bouillon
1 Tbs. parsley
4 Tbs. lemon juice

4 ozs. low sodium Gouda cheese, sliced
  thin
1 Tbs. paprika

Preheat oven to 425°.
Scoop out and discard seeds from zucchini. Scoop out pulp, leaving ½″ all around. Chop pulp and set aside.
In skillet, heat oil. Sauté onion over low heat till wilted.
Add meat and cook, stirring often, till it loses its pink color.
Add zucchini pulp and cook 5 minutes, stirring often.
Stir in Bread Crumbs, pepper, and bouillon. Stir in parsley. Blend thoroughly.
Fill zucchini boats with meat mixture. Sprinkle with lemon juice.
Top with cheese slices. Sprinkle with paprika and bake 35 minutes.
Cut each zucchini boat into 4 wedges.
Serve with Tomato Sauce (See Page 298), if desired.

Beef: Calories per serving: 89
Pork: Calories per serving: 95
Veal: Calories per serving: 95

Sodium per serving: 16 mgs.
Sodium per serving: 16 mgs.
Sodium per serving: 18 mgs.

SPICED EGGPLANT DIP

Makes 2½ Cups

1 Tbs. unsalted butter or margarine
1 Tbs. oil
2 medium-size onions, minced
1 1-lb. eggplant, peeled and chopped
⅛ tsp. garlic powder
Coarse black pepper to taste
Dash of hot pepper flakes

8 mushrooms, chopped
3 Tbs. low sodium chili ketchup
3 low sodium cucumber pickles, minced
1 tsp. basil
1 tsp. parsley
½ tsp. thyme

Heat butter and oil in medium-size skillet. Add onions and cook over low heat, stirring often, 5 minutes.
Add eggplant and cook, stirring often, till eggplant is soft, about 6 minutes.
Stir in remaining ingredients and simmer over low heat, stirring often, for 5 minutes.
Serve hot or chilled with low sodium crackers.

Calories per recipe: 386
Calories per Tbs.: 16

Sodium per recipe: 65 mgs.
Sodium per Tbs.: 3 mgs.

Jewish

To the Jewish family, appetizers are meal starters. They are tongue tantalizers—sweetly rich chopped chicken liver, puckery herring, seductive creamy cheese—to tease the appetite and heighten pleasure in the meal to come.

CHICKEN NUT SPREAD

Makes 2¼ Cups

1 cup leftover chicken or lamb, chopped
6 low sodium cucumber pickles, minced
½ cup low sodium mayonnaise
2 Tbs. lemon juice
2 Tbs. cider vinegar
¼ cup chopped almonds

1 Tbs. low sodium chicken bouillon
Black pepper to taste
½ tsp. mustard powder
½ tsp. garlic powder
1 tsp. dill
1 tsp. tarragon

Combine all ingredients, stirring to blend. Chill 1 hour.
Serve with low sodium crackers.

Chicken: Calories per recipe: 1462	Sodium per recipe: 242 mgs.
Calories per Tbs.: 41	Sodium per Tbs.: 7 mgs.

Lamb: Calories per recipe: 1761	Sodium per recipe: 252
Calories per Tbs.: 49	Sodium per Tbs.: 7 mgs.

CHOPPED CHICKEN LIVER

Makes 2 Cups

2 Tbs. Chicken Fat (See Page 285),
    unsalted butter, or margarine
3 medium-size onions, minced
1 lb. chicken livers
1 tsp. sage
½ tsp. rosemary, crushed

½ tsp. thyme
1 tsp. mustard powder
Black pepper to taste
2 tsps. low sodium chicken bouillon
3 Tbs. dry sherry
4 hard boiled eggs, coarsely grated

In large skillet, heat fat. Sauté onions and livers till livers lose their pink color.
Remove from heat and chop livers.
Stir in herbs, spices, and bouillon.
Return to heat. Stir in sherry and cook 2 minutes, stirring often.
Scrape liver mixture into bowl. Mash to a paste. Stir in grated eggs, blending thoroughly.
Serve with low sodium crackers.

Calories per recipe: 1251
Calories per Tbs.: 39

Sodium per recipe: 581 mgs.
Sodium per Tbs.: 18 mgs.

CREAMED AVOCADO DIP

Makes 1½ Cups

1 avocado, peeled, pitted, and chopped
2 Tbs. heavy cream
1 Tbs. lemon juice
White pepper to taste

⅛ tsp. allspice
2 tsps. low sodium chicken bouillon
2 tsps. mustard powder
¼ cup chopped walnuts

In blender, combine all ingredients. Purée till smooth.
Transfer to bowl. Cover and chill at least 2 hours before serving.
Serve as raw vegetable dip or with low sodium crackers.

Calories per recipe: 859
Calories per Tbs.: 36

Sodium per recipe: 39 mgs.
Sodium per Tbs.: 2 mgs.

Mexican

The Mexicans have a lovely word for them: antojitos, which means little whims. These munching fancies include the delectable, finger-licking tacos and empanadas, as well as succulent tidbits of fried or marinated meat or fish. Antojitos are perfect anytime, anywhere—wonderful companions on a leisurely stroll, welcome guests at a happy hour. They are little whims that live up to your expectations.

CHILI RICE DIP

Makes 2½ Cups

½ lb. low sodium cottage cheese
¼ cup sour cream*
2 chili peppers, minced
1 medium-size onion, minced
1 tomato, chopped
½ tsp. thyme

1 tsp. oregano
Black pepper to taste
1 Tbs. low sodium chicken bouillon
1½ cups cooked rice
2 ozs. low sodium Cheddar cheese, sliced thin

*Preserved in non-sodium ingredient
Preheat oven to 350°.
In oven-proof casserole, combine all ingredients except Cheddar cheese. Blend thoroughly. Cover and bake 15 minutes.
Remove cover. Top with cheese and bake 10 minutes more, or till top is bubbly.
Serve hot as a dip with low sodium crackers or raw vegetables.

Calories per recipe: 976
Calories per Tbs.: 49

Sodium per recipe: 192 mgs.
Sodium per Tbs.: 10 mgs.

GUACAMOLE

Makes 2 Cups

2 avocados, peeled, pitted, and chopped
1 medium-size onion, chopped
2 cloves garlic, chopped
2 chili peppers, chopped
1 tomato, chopped

2 Tbs. lemon juice
1 tsp. sugar
1/16 tsp. ground coriander
1 Tbs. low sodium chicken bouillon
Cayenne pepper to taste

In large bowl, mash avocados with fork, but leave them slightly lumpy.
In blender, grind remaining ingredients. Stir into avocados. Blend thoroughly.

Cover and chill 2 hours.
Serve with raw vegetables or low sodium crackers.

Calories per recipe: 659	Sodium per recipe: 47 mgs.
Calories per Tbs.: 2	Sodium per Tbs.: 2 mgs.

SEVICHE

Makes 26 Hors d'oeuvres

1 lb. flounder fillets, cut into 1" chunks
½ cup lime juice
1 tsp. sugar
1 tsp. oregano
1 tsp. basil
2 Tbs. low sodium chicken bouillon

2 tsps. garlic powder
Cayenne pepper to taste
White pepper to taste
3 chili peppers, minced
1 medium-size onion, minced

In large bowl, combine all ingredients. Cover and refrigerate at least 8 hours, turning occasionally.
Skewer fish chunks with toothpicks.

Calories per serving: 34	Sodium per serving: 26 mgs.

Spanish

When evening comes, the Spanish happily converge in the tiny bars dotting every street. There they convivially spend the many pleasant hours between the noonday meal and the late supper socializing while sipping creamy Spanish sherry and nibbling tapas—the Spanish version of hors d'oeuvres. These delightful cocktail tidbits, predominantly seafood, are as much the custom in Spain as they are in the United States.

COCKTAIL CHICKEN VINAIGRETTE

Makes 24 Canapes

1 lb. leftover chicken, cut into 1" chunks
¼ cup Vinaigrette Dressing (See Page 299)
Cayenne pepper to taste
2 Tbs. parsley

1 tsp. dill
Dash of hot pepper flakes
4 scallions, chopped, including greens
Coarse black pepper to taste

In bowl, combine all ingredients. Cover and chill overnight.
Skewer chicken pieces with toothpicks.

Calories per serving: 43   Sodium per serving: 13 mgs.

FISH AND CORN FRITTERS

Makes 30 Hors d'oeuvres

½ cup all-purpose flour
2 eggs
2 Tbs. lemon juice
2 Tbs. water
1 Tbs. plus ¼ cup oil, divided
1 lb. halibut fillets, minced
8 scallions, chopped, including greens
2 cloves garlic, minced

2 cans (8 ozs. each) low sodium corn
    niblets, drained
1 Tbs. parsley
1 Tbs. tarragon
2 Tbs. low sodium beef bouillon
1 tsp. dill
1 tsp. thyme
Black pepper to taste

Combine flour, eggs, lemon juice, water, and 1 Tbs. oil. Blend well.
Combine remaining ingredients except oil. Blend into flour mixture.
Heat oil in large skillet till bubbly. Drop in batter, a heaping teaspoonful at a time.
Deep fry till fritters are golden. Drain.
Serve immediately, skewered on toothpicks.

Calories per serving: 67   Sodium per serving: 29

SPANISH MEAT PÂTÉ

Makes 64 Canapes

2 lbs. ground beef
½ cup cooked rice
1 egg, lightly beaten
1 medium-size onion, minced
3 Tbs. low sodium beef bouillon
4 Tbs. dry sherry
1 tsp. basil
1 tsp. parsley

1 tsp. tarragon
¼ tsp. rosemary, crushed
¼ tsp. thyme
¾ tsp. coarse black pepper or to taste
¾ cup dry red wine
3 bay leaves
1 cup Tomato Aspic (See Page 298)
64 low sodium crackers

Preheat oven to 350°.
In bowl, combine first 12 ingredients. Blend well and shape into loaf.
Place loaf in 9″ × 13″ oven-proof casserole. Pour wine around loaf. Add bay leaves.
Cover loosely with tin foil and bake 30 minutes.

41

Remove tin foil. Baste loaf and bake, uncovered, 30 minutes more. Let cool.
While loaf is baking, pour 1″ of Parsley Aspic into a 5 × 9″ pan. Chill till jellylike.
Place loaf on aspic layer and spoon additional aspic over loaf. Chill till aspic is firm.
Repeat till all aspic is used.
Unmold. Slice loaf and quarter each slice. Place pâté on low sodium crackers.

Calories per serving: 55   Sodium per serving: 14 mgs.

SOUPS

The versatility of soups is really marvelous. Fruits or vegetables, puréed or whole, are usually the main ingredients. But add some meat, fish, or chicken, and you have a sumptuous yet light main dish.

Even bones—from meat or chicken—simmered in water with some low sodium bouillon, herbs, spices, and a dash of wine make a beautiful broth. Serve as a consommé or use as a base for other soups.

Add some cream, low sodium cheese, cornstarch, flour, or puréed potato and you have a rich and luscious creamy broth, gravy, or sauce to savor for its own sake or to crown entrees and vegetables. For the gourmet touch, flavor with a hint of white wine, red wine, or sherry. And don't forget leftovers. Soups offer the perfect way to discover how good and special food can taste the second time around.

Nothing really hurts a good basic soup. Anything goes. So let the spirit move you and create your own recipe treasures.

In this book, low sodium beef or chicken bouillon, used in the broth base of all soups, is the key to a salted soup taste. Other seasonings that will give you salty results are pepper (black or white), garlic powder, mustard powder, and onion powder. Used separately or together, these seasonings will virtually eliminate the request to "pass the salt, please" at your table. Let your own taste determine the quantity, and don't worry. Herbs, spices, and low sodium bouillon contain so little sodium and calories, they are almost negligible. Just be aware of what you're doing for your own daily menu planning and your recipe collection.

Another good thing about soups is they can be frozen. So you can plan ahead, defrost a broth, and whip up a delicious concoction at a moment's notice. The motto: make more than you need so the soup you enjoy today you can savor again weeks from now with no special effort.

Soups that do not contain cream or other dairy products may be frozen as long as six months. Just remember some of the flavor may be lost as excess moisture is absorbed in the freezing process. If this happens, simply refresh the soup with an extra teaspoon or two of low sodium bouillon when you reheat.

Cream or dairy based soups should be used within two weeks of freezing and should be defrosted in the refrigerator. Better yet, if you don't plan to use the cream broth soon, prepare it up to the addition of the cream and freeze at this point up to six months. Stir in the cream while reheating.

There will be lots of recipes of your own you'll want to adapt. Just remember the hints for salty taste. And in those calling for stock or water, you can substitute Beef or Chicken Broth given in this chapter for a flavorful goodness that makes the soup your own. For a real shortcut, for every cup of broth called for in a recipe, dissolve one tablespoon of beef or chicken bouillon in one cup of boiling water.

If you want the convenience of canned, try some of the low sodium soups available. They may not taste exactly as you want them to. So doctor them with any of the hints we've described for preparing soups from scratch.

Above all, do not buy regular canned soups or bouillon. These are so heavily salted that most of them contain as much as one fourth the suggested salt intake for the average person. For example, one regular bouillon cube contains 914 mgs. of sodium compared to 10 mgs. and 5 mgs. for low sodium beef and chicken bouillon, respectively.

But there's nothing as good as homemade soup. Hot or cold, soups are an elegant way to enhance or make a meal. So don't wait. It's a lot easier than you think, not only to make soup, but to turn it into a delicate, delectable star performance.

American

Of all people, Americans hold soups in the lightest regard. Soups seem to be reserved for holidays or eating out, perhaps because Americans want to dive right into the main course or because American cooks believe soups are too much of a bother to prepare.

Nevertheless, some of the most delicious soups are made in American kitchens.

BEEF BROTH

Serves 6 (Makes 4 Cups)

1 lb. beef marrow bones or bones,
   carcass, and giblets from 1 chicken
1 large onion, minced
3 bay leaves
5 cups water

4 Tbs. low sodium beef bouillon
Black pepper to taste
¼ tsp. basil
⅛ tsp. thyme
3 Tbs. dry red or white wine (optional)

In large saucepan, combine bones, carcass, giblets, onion, bay leaves, and water. Bring to a slow boil over medium heat.

Reduce heat. Cover and simmer over low heat 20 minutes.

Stir in all other ingredients except wine. Cover and simmer 15 minutes more.

Discard bones, reserving giblets, if desired, for Chicken Gravy (See Page 285). Stir in wine.

Cover and refrigerate 1 hour. Skim off fat. Reheat over low heat. Serve as is, strain for consommé, or use as directed in other recipes. Broth made without wine may be frozen up to 6 months, but should be reheated with extra low sodium bouillon to taste.

Calories per serving: 32	Sodium per serving: 22 mgs.
Calories per cup: 49	Sodium per cup: 34 mgs.

CHICKEN BROTH

Serves 6 (Makes 4 Cups)

Bones, carcass, and giblets from
  1 chicken
5 cups water
2 medium-size onions, minced, or 2 tsps.
  onion powder

Coarse black pepper to taste
4 Tbs. low sodium chicken bouillon

In large saucepan, combine first 2 ingredients. Add onions and pepper. Bring to a slow boil over medium heat.

Reduce heat. Cover and simmer over low heat 30 minutes.

Stir in bouillon. Turn off heat. Cover and let stand 30 minutes.

Chop giblets and strip meat from carcass. Return to broth. Discard bones.

Cover and refrigerate 1 hour. Skim off fat. Reheat over low heat, strain and serve as consommé, or use as directed in other recipes. Broth may be frozen up to 6 months, but should be reheated with additional low sodium chicken bouillon to taste.

Calories per serving: 37	Sodium per serving: 13 mgs.
Calories per cup: 55	Sodium per cup: 20 mgs.

EASY FISH STOCK

Makes 2½ Cups

1 tsp. olive oil
1 carrot, scraped and diced
2 shallots, minced
2 Tbs. dry white wine
1 cup Chicken Broth (See above)
½ cup oyster liquid (optional)
1 cup water
4 tsps. low sodium chicken bouillon
½ lb. fish bones, heads, etc.

½ tsp. basil
½ tsp. parsley
½ tsp. thyme
1 clove
4 black peppercorns or ground black
  pepper to taste
Dash of white pepper
1 bay leaf

In medium saucepan, heat oil. Add carrot and shallots. Cook over low heat till shallots begin to wilt.

Add wine and simmer 2 minutes. Add remaining ingredients and cook 10 minutes, stirring occasionally. Strain.

Calories per cup: 178   Sodium per cup: 108 mgs.

GOLDEN MUSHROOM SOUP

Serves 8

This soup is especially good as a sauce base for chicken, fish, or vegetables. Thicken by adding flour or cornstarch mixed with a little cold water.

1 Tbs. unsalted butter or margarine
1 lb. mushrooms, sliced
2 shallots, minced
3½ cups Chicken Broth (See Page 45)
¼ cup heavy cream

2 Tbs. dry sherry
White pepper to taste
¾ tsp. onion powder
½ tsp. mustard powder
1 Tbs. low sodium chicken bouillon

In saucepan, melt butter, add mushrooms and cook over low heat 7 minutes, stirring often.

Stir in remaining ingredients except bouillon. Bring to a boil. Cover. Reduce heat and simmer 20 minutes.

Stir in bouillon and simmer 5 minutes more, stirring occasionally.

Calories per serving: 95   Sodium per serving: 24 mgs.

SALMON SOUP

Serves 6

3½ cups Chicken Broth (See Page 45)
½ cup fresh chopped dill
½ lb. new potatoes, cubed
3 carrots, scraped and sliced thin
2 leeks, sliced, including greens
1 Tbs. tarragon

3 Tbs. lemon juice
1 lb. salmon fillets, cut into 1¼" chunks
White pepper to taste
2 tsps. parsley
⅛ tsp. mace
2 tsps. low sodium chicken bouillon

In Dutch oven, combine Chicken Broth and dill. Simmer 15 minutes.

Add potatoes, carrots, and leeks. Bring to a boil. Reduce heat. Cover and simmer 30 minutes.

Add tarragon, lemon juice, salmon, pepper, parsley, mace, and bouillon. Simmer 10 minutes, or till bubbly around edges.
Serve as main dish with salad.

Calories per serving: 190	Sodium per serving: 93 mgs.

SIMPLY LUSCIOUS OYSTER STEW

Serves 8

2 pts. oysters, including liquid
2 potatoes, parboiled, peeled, and diced
1 medium-size onion, chopped
3 cups boiling water
4 Tbs. low sodium chicken bouillon
6 Tbs. dry white wine

2 Tbs. lemon juice
White pepper to taste
¼ tsp. sage
¼ tsp. thyme
Dash of ground coriander
2 Tbs. unsalted butter or margarine

In large saucepan, combine all ingredients except butter. Bring to a boil.
Reduce heat and stir in butter. Cook till butter completely melts, stirring often.
Serve as main course with salad.

Calories per serving: 185	Sodium per serving: 97 mgs.

Chinese

In China, soup is served throughout the meal in place of other drinks. Soups are also traditionally served as a dessert course. Other countries, like the United States, have applied their own customs, and relish such delicacies as won ton, shark's fin, and winter melon soups as a separate first course that whets the appetite for the meal to follow.

BEEF AND LETTUCE SOUP

Serves 4

4 scallions, chopped, including greens
Boiling water
⅔ lb. ground beef
1 Tbs. cornstarch
1 Tbs. low sodium beef bouillon
1 square of bean curd

4 cups Chicken Broth (See Page 45)
¼ tsp. ground coriander
8 romaine lettuce leaves, torn into pieces
¼ lb. vermicelli, cooked al dente*
Black pepper to taste

Do not add salt to boiling water.

In bowl, place scallions and cover with boiling water. Let stand 5 minutes.
In second bowl, combine beef, cornstarch, and beef bouillon. Blend thoroughly.
Drain scallions and work them into the beef mixture.
Work bean curd into beef mixture till blended thoroughly. Shape into 20 miniature balls.
In large saucepan, bring Chicken Broth to a boil. Reduce heat and cook 15 minutes.
Stir in coriander.
Drop in beef balls and cook over low heat 20 minutes.
Divide lettuce and vermicelli into 8 bowls. Sprinkle with pepper.
Pour in soup and beef balls.
Serve as a main dish accompanied by a salad or vegetables.

Calories per serving: 353   Sodium per serving: 85 mgs.

SZECHWAN PORK SOUP

Serves 4

6 cups Beef Broth (See Page 44)
Black pepper to taste
Dash of hot pepper flakes
2 Tbs. long grain rice
1 Tbs. oil
½ lb. ground pork
6 mushrooms, sliced

⅛ tsp. Five Spice Powder (See Page 289)
2 Tbs. dry sherry
1 tsp. cider vinegar
½ lb. snow pea pods
4 tsps. low sodium beef bouillon

In large saucepan, bring Beef Broth to a boil. Reduce heat. Stir in black pepper and hot pepper flakes.
Stir in rice. Cover and simmer 10 minutes.
While soup is cooking, heat oil in wok or skillet. Add pork and mushrooms. Stir fry 5 minutes, breaking up pork. Add Five Spice Powder.
Stir in sherry and vinegar. Scrape into soup.
Add snow pea pods and bouillon to soup. Stir well. Cook 7 minutes, covered.
Serve as main dish accompanied by individual bowls of rice.

Calories per serving: 304   Sodium per serving: 30 mgs.

WON TON SOUP

Serves 8

3 cups Chicken Broth (See Page 45)
8 Won Tons (See Page 66) with Egg Roll filling (See Page 29)
2 stalks broccoli, trimmed and separated into flowerets, stalks peeled and cut into 1″ rounds

2 Tbs. dry sherry
½ can (4 ozs.) water chestnuts, sliced in half
2 scallions, chopped, including greens
4 mushrooms, sliced

Bring Chicken Broth to a boil in Dutch oven.
Reduce heat to low. Add remaining ingredients and simmer 15 minutes.

Pork: Calories per serving: 178
Beef: Calories per serving: 179
Chicken: Calories per serving: 170

Sodium per serving: 20 mgs.
Sodium per serving: 20 mgs.
Sodium per serving: 20 mgs.

French

Soups play a critical role in the life of every Frenchman. They are savored at every meal, including breakfast. They are often the main dish. And they are starters for innumerable sauces. Learning to make soups is one basic lesson for every French cook.

COD BISQUE

Serves 8

If serving as a main dish, double the amount of fish.

2 Tbs. unsalted butter or margarine
1 Tbs. all-purpose flour
¾ Tbs. dried or fresh grated lemon peel
3 hard boiled eggs, mashed
1½ cups milk
½ lb. cod fillets, cut into 1″ chunks
⅛ tsp. mace

½ tsp. mustard powder
⅛ tsp. sage
2 cups boiling water
2 Tbs. low sodium chicken bouillon
½ cup heavy cream
½ cup dry sherry

In bowl, combine first 4 ingredients.
In saucepan, bring milk to slow boil. Slowly stir in egg mixture.

Add all but last 2 ingredients. Cook over low heat 10 minutes.
Stir in cream and sherry. Cook 10 minutes more, stirring regularly.

Calories per serving: 165	Sodium per serving: 75 mgs.

LOVELY ONION SOUP

Serves 10

This makes a surprisingly filling main dish when accompanied by a salad and vegetable.

1 Tbs. unsalted butter or margarine
1 Tbs. oil
6 medium-size onions, sliced into rings
Black pepper to taste
2 Tbs. dry sherry
1 tsp. mustard powder
7½ cups boiling water, divided

7½ Tbs. low sodium beef bouillon
½ cup dry white wine
½ tsp. thyme
2½ slices low sodium bread, toasted and
   cut into 10 triangles
5 ozs. low sodium Cheddar cheese, cut
   into 10 thin triangles

In large saucepan, heat butter and oil. Add onion rings. Sprinkle with pepper. Cover and simmer over low heat 25 minutes, or till onions start to brown, stirring regularly.
   Add sherry, mustard powder, and ½ cup boiling water. Stir to blend. Simmer 15 minutes.
   Stir in bouillon, remaining 7 cups water, and wine. Cover and simmer 30 minutes. Stir in thyme.
   Top each toast triangle with slice of cheese. Place on shallow baking sheet and broil 2 minutes, or till cheese starts to bubble.
   Pour soup into 10 bowls. Top with toast.

Calories per serving: 162	Sodium per serving: 33 mgs.

MADRILÈNE

Serves 8

2 cans (16 ozs. each) low sodium
   tomatoes, including liquid
3 cups boiling water
7 tsps. low sodium chicken bouillon
1 Tbs. low sodium beef bouillon
½ cup dry white wine
4 pkges. unflavored gelatin
¼ cup lemon juice

¼ cup dry sherry
1/16 tsp. allspice
½ tsp. basil
½ tsp. thyme
Black pepper to taste
2 Tbs. fresh chopped chives
2 Tbs. fresh chopped parsley
2 lemons, cut into wedges

Chop tomatoes. Place in large saucepan with their liquid. Add boiling water, chicken and beef bouillon. Cook over low heat 10 minutes, stirring occasionally.

In second saucepan, combine wine and gelatin. Cook over very low heat, stirring to dissolve.

Add gelatin mixture to tomato mixture. Stir to blend.

Stir in all but last 3 ingredients. Cook 10 minutes, stirring often. Cover and chill 4 hours.

Garnish with chives, parsley, and lemon wedges.

Calories per serving: 81   Sodium per serving: 32 mgs.

SQUASH SOUP

Serves 6

3 small butternut squash, baked and
  seeded
1 cup milk
2½ cups boiling water
3 Tbs. low sodium chicken bouillon

1 Tbs. lemon juice
¼ tsp. nutmeg
¼ tsp. aniseed
Black pepper to taste
1 Tbs. dry sherry

In large saucepan, combine squash pulp, milk, and water. Cook over low heat 5 minutes, mashing squash with fork.

Add remaining ingredients and cook 15 minutes over low heat, stirring often.

Calories per serving: 62   Sodium per serving: 29 mgs.

VICHYSSOISE

Serves 8

2 Tbs. unsalted butter or margarine
2 leeks, chopped, including greens
1 medium-size onion, chopped
4 potatoes, parboiled, peeled, and
  chopped
3½ cups boiling water
3½ Tbs. low sodium chicken bouillon

White pepper to taste
¼ tsp. garlic powder
2 Tbs. dry sherry
2 Tbs. lemon juice
½ cup heavy cream
4 Tbs. fresh chopped chives

In medium saucepan, melt butter. Add leeks and onion. Cook over low heat, stirring often, till onion is wilted.

Add all but last 2 ingredients. Cook over medium heat 15 minutes, stirring often.

In blender, purée, a little at a time, and return to pan.

Stir in cream.

Serve hot or chill 2 hours.
Garnish with chives.

Calories per serving: 160   Sodium per serving: 17 mgs.

German

The Germans enjoy soups as they do everything else—with gusto. For them, soups are a hearty and heartening warming-the-bones affair. They are eaten for lunch and for dinner as clear broths, and they serve as bases for stews and sauces. Soups are, indeed, an integral part of every German meal.

CHILLED TOMATO SOUP

Serves 6

4 tomatoes, chopped
2 cans (12 ozs. each) low sodium tomato
  juice
1½ cups dry white wine
½ cup dry sherry
1 Tbs. low sodium chicken bouillon

2 tsps. lemon juice
2 tsps. dill
Black pepper to taste
1 Tbs. sugar
6 Tbs. heavy cream

In blender, purée tomatoes, two at a time. Transfer to large saucepan.
Add all other ingredients except sugar and cream. Cook over low heat 5 minutes, stirring often.
Stir in sugar. Cover and chill at least 2 hours.
Pour into 6 bowls. Float 1 Tbs. cream in each bowl.

Calories per serving: 175   Sodium per serving: 19 mgs.

FRUIT SOUP

Serves 8

2 apples, peeled, cored, and chopped
1 cinnamon stick
1 Tbs. sugar
1 tsp. dried or fresh grated lemon peel
4 peaches, pitted and chopped
½ cup orange juice

½ cup dry red wine
2½ cups boiling water
2 Tbs. all-purpose flour
3 Tbs. cold water
¼ cup heavy cream

In large saucepan, combine first 8 ingredients. Cook over low heat 20 minutes.
Combine flour and cold water. Blend thoroughly. Stir into soup and simmer 5 minutes longer, stirring often.
Cover and chill at least 2 hours.
Discard cinnamon. Stir in cream.

Calories per serving: 112   Sodium per serving: 5 mgs.

Greek

Because Greece is a relatively poor country, except in spirit, soups are an important food staple. Leftovers are often turned into main meals when added to a hearty broth, nourishing the body as they do the senses with relatively little expense.

GREEK LEMON SOUP

Serves 6

3 cups Chicken Broth (See Page 45)
2 Tbs. lemon juice
1 egg, beaten
2 Tbs. water

¼ cup dry white wine
Black pepper to taste
1 Tbs. low sodium chicken bouillon
1 cup cooked rice

In saucepan, bring broth to a boil. Stir in lemon juice. Remove from heat.
In bowl, beat egg and water. Beat in ½ cup broth. Return to saucepan.
Stir in wine, pepper, and bouillon. Cook over low heat 10 minutes, or till mixture starts to bubble around the edges, stirring often.
Divide rice among 6 bowls. Add soup.

Calories per serving: 85   Sodium per serving: 24 mgs.

LIMA BEAN SOUP

Serves 8

1½ cups dried lima beans
8 cups water
1 Tbs. olive oil
2 medium-size onions, minced
2 cloves garlic, minced
3 cups Beef Broth (See Page 44)
4 tsps. low sodium chicken bouillon

2 bay leaves
1 Tbs. parsley
Black pepper to taste
1 can (6 ozs.) low sodium tomato paste
¼ cup red wine vinegar
1 tsp. oregano

Cover beans with water. Let stand overnight.
Bring beans to a boil in water in which they were soaked. Cover. Reduce heat and simmer 1½ hours, or till beans are tender. Drain, reserving ½ cup liquid.
In large saucepan, heat oil. Cook onions and garlic till onions are wilted. Add all remaining ingredients except tomato paste, vinegar, and oregano. Cover and simmer 30 minutes.
Stir in remaining ingredients. Cover and simmer 30 minutes more.

Calories per serving: 222   Sodium per serving: 24 mgs.

Indian

Soups are not normally included in the Indian meal, although many of their special stews, such as the famous mulligatawny, serve as robust main courses.

CHICKEN AND BARLEY SOUP

Serves 8

To make a wonderfully zesty main dish, add 1 lb. leftover chicken or lamb, cut into small chunks, just before serving.

2 cups water
⅔ cup barley
1 medium-size onion, minced
1 carrot, scraped and diced
Black pepper to taste
¼ tsp. garlic powder
3 cups Chicken Broth (See Page 45)

2 Tbs. low sodium chicken bouillon
1 leek, chopped, including greens
¼ tsp. Curry Powder (See Page 288)
Cayenne pepper to taste
¼ cup heavy cream
1½ Tbs. parsley

In large saucepan, combine water and barley. Bring to a boil. Reduce heat and simmer 30 minutes.

Add onion, carrot, black pepper, garlic powder, and Chicken Broth. Simmer 30 minutes more.

Add bouillon, leek, Curry Powder, and cayenne. Stir to blend well. Cover and simmer 20 minutes more.

Gradually stir in cream. Then stir in parsley. Cook 10 minutes more, stirring frequently.

Calories per serving: 133	Sodium per serving: 22 mgs.

MULLIGATAWNY SOUP

Serves 4

This is more stew than soup and should really be served as a main course with a side dish of vegetables.

1 Tbs. chopped ginger root or ¼ tsp.
  ginger powder
4 cloves garlic, chopped
3 Tbs. water
½ lb. stewing lamb, cut into 1″ chunks
½ tsp. ground coriander
½ tsp. cumin seed
1½ tsps. turmeric

Black pepper to taste
Cayenne pepper to taste
1 Tbs. cornstarch
2½ cups Chicken Broth (See Page 45)
2½ Tbs. long grain rice
2 tsps. low sodium chicken bouillon
2 Tbs. lemon juice
2 Tbs. dry white wine

In blender, combine first 3 ingredients. Grind to a paste. Set aside.

In large, ungreased saucepan, brown lamb over very low heat, turning often. Transfer to platter.

Add coriander, cumin, and turmeric to fat in pan, plus garlic paste. Fry over medium heat 1 minute, stirring to blend.

Reduce to low heat. Return lamb to pan. Stir in black pepper and cayenne.

Stir cornstarch into Chicken Broth, blending well. Slowly stir into lamb mixture.

Bring soup to a boil. Cover. Reduce heat and simmer 40 minutes.

Stir in remaining ingredients. Simmer 5 minutes more.

Calories per serving: 230	Sodium per serving: 79 mgs.

Italian

From the days the monks served soups to greet weary travelers or speed them on their way, soups have established themselves as an important part of Italian cuisine. Though never served at the same meal as pasta, some—such as the classic minestrone—contain pasta, rice, vegetables, or meat. These additions change a soup from what the Italians call light to thick—the latter often served as a main dish. Whichever the consistency, Italians have created a wealth of soups, and heartily enjoy them all.

CREAM OF ASPARAGUS SOUP

Serves 6

1 Tbs. unsalted butter or margarine
1 lb. asparagus, ends trimmed
2 potatoes, parboiled, peeled, and
   chopped
3½ cups boiling water

4 Tbs. low sodium chicken bouillon
2 tsps. lemon juice
White pepper to taste
1 tsp. basil
2 Tbs. chives

In saucepan, combine first 5 ingredients. Simmer 20 minutes, or till asparagus is tender, stirring occasionally.

In blender, purée asparagus mixture, a little at a time. Return to saucepan. Stir in remaining ingredients and simmer 10 minutes more, stirring often.

Calories per serving: 84	Sodium per serving: 14 mgs.

MINESTRONE

Serves 8

1 Tbs. unsalted butter or margarine
1 Tbs. olive oil
2 sprigs watercress, chopped
1 endive, chopped
½ large head cauliflower, separated into
   flowerets
2 medium-size onions, chopped

½ cup water
1 tsp. basil
Black pepper to taste
1 Tbs. low sodium beef bouillon
3 cups Chicken Broth (See Page 45)
1 lb. green beans, cut into 1″ lengths
⅛ tsp. nutmeg

In Dutch oven, heat butter and olive oil. Add all vegetables except green beans. Toss to coat well. Cover and sauté over very low heat 7 minutes.

Add water, basil, pepper and bouillon. Stir to blend. Cover and cook over low heat 20 minutes, adding more water, if necessary, to maintain 2″ water in pan.

Stir in Chicken Broth. Cover and simmer 10 minutes.
Stir in green beans and nutmeg. Cover and simmer 10 minutes more.

Calories per serving: 86	Sodium per serving: 25 mgs.

Jewish

There's no soup as Jewish as Matzo Ball Soup. It welcomes the Sabbath, cures colds, and generally presides at all important Jewish celebrations. The history of Jewish soup is as old as Judaism itself, starting as broths from boiling meat, simply flavored with herbs and spices, and nourishing its people throughout the centuries.

BORSCHT

Serves 8

3 cans (8 ozs. each) low sodium beets,
  including liquid
½ cup water
2 Tbs. sugar
2 Tbs. lemon juice
1½ tsps. dried or fresh grated lemon peel

Black pepper to taste
1 cup Chicken Broth (See Page 45)
3 Tbs. cranberry juice (optional)
8 strips of lemon peel
2 Tbs. fresh chopped parsley
1 Tbs. fresh chopped dill

In blender, combine beets and their liquid, water, sugar, lemon juice, lemon peel, and pepper. Grind coarse. Transfer to large saucepan.
Add remaining ingredients and cook over low heat till boiling.
Serve hot or cold garnished with lemon peel, parsley, or dill and a dollop of sour cream, if desired.

Calories per serving: 50	Sodium per serving: 45 mgs.

MATZO BALL SOUP

Serves 8

4 cups Chicken Broth (See Page 45)
1 Tbs. dill
2 tsps. parsley
Dash of sage (optional)

1 carrot, scraped, cut into ¼" rounds,
  and parboiled
8 Matzo Balls (See Page 80)

In large saucepan, combine all ingredients except Matzo Balls. Cook over low heat till steaming.

Place a Matzo Ball into each of 8 soup plates. Pour soup and carrots into plates.

Calories per serving: 119   Sodium per serving: 31 mgs.

SORREL SOUP (SCHAV)

Serves 8

1 lb. sorrel, chopped coarse
1 medium-size onion, minced
4 cups water
4½ Tbs. low sodium chicken bouillon

2 Tbs. sugar
¼ cup lemon juice
White pepper to taste
½ cup sour cream*

Preserved in non-sodium ingredient

In large saucepan, combine first 4 ingredients. Cover and simmer 25 minutes, stirring occasionally.

Stir in sugar, lemon juice, and pepper. Simmer 10 minutes more. Pour into pint jars.
Stir equal amounts of sour cream into jars. Cover and refrigerate overnight.
Shake before serving.

Calories per serving: 80   Sodium per serving: 19 mgs.

Mexican

Soups are part of every midday meal in Mexico, ladled from pots that simmer all day, perfuming the air. The variety is infinite, and one specialty or another is served, no matter the weather.

APPLE AND CHEESE SOUP

Serves 8

3 apples, peeled, cored, and chopped
2 medium-size onions, chopped
4 cups Chicken Broth (See Page 45)
½ cup dry sherry
Black pepper to taste
⅛ tsp. nutmeg

4 ozs. low sodium Gouda cheese, chopped
1 Tbs. low sodium beef bouillon
4 Tbs. heavy cream
1 tsp. mustard powder
2 Tbs. fresh chopped parsley

In large saucepan, combine apples, onions, and Chicken Broth. Cook over medium heat 10 minutes.

Stir in sherry, pepper, and nutmeg. Cook 5 minutes more, stirring occasionally.

Add cheese and bouillon. Cook over low heat, stirring often, till cheese melts, about 15 minutes.

Stir in cream and mustard powder. Cook 5 minutes more, stirring frequently.

Garnish with parsley.

Calories per serving: 167   Sodium per serving: 23 mgs.

SPICY CORN SOUP

Serves 8

1 Tbs. unsalted butter or margarine
1 medium-size onion, minced
3 cans (8 ozs. each) low sodium corn
  niblets, including liquid
2 Tbs. lemon juice
2 Tbs. dry sherry

3 cups Chicken Broth (See Page 45)
Black pepper to taste
Dash of hot pepper flakes
2 tsps. mustard powder
⅛ tsp. nutmeg
¼ cup heavy cream

In large saucepan, melt butter. Sauté onion till wilted.

Stir in corn and liquid, lemon juice, sherry, Chicken Broth, and all other ingredients except cream. Bring to a boil. Cover and simmer over low heat 15 minutes, or till mixture is bubbly.

Stir in cream.

Serve immediately. Or cover, chill overnight, and serve cold.

Calories per serving: 120   Sodium per serving: 14 mgs.

Spanish

Soups are an important part of the Spanish diet. Light broths appear at nearly every meal. Heartier varieties generally are a main dish.

Of the latter, the most popular worldwide is gazpacho, a rich, thick tomato broth garnished with chopped cucumbers, scallions, hard boiled eggs, and croutons. But in Spain, there are as many varieties of gazpacho as there are regions. Fish soups are, of course, among the most popular in this coastal land. But, along with gazpacho, garlic soup is the most representative of Spain.

FISH SOUP WITH CITRUS

Serves 6

4 cups Easy Fish Stock (See Page 45)
1 cup Chicken Broth (See Page 45)
1 medium-size onion, chopped
2 cloves garlic, minced
½ lb. cod fillets, cut into 1″ pieces
½ lb. haddock fillets, cut into 1″ pieces

Black pepper to taste
¼ tsp. nutmeg
2 cloves
1 orange, unpeeled, cut into wedges
1 Tbs. raisins*
½ cup orange juice

Preserved in non-sodium ingredient

In Dutch oven, combine Fish Stock, Chicken Broth, onion, and garlic. Bring to a boil and continue boiling 5 minutes.

Add all other ingredients except orange juice. Simmer over low heat 15 minutes.

Discard orange wedges. Stir in orange juice. Cook 5 minutes more, stirring occasionally. Discard cloves.

Serve as a main course with potatoes and salad.

Calories per serving: 222   Sodium per serving: 127 mgs.

GARLIC SOUP

Serves 6

4 Tbs. oil
4 cloves garlic
4 slices low sodium bread, cut into
  bite-size pieces
2 tsps. paprika

1 Tbs. low sodium beef bouillon
1 tomato, chopped
Coarse black pepper to taste
4 cups Chicken Broth (See Page 45)

In large saucepan, heat oil. Fry garlic till golden and mushy. Discard.

Add bread pieces and fry till brown on both sides. Transfer to plate.

Remove skillet from heat. Stir in paprika and bouillon.

Return to heat. Raise to high. Stir in tomato, pepper, and Chicken Broth. Bring to a boil. Reduce heat and cook over medium heat 10 minutes.

Return bread pieces to mixture. Cook 10 minutes more.

Calories per serving: 145   Sodium per serving: 24 mgs.

GAZPACHO

Serves 6

3 cloves garlic, minced
1 Tbs. paprika
1 tsp. sugar
2 tsps. low sodium beef bouillon
Cayenne pepper to taste
¼ tsp. cumin seed
3 large tomatoes, chopped coarse
1 Tbs. red wine vinegar
1 Tbs. olive oil
1 can (16 ozs.) low sodium canned
   tomatoes

1 can (6 ozs.) low sodium tomato paste
1½ cups boiling water
2 Tbs. low sodium chicken bouillon
4 scallions, chopped, including greens
1 cucumber, scraped and chopped
1 green pepper, minced
1 hard boiled egg, grated
2 slices low sodium bread, toasted and
   cubed

In bowl, combine first 6 ingredients. Stir to blend. Set aside.

In blender, combine tomatoes, vinegar, oil, canned tomatoes, tomato paste, and garlic mixture. Purée. Transfer to saucepan.

Add boiling water and bouillon. Cook over low heat 5 minutes, stirring frequently. Cover and chill 4 hours.

Place scallions, cucumber, green pepper, egg, and bread cubes in separate bowls. Serve as garnishes.

Calories per serving: 172   Sodium per serving: 48 mgs.

BREADS, ROLLS, AND DUMPLINGS

There's something comforting about a piece of bread—whether it's plain or herbed, with cheese or fruit. It's delectable.

Breads, especially homemade, are wondrous from the moment their hearty aroma starts to rise from the oven to the moment that first delicious morsel melts in your mouth. Moreover, prepared without salt and sliced thin, they are not a threat to your figure. But don't gorge yourself on bread just because it's healthy. Too much of anything is not good.

Most people love to eat bread but not to make it—kneading and flouring, letting it rise, and punching it down only to start over again. It is a chore. So if you'd rather, try one of the many salt free breads available. Plain or toasted. They're very good —with fewer calories and more nutrition than the commercial varieties—in puddings, stuffing, or for French toast or topped with your choice of herbs or spices for different taste delights.

But if you lust after homemade, don't be scared. Many breads can be started one day and left overnight. The work is the same, but it seems like less. And some bread batters can be poured directly from mixing bowl to loaf pan. Check your recipes and select those suitable to your needs and ambitions. Pick a dreary, stay-at-home day, and turn it into a cozy adventure by baking bread and letting its fragrance waft through your home and senses.

Don't forget however, that these breads, because they're salt free, should always be refrigerated to avoid molding. And even bread can be frozen and reheated as toast.

Store-bought is fine if you don't have the time. But no store-bought bread can ever compare in taste or satisfaction to the sensuous thrill of your own oven-baked loaf. Try it. It's definitely worth it.

American

Americans love bread. Bread is generally served at every meal. It is the first food selection your waiter offers in a restaurant. It is mother's standby for a quick sandwich meal.

Quick breads—biscuits, for example—are made with fast acting baking powder instead of yeast and are still a treat prepared at home. Yeast breads are generally left to professional bakers, though modern methods have taken the time out of this finer art.

But whoever makes them, breads are as much a part of American cuisine as meat and potatoes.

BLUEBERRY MUFFINS

Serves 24

2½ cups all-purpose flour
¾ cup sugar
1½ Tbs. low sodium baking powder
2 tsps. lemon juice
6 Tbs. unsalted butter or margarine
2 eggs

½ cup milk
1 tsp. vanilla extract
½ cup warm water
1 Tbs. low sodium chicken bouillon
1½ cups fresh blueberries or raspberries

Preheat oven to 400°.
Grease two 12-cup muffin pans. Line cups with waxed paper.
In large bowl, mix first 4 ingredients with fork.
Cut in butter till mixture resembles fine crumbs.
In small bowl, beat eggs, milk, vanilla, water, and bouillon. Stir into flour mixture to moisten.
Stir in blueberries. Spoon batter into muffin cups two-thirds full.
Bake 20 minutes, or till tops are golden.

Calories per serving: 126   Sodium per serving: 12 mgs.

CARROT LOAF

Serves 36

2½ cups whole wheat or all-purpose flour
3 tsps. low sodium baking powder
1½ tsps. cinnamon
¼ tsp. nutmeg
4 eggs
2 tsps. lemon juice

½ tsp. vanilla extract
2 cups sugar
1 cup oil
6 carrots, peeled and grated
¾ cup raisins*
¼ cup coconut, shredded

Preserved in non-sodium ingredient
   Preheat oven to 375°.
   In medium bowl, mix first 4 ingredients with a fork.
   In large bowl, beat eggs, lemon juice, vanilla, and sugar with a whisk till mixture is frothy.
   Gradually beat flour mixture then oil alternately into egg mixture.
   Stir in carrots, then raisins, then coconut. Pour batter into two greased 5″ × 9″ loaf pans. Bake 1 hour, or till toothpick inserted in center comes out clean.

Calories per serving: 159   Sodium per serving: 13 mgs.

HERBED COTTAGE CHEESE BISCUITS

Serves 24

3 cups all-purpose flour
10 tsps. low sodium baking powder
1 Tbs. sugar
1 Tbs. chives
1 Tbs. lemon juice
2 tsps. basil
2 tsps. oregano
½ tsp. sage

½ tsp. savory
½ tsp. thyme
½ tsp. garlic powder
⅛ tsp. rosemary, crushed
Black pepper to taste
¼ cup unsalted butter or margarine
1 lb. low sodium cottage cheese
2 eggs

   In large bowl, combine all but last 3 ingredients. Stir with fork to blend.
   Cut in butter till mixture resembles coarse crumbs.
   Stir in cottage cheese and eggs with fork, blending till soft dough forms. Add warm water, if necessary, to make dough pliable.
   Preheat oven to 450°.
   Turn dough onto lightly floured board. Knead 5 minutes. Form dough into balls the size of a tablespoon and place on cookie sheet 2″ apart.
   Bake 20 minutes, or till tops are golden brown.

Calories per serving: 122   Sodium per serving: 17 mgs.

MUFFINS

Serves 12

1 Tbs. low sodium chicken bouillon
2 cups all-purpose flour
2 Tbs. sugar
1½ Tbs. low sodium baking powder

2½ tsps. lemon juice
1 egg
1 cup water
¼ cup salad oil

Preheat oven to 400°.
Grease 12-cup muffin pan.
In large bowl, mix first 4 ingredients with fork.
In small bowl, beat remaining ingredients with fork till blended.
Stir egg mixture into flour mixture till flour is just moistened. (Batter will be lumpy.)
Spoon batter into muffin cups two-thirds full.
Bake 25 to 30 minutes, till golden, or till toothpick inserted in center comes out clean.

For Caraway Muffins, add 2 tsps. caraway seed to dry ingredients.

Calories per serving: 138   Sodium per serving: 10 mgs.

Chinese

Breads in China are the same as anywhere else in the world with one difference: they are generally steamed as small buns. These lovely mouthfuls are never served with butter, but rather with a variety of spicy sauces.

These dainty breads are often turned into separate courses when stuffed, before steaming, with blendings of meats and vegetables or fruit. A new and very pleasurable way, indeed, for western tongues to savor bread.

HONEY BUNS

Serves 30

1 pkge. active dry yeast
2 cups warm water, divided
5 cups all-purpose flour
10 tsps. sesame oil

3 Tbs. honey
¼ cup water
1 cup sesame seed

In large bowl, place yeast. Pour on ¾ cup warm water. Stir to blend.
Add flour and stir vigorously.
Add remaining 1¼ cups warm water and continue to stir till dough forms.

Knead firmly and shape into a ball. Place in second bowl. Cover with damp cloth and let stand 1¼ hours.

Turn onto floured board. Knead briefly.

Break off a heaping teaspoon of dough. Flatten and make a depression in the center. Brush with sesame oil and close over the depression by pinching dough with your fingers. Remove to platter.

Repeat till all dough is used.

Preheat oven to 450°.

In small saucepan, combine honey and ¼ cup water. Cook 1 minute over low heat, stirring to blend well.

Brush each bun with honey mixture. Sprinkle liberally with sesame seed.

Place buns, seeded side up, on lightly greased shallow baking pan. Bake 20 minutes, or till golden brown.

Calories per serving: 142   Sodium per serving: 6 mgs.

SWEET AND SOUR WON TONS

Serves 18

¾ cup oil
18 Won Tons (See below)
1 medium-size onion, chopped
3 cloves garlic, minced
3 mushrooms, sliced
½ green pepper, chopped

½ cup boiling water
1 Tbs. low sodium beef bouillon
2 Tbs. white vinegar
2 Tbs. sugar
1 Tbs. cornstarch

In wok, heat a third of the oil. When hot, add 6 Won Tons and cook over low heat till both sides are browned. Transfer to platter.

Repeat with remaining oil and Won Tons.

To wok, add onion, garlic, mushrooms, and green pepper. Stir fry 1 minute. Transfer to bowl.

In bowl, combine remaining ingredients. Add to wok. Bring to a boil, stirring constantly. Pour over vegetables.

Serve vegetable sauce on the side as dip for Won Tons.

Calories per serving: 148   Sodium per serving: 9 mgs.

WON TONS

Serves 18

2 cups all-purpose flour
1 egg, lightly beaten

4 tsps. low sodium chicken bouillon
⅓ cup water

Sift the flour into a bowl. Stir in egg and bouillon.
Gradually stir in water till dough is formed. Do not let it get pasty.
Turn dough onto lightly floured board and knead well.
Cover with damp cloth and let stand in warm place for 30 minutes.
Roll out very, very thin on lightly floured board. Cut into 2″ squares.
Place 1 Tbs. of Egg Roll Filling (See Page 29) in center of each square. Fold into a triangle and crimp the edges together.
Cook 20 minutes in boiling water or soup.

Calories per serving: 53*
*Does not include filling

Sodium per serving: 5 mgs.*

French

The baker and his wares are essential to the Frenchman's daily well being. Breads are not sold in the same shop as pastries. They, along with their respective chefs, are accorded separate places of culinary honor.

The baker prides himself on having an intimate feel for his ingredients. Independent of a given recipe, he instinctively knows when to add a little more of this, a little less of that. The light, melt-in-the-mouth French breads, croissants, and brioches are well-savored testaments to his skill.

BRIOCHE

Serves 16

¼ cup warm water
2 pkges. active dry yeast
2 Tbs. sugar
3 eggs

1 Tbs. low sodium chicken bouillon
2 cups all-purpose flour
½ cup unsalted butter or margarine

In large bowl, combine water and yeast, stirring to dissolve. Let stand 20 minutes.
In second bowl, combine sugar and eggs. Beat well.
To egg mixture, add remaining ingredients, creaming in butter till smooth.
Add yeast mixture. Beat vigorously 5 minutes.
Pour batter into 5″ × 9″ loaf pan. Let rise 3 hours.
Preheat oven to 450°.
Bake 20 minutes, or till toothpick inserted in center comes out clean.

Calories per serving: 133

Sodium per serving: 15 mgs.

FRENCH BREAD

Serves 16 (Makes 4 loaves)

½ cup Chicken Broth (See Page 45) or milk
1 Tbs. unsalted butter or margarine
1½ Tbs. sugar
3 Tbs. low sodium chicken bouillon

1¼ cups warm water
2 pkges. active dry yeast
5 cups all-purpose flour
1 Tbs. oil
4 Tbs. milk

In saucepan, bring Chicken Broth to a boil. Stir in butter, sugar, and bouillon. Let stand 15 minutes.

In second bowl, combine warm water and yeast, stirring to dissolve. Pour into broth mixture.

Gradually stir in flour, mixing till dough is formed.

Turn dough onto floured board. Knead till rubbery. Place in greased bowl. Brush top with oil. Cover and let rise 2 hours.

Punch down. Cover and let rise again 45 minutes.

Turn onto floured board and divide into 4 sections. Shape each into elongated oval.

Place loaves on greased baking sheet. Cover with towel and again let rise for 45 minutes.

Preheat oven to 400°.

Cut several diagonals in each loaf. Brush with milk and bake 20 minutes, or till loaves are browned.

Calories per serving: 148   Sodium per serving: 5 mgs.

SWEET ROLLS

Serves 26

1 pkge. active dry yeast
1 cup warm water
4 cups all-purpose flour
2 Tbs. low sodium chicken bouillon
1 egg

3 Tbs. sugar
½ cup unsalted butter or margarine
1 cup raisins*
¼ cup heavy cream

Preserved in non-sodium ingredient

Place yeast in bowl. Pour on warm water. Let stand 15 minutes.

Stir in remaining ingredients. Beat vigorously till dough is smooth and completely blended.

Turn dough into greased bowl. Cover with greased waxed paper. Chill overnight in refrigerator.

Preheat oven to 400°.
Turn dough onto floured board and roll to ½" thickness. Cut into circles, 2" in diameter.
Place circles on greased baking sheet.
Bake 15 minutes, or till rolls are golden brown.

Calories per serving: 116   Sodium per serving: 6 mgs.

German

It's hard to believe, but the people who bestowed dark rye on the world rarely bake bread at home. That's because it is easier to buy commercial breads or to visit the many bake shops which exude the sweet smell of baking bread.

BREAD PUFFS

Serves 24

1 pkge. active dry yeast
1¼ cups warm water
1 cup whole wheat flour
1 cup all-purpose flour
2 eggs

3 Tbs. maple syrup
¼ cup brandy
2 tsps. low sodium beef bouillon
½ cup unsalted butter or margarine, melted, divided

In medium-size bowl, combine yeast and water, stirring to dissolve.
Stir in whole wheat and all-purpose flour, eggs, maple syrup, brandy, bouillon, and half the melted butter. Blend to a smooth batter.
Cover and let stand 1 hour to rise. Stir down again.
In large skillet, pour half the remaining butter, tipping pan to cover entire surface.
Drop batter onto skillet. Cook over medium heat, turning to brown on all sides. Transfer to warm platter.
Repeat with remaining butter and batter. Cut puffs into wedges.

Calories per serving: 78   Sodium per serving: 8 mgs.

DARK RYE BREAD

Serves 20

1 pkge. active dry yeast
1 cup warm water, divided
2 cups all-purpose flour, divided
3 Tbs. molasses
2 Tbs. sugar
1 Tbs. unsalted butter or margarine

2 Tbs. low sodium beef bouillon
2 tsps. carob powder
2 tsps. caraway seed
½ cup raisins* (optional)
1½ cups rye flour

Preserved in non-sodium ingredient

In large bowl, dissolve yeast in ¼ cup warm water. Let stand 10 minutes.

Stir in 1 cup all-purpose flour, remaining warm water, molasses, sugar, butter, bouillon, carob powder, caraway, and raisins. Beat vigorously 5 minutes.

Stir in rye flour and remaining all-purpose flour. Beat till a soft dough is formed. Turn onto lightly floured board and knead 5 minutes, or till dough is spongy yet firm.

Turn dough into greased bowl. Cover with cloth and let stand 30 minutes.

Punch down dough. Turn onto lightly greased baking sheet and form into plump round loaf. Cover and refrigerate at least 4 hours.

Slash an "X" on the top of the loaf. Let stand at room temperature 30 minutes.

Preheat oven to 400°.

Bake 45 minutes, or till bottom sounds hollow when tapped.

Calories per serving: 110   Sodium per serving: 10 mgs.

SOUR CREAM BISCUITS

Serves 20

2 Tbs. water
1 tsp. sugar
1½ tsps. active dry yeast
2 tsps. low sodium chicken bouillon
1 Tbs. low sodium beef bouillon
Black pepper to taste

2 Tbs. lemon juice
2 eggs
½ cup sour cream*
2 Tbs. chives
2 cups all-purpose flour

Preserved in non-sodium ingredient

In large bowl, combine water, sugar, and yeast, stirring to dissolve.

Stir in chicken and beef bouillon, pepper, lemon juice, eggs, sour cream, and chives.

Stir in flour, mixing thoroughly till dough is formed.

Turn dough onto lightly floured board and roll to ¼" thickness. Cut into 1½" rounds. Transfer to baking sheet.

Cut a cross in center of each biscuit. Let rise 40 minutes.

Preheat oven to 350°.
Bake 15 minutes, or till biscuits are golden brown.

Calories per serving: 66   Sodium per serving: 11 mgs.

Greek

Bread is, indeed, the staff of life for many poor Greeks. But for rich and poor alike, it is part of every meal.

Many Greek breads are traditionally decorated and shaped to commemorate holidays, especially religious ones such as Christmas and Easter. But the most famous of all is the everyday pita—so popular as sandwich pockets.

DOUGHNUT BREAD

Serves 10

2 pkges. active dry yeast
1½ cups warm water
¾ cup milk
1 Tbs. sugar
3 Tbs. oil
1 tsp. aniseed

1 tsp. cinnamon
1 tsp. vanilla extract
5 cups all-purpose flour
1 egg yolk
2 Tbs. cool water

In bowl, combine yeast and ½ cup warm water. Stir to dissolve.
Slowly stir in remaining warm water, milk, sugar, oil, aniseed, cinnamon, and vanilla. Beat thoroughly.
Gradually beat in flour, beating vigorously till batter is smooth.
Turn dough onto lightly floured board and knead till dough loses stickiness. Cover and let stand 30 minutes.
Preheat oven to 350°.
Turn onto floured board, knead briefly, and divide dough in half.
Form each half into a flat ball. Roll each ball into a 12" rope.
Join ends of ropes and shape dough into two circles. Place on greased baking sheets and flatten circles to 9" in diameter. Cover and let stand 45 minutes, or till dough springs back to the touch.
In bowl, combine egg yolk and water. Brush mixture over dough circles. Bake, one at a time, on lowest oven rack.

Calories per serving: 90   Sodium per serving: 16 mgs.

NEW YEAR'S BREAD

Serves 18

1 pkge. active dry yeast
¼ cup warm water
½ cup milk
4 Tbs. unsalted butter or margarine
⅓ cup sugar
3 eggs
2 Tbs. lemon juice
2 tsps. dried or fresh grated lemon peel

2 tsps. dried or fresh grated orange peel
½ tsp. allspice
½ tsp. nutmeg
⅛ tsp. ground cloves
1 tsp. vanilla extract
3 cups all-purpose flour
¼ cup slivered almonds

In bowl, combine yeast and warm water. Stir to dissolve.

In saucepan, heat milk and butter till butter is melted, stirring often. Transfer to bowl.

Stir in sugar. Then beat in eggs, one at a time.

Stir in yeast mixture, lemon juice, lemon and orange peel, spices, and vanilla.

Slowly beat in flour, beating thoroughly.

Turn dough onto lightly floured board and knead till dough is pliable but not sticky.

Place dough in lightly greased bowl. Cover with damp cloth and let rise 1¾ hours. Preheat over to 350°.

Turn dough onto lightly floured board. Knead briefly. Shape into large round.

Place dough in lightly greased, deep 9" round cake pan. Cover and let rise again—about 45 minutes.

Moisten top with water. Sprinkle with almonds. Bake 40 minutes, or till top is lightly browned.

Calories per serving: 152   Sodium per serving: 15 mgs.

PITA BREAD

Serves 12

1 pkge. active dry yeast
1 tsp. sugar
¾ cup warm water, divided
3 cups all-purpose flour

2 Tbs. olive oil
1 Tbs. low sodium beef bouillon
½ cup Chicken Broth (See Page 45)

In bowl, combine yeast, sugar, and ¼ cup water. Stir to dissolve.

In second bowl, combine flour and oil. Beat in yeast mixture, bouillon, remaining ½ cup water, and Chicken Broth. Continue beating till dough is formed. Cover with damp cloth and let rise 1½ hours.

Turn dough onto lightly floured board. Knead briefly.

Divide dough into 12 equal sections. Roll each section to about 4½″ in diameter and ⅛″ thick.

Line a baking sheet with tin foil. Place rounds on sheet. Let stand 1 hour.

Preheat oven to 500°.

Bake rounds on lowest oven rack 5 minutes, or till puffy. Repeat till all pita is made.

Serve at once or stack, wrap in tin foil, and freeze. If reheating, bake pita, wrapped in foil, at 375° for 15 minutes.

Calories per serving: 146   Sodium per serving: 5 mgs.

Indian

Most Indian breads are unleavened and, therefore, flat—much like slightly oversize pancakes. They are best when eaten hot from the oven or grill and wrapped around a spicy morsel of Indian food.

BAKED INDIAN BREAD

Serves 16

3 cups all-purpose flour
1 egg, lightly beaten
4 tsps. low sodium chicken bouillon
2 tsps. sugar
1½ tsps. low sodium baking powder
1½ tsps. active dry yeast
3 Tbs. oil, divided

Cayenne pepper to taste
¼ tsp. nutmeg
5 Tbs. plus ¼ cup milk, divided
1 medium-size onion, minced
1 Tbs. lemon juice
¾ cup water, divided

Sift flour into large bowl.

In second bowl, combine egg, bouillon, sugar, baking powder, yeast, 2 Tbs. oil, cayenne, nutmeg, and 5 Tbs. milk.

Pour over flour and stir lightly.

Add onion and lemon juice.

Gradually add remaining ¼ cup milk and ¼ cup water. Knead well for 5 to 10 minutes, or till dough is spongy and elastic. Form into ball.

Turn dough into greased bowl. Brush with remaining Tbs. oil. Cover with damp cloth and let rise 2¾ hours in warm place.

Lightly grease a shallow pan.

Divide dough into 8 sections. Flatten, one at a time, on lightly floured board and shape into a long, thin oval. Place on pan. Cover with damp cloth and let stand 20 minutes at room temperature.

Preheat oven to broil.

Brush each bread with 1 Tbs. water, leaving ½" border all around. Bake under the broiler 6" from heat till each side is lightly browned.

Calories per serving: 144	Sodium per serving: 10 mgs.

GRIDDLE BREAD

Serves 8

½ cup whole wheat flour
½ cup all-purpose flour

½ cup water
Flour for dusting

In large bowl, combine whole wheat and all-purpose flour.

Slowly add the water, stirring to blend well, till dough is formed.

Knead well for 10 minutes. Form into ball. Cover with damp cloth and let stand 4 hours.

Slowly heat large cast iron or other heavy skillet over low heat.

Knead dough a second time for 2 minutes. Divide into 8 sections. Form into balls.

Place one ball at a time on floured board. Flatten. Dust with flour and roll to 4½" in diameter. Dust with more flour whenever dough starts to stick.

Place the flattened roll on the griddle. When bubbly, turn with tongs or wide spatula. Cook 30 seconds.

Remove from griddle with tongs and place directly over flame of second burner.

Hold over flame till it puffs up. Turn and flame second side briefly.

Place on warm platter.

Calories per serving: 59	Sodium per serving: 2 mgs.

WHOLE WHEAT PANCAKES

Serves 8

1½ cups whole wheat flour
2 Tbs. oil
2 tsps. low sodium beef bouillon
2 tsps. low sodium chicken bouillon
⅔ cup raisins*
½ tsp. cinnamon

⅛ tsp. nutmeg
½ cup water
Flour for dusting
10 Tbs. unsalted butter or margarine, melted

*Preserved in non-sodium ingredient

In large bowl, place flour. Pour on oil.

Stir in beef and chicken bouillon, raisins, and spices and gradually add water, mixing thoroughly till dough is formed.

Knead dough 10 minutes. Cover with damp cloth and let stand 20 minutes. Knead again briefly.

Heat a heavy skillet.

Divide dough into 8 sections.

Place one section at a time on floured board. Flatten.

Dust with flour and roll to 4″ in diameter.

Brush gently with butter. Fold in half.

Brush again with butter. Fold again.

Roll out a second time, dusting with flour to keep dough from sticking.

Brush griddle with melted butter. Add pancake and cook till golden brown. Turn and cook second side.

When all pancakes are done, stack and wrap in tin foil. To serve, heat in 250° oven 10 minutes.

Calories per serving: 153 Sodium per serving: 15 mgs.

Italian

Italians love their bread as much as anyone and especially love making special breads for every holiday occasion and religious feast days.

BREAD STICKS

Serves 36

3 Tbs. unsalted butter or margarine
1 cup warm water, divided
1 pkge. active dry yeast
1½ Tbs. garlic powder

1 Tbs. low sodium chicken bouillon
3 cups all-purpose flour, divided
2 egg whites, beaten stiff
½ cup sesame seed

In bowl, combine butter and ½ cup water. Stir to blend.

In second bowl, combine yeast and remaining water. Stir to dissolve.

Stir yeast mixture into butter mixture. Stir in garlic powder and bouillon.

Beat in 1 cup flour. Fold in egg whites.

Gradually beat in remaining flour. Turn dough into greased bowl. Cover with damp cloth and let rise 1¾ hours.

Punch dough down. Cover and let rise again 45 minutes.

Punch dough down. Cover and let stand 20 minutes.

Turn dough onto lightly floured board. Divide in half and roll each half ¼″ thick.

Cut dough into 2½″ pieces and roll to shape of thin pencils.

Sprinkle sticks with sesame seed. Place on greased baking sheet. Let stand 20 minutes.
   Preheat oven to 350°.
   Bake sticks 20 minutes, or till golden brown.

Calories per serving: 65   Sodium per serving: 5 mgs.

CRISPY BUNS

Serves 30

2 pkges. active dry yeast
3 Tbs. warm water
1 cup boiling water
2 Tbs. sugar
2 Tbs. vegetable shortening

1 Tbs. low sodium beef bouillon
3 ozs. low sodium Gouda cheese, shredded
5 cups all-purpose flour
1 egg, lightly beaten

   In bowl, combine yeast and 3 Tbs. warm water. Stir to dissolve. Set aside.
   In second bowl, combine boiling water, sugar, shortening, and bouillon. Stir to blend thoroughly.
   Add yeast mixture, cheese, and half the flour. Beat vigorously.
   Gradually beat in remaining flour. Place in greased bowl. Cover with damp cloth and let rise 1¾ hours.
   Punch down dough. Cover and let rise 45 minutes.
   Break off tablespoonfuls of dough. Form into balls. Place on baking sheet. Cover and let stand 30 minutes.
   Preheat oven to 350°.
   Brush dough balls with beaten egg and bake 20 minutes, or till golden brown.

Calories per serving: 104   Sodium per serving: 5 mgs.

GNOCCHI

Serves 12

1 cup water
4 Tbs. unsalted butter or margarine
2 tsps. low sodium beef bouillon
2 Tbs. low sodium chicken bouillon
⅛ tsp. nutmeg

1 cup all-purpose flour
2 eggs
6 ozs. low sodium Gouda cheese, minced
2 quarts water

   Put water, butter, beef and chicken bouillon, and nutmeg in medium-size saucepan. Bring to a boil.
   Add the flour, stirring vigorously, till a ball is formed that clears the sides of the pan.

Add eggs, one at a time, beating well to blend thoroughly.

Add cheese, beating in well.

Bring 2 quarts water to boil.

Form dough into cylinders ½" thick and 2" long.

Drop gnocchi into barely simmering water. Simmer 4 minutes. Drain.

Place gnocchi in 9" × 13" oven-proof casserole.

Preheat oven to 400°.

Pour 2 cups Mornay Sauce (See Page 292) over all. Bake 15 minutes, or till sauce bubbles.

Serve as light main course with salad and vegetable.

Calories per serving: 143*
*Does not include Mornay Sauce

Sodium per serving: 20 mgs.*

PIZZA

Serves 12

1½ tsps. active dry yeast
⅓ cup warm water
1 Tbs. lemon juice
1 Tbs. olive oil
5 tsps. low sodium chicken bouillon
3 Tbs. boiling water
1½ cups all-purpose flour, sifted
1 egg
2½ cups Tomato Sauce (See Page 298)
Dash of hot pepper flakes (optional)
2 tsps. low sodium beef bouillon

½ lb. mushrooms, sliced
1 medium-size onion, sliced thin
1 green pepper, sliced
½ red pepper, sliced
Hot Pepper Meatballs (See Page 187), halved
½ can (2⅕ ozs.) low sodium sardines (optional)
2 Tbs. oil
4 ozs. low sodium mozzarella cheese, sliced thin

In bowl, sprinkle yeast over warm water. Stir to dissolve.

In second bowl, combine lemon juice, oil, chicken bouillon, boiling water, flour, and egg. Mix well to form dough. Turn onto lightly floured board and knead till smooth and elastic. Form into ball and place in lightly oiled bowl. Cover with towel and let rise in warm place 2 hours, or till doubled in size.

Preheat oven to 400°.

Place dough on shallow baking sheet. Gently pat and stretch dough over sheet.

Spoon Tomato Sauce over dough. Sprinkle with pepper flakes and beef bouillon. Top with all remaining ingredients except oil and cheese.

Drizzle with oil and bake 20 minutes. Top with cheese and bake 5 minutes more, or till dough is browned and cheese melted.

Calories per serving: 388

Sodium per serving: 79 mgs.

Jewish

Bagels, rye bread, onion rolls, challah, not to mention matzo which dates back to the first Passover. These breads—and many others—universal in appeal, all started in a Jewish kitchen many years ago.

CHALLAH

Serves 18

1 cup warm water
4 cups all-purpose flour, divided
4 tsps. sugar
1 pkge. active dry yeast
1 Tbs. low sodium beef bouillon

1 Tbs. low sodium chicken bouillon
2 Tbs. oil
2 eggs, lightly beaten
2 tsps. water

In large bowl, combine warm water, 1⅓ cups flour, sugar, and yeast. Stir to a smooth blend.
Cover and let stand 20 minutes, or till air bubbles form.
Stir in remaining 2⅔ cups flour, beef and chicken bouillon, oil, and three quarters of the egg. Mix 5 minutes at medium speed or knead steadily 7 minutes.
Turn dough onto floured board and knead 5 minutes.
Form dough into ball. Cover with greased waxed paper, wrapped very loosely to allow dough to double.
Refrigerate overnight. Remove and let stand at room temperature 45 minutes.
Divide dough into 3 equal sections. Knead well and, with hands, roll into three 12″ ropes.
Press the ropes together at one end and then braid them, fastening together at the other end.
Cover loosely with greased waxed paper. Let stand 45 minutes, or till dough springs back to the touch.
Preheat oven to 425°.
Lightly grease a shallow pan.
Combine remaining egg with 2 tsps. water. Beat lightly. Brush over dough.
Place on greased baking sheet and bake 20 minutes.
Reduce heat to 375° and bake 40 to 45 minutes, or till challah is golden brown.

Calories per serving: 141   Sodium per serving: 10 mgs.

CHEESE BLINTZES

Serves 6 (Makes 12 Blintzes)

2 eggs
½ cup all-purpose flour
¾ cup water
2 tsps. oil
1 Tbs. low sodium chicken bouillon
1 lb. low sodium cottage cheese, drained

2 Tbs. heavy cream
2 Tbs. sugar
½ tsp. cinnamon
½ tsp. vanilla extract
1 Tbs. lemon juice
8 Tbs. unsalted butter or margarine

In bowl, beat together first 5 ingredients till batter is smooth.

In second bowl, combine cottage cheese, cream, sugar, cinnamon, vanilla, and lemon juice. Set aside.

Heat a small skillet. Brush lightly with butter. Pour a light coating of batter into center of pan, rolling it evenly across the bottom. Cook over low heat till underside is lightly browned.

Repeat using all but 2 Tbs. butter, turning blintzes onto a kitchen towel.

Place 1½ Tbs. cottage cheese mixture down center of browned side of each blintz. Fold toward the center.

Heat remaining 2 Tbs. butter in large skillet. Add blintzes, seam side down, and brown over low heat about 3 minutes.

Turn and brown second side.

Serve with stewed fruit or sour cream as luncheon meal.

Calories per serving: 319   Sodium per serving: 57 mgs.

EGG BAGELS

Serves 20

Recipe for Challah (See Page 78), using 4½ cups of flour instead of 4 cups.

Follow directions for preparation of Challah through removal of chilled dough from refrigerator.

Divide chilled dough into 20 sections. Knead each piece into a ball and roll into a rope.

Bring both ends of rope together and roll back and forth on table.

Place bagels on floured board. Let stand 1 hour.

Preheat oven to 500°.

Boil water in Dutch oven.

Add bagels to boiling water, a few at a time, and boil 2 minutes, or till they rise to the top. Turn over with slotted spoon and boil 30 seconds more. Remove to floured tray and bake 5 minutes, or till bagels are browned and crisp.

For Onion Bagels, work 2 medium-size onions, minced, into dough before dividing.

Egg bagels: Calories per serving: 126	Sodium per serving: 9 mgs.
Onion bagels: Calories per serving: 129	Sodium per serving: 10 mgs.

FLUFFY MATZO BALLS

Serves 10

½ cup matzo meal
1½ Tbs. low sodium chicken bouillon
1 tsp. dill
1 tsp. parsley
1 tsp. onion powder

Black pepper to taste
2½ Tbs. boiling water
2 Tbs. oil
2 eggs, lightly beaten

Place matzo meal in bowl. Stir in bouillon, herbs, and spices.
Stir in boiling water.
Add oil and blend thoroughly.
Stir in eggs and combine well. Mixture will be pasty.
Cover bowl and place in refrigerator 30 to 45 minutes. Form into 10 balls.
Bring 2 quarts water to a boil. Reduce heat to medium/low and drop in matzo balls. Cover pot and cook 40 minutes.
Remove matzo balls to soup pot and simmer 7 to 10 minutes in soup before serving.

Calories per serving: 86	Sodium per serving: 15 mgs.

ONION ROLLS

Serves 20

Recipe for Challah (See Page 78)

2 medium-size onions, minced

Follow recipe for Challah, leaving aside a quarter of the egg for glazing.

Divide dough into 20 sections. Form into rolls, flattened on the bottom.
Cover loosely with greased waxed paper. Let stand 45 minutes, or till dough springs back to the touch.
Glaze each roll with egg.
Sprinkle with minced onion.
Bake at 375° 20 to 25 minutes, or till tops are browned.

Calories per serving: 129	Sodium per serving: 10 mgs.

Mexican

Before the Spanish brought wheat into Mexico, corn was the basis for all breads. Today corn and wheat flours are used equally, and, whether corn or wheat, tortillas are still the most popular form of bread. Tortillas are eaten with breakfast, in sandwiches, and fried for hors d'oeuvres snacks.

Call them tortillas, tostadas, or enchiladas—breads are an important part of Mexican cuisine.

BREAD PUDDING MEXICANA

Serves 12

3 Tbs. unsalted butter or margarine,
   divided
1 cup milk
¼ cup dry sherry
1 cup Chicken Broth (See Page 45)
4 slices low sodium bread, toasted and
   broken
3 Tbs. chopped almonds

3 Tbs. raisins*
1 tsp. cinnamon
⅛ tsp. nutmeg
1 tsp. vanilla extract
1 tsp. low sodium beef bouillon
1 tsp. low sodium chicken bouillon
¼ lb. low sodium cottage cheese, drained
2 eggs, beaten

Preserved in non-sodium ingredient

Preheat oven to 350°.

In saucepan, combine 1 Tbs. butter, the milk, sherry, and Chicken Broth. Bring to a scalding boil.

Pour into buttered oven-proof casserole. Add bread pieces.

Stir in remaining ingredients except butter.

Dot remaining 2 Tbs. butter over the top.

Bake 35 minutes, or till top is lightly browned and firm.

Calories per serving: 136   Sodium per serving: 31 mgs.

DEVILISH CORN BREAD

Serves 16

1 cup cornmeal
1½ Tbs. low sodium baking powder
4 ozs. low sodium Cheddar cheese,
   grated
½ cup milk
2 eggs

2 chili peppers, chopped, or dash of hot
   pepper flakes
½ cup water
½ cup low sodium cottage cheese
4 Tbs. lemon juice
1 Tbs. cider vinegar

Grease a 9″ square oven-proof casserole.
Preheat oven to 400°.
In large bowl, combine cornmeal, baking powder, and cheese. Stir to blend.
In second bowl, combine remaining ingredients, blending thoroughly.
Stir egg mixture into cornmeal mixture. Stir to combine thoroughly.
Pour batter into casserole. Bake 50 minutes, or till top is firm and browned and toothpick inserted in center comes out clean.
Cool 20 minutes.

Calories per serving: 100   Sodium per serving: 17 mgs.

TORTILLAS

Serves 12

2 cups masa harina*
1⅛ cups Chicken Broth (See Page 45) or
  warm water
2 tsps. low sodium beef bouillon

2 tsps. low sodium chicken bouillon
1 tsp. garlic powder
Black pepper to taste

In bowl, combine masa, Chicken Broth, and the beef and chicken bouillon. Blend with hands till dough loses its stickiness.
Work in remaining ingredients.
Divide into 12 sections. Flatten each section as thin as possible between two pieces of waxed paper with a salad plate, or use a tortilla press.*
Heat a cast iron or other heavy skillet over low heat and cook tortillas, one at a time, till edges start to curl.
Flip tortilla with spatula and cook till edges start to lift again. Both sides should be browned.
Stack or wrap till needed. Tortillas may be frozen up to 4 months or refrigerated up to 3 weeks.
Note: To reheat, wrap damp cloth around foil and warm at 200° for 20 minutes.

Available in Mexican markets and in some specialty food stores.

Calories per serving: 81**   Sodium per serving: 5 mgs.***
**75 if water replaces Chicken Broth.*
***3 mgs. if water replaces Chicken Broth.*

Spanish

Perhaps because they expend so much time and lavish so much enthusiasm on their meals, the Spanish are not overly indulgent bread makers. Nevertheless, they do enjoy French toast, Spanish style, of course, bread puddings, and toast lavished with olive oil and garlic.

TOMATO BREAD

Serves 8

8 slices low sodium bread, toasted
8 cloves garlic, halved
1½ Tbs. olive oil
1 tsp. garlic powder

1 Tbs. low sodium chicken bouillon
1 large tomato, cut into 8 slices
1 Tbs. fresh chopped parsley

Rub toast on both sides with cut side of garlic cloves. Brush on oil.
Sprinkle toast with garlic powder and bouillon. Top with tomato slice and parsley.

Calories per serving: 151 — Sodium per serving: 15 mgs.

SQUASH BREAD

Serves 18

1½ cups all-purpose flour
1 cup sugar
3¾ tsps. low sodium baking powder
1/16 tsp. ground cloves
½ tsp. cinnamon
¼ tsp. nutmeg

2 Tbs. lemon juice
1 Tbs. dry sherry
1 egg
½ lb. cooked, drained, butternut squash
⅓ cup salad oil

Preheat oven to 350°.
Grease a 5″ × 9″ loaf pan.
In large bowl, mix all but last 3 ingredients.
In second bowl, beat egg, squash, and oil with fork or whisk till blended. Stir into flour mixture.
Pour batter into pan. Bake 1 hour, or till toothpick inserted in center comes out clean.

Calories per serving: 132 — Sodium per serving: 7 mgs.

VEGETABLE BISCUITS

Serves 28

1 recipe Herbed Cottage Cheese Biscuits
  (See Page 64)
1 carrot, scraped and chopped fine

1 medium-size onion, minced
½ green pepper, minced

Follow recipe for Herbed Cottage Cheese Biscuits, adding vegetables along with cottage cheese.
Bake according to directions for Herbed Cottage Cheese Biscuits.

Calories per serving: 108

Sodium per serving: 17 mgs.

SALADS

Crisp and crunchy, hot or cold, sweet or spicy, main dish or side, salads are a treasure. Filling, rich in protein and fiber, low in sodium and calories—with dressing or without—they are to be enjoyed for the healthy, tasty, and slimming delights they are. What's more, they can turn a simple meal into a fancy one.

Like soups, salads can be turned into a main course in minutes. They're a boon for those tired evenings when you just don't feel like cooking or can't make up your mind what to eat. Combine vegetables to please your eye as well as your palate, or turn a cold plate into a hot main dish by combining your favorite vegetables with pasta, potatoes, or boiled rice. Add some wine or bouillon and cheese and let it steam in the oven to mouth-watering, crispy tenderness while you relax.

Or add leftover meat, fish, or fowl and toss with your favorite dressing (already bottled in the refrigerator) and you have a full-course meal in one dish.

Whether side dish or main course, salads are easy. They are as varied in taste and texture as your vegetable bin and imagination can make them. So make whatever variety of chef's salad that strikes your fancy because this time you are the chef.

American

Unfortunately, Americans eat salads primarily to fill time between the appetizer and the main meal. Perhaps this trait stems from their impatient and eager desire to get to the heart of a situation or, in this case, meal.

This habit is changing, however. As Americans have become more conscious of and involved in physical fitness, they have learned to appreciate and enjoy salads for their nutritional, low calorie values. Moreover, they have come to relish the slightly chilled, crisp freshness of vegetables and regard their myriad tastes and textures as pleasing satisfiers of appetite, as well as hunger.

BEAN SALAD

Serves 8

1 lb. green beans, cut into 1″ lengths
1 lb. yellow (wax) beans, cut into 1″ lengths

2 medium-size onions, sliced into rings
¾ cup Vinaigrette Dressing (See Page 299)

Cook beans in boiling water till tender crisp, about 20 minutes.
In large bowl, combine beans and remaining ingredients. Cover and refrigerate 3 hours or more.

Calories per serving: 160   Sodium per serving: 8 mgs.

CARROT SALAD

Serves 8

½ head romaine lettuce, torn into pieces
3 carrots, peeled and grated
1 Bermuda onion, sliced thin
3 Tbs. oil

1 Tbs. cider vinegar
1½ tsps. honey
6 Tbs. Herbed Mayonnaise (See Page 290)

Combine first 6 ingredients. Blend well.
Add mayonnaise and mix.
Serve on a bed of lettuce.

Calories per serving: 130   Sodium per serving: 25 mgs.

CHICKEN SALAD

Serves 4

¾ lb. leftover chicken, cut into small
   chunks
½ cup Green Sauce (See Page 289)
1 cucumber, scraped and chopped

4 scallions, chopped, including greens
½ green pepper, minced
1 tsp. mustard powder
1 Tbs. tarragon

In bowl, combine first 2 ingredients, blending well.
Stir in remaining ingredients. Cover and chill 1 hour.
Serve as main dish with potatoes or pasta and vegetable.

Calories per serving: 235   Sodium per serving: 76 mgs.

CREAMY COLESLAW

Serves 12

½ large head cabbage, shredded
1¼ cups low sodium mayonnaise
6 Tbs. cider vinegar
1¼ tsps. sugar
Black pepper to taste

¼ tsp. garlic powder
1 tsp. mustard powder
1 carrot, scraped and diced
1 medium-size onion, minced
1 green pepper, chopped

Combine all ingredients. Stir thoroughly with fork to blend well.
Chill overnight to heighten flavor.
Note: For potato salad, substitute 6 potatoes, parboiled, pealed, and cubed, for
cabbage. Add 2 Tbs. parsley and omit carrot.

Calories per serving: 214   Sodium per serving: 14 mgs.

TOMATO AND OYSTER SALAD

Serves 4

1 Tbs. unsalted butter or margarine
1 pt. oysters, drained, liquid reserved for
   other use
Black pepper to taste
¼ tsp. fennel seed
¼ tsp. garlic powder

2 tsps. low sodium chicken bouillon
2 Tbs. lemon juice
3 Tbs. Tartar Sauce (See Page 297)
2 tsps. fresh chopped parsley
2 tomatoes
2 hard boiled eggs, cut into wedges

In skillet, melt butter. Sauté oysters, seasoned with pepper, fennel, and garlic powder, 30 seconds.
Remove from heat. Chop oysters coarsely.
Stir in bouillon, lemon juice, Tartar Sauce, and parsley.
Cut ½" cap off tomatoes. Scoop out pulp and add to oyster mixture. Blend well.
Stuff tomatoes with oyster mixture.
Replace tomato cap and chill 30 minutes.
Serve on bed of lettuce.
Garnish with egg wedges.
Serve as main dish with rice.

Calories per serving: 221   Sodium per serving: 87 mgs.

Chinese

Salads consisting of raw, fresh vegetables are virtually unknown in China. Even when vegetables are served as separate dishes, they are cooked or marinated in some fashion.

Thus, the recipes in this section are by no means authentic. They are simply flavored in the Chinese manner to enable you to add a touch of the Orient to your salad plate.

HOT WATERCRESS AND TOMATO SALAD

Serves 4

1 Tbs. oil
1 can (8 ozs.) bamboo shoots, drained
½ can (4 ozs.) water chestnuts, sliced
8 mushrooms, sliced
2 bunches watercress, stems trimmed

2 tomatoes, cut into wedges
1 tsp. sugar
2 Tbs. dry sherry
2 tsps. low sodium chicken bouillon
2 Tbs. boiling water

In wok or skillet, heat oil. Add bamboo shoots, water chestnuts, and mushrooms. Stir fry over medium heat 1 minute.
Add watercress, tomatoes, sugar, and sherry. Stir fry 1 minute more.
Combine bouillon and boiling water. Add to wok and stir fry briefly.
Serve with 1 hard boiled egg per person to turn dish into light lunch.

Calories per serving: 110   Sodium per serving: 33 mgs.

NOODLE AND PEANUT SALAD

Serves 8

½ lb. vermicelli, cooked al dente*
½ lb. fresh bean sprouts, chopped
16 lettuce leaves, torn into pieces
4 mushrooms, sliced
1 lb. asparagus, trimmed, steamed, and
  chopped
2 Tbs. low sodium peanut butter

4 scallions, chopped, including greens
⅓ cup hot water
2 tsps. low sodium beef bouillon
1 tsp. sesame oil
1 tsp. cider vinegar
1 Tbs. dry sherry
Dash of hot pepper flakes

Do not add salt to boiling water.
  In large bowl, combine first 5 ingredients. Toss to blend.
  In saucepan, combine remaining ingredients. Cook over low heat, stirring constantly, till peanut butter is blended smoothly. Pour over noodle mixture. Toss to blend well.
  Cover and chill 1 hour.

Calories per serving: 186   Sodium per serving: 12 mgs.

SZECHWAN SALAD

Serves 4

1 Tbs. oil
½ lb. sirloin steak, sliced thin
2 cloves garlic, minced
½ tsp. garlic powder
½ can (4 ozs.) water chestnuts, chopped
Dash of hot pepper flakes

Dash of ginger powder
3 Tbs. dry sherry
½ cup Chicken Broth (See Page 45),
  divided
1 head Bibb lettuce, torn into pieces
2 Tbs. heavy cream

  In skillet, heat oil. Add beef and stir fry over medium heat till both sides lose their pink color.
  Add garlic, garlic powder, water chestnuts, pepper flakes, ginger powder, and sherry. Stir fry 1 minute.
  Add 2 Tbs. Chicken Broth and cook 1 minute more. Transfer to bowl.
  Add lettuce, remaining Broth, and cream. Stir to blend. Cover and refrigerate 1 hour.
  Serve as main dish with rice and broccoli.

Calories per serving: 272   Sodium per serving: 59 mgs.

French

In the case of salads, the French believe more is better. Theirs is the true mixed salad, often combining several types of crisp, fresh greens along with an occasional tomato or onion. A simple vinaigrette dressing flavored with mustard or other spices and tossed with romaine, escarole, or any raw vegetables you choose are a delightful refreshment, the perfect ending to any meal.

CAULIFLOWER AND PORK SALAD

Serves 6

1 head cauliflower, separated into flowerets
2 Tbs. low sodium mayonnaise
¼ cup Vinaigrette Dressing (See Page 299)
1 Tbs. low sodium chili ketchup

2 Tbs. dry sherry
½ tsp. turmeric
⅛ tsp. mace
⅛ tsp. nutmeg
¾ lb. leftover pork, chopped
2 scallions, chopped, including greens

Cook cauliflower in boiling water till tender crisp, about 15 minutes. Drain.
In bowl, combine all remaining ingredients except pork and scallions. Cover and chill 1 hour, stirring occasionally.
Stir in pork and scallions. Let stand 5 minutes.
Serve as main dish with pasta or rice.

Calories per serving: 266	Sodium per serving: 50 mgs.

SALADE NIÇOISE

Serves 6

2 cans (6½ ozs. each) low sodium tuna
4 scallions, chopped, including greens
2 lbs. green beans, steamed tender crisp
1 carrot, cut into ¼" rounds
3 tomatoes, quartered
1 green pepper, sliced thin

2 potatoes, parboiled, peeled, and cubed
1 head romaine lettuce, torn into pieces
½ cup Vinaigrette Dressing (See Page 299)
3 hard boiled eggs, quartered
6 slices red onion

In large salad bowl, flake tuna.
Add all but last 3 ingredients. Toss to blend.
Pour on Vinaigrette Dressing. Toss to blend.

Place egg wedges on top of salad.
Garnish with onion slices.
Serve as main dish.

Calories per serving: 270	Sodium per serving: 89 mgs.

WATERCRESS SALAD

Serves 6

2 bunches watercress, stems trimmed,
  chopped
2 zucchini, cut into ¼″ rounds
4 mushrooms, sliced

12 cherry tomatoes, sliced in half
1 tangerine, peeled and sectioned
⅓ cup Creamy Mustard Dressing (See
  Page 287)

In large bowl, combine all ingredients. Stir to blend well.

Calories per serving: 106	Sodium per serving: 28 mgs.

German

In Germany, salads usually accompany rather than precede the main meal. In fact, they are almost like relishes, accenting the total eating experience with additional tastes and textures.

Because root plants—such as beets, cabbage, cauliflower, carrots, parsnips, and Brussels sprouts—grow abundantly in the northern German climate, they are usually featured in salads, enhanced by a tangy dressing, using as much vinegar as oil, often tempered by a small amount of sugar. As such, salads heighten the appreciation of the main course.

CREAMY CUCUMBER SALAD

Serves 6

2 cucumbers, scraped and sliced thin
¼ cup sour cream*
2 Tbs. lemon juice
1 tsp. paprika
1 tsp. dill

Black pepper to taste
½ tsp. sugar
1 Tbs. chives
2 ozs. raisins*

*Preserved in non-sodium ingredient

In bowl, combine all ingredients. Toss to blend well.
Chill 30 minutes before serving.

Calories per serving: 56   Sodium per serving: 11 mgs.

HOT CABBAGE AND APPLE SALAD

Serves 10

1 large head cabbage, shredded
3 cups water
1 cup Chicken Broth (See Page 45)
½ tsp. caraway seed
2 Tbs. low sodium ketchup
2 Tbs. lemon juice

⅛ tsp. allspice
2 tsps. sugar
⅛ tsp. hot pepper flakes
¼ cup heavy cream
3 apples, cored and sliced thin
¼ cup chopped walnuts

In Dutch oven, combine cabbage and water. Bring to a boil. Cover. Reduce heat and simmer 10 minutes. Drain. Set aside.

In saucepan, combine Chicken Broth, caraway seed, ketchup, lemon juice, allspice, sugar, and pepper flakes. Bring to a boil. Reduce heat and simmer 10 minutes. Stir in cream.

Place cabbage in large bowl. Add apples and walnuts. Pour on dressing. Stir to blend well.

Calories per serving: 83   Sodium per serving: 18 mgs.

SWEET AND SOUR BEET SALAD

Serves 6

⅓ cup cider vinegar
2 Tbs. brown sugar
4 cloves
½ tsp. thyme

Coarse black pepper to taste
2 cans (8 ozs. each) low sodium beets,
   including liquid
1 Tbs. lemon juice

In small saucepan, combine all ingredients except beets and their liquid and lemon juice. Bring to a boil. Reduce heat and simmer 3 minutes.

Add beets and their liquid and lemon juice. Stir to blend. Cook over low heat 5 minutes.

Pour into bowl. Cover and refrigerate overnight. Discard cloves.

Calories per serving: 42   Sodium per serving: 36 mgs.

Greek

Vegetables are varied and plentiful in Greece, often waiting to be plucked from a backyard garden. They are presented on platters—artistic juxtapositions of colors and forms, designed to please the eye as well as the palate.

The simplest dressings are preferred. A light blend of oil and vinegar or lemon juice a touch of spice, are all that's required to awaken and enhance the natural flavors of the vegetables. Cubes of feta cheese (for which we substitute low sodium Gouda or Monterey Jack) often lend a piquant touch.

Salads are so popular that the Greeks often turn them into main courses, usually punctuated with chunks of seafood.

AVOCADO WITH MINCED FISH

Serves 4

2 avocados, halved and pitted
2 tsps. lemon juice

1 cup Minced Fish (See Page 27)
1 lemon, quartered

Fill each avocado half with ½ tsp. lemon juice.
Spoon a quarter of the Minced Fish into each avocado half.
Chill 1 hour.
Garnish with lemon wedges.
Serve as main dish with tomatoes and cauliflower.

Calories per serving: 298   Sodium per serving: 28 mgs.

DILLED CUCUMBER SALAD

Serves 6

4 Tbs. low sodium chili ketchup
1 Tbs. cider vinegar
3 Tbs. heavy cream
3 Tbs. lemon juice
1 can (4⅜ ozs.) low sodium sardines,
  including liquid

2 cucumbers, scraped and sliced thin
½ tsp. garlic powder
1 tsp. dill
½ tsp. mustard powder
2 tsps. fresh chopped parsley

In small bowl, combine ketchup, vinegar, cream, lemon juice, and liquid from sardine can. Stir to blend.

In a bowl, place cucumbers. Sprinkle with garlic powder, dill, and mustard powder. Toss lightly.

Divide cucumber mixture among 6 plates. Top with sardines. Spoon ketchup mixture on each. Sprinkle with parsley.

Calories per serving: 60   Sodium per serving: 26 mgs.

GREEK EGGPLANT SALAD

Serves 8

1 1-lb. eggplant
1 medium-size onion, minced
2 cloves garlic, minced
1 tomato, chopped
2 Tbs. red wine vinegar
6 Tbs. oil
6 Tbs. warm water
2 Tbs. heavy cream
2 Tbs. lemon juice

3 Tbs. parsley
½ tsp. sugar
¼ tsp. marjoram
⅛ tsp. nutmeg
Coarse black pepper to taste
¼ Tbs. raisins*
1 carrot, scraped and cut into 1″ rounds
1 head lettuce

Preserved in non-sodium ingredient

Preheat oven to 350°.

Bake eggplant 45 minutes. Hold under cold water and peel skin.

In large bowl, chop eggplant. Add all remaining ingredients except carrot and lettuce. Blend thoroughly.

In small saucepan, cover carrot with water and cook till tender. Chop and stir into eggplant mixture. Cover and chill overnight.

Divide lettuce among 6 plates. Mound eggplant mixture on top.

Calories per serving: 127   Sodium per serving: 18 mgs.

Indian

Salads are virtually unknown in India as we know them in the States. Perhaps because there are so many vegetarians in India who like the flavor of spices to permeate their meals, and this is best accomplished by cooking. Perhaps because the Indians are so conscious of the seasonality of their vegetables and would rather pickle or otherwise preserve them to be enjoyed when they are no longer available.

Consequently, using Indian spices, we have developed some salads, Western style, that, we hope, will give you a touch of that mysterious land.

EGGPLANT AND RICE SALAD

Serves 8

1 cup long grain rice
2 cups Chicken Broth (See Page 45)
1 Tbs. unsalted butter or margarine
1 1-lb. eggplant, peeled and chopped
1 cinnamon stick
1 medium-size onion, minced

2 cloves garlic, minced
3 Tbs. lemon juice
1 tsp. sugar
1 Tbs. honey
2 tsps. low sodium beef bouillon
1 head romaine lettuce, torn into pieces

In saucepan, combine rice and Chicken Broth. Bring to a boil. Cover. Reduce heat and simmer till liquid is absorbed.

While rice is cooking, melt butter in wok or skillet. Add eggplant, cinnamon, onion, and garlic. Cook over low heat 5 minutes, stirring occasionally.

Raise to medium heat. Stir in lemon juice, sugar, and honey. Stir fry 1 minute.

Stir in bouillon, blending well. Discard cinnamon.

In bowl, combine rice and eggplant mixture. Blend thoroughly.

Toss eggplant mixture with lettuce.

Calories per serving: 154   Sodium per serving: 18 mgs.

GREEN BEANS AND POTATO SALAD

Serves 6

1 Tbs. oil
1 tsp. turmeric
¼ tsp. ground cumin
½ tsp. ground coriander
2 potatoes, parboiled, peeled, and diced

1 lb. green beans, cut into 1″ lengths,
  and steamed
2 tsps. low sodium chicken bouillon
6 hard boiled eggs, cut into wedges
2 lemons, cut into wedges

95

In wok or skillet, heat oil. Add turmeric, cumin, and coriander. Then add potatoes. Stir fry over low heat 1 minute, being sure to coat all potatoes.

Add green beans and chicken bouillon. Stir to blend. Transfer to salad bowl. Cover and chill 30 minutes.

Divide salad among 6 salad plates. Garnish with egg and lemon wedges.

Calories per serving: 142   Sodium per serving: 62 mgs.

YELLOW CAULIFLOWER SALAD

Serves 8

2 Tbs. plus ¼ cup oil, divided
2 tomatoes, chopped
1 Tbs. turmeric
½ tsp. ground coriander
¼ tsp. Indian Spice (See Page 291)
2 tsps. low sodium ketchup

1 head cauliflower, broken into flowerets
 and steamed tender crisp
¼ cup hot water
3 Tbs. lemon juice
⅛ tsp. nutmeg

In wok or skillet, heat 2 Tbs. oil. Add tomatoes, turmeric, coriander, and Indian Spice. Stir fry 1 minute.

Add ketchup and cauliflower. Stir fry to coat cauliflower. Transfer to bowl.

In small bowl, beat together remaining ingredients. Pour on cauliflower mixture. Toss to coat thoroughly. Chill 1 hour.

Calories per serving: 113   Sodium per serving: 7 mgs.

Italian

The Italians love their vegetables, and for salads, they love greens above all. But whatever vegetables they choose, they carefully select only unblemished, small produce, finding them the sweetest.

Italians are especially particular about the dressings for these tender greens. They use at least twice as much oil as vinegar, a clove of garlic to perfume the bowl and a light dash of seasonings. To insure that each ingredient is thoroughly blended into the salad, they add them one at a time. The care they take is quite worthwhile.

OYSTER SALAD

Serves 6

½ lb. spaghetti
1 Tbs. olive oil
2 pts. oysters, drained, liquid reserved
White pepper to taste
2 small onions, minced
6 cloves garlic, minced
2 tomatoes, chopped
½ cup dry white wine

1 tsp. oregano
2 tsps. tarragon
1 Tbs. parsley
½ tsp. thyme
Dash of hot pepper flakes
1 Tbs. low sodium beef bouillon
2 Tbs. lemon juice

Cook spaghetti al dente.* Drain. Set aside.

While spaghetti is cooking, heat oil in large skillet. Add oysters. Sprinkle with pepper and cook over medium heat 10 seconds each side. Remove to deep dish and chop.

To same skillet, add onions and garlic. Cook over very low heat till onions are wilted, stirring often.

Add tomatoes. Cook 2 minutes.

Stir in remaining ingredients, including oyster liquid. Cook over medium heat, stirring often, till mixture bubbles around the edges.

Add spaghetti to oysters. Toss to blend thoroughly.

Serve as main dish.

Do not add salt to boiling water.

Calories per serving: 321   Sodium per serving: 96 mgs.

PORK AND RICE ANTIPASTO

Serves 8

1 cup long grain rice
3 cups water
2 Tbs. oil
2 medium-size onions, minced
8 cloves garlic, minced
1 lb. ground pork
6 mushrooms, sliced
⅓ cup Vinaigrette Dressing (See Page 299)

2 tsps. oregano
1 Tbs. low sodium beef bouillon
3 ozs. low sodium Gouda cheese, cut into 1″ chunks
½ green pepper, sliced
½ red pepper, sliced

In medium saucepan, combine rice and water. Bring to a boil. Cover. Reduce heat and simmer till liquid is absorbed, about 20 minutes. Fluff with fork. Set aside.

While rice is cooking, heat oil in large skillet. Add onions and garlic and cook over low heat till onions are wilted.

Add pork and mushrooms. Cook till pork loses its pink color, breaking it up with fork.

Combine rice, pork mixture, Vinaigrette, oregano, bouillon, and cheese in large bowl. Toss to blend well. Let stand at room temperature.

Place peppers on tin foil, skin side up. Run under broiler till skins start to blacken. Add to salad.

Serve as main dish.

Calories per serving: 387   Sodium per serving: 52 mgs.

Jewish

The Jews have cultivated a wide range of taste in food because of their divergent backgrounds. The development of salads in their cuisine is no exception. Originally, salads were no more than a chopped cucumber and scallions, with perhaps a radish or carrot or two. But thanks to their German, Egyptian, and American heritage, Jews have become more sophisticated in their appreciation of the wide variety of salads that can and do provide delightful prologues to the main meal.

CHICKEN, RAISIN, AND ALMOND SALAD

Serves 6

¼ cup low sodium mayonnaise
2 Tbs. lemon juice
3 Tbs. dry sherry
1 tsp. mustard powder
1 lb. leftover chicken, cut into 1″ chunks

¼ cup chopped almonds
¼ cup raisins*
½ green pepper, chopped
¼ large cantaloupe, cut into 1″ chunks

Preserved in non-sodium ingredient
In bowl, combine mayonnaise, lemon juice, sherry, and mustard. Stir to blend.
Add remaining ingredients. Toss to blend thoroughly.
Serve as main dish.

Calories per serving: 268   Sodium per serving: 59 mgs.

HONEY BEET SALAD

Serves 4

1 can (8 ozs.) low sodium beets, including liquid
2 Tbs. lemon juice
2 Tbs. honey

½ head romaine lettuce, torn into pieces
1 orange, peeled and sectioned
2 scallions, chopped, including greens

In large bowl, combine beet liquid, lemon juice, and honey, blending thoroughly.
Add remaining ingredients. Blend well.

Calories per serving: 85   Sodium per serving: 33 mgs.

MOLDED CUCUMBER SALAD

Serves 6

1 pkge. unflavored gelatin
¾ cup boiling water
2 Tbs. lemon juice
2 Tbs. lime juice
1 cucumber, scraped and chopped

1 Tbs. parsley
1 can (8 ozs.) fruit salad, drained
1 apple, peeled, cored, and chopped
1 grapefruit, peeled and sectioned

In bowl, combine gelatin and boiling water, stirring to dissolve.
Stir in lemon and lime juice. Stir in remaining ingredients except grapefruit. Pour into mold. Chill until firm.
Unmold by placing mold in warm water and running knife around edges to loosen. Place plate on top and invert gelatin.
Garnish with grapefruit sections.

Calories per serving: 86   Sodium per serving: 5 mgs.

Mexican

Mexicans incorporate so many vegetables in preparing the main meal and in garnishing it, a separate salad would be redundant. That's not to say they don't enjoy salads. They do. So much so, they often arrange a beautiful and colorful selection of crisp, raw vegetables as a main dish.

AVOCADO AND TACO SALAD

Serves 8

1 head romaine lettuce, torn into pieces
1 orange, peeled and sectioned
1 avocado, peeled and cut into 1″ chunks
8 slices red onion, chopped
2 cups Bean Salad (See Page 86)

4 ozs. low sodium Cheddar cheese, cut
  into ½″ chunks
8 cherry tomatoes, sliced in half
1 tsp. paprika
Low sodium taco chips

In large bowl, combine all ingredients except taco chips.
Cover and chill 30 minutes.
Serve with taco chips.

Calories per serving: 132   Sodium per serving: 14 mgs.

BEAN AND CORN SALAD

Serves 10

½ cup kidney beans
4 cups water
3 cans (8 ozs. each) low sodium corn
   niblets, including liquid
2 chili peppers, minced
½ cup low sodium mayonnaise
½ medium-size red onion, chopped
¼ tsp. cumin seed

¼ tsp. cinnamon
½ tsp. fennel seed
1 Tbs. turmeric
2 Tbs. cider vinegar
2 tsps. mustard powder
1 tsp. onion powder
1½ Tbs. low sodium chili ketchup
1 head romaine lettuce, torn into pieces

Combine kidney beans and water. Soak overnight.
   Cook beans in water in which they were soaked, uncovered, over low heat 1½ hours, or till beans start to burst and are tender. Drain.
   Combine beans, corn and its liquid, and chili peppers. Cover and chill 1 hour.
   Combine mayonnaise and all remaining ingredients except lettuce. Blend thoroughly. Stir in bean mixture.
   Divide lettuce among 10 salad plates. Spoon bean mixture on top.

Calories per serving: 169   Sodium per serving: 14 mgs.

FRUIT SALAD

Serves 8

¼ cup lemon juice
¼ cup honey
3 Tbs. oil
¼ cup orange juice
2 Tbs. low sodium mayonnaise
1 tsp. mustard powder
1 Tbs. paprika
¾ lb. low sodium cottage cheese

1 grapefruit, peeled and sectioned
1 banana, peeled and sliced
½ lb. seedless grapes
1 avocado, peeled, pitted, and sliced
½ head escarole, torn into pieces
4 hard boiled eggs, cut into wedges
2 limes, cut into wedges

In large bowl, beat together first 7 ingredients.
Fold in cottage cheese.
Stir in remaining ingredients except escarole, eggs, and limes.
Divide escarole among 8 salad plates. Spoon salad mixture in center.
Garnish with egg and lime wedges.
Serve as main dish.

Calories per serving: 261   Sodium per serving: 50 mgs.

Spanish

Salad is typically a first course in Spain. Atypically, it often contains a wide assortment of vegetables, of which lettuce is but one. They are prettily arranged on a platter, lightly touched with oil and vinegar; so each diner can, in fact, put his favorite combination together. In Spain, salad is an invitation to dine.

MIXED GREEN SALAD

Serves 8

1 endive, torn into pieces
1 medium-size onion, sliced into rings
3 tomatoes, cut into wedges
½ green pepper, chopped
6 Tbs. oil
6 Tbs. water
4 Tbs. red wine vinegar

1 Tbs. dry sherry
1 Tbs. lemon juice
1 Tbs. dry red wine
1 Tbs. parsley
1 tsp. mustard powder
1 Tbs. low sodium beef bouillon
Cayenne pepper to taste

In bowl, combine first 4 ingredients. Toss to blend.
In jar, combine remaining ingredients, cover, and shake well. Pour over salad. Toss to blend well.

Calories per serving: 124   Sodium per serving: 11 mgs.

PICKLED FISH SALAD

Serves 6

3 Tbs. oil, divided
1¼ lbs. sea bass fillets
1 Tbs. parsley
¼ tsp. cumin seed
4 cloves garlic
Dash of ginger powder
1 Tbs. paprika

Cayenne pepper to taste
¼ cup cider vinegar
2 Tbs. water
2 bay leaves
1 head romaine lettuce, torn into pieces
2 lemons, cut into wedges

In skillet, heat 1 Tbs. oil. Add fish and cook over low heat 5 minutes each side, or till lightly browned. Transfer to platter and cut into 1″ chunks.
In blender or food processor, combine parsley, cumin, garlic, and ginger powder. Blend briefly. Transfer to bowl.
Stir in paprika, cayenne, vinegar, remaining oil, and water. Blend well.
Add fish chunks and bay leaves. Cover and refrigerate overnight.

Divide lettuce among 6 salad plates. Mound fish mixture on top.
Garnish with lemon wedges.
Serve as main course with boiled potatoes and vegetable.

Calories per serving: 165   Sodium per serving: 72 mgs.

STUFFED TOMATO SALAD

Serves 6

6 tomatoes
3 Tbs. low sodium mayonnaise
1 can (4⅜ ozs.) low sodium sardines
1 medium-size onion, minced
½ tsp. cider vinegar

2 tsps. parsley
2 tsps. tarragon
Cayenne pepper to taste
½ cup cooked rice

Cut ½" top off tomatoes. Scoop out pulp and transfer to bowl.
To pulp, add remaining ingredients except rice. Mash thoroughly.
Add rice and blend well.
Stuff tomatoes with rice mixture.
Precede with soup and serve as main course lunch with hard boiled eggs.

Calories per serving: 130   Sodium per serving: 19 mgs.

AMERICAN

There's nothing like a meal "just like mother made." But mother and father, too, have inherited cultures, traditions, cooking methods and secrets from all over the world. That's why—with the possible exception of hamburgers and hot dogs—there is really no such thing as American food.

There are, however, uniquely American types of food. Stews laden with potatoes and other vegetables, to cite one example. Casseroles for another. And regional dishes we call our own, including New England boiled dinner, creole cooking, southern fried chicken, chili, beef pot pie, health food salads bursting with sprouts and seeds.

American cooking is also a potpourri of ethnic tastes, of cooking traditions handed down through generations and across oceans, enhanced and enriched from cross pollination and imaginative adaptations. The result is a variety of tastes and textures derived from a common base. For example, Americans enjoy beans Boston, creole and Mexican style; cabbage rolls with German, Polish, or Russian flair; or tomato sauce that smacks of southern Italy, the Spanish coast, or northern France. And in the making, they become as American as the venerable apple pie.

By following the basic tips for low sodium cooking, you can adapt your own favorites and develop a personal recipe collection.

BAKED STUFFED FISH

Serves 2

1 1-lb. bluefish, brook trout, or snapper; head and tail intact
¼ cup lemon juice, divided
¼ tsp. white pepper, divided

½ cup Bread Stuffing (See Page 259), divided
2 Tbs. unsalted butter or margarine
⅓ cup dry white wine, divided

Have butcher scale and clean fish and slit pocket down the front.
Preheat oven to 400°.
Place fish in foil lined pan. Pour on half the lemon juice. Sprinkle with half the pepper. Let stand 15 minutes.
Turn fish. Pour on remaining lemon juice. Sprinkle with pepper. Let stand an additional 15 minutes.
Fill pocket with Bread Stuffing (extra stuffing may be wrapped in tin foil and baked same time as fish).
Dot fish with butter. Pour half the wine in pan. Bake 10 minutes.
Baste with remaining wine. Bake 10 minutes more.
Serve with pan juices on side.

Bluefish: Calories per serving: 403	Sodium per serving: 121 mgs.
Brook Trout: Calories per serving: 355	Sodium per serving: 18 mgs.
Snapper: Calories per serving: 352	Sodium per serving: 110 mgs.

BREADED OYSTERS

Serves 4

2 pts. oysters, liquid reserved for other use
1 cup low sodium Seasoned Bread Crumbs (See Page 296)

4 Tbs. olive oil, divided
1 lemon, cut into wedges

Roll oysters in Bread Crumbs. Let stand 10 minutes.
In large skillet, heat half the oil. Add half the oysters and fry over medium heat till brown on both sides. Transfer to platter.
Repeat with remaining oil and oysters.
Garnish with lemon wedges. Serve with Tartar Sauce (See Page 297).

Calories per serving: 332	Sodium per serving: 151 mgs.

FISH IN MAYONNAISE SAUCE

Serves 8

2 lbs. red snapper, pollack, or flounder
   fillets
Juice of 4 lemons
1 Tbs. oregano
Black pepper to taste

1 tsp. garlic powder
½ tsp. mace
¼ cup low sodium mayonnaise
1 tsp. paprika

Put fillets in large bowl. Pour lemon juice over all.
Mix to coat fish thoroughly. Add all remaining ingredients except mayonnaise and paprika.
Let stand 20 minutes, stirring often.
Preheat oven to 350°.
Place fish in single layer in shallow baking pan.
To lemon juice mixture in bowl, add mayonnaise, stirring to form a smooth sauce. Spoon over fish.
Sprinkle paprika on top and bake 20 minutes, or till fish flakes easily.

Red Snapper: Calories per serving: 171	Sodium per serving: 83 mgs.
Pollack: Calories per serving: 173	Sodium per serving: 61 mgs.
Flounder: Calories per serving: 154	Sodium per serving: 95 mgs.

POACHED SALMON WITH CRUDITÉS

Serves 8

1 3-lb. salmon, sea bass, brook trout, or
   bluefish, cleaned, head and tail intact
3 cups Easy Fish Stock (See Page 45)
2 sprigs parsley
2 sprigs watercress

1 bay leaf
Dry white wine (optional)
12 radishes, sliced thin
2 cucumbers, unpeeled, sliced thin
2 lemons, cut into wedges

Place fish in poacher, add Fish Stock, parsley, watercress, and bay leaf, plus enough dry white wine to cover fish, if necessary.
Bring to a boil. Reduce heat and poach at a simmer 30 to 40 minutes, or till fish flakes but does not break.
Cool fish in poacher. Drain and carefully remove skin from body. Transfer to serving dish.
Place radishes, overlapping, down the spine.
Place cucumbers, overlapping, over the rest of the body.

Garnish with lemon wedges.
Serve with Tartar Sauce (See Page 297) or Herbed Mayonnaise (See Page 290).

Salmon: Calories per serving: 350	Sodium per serving: 119 mgs.
Sea Bass: Calories per serving: 172	Sodium per serving: 143 mgs.
Brook Trout: Calories per serving: 194	Sodium per serving: 73 mgs.
Bluefish: Calories per serving: 229	Sodium per serving: 149 mgs.

SWORDFISH IN CHAMPAGNE SAUCE

Serves 4

1 1-lb. swordfish steak
½ cup Champagne or dry white wine
2 Tbs. lemon juice
¾ tsp. oregano, divided
1 tsp. mustard powder, divided

2 tsps. low sodium beef bouillon, divided
2 tsps. low sodium chicken bouillon, divided
½ tsp. garlic powder, divided

Preheat oven to broil.
Place swordfish in shallow pan. Pour on Champagne or wine and lemon juice.
Sprinkle fish with half the oregano, mustard, beef and chicken bouillon, and garlic powder. Broil 7 minutes, or till top is lightly browned.
Turn fish. Sprinkle with remaining oregano, mustard, and bouillon and broil 6 minutes more, or till top is lightly browned.
Serve with Piquant Spice Sauce (See Page 294).

Calories per serving: 174	Sodium per serving: 9 mgs.

TUNA CASSEROLE

Serves 6

2 cans (6½ ozs. each) low sodium tuna, drained
3 cups Golden Mushroom Soup (See Page 46)
1 large onion, chopped
Dash of ginger powder
½ tsp. mustard powder
Black pepper to taste

1½ lbs. fresh bean sprouts
4 stalks Chinese cabbage, chopped (optional)
2 tsps. low sodium beef bouillon
¼ cup boiling water
1 Tbs. cornstarch
2 Tbs. cold water
2 Tbs. dry sherry

Preheat oven to 350°.
In large bowl, combine the tuna, Mushroom Soup, onion, spices, bean sprouts, and cabbage.
Dissolve bouillon in boiling water.
Combine cornstarch and cold water. When thoroughly blended, stir into bouillon mixture.

Add sherry to bouillon mixture. Pour over tuna mixture. Blend thoroughly.
Pour into a 9″ square oven-proof casserole.
Bake 45 to 60 minutes, or till tuna starts to bubble and brown around the edges.
Serve with rice and Sweet and Sour Sauce (See Page 286).

Calories per serving: 214   Sodium per serving: 66 mgs.

BREAST OF VEAL

Serves 6

1 Tbs. oil
1½ lbs. stewing veal, cut into 1″ chunks
½ tsp. black pepper, divided
1 tsp. garlic powder, divided
2 medium-size onions, cut into rings
3 small apples, cored, peeled, and sliced
    thin
2 tsps. mustard powder
½ tsp. marjoram

½ tsp. thyme
½ tsp. basil
½ tsp. sage
1 tsp. savory
1 cup water
½ cup apple juice
½ cup Champagne
½ cup dry vermouth
½ cup dry white wine

In Dutch oven, heat oil.
Sprinkle veal with half the black pepper and garlic powder. Sear, seasoned side down.
Sprinkle remaining pepper and garlic powder on top of veal. Turn and sear. Remove to warm platter.
Line Dutch oven with onion rings and apple slices.
Sprinkle mustard, marjoram, and thyme on top.
Add veal, fat side up. Sprinkle top with basil, sage, and savory.
Add enough water to cover, up to 1 cup.
Cover and simmer 3½ hours, adding more water as necessary to maintain about 3″ liquid in pan.
After 3½ hours, add the apple juice and all wines. Simmer 30 minutes more, or till veal is tender.

Calories per serving: 315   Sodium per serving: 108 mgs.

CHIVE-LEMON STEAK

Serves 8

1 2-lb. beef sirloin steak ¾″ thick
Black pepper to taste
1 tsp. garlic powder
1 tsp. mustard powder

3 Tbs. lemon juice
2 Tbs. chives
2 Tbs. unsalted butter or margarine,
    melted

Preheat oven to broil.
Season steak with pepper and garlic and mustard powder.
Broil near flame 5 minutes each side for medium rare.
Stir lemon juice and chives into melted butter. Pour over steak and broil 30 seconds longer. Serve sliced thin.

Calories per serving: 356   Sodium per serving: 70 mgs.

CRANBERRY MEAT BALLS

Serves 8

1½ lbs. ground beef
½ tsp. black pepper, divided
1 Tbs. garlic powder
1 Tbs. basil
1½ tsps. thyme
2 Tbs. olive oil

3 medium-size onions, sliced into rings
1 can (16 ozs.) whole berry cranberry sauce
2 cans (12 ozs. each) low sodium tomato juice
2 cups water

Combine beef, ¼ tsp. pepper, garlic powder, basil, and thyme. Blend well and form into small meatballs. Set aside.

In Dutch oven, heat oil. Line with onion rings. Sprinkle with remaining pepper and cook over low heat till slightly brown, turning often.

Add meatballs and cook, turning to brown all sides lightly, being careful not to let onions burn.

Add cranberry sauce, tomato juice, and water. Cover and simmer 1 hour, stirring occasionally. Cover and refrigerate overnight.

Skim fat off top. Cover and reheat over very low heat 1 hour, stirring occasionally. Serve with rice and squash.

Calories per serving: 373   Sodium per serving: 70 mgs.

GLAZED PORK ROAST

Serves 8

1 2-lb. boneless pork loin or shoulder
Coarse black pepper to taste
1 tsp. mustard powder
1 tsp. rosemary, crushed
1 tsp. sage
½ cup dry sherry, divided
½ cup dry red wine, divided

½ cup water, divided
1 large onion, minced
1 carrot, scraped and chopped
½ can (8 ozs.) whole berry cranberry sauce
1 whole orange, unpeeled, sectioned
2 Tbs. honey

Preheat oven to 475°.

Place pork on rack in roasting pan. Sprinkle with seasonings. Pour half the sherry, wine, and water in the pan. Add onion and carrot.

Roast 20 minutes. Reduce heat to 350° and roast 1½ hours, or till pork is gray/white, basting occasionally with remaining sherry, wine, and water.

During last 30 minutes of roasting, combine remaining ingredients in medium saucepan. Heat over low flame till bubbly, stirring occasionally.

Carve roast. Spoon on some of the glaze. Serve remaining glaze in a gravy boat.

Calories per serving: 440   Sodium per serving: 88 mgs.

HERBED LAMB CHOPS

Serves 4

4 lamb chops, center cut, ¾" thick
Black pepper, to taste, divided
½ tsp. mustard powder, divided
½ tsp. garlic powder, divided

1 Tbs. mint, divided
4 Tbs. dry vermouth
2 Tbs. lemon juice

Preheat oven to broil.
Sprinkle chops with half the seasonings. Broil 4 minutes.
Turn. Sprinkle with remaining seasonings and vermouth. Broil 6 minutes more.
Sprinkle with lemon juice.

Calories per serving: 296   Sodium per serving: 86 mgs.

LONDON BROIL WITH SPICE SAUCE

Serves 8

1 2-lb. beef steak cut for London broil,
    1" thick
3 cups boiling water
3½ Tbs. low sodium beef bouillon
3 Tbs. white vinegar

¼ cup dry red wine
¾ tsp. garlic powder, divided
Black pepper to taste
1 tsp. mustard powder, divided
2 tsps. basil, divided

Place beef in large casserole. Pour boiling water all around. Stir in bouillon, vinegar, and wine.

Season beef with half the seasonings. Let stand 15 minutes. Turn. Season with remaining seasonings. Cover and refrigerate 4 hours or overnight, turning occasionally.

Preheat oven to broil.

Place beef in broiling pan and broil in marinade close to heat 6 minutes. Turn and broil 4 minutes more. Steak will be medium rare.
Transfer beef to platter. Carve thin. Serve marinade on the side as gravy.
Serve with potatoes or rice.

Calories per serving: 186   Sodium per serving: 88 mgs.

POT ROAST

Serves 8

6 cloves garlic, slivered
12 black peppercorns, crushed
1 2-lb. beef chuck roast
½ cup dried onion flakes
Black pepper to taste

2 Tbs. garlic powder
2 Tbs. paprika
3 Tbs. low sodium beef bouillon
¾ cup boiling water
4 Tbs. low sodium ketchup

Preheat oven to 350°.
Gash beef all around and insert garlic and peppercorns in gashes. In Dutch oven, sear beef on all sides.
Place beef on top of 2 large sheets of double duty tin foil in roasting pan. Season with onion flakes, pepper, garlic powder, paprika, and bouillon.
Pour in water. Spread ketchup on roast. Fold tin foil, tentlike, around roast. Roast 2 hours, or until roast is tender, adding water to moisten if necessary.

Calories per serving: 418   Sodium per serving: 87 mgs.

ROAST BEEF

Serves 12

1 4-lb. standing rib roast
Black pepper to taste
1½ tsps. garlic powder

2 Tbs. low sodium beef or chicken
   bouillon
1 Tbs. dry red or white wine or sherry

Let meat stand at room temperature 2 hours before roasting. Then place, fat side up, on rack in roasting pan. Rub top and sides with pepper, garlic powder, and bouillon.
Preheat oven to 550°.
Insert meat thermometer so that tip is in the thickest section, but not touching fat or bone. Place meat in oven. Reduce heat to 350° and roast 18 minutes per lb., or till thermometer reads 155° for medium rare. Note: 140° is rare; 170°, well done.
Remove roast to platter. Pour pan juices into heat-proof beaker. Plunge beaker into cold water and skim off fat that rises to the top.

Pour pan juices back into roasting pan, scraping particles from bottom and sides. Stir in wine and return pan to oven for 5 minutes, or until hot.

Spoon some of the sauce over carved beef. Serve remainder on the side.

Calories per serving: 379   Sodium per serving: 74 mgs.

SHERRIED HAMBURGER

Serves 6

1¼ lbs. ground beef
1 Tbs. garlic powder
1 tsp. basil
¼ tsp. marjoram
1 tsp. mustard powder

½ tsp. tarragon
½ tsp. sage
Black pepper to taste
¼ cup dry sherry

Combine first 8 ingredients, blending well.

Form beef into 6 patties.

In large skillet, brown hamburgers in own fat over medium heat till brown on both sides, pink in the middle.

Turn heat to high. Add sherry and cook 1 minute more.

Calories per serving: 312   Sodium per serving: 74 mgs.

WHEAT GERM MEAT LOAF

Serves 8

1 Tbs. low sodium beef bouillon
¼ cup boiling water
1 lb. ground beef
½ cup dry red wine
1 cup wheat germ and honey mix
1 Tbs. garlic powder
½ tsp. basil

½ tsp. thyme
½ tsp. sage
½ tsp. rosemary, crushed
Black pepper to taste
¼ tsp. marjoram
2 Tbs. low sodium ketchup

Preheat oven to 350°.

Dissolve bouillon in boiling water.

In large bowl, combine all ingredients. Mix well.

Place mixture in 9″ × 13″ casserole. Shape into loaf. (It will be soft, not firm.)

Bake, uncovered, 45 minutes, or till brown on top and firm.

Calories per serving: 273   Sodium per serving: 43 mgs.

BROWN BAGGED CHICKEN

Serves 4

1 2-lb. chicken
Black pepper to taste
2 tsps. garlic powder
1 tsp. sage

2 tsps. onion powder
1 Tbs. paprika
2 Tbs. low sodium chicken bouillon

Preheat oven to 375°.
Season chicken inside and out with pepper and garlic powder.
Sprinkle remaining ingredients over outside of chicken. Place in brown bag and close bag loosely, folding under chicken.
Place chicken, breast side up, in roasting pan. Roast 1 hour.

Calories per serving: 188   Sodium per serving: 97 mgs.

CHICKEN OREGANO

Serves 4

1 2-lb. chicken, cut into quarters
2 Tbs. oregano, divided
½ tsp. sage, divided
½ tsp. thyme, divided
½ tsp. rosemary, crushed, divided
Black pepper to taste

1 tsp. garlic powder, divided
1 Tbs. low sodium beef bouillon, divided
1 Tbs. low sodium chicken bouillon, divided
¼ cup lemon juice, divided

Preheat oven to broil.
Line roasting pan with tin foil. Place chicken in pan, skin side down.
Sprinkle with half the seasonings and bouillon and half the lemon juice. Broil till skin browns and bubbles, about 5 minutes.
Turn chicken. Sprinkle with remaining ingredients and broil 6 minutes more.

Calories per serving: 196   Sodium per serving: 103 mgs.

COUNTRY CHICKEN

Serves 6

1 3-lb. chicken
1 tsp. garlic powder, divided
2 tsps. black pepper or to taste, divided
1 Tbs. sage, divided
2 Tbs. paprika, divided
4 cups water, divided

2 medium-size onions, sliced
2 Tbs. low sodium chicken bouillon
2 zucchini or yellow squash, cut into ½"
  rounds
3 potatoes, parboiled, peeled, and sliced

Preheat oven to 325°.
Line a roasting pan with tin foil. Truss chicken and place, breast side down, on rack in pan. Season with half the pepper, sage, and paprika.
Pour 3 cups water into pan. Scatter onions around.
Bake chicken 45 minutes, or till skin is brown and crispy.
Stir bouillon into pan juices, being careful not to tear the foil. Add zucchini and potatoes.
Turn chicken, breast side up. Season with remaining pepper, sage, and paprika.
Pour remaining water into pan. Bake 45 minutes more, or till skin is browned and crispy and juices run clear. Remove to platter.
Carve chicken. Spoon vegetables around chicken. Spoon pan juices over all. Serve remaining sauce on the side.

Calories per serving: 250   Sodium per serving: 99 mgs.

CRUNCHY PEANUT CHICKEN

Serves 8

¼ cup low sodium peanut butter
1 egg
6 Tbs. low sodium mayonnaise
3 Tbs. dry sherry
4 tsps. low sodium beef bouillon
¼ tsp. hot pepper flakes
1¾ tsps. basil
1¾ tsps. dill
½ tsp. rosemary, crushed
1 tsp. sage

¾ tsp. dried or fresh grated lemon peel
¾ tsp. mustard powder
1 tsp. garlic powder
1 tsp. nutmeg
Black pepper to taste
White pepper to taste
1¼ cups low sodium wheat cracker
  crumbs, crushed fine with rolling pin
8 pieces chicken (4 half breasts, 4 whole
  legs)

Preheat oven to 350°.
In medium-size bowl, combine first six ingredients. Cream with back of spoon to blend well.
In second bowl, combine remaining ingredients except chicken.

Dip chicken in peanut butter mixture, then in cracker mixture.
Place in shallow baking pan. Bake 45 to 60 minutes, or till fork tender, turning occasionally.

Calories per serving: 319	Sodium per serving: 103 mgs.

LEMON CHICKEN

Serves 6

1 3-lb. chicken
4 Tbs. garlic powder
Black pepper to taste
½ cup lemon juice, divided
1¾ cups water

5 tsps. low sodium chicken bouillon
¼ cup boiling water
2 Tbs. cornstarch
2 Tbs. cold water

Preheat oven to 350°.

Sprinkle chicken inside and out with garlic powder and pepper. Place, breast side down, on rack in roasting pan. Pour on half the lemon juice. Add 1¾ cups water to pan and roast 40 minutes, or till skin is browned.

Turn chicken. Pour on remaining lemon juice and roast 30 minutes more, or till juices run clear and skin is golden brown. Remove chicken to platter and carve.

Skim off fat from pan juices.

In bowl, combine boiling water and bouillon. Stir into pan juices.

In second bowl, combine cornstarch and cold water. Stir into pan juices. Spoon some of pan juices over chicken.

Serve remaining gravy on the side.

Calories per serving: 200	Sodium per serving: 96 mgs.

ONION BAKED CHICKEN

Serves 6

1 3-lb. chicken, cut into serving pieces
8 tsps. low sodium beef bouillon
1 medium-size onion, minced
2 tsps. garlic powder
2 tsps. dried or fresh grated lemon peel
1 tsp. rosemary, crushed
1 tsp. thyme

1 tsp. ground coriander (optional)
1 tsp. coarse black pepper
¾ cup low sodium Bread Crumbs (See Page 291)
1½ Tbs. oil
4 Tbs. unsalted butter or margarine, melted

Preheat oven to 375°.

Moisten chicken pieces with water. Set aside.

In shallow dish, combine bouillon, onion, garlic powder, lemon peel, rosemary, thyme, coriander, pepper, and Bread Crumbs.

Grease a shallow baking tray with oil. Coat chicken in crumb mixture. Place on tray. Drizzle with butter. Cover loosely with tin foil and bake 45 minutes, or till chicken is tender.

Calories per serving: 326   Sodium per serving: 110 mgs.

ROAST DUCK WITH FRUIT SAUCE

Serves 6

1 4-lb. duck
1½ tsps. black pepper, divided
2 Tbs. garlic powder, divided
2 tsps. sage, divided
1 tsp. rosemary, crushed, divided
2 Tbs. paprika, divided
4 tsps. low sodium beef bouillon, divided
2 cups plus 3 tbs. cold water, divided
1 cup dry white wine

1 cup boiling water
1½ Tbs. low sodium chicken bouillon
1 tangerine, peeled and sectioned, plus ¼ peel, chopped
2 cans (16 ozs. each) plums, pitted and chopped, including liquid
2½ tsps. cornstarch
2 Tbs. strawberry preserves*
2 Tbs. honey

Preserved without pectin or sodium

Preheat oven to 450°.

Wash duck thoroughly. Sprinkle cavity with a little of the pepper and garlic powder.

Place duck, breast side down, on rack in roasting pan. Season with half the remaining pepper and garlic powder, plus half the sage, rosemary, paprika, and beef bouillon. Roast duck 20 minutes, or till skin is browned. Reduce heat to 350°.

Turn duck, breast side up. Season with remaining pepper, garlic powder, sage, rosemary, paprika, and beef bouillon. Pour 2 cups cold water in pan and roast 20 minutes more, or till skin is browned.

While duck is roasting, in saucepan, combine wine, boiling water, chicken bouillon, tangerine sections and rind, and the plums and their liquid. Simmer over low heat 15 minutes, stirring occasionally.

In bowl, combine cornstarch and 3 Tbs. cold water. Stir into plum mixture. Stir in strawberry preserves and honey. Simmer till sauce is bubbly.

Baste duck with sauce every 20 minutes till duck is done (total time: 3 hours, 20 minutes).

Carve duck. Spoon on pan juices. Serve remaining sauce on side.

Calories per serving: 480   Sodium per serving: 151 mgs.

SHERRY PEPPER CHICKEN

Serves 6

1 3-lb. chicken
½ recipe for Orange Rice (See Page 278)
1 tsp. coarse black pepper, divided
1 tsp. tarragon, divided

½ tsp. sage, divided
1 Tbs. paprika, divided
3 cups dry sherry, divided

Preheat oven to 350°.
Stuff chicken with Three Color Rice. Truss and place, breast side down, on rack in roasting pan. Season with half the pepper, tarragon, sage, and paprika.
Pour 2 cups sherry into pan and roast 30 minutes, or till skin is browned. Baste with pan juices.
Turn chicken, breast side up. Season with remaining pepper and herbs. Add remaining sherry and bake 30 minutes more, or till skin is browned and juices run clear.
Remove stuffing to bowl. Carve chicken and spoon on pan juices.

Calories per serving: 405	Sodium per serving: 105 mgs.

SPICY FRIED CHICKEN

Serves 8

1 Tbs. low sodium chicken bouillon
⅓ cup boiling water
2 Tbs. lemon juice
2 Tbs. low sodium mayonnaise
¾ cup low sodium Bread Crumbs (See Page 291)
2 Tbs. low sodium chili ketchup
½ tsp. garlic powder
½ tsp. tarragon

½ tsp. thyme
½ tsp. sage
½ tsp. oregano
½ tsp. dill
White pepper to taste
8 pieces chicken (4 half breasts, 4 whole legs)
½ cup oil

Combine first 4 ingredients. Set aside.
In bowl, combine Bread Crumbs, ketchup, and seasonings. Set aside.
Dip chicken in mayonnaise mixture. Then coat thoroughly with crumbs. Set remaining mayonnaise mixture aside.
Heat oil in large skillet. When bubbling hot, add chicken. Fry till dark brown on both sides.
Over low heat, simmer remaining mayonnaise mixture in small saucepan till bubbly.
Drain chicken on brown bags. Serve sauce on the side.

Calories per serving: 314	Sodium per serving: 82 mgs.

CHINESE

Of all the mysteries of China, food is not among them. It is one secret shared and relished by people all over the world.

It is no surprise that a country as vast as China should produce many styles of cooking based on climate, geography, and cultural background. The five principal schools of Chinese cooking include:

Fukien. Most famous for its soups, it is least well known in this country. Its sweet taste, created from a liberal use of sugar, and soft rather than crunchy, crisp vegetables offers a different experience from the Chinese dishes generally enjoyed here.

Shanghai is another cooking method not frequently practiced in the United States. As in Fukien meals, sugar is often used but contrasted with a generous, salty dose of soy sauce. What's more, steaming and sautéeing are favored, the latter primarily reserved for finely minced vegetables so popular in the port city of Shanghai.

Mandarin, Szechwan, and Cantonese are the cuisines most often savored by the American palate.

Mandarin (or Peking) cuisine gave us the popular egg roll, noodle, and dumpling specialties. For of all the regions, wheat is the staple of this northern China province. Heavy spicing, as well as the famous Peking duck, also marks the style distinguished by dark soy sauce, bean paste, and garlic. Likewise, the delicate fragrance of wine regularly permeates the food.

Szechwan cooking owes its zesty sting to the liberal use of garlic, ginger, hot peppers, and peppercorns. The people of this western land have made full and exotic use of the spices produced so abundantly in what is otherwise an unwelcoming agricultural climate. Szechwan food is hot and spicy, sometimes even fiery, and always unmistakable.

Cantonese is the best known of Chinese cuisines, probably because the people of this region were the first to emigrate here. It is also the most varied because of the region's easy access to fresh and salt water fish and the richness of its soil. Food is generally stir fried just long enough to lock in its natural flavors, although the Cantonese are also renowned for their roasted and grilled dishes. Very often a Cantonese dish is floated in a mild sauce, delicately spiced to enhance the original flavors.

Without the soy sauce and MSG, Chinese food is one of the healthiest in the world because it blends small amounts of meat with large quantities of vegetables. At the same time, it offers something for everyone. Chinese food is crunchy or tender, sweet or sour, dry fried or saucy. There's a taste and texture to satisfy any eating whim.

We propose to retain the flavors and consistencies while eliminating the salty offenders. It's not impossible. In fact, it's downright believable with a few ingredient changes and no extra work.

A complete Chinese meal is a brief few minutes from wok (or skillet) to table. The time is spent, not in the cooking, but in preparation, which, by the way, can be suited to your schedule.

In Chinese cooking, ingredients are often sliced, chopped, or minced, and frequently marinated.

You'll need a sharp knife for cutting vegetables. The Chinese cut certain vegetables on the diagonal and slice others straight for either aesthetic or practical reasons. However, we're not pretending to be authentic in any way but taste, so we simply suggest you cut uniformly to create an attractive presentation and to insure even cooking. A food processor serves this purpose admirably. Either way—by hand or machine—when you have five minutes to spare, prepare. Then wrap each ingredient individually and store in the refrigerator up to three days before use.

Always cook first the more fibrous vegetables, such as onions, broccoli stalks, carrots, and cauliflower; and last, the more tender garnishes, like lettuce, peapods, water chestnuts, and scallions.

You can whip up a marinade in an equally short period of time. Add fresh or cooked food, cut as you prefer. Cover and marinate in the refrigerator for two or three days.

When prepared in stages, it will seem like nothing at all to actually cook your favorite dishes.

The special joy of Chinese food is that it can be prepared at a moment's notice. In fact, it's probably the easiest kind of last minute meal to prepare when you want something as fast as it is special. For example, make a marinade or batter. Cut and add a fresh or cooked main ingredient. Cover and refrigerate one half hour. Meanwhile, chop some vegetables. Then you're ready to cook.

Drain the main ingredient (reserving the sauce), stir fry, and drain it. Stir fry the vegetables. Add the marinade. When bubbly, add the drained food. Thicken with a mixture of cornstarch and cold water. And almost before you can say chop suey, you'll have an exotic feast on the table.

Now for a few tips. When steaming, always place the food two inches above boiling water. Cover; reduce heat and cook as directed. As with any food, do not allow the water to evaporate completely.

Stir frying is always done in a wok with very little oil over high heat to preserve the color, texture, and nutritional value of the food. Just remember, heat the wok (or skillet) before adding the oil. (For skillet frying, use a little more oil, to cover the bigger surface, and lower heat.) Heat the oil before adding the food. If you need more oil, add instead one or two tablespoons of white wine, sherry, or sauce. Each will add flavor while cooking and reduce excess fat and cholesterol at the same time. Oil used for deep frying can be bottled, labelled, and used again for cooking the same type food.

Combine a spicy firecracker of Szechwan origin with the more subtly flavored Cantonese stir fry. It's slimming and healthy. What's more, whether you fry it, steam it, or bake it, there's no food quite as pretty to look at, as wonderfully varied in taste, as totally delightful to the senses as Chinese.

BRAISED FISH IN SHERRY

Serves 6

1½ lbs. red snapper fillets
2 tsps. lemon juice
1 tsp. garlic powder
3 Tbs. oil
2 cloves garlic
4 Tbs. dry sherry
4 Tbs. Soy Sauce Substitute (See Page 297)

1 tsp. sugar
4 tsps. low sodium chicken bouillon
1 cup boiling water
1 can (8 ozs.) bamboo shoots, drained
6 mushrooms, sliced
2 slices ginger root, ⅛" thick, or dash of ginger powder
2 scallions, cut into 2" pieces

Rub fillets with lemon juice and garlic powder on both sides.
Heat oil in large skillet 1 minute. Add garlic and cook 30 seconds.
Add fish and brown each side 2 to 3 minutes.
Add sherry, Soy Sauce Substitute, sugar, bouillon, and boiling water. Reduce to medium heat and cook 30 seconds.
Add remaining ingredients. Cover and cook over medium heat 10 minutes.
Remove cover. Baste fish. Cover and simmer on low heat 10 minutes more.

Calories per serving: 205   Sodium per serving: 86 mgs.

FISH PUFFS WITH VEGETABLES

Serves 8

1½ lbs. cod fillets, cut into 1" chunks
1½ tsps. garlic powder
¼ cup lemon juice
½ cup all-purpose flour
3 Tbs. low sodium baking powder
6 Tbs. plus 1 cup oil, divided
3 stalks broccoli, broken into flowerets, stalks peeled and cut into ½" rounds

8 mushrooms, sliced
1 can (8 ozs.) water chestnuts, sliced
¼ tsp. black pepper
5 tsps. low sodium chicken bouillon
1 cup boiling water
1 Tbs. cornstarch
¼ cup cold water

In bowl, combine fish, garlic powder, and lemon juice. Let stand 15 minutes.

In bowl, make a batter by combining flour, baking powder, and 6 Tbs. oil.

Heat wok over high heat. Add 1 cup oil. Heat till small bubbles form.

Dip fish in batter. Add to hot oil, a few pieces at a time, and fry till lightly browned. Transfer to platter and repeat till all fish is fried.

Pour off all but 2 Tbs. oil. Add vegetables and pepper. Stir fry over medium heat 1½ minutes.

In bowl, combine bouillon and boiling water. Stir into vegetable mixture. Bring to a boil.

In bowl, combine cornstarch and cold water. Stir into vegetable mixture. Add fish and cook till mixture thickens.

Calories per serving: 300   Sodium per serving: 88 mgs.

ORIENTAL FRIED FISH

Serves 8

1 3-lb. bass, boned, cut into 1″ chunks,
  head and tail discarded
5 Tbs. cornstarch, divided
1 cup oil
1 medium-size onion, chopped
1 red pepper, chopped
⅛ tsp. sage
Dash of hot pepper flakes

2 Tbs. lemon juice
1 Tbs. paprika
1 Tbs. dry sherry
1 cup boiling water
2 tsps. low sodium beef bouillon
2 tsps. low sodium chicken bouillon
2 tsps. cider vinegar
¼ cup cold water

Sprinkle fish with 4 Tbs. cornstarch. Set aside.

Heat wok over high heat. Add oil and heat till small bubbles form. Fry fish, a few pieces at a time, till all fish is browned. Transfer to platter.

Pour off all but 2 Tbs. oil. Add onion, red pepper, sage, and pepper flakes. Stir fry over medium heat 1 minute. Stir in lemon juice, paprika, and sherry.

In bowl, combine boiling water, beef and chicken bouillon, and vinegar. Stir into wok. Bring to a boil.

In bowl, combine remaining Tbs. cornstarch and cold water. Stir into wok. Add fish and cook till mixture thickens. Serve over white rice.

Calories per serving: 217   Sodium per serving: 76 mgs.

OYSTERS CANTONESE

Serves 6

¾ cup boiling water
1 Tbs. low sodium chicken bouillon
2 Tbs. low sodium beef bouillon
4 scallions, chopped, including greens
1 egg, lightly beaten
3 Tbs. dry sherry
1½ tsps. minced ginger root or dash of
   ginger powder

2 cloves garlic, minced
2 Tbs. oil
½ lb. ground pork
3 pts. oysters, drained, liquid reserved
1 tsp. lemon juice
⅓ cup cold water
1 Tbs. cornstarch

Combine boiling water, chicken and beef bouillon, scallions, egg, sherry, ginger, and garlic. Set aside.

In wok, heat oil. Add pork and stir fry over medium/low heat 5 minutes, stirring to prevent lumping.

Add oysters and lemon juice. Stir fry over medium heat 30 seconds.

Stir in oyster liquid and bouillon mixture. Heat, stirring frequently, 3 minutes.

Combine cold water and cornstarch. Add to wok and stir till thickened.

Calories per serving: 321   Sodium per serving: 175 mgs.

STEAMED GINGER FISH

Serves 4

1 2-lb. snapper, cleaned, head and tail
   intact
2 Tbs. sesame oil
1 tsp. white vinegar
2 tsps. mustard powder

1 Tbs. dry white wine
1 Tbs. minced ginger root or ⅛ tsp.
   ground ginger
6 scallions, minced
2 Tbs. low sodium beef bouillon

Put ¾" of water in bottom of wok or large skillet. Place steaming tray over, but not touching, water. Bring water to boil.*

Place fish in heat-proof casserole. Set on top of steamer, once steam is at high. Cover tightly and steam 15 minutes.

In small saucepan, heat remaining ingredients, stirring often. Pour juices from fish into saucepan. Heat. Pour over fish.

Check to make sure water does not evaporate. Add boiling water if necessary.

Calories per serving: 203   Sodium per serving: 109 mgs.

BARBEQUED SPARERIBS

Serves 6

6 large spareribs
¼ tsp. black pepper, divided
2 tsps. mustard powder, divided
1 whole head garlic, minced, divided

1¼ Tbs. low sodium chicken bouillon,
   divided
6 Tbs. honey

Preheat oven to 350°.

Line a roasting pan with tin foil. Place ribs on rack in roasting pan. Sprinkle with half the pepper, mustard powder, garlic, and bouillon. Bake 40 minutes.

Turn ribs. Sprinkle with remaining pepper, mustard powder, garlic, and bouillon. Bake 20 minutes more.

Spoon honey over ribs and bake 1 minute more.

Serve with boiled white rice and Chinese Vegetables (See Page 241).

Calories per serving: 381   Sodium per serving: 113 mgs.

BEEF AND OYSTERS

Serves 8

1 lb. flank or other beef steak cut for
   London broil, sliced into ½" strips
1½ cups boiling water
2 Tbs. low sodium beef bouillon
4 Tbs. dry sherry
1 Tbs. sesame oil (optional)
1 tsp. mustard powder
½ tsp. chopped ginger root or dash of
   ginger powder
Dash of hot pepper flakes
10 scallions, chopped, including greens

2 Tbs. sesame or vegetable oil
1 medium-size onion, sliced
2 cloves garlic, minced
8 mushrooms, sliced
Black pepper to taste
2 pts. oysters, chopped, liquid reserved
2 stalks broccoli, broken into flowerets,
   stalks peeled and cut into ½" rounds
1 Tbs. cornstarch
¼ cup cold water

In large bowl, combine first 9 ingredients. Stir to blend. Cover and refrigerate overnight. Drain. Reserve marinade, but discard ginger root.

In wok or large skillet, heat 2 Tbs. oil. Add beef, onion, garlic, and mushrooms. Stir fry over medium/low heat till beef loses its pink color. Transfer mixture to bowl.

Add pepper and oysters to wok. Stir fry over high heat 10 seconds. Transfer to beef mixture.

Add 2 Tbs. marinade to wok. Add broccoli. Stir fry over high heat 1 minute. Add remaining marinade. Bring to a boil.

In bowl, combine cornstarch and cold water. Set aside.

Return beef and oyster mixture to wok. Stir in cornstarch mixture and heat till thickened.

Stir in oyster liquid.

Calories per serving: 231   Sodium per serving: 118 mgs.

BEEF AND SNOW PEA PODS

Serves 8

3 Tbs. oil, divided
2 medium-size onions, sliced thin
12 mushrooms, sliced
½ tsp. garlic powder
½ tsp. mustard powder
Black pepper to taste
2 Tbs. dry sherry
1 lb. beef sirloin, sliced into ½" strips

½ tsp. sugar
1 lb. snow pea pods
1 cup boiling water
2 Tbs. low sodium beef bouillon
1 Tbs. cornstarch
¼ cup cold water
4 Tbs. dry red wine

In wok or large skillet, heat 2 Tbs. oil. Add onions and stir fry over medium/low heat 1 minute.

Add mushrooms. Stir in garlic and mustard powder and pepper. Stir fry 1 minute more. Remove vegetables to platter.

Add remaining oil and sherry. Add beef. Stir fry over high heat 1 minute, or till beef has lost its color. Remove to platter.

Add sugar and pea pods. Fry over low heat 1 minute, stirring often.

In bowl, combine boiling water and bouillon. Add 4 Tbs. of mixture to pea pods and fry 1 minute more.

Return vegetables and sirloin to wok. Toss to blend. Add remaining bouillon mixture and cook over high heat till bubbly.

In bowl, combine cornstarch and cold water. Stir into wok.

Stir in red wine and cook till mixture thickens.

Serve over white rice.

Calories per serving: 343   Sodium per serving: 66 mgs.

BEEF LO MEIN

Serves 6

½ lb. Chinese noodles or spaghetti
¾ lb. beef steak cut for London broil, sliced very thin
½ cup oyster liquid

Black pepper to taste
1 tsp. plus 4 Tbs. sesame or peanut oil, divided
½ tsp. mustard powder

(continued next page)

½ can (4 ozs.) bamboo shoots, drained and chopped
¼ small head cabbage, shredded
½ tsp. sugar
6 mushrooms, sliced
1 Tbs. dry sherry

¾ cup boiling water, divided
1½ Tbs. low sodium beef bouillon
1½ Tbs. low sodium chicken bouillon
½ lb. fresh bean sprouts, chopped
4 scallions, chopped, including greens

Cook noodles according to package directions.* Drain. Set aside.

In bowl, combine beef, oyster liquid, pepper, 1 tsp. oil, and mustard powder. Stir to blend. Let stand 10 minutes.

In wok or large skillet, heat 2 Tbs. oil. Add beef mixture and stir fry over medium heat 1 minute, or till beef loses its color. Transfer to sieve and let drain over bowl.

Add bamboo shoots, cabbage, sugar, mushrooms, 2 Tbs. oil, and sherry to wok. Stir fry over medium/low heat 2 minutes.

In bowl, combine ¼ cup boiling water and beef bouillon. Stir into wok. Raise heat to high and cook 1 minute. Transfer to bowl.

To wok, add beef drippings and noodles. Cook over medium/low heat 2 minutes, stirring constantly.

In bowl, combine ½ cup boiling water and chicken bouillon. Stir into wok. Stir to blend.

Add cabbage mixture, beef, bean sprouts, and scallions. Cook over medium heat 5 minutes, stirring constantly.

Do not add salt to boiling water.

Calories per serving: 300	Sodium per serving: 65 mgs.

PEPPER STEAK AND TOMATOES

Serves 6

1¼ lbs. flank steak, cut into ½" wide strips
1 Tbs. paprika
2 Tbs. unsalted butter or margarine
2 cloves garlic, minced
1½ cups boiling water
1 Tbs. low sodium beef bouillon
Dash of ginger powder

10 scallions, sliced, including greens
2 green peppers, cut into strips
2 tomatoes, cut into wedges
1 Tbs. cornstarch
¼ cup water
¼ cup Soy Sauce Substitute (See Page 297)
1 Tbs. low sodium tomato ketchup

Sprinkle steak with paprika. Let stand 30 minutes.

In large skillet, over medium heat, stir fry meat in butter till brown, about 2 minutes.

Add garlic, boiling water, bouillon, and ginger. Lower heat and simmer 30 minutes.

Stir in scallions, peppers, and tomatoes. Cover and simmer 5 minutes more.
Blend cornstarch, water, Soy Sauce Substitute, and ketchup. Stir into meat mixture till thickened.

Calories per serving: 224   Sodium per serving: 78 mgs.

PORK AND CORN SHANGHAI

Serves 6

6 pork chops, ½" thick
4 cloves garlic, minced, divided
¼ tsp. black pepper, divided
1 large onion, sliced
1 can (16 ozs.) low sodium corn niblets, drained

½ cup dry sherry
½ cup lemon juice
2 Tbs. low sodium chicken bouillon.
4 Tbs. honey

Preheat oven to broil.
Place pork chops in shallow broiling pan. Season with half the garlic and pepper. Broil close to heat 5 minutes.
Turn pork. Season with remaining garlic and pepper. Broil 5 minutes more. Remove to oven-proof casserole.
Reduce heat to 350°. Surround chops with onion and corn. Pour sherry over all.
Sprinkle chops with lemon juice, then with chicken bouillon.
Bake, uncovered, 35 minutes.
Spoon honey over chops. Bake, uncovered, 10 minutes more.

Calories per serving: 372   Sodium per serving: 77 mgs.

PORK IN GINGER TOMATO SAUCE

Serves 8

1 egg white, lightly beaten
1½ tsps. cornstarch
6 Tbs. dry sherry
1 Tbs. low sodium chicken bouillon
1 cup boiling water, divided
1¼ lbs. pork, cut into 1" cubes
5 tsps. low sodium chicken bouillon
1 Tbs. red wine vinegar
2 Tbs. lemon juice
2 tsps. low sodium beef bouillon
¼ cup cold water

2 tsps. cornstarch
4 Tbs. sesame or peanut oil, divided
2 medium-size onions, sliced
1 green pepper, chopped
2 cloves garlic, minced
1 can (8 ozs.) water chestnuts, drained
1 tsp. minced ginger root or dash of ginger powder
½ cup low sodium chili ketchup
2 tsps. sugar

In large bowl, combine first 4 ingredients. Add ½ cup boiling water. Stir to blend. Add pork, turning to coat well. Cover and refrigerate 1 hour.

In bowl, combine chicken bouillon and ½ cup boiling water. Set aside.

In another bowl, combine vinegar, lemon juice, and beef bouillon. Set aside.

Combine cold water and cornstarch. Set aside.

In wok or large skillet, heat 2 Tbs. oil. Add onions, green pepper, garlic, water chestnuts, and ginger. Stir fry over medium heat 1 minute. Transfer to platter.

Heat remaining oil. Add pork mixture and stir fry over medium/low heat till pork is lightly browned on all sides.

Add chicken bouillon mixture, beef bouillon mixture, chili ketchup, and sugar. Raise heat to high and cook till mixture bubbles. Stir in vegetables and cornstarch mixture. Cook till mixture thickens, stirring often.

Serve over white rice.

Calories per serving: 345	Sodium per serving: 82 mgs.

SPARERIBS IN PLUM SAUCE

Serves 12

1 Tbs. sesame or peanut oil
2 medium-size onions, diced
6 cloves garlic, minced
10 Tbs. white vinegar
10 Tbs. low sodium chili ketchup
¼ cup lemon juice
½ cup Imitation Worcestershire Sauce
  (See Page 291)

1 Tbs. low sodium beef bouillon
2 cans (16 ozs. each) purple plums, pitted
  and chopped, including liquid
12 large spareribs
2 Tbs. low sodium chicken bouillon,
  divided

In bowl, combine first 9 ingredients. Stir to blend.

In large casserole, place spareribs. Pour on sauce. Cover and marinate at least 4 hours.

Preheat oven to broil.

Remove spareribs and place in shallow pan. Sprinkle with half the chicken bouillon. Broil 5 minutes, or till top is browned. Turn ribs. Sprinkle with remaining bouillon and broil 5 minutes more.

Reduce heat to 350°. Spoon marinade over ribs and bake 10 minutes, or till sauce is bubbly.

Calories per serving: 423	Sodium per serving: 72 mgs.

CHICKEN AND CHINESE VEGETABLES

Serves 6

2 Tbs. oil, divided
3 chicken breasts, skinned, boned, and
  cut into 1″ pieces, divided
1 medium-size onion, sliced
1 tsp. minced ginger root or dash of
  ginger powder
¼ green pepper
¼ red pepper
2 stalks broccoli, broken into flowerets
  and stalks cut into rounds
6 mushrooms, sliced

½ can (4 ozs.) water chestnuts, sliced
½ tsp. garlic powder
¾ tsp. mustard powder
Black pepper to taste
3 Tbs. dry sherry
¾ cup boiling water
5 tsps. low sodium chicken bouillon
4 scallions, chopped, including greens
4 Tbs. cold water
½ Tbs. cornstarch

In wok, heat 1 Tbs. oil. Add half the chicken and stir fry over high heat till all sides are white. Remove to platter.

Repeat with remaining oil and chicken. Remove to platter.

Add onion, ginger, red and green pepper, broccoli, mushrooms, and water chestnuts to wok. Sprinkle with garlic and mustard powder and black pepper.

Add sherry and stir fry 30 seconds.

Combine boiling water and chicken bouillon. Add 2 Tbs. to wok and stir fry over medium/low heat 1 minute.

Add remaining bouillon mixture and scallions to wok. Bring to a boil. Add chicken. Combine cold water and cornstarch. Stir into wok. Heat, stirring often, till bubbly.

Calories per serving: 200   Sodium per serving: 78 mgs.

CHICKEN IN TOMATO SAUCE

Serves 4

2 chicken breasts, skinned, boned, and
  cut into 1″ pieces
1 egg white, lightly beaten
1 Tbs. low sodium beef bouillon, divided
1 Tbs. low sodium chicken bouillon,
  divided
1 Tbs. cornstarch
3 Tbs. oil, divided
6 cloves garlic, minced

Dash of anise powder
4½ tsps. minced ginger root or dash of
  ginger powder
2 tsps. sugar
½ lb. snow pea pods, cut in half
  crosswise
4 tomatoes, diced
½ can (4 ozs.) water chestnuts, sliced
¼ cup dry sherry

Place chicken in large bowl. Add egg white, 2 tsps. each beef and chicken bouillon and cornstarch. Toss to blend well. Refrigerate 1 hour.

In wok, heat 1 Tbs. oil. Add half the chicken and stir fry over medium/low heat till chicken turns white. Remove to warm platter.

Heat 1 more Tbs. oil and stir fry remaining chicken.
Remove to warm platter.

Add remaining oil and all ingredients except sherry and chicken. Stir fry 2 minutes.
Add chicken and sherry. Heat through.

Calories per serving: 312　　　　Sodium per serving: 95 mgs.

COCONUT CHICKEN

Serves 8

3 Tbs. oil, divided
4 cloves garlic, minced
4 chicken breasts, skinned, boned, and
　cut into 1" chunks
2 Tbs. lemon juice
Dash of hot pepper flakes
2 lbs. asparagus, trimmed and cut into 2"
　lengths
1 tsp. sugar
½ tsp. mustard powder
Dash of Five Spice Powder (See Page
　289)

2 Tbs. cider vinegar
1 can (8 ozs.) bamboo shoots, drained
1 Tbs. paprika
2 Tbs. shredded coconut
¾ cup boiling water
1 Tbs. low sodium beef bouillon
2 Tbs. dry sherry
2 tsps. cornstarch
2 Tbs. cold water

In wok or large skillet, heat 2 Tbs. oil. Add garlic and chicken. Stir fry over medium heat till chicken turns white. Transfer to platter. Sprinkle with lemon juice and pepper flakes.

Add remaining oil to wok. Stir in asparagus, sugar, mustard, and Five Spice Powder. Stir fry over medium/low heat 1 minute.

Stir in vinegar and bamboo shoots. Stir fry 1 minute more.

Return chicken mixture to wok. Stir in paprika and shredded coconut.

Combine boiling water and bouillon. Add to chicken mixture. Cook over high heat till mixture bubbles.

Stir in sherry.

Combine cornstarch and cold water. Stir into chicken mixture till thickened.

Calories per serving: 217　　　　Sodium per serving: 82 mgs.

DRUNKEN CHICKEN

Serves 6

2 Tbs. low sodium beef bouillon
2 Tbs. low sodium chicken bouillon
½ cup boiling water
2 tsps. garlic powder
1 3-lb. chicken
Dash of ginger powder

12 scallions, chopped into ¾″ lengths,
   including greens
3 cups dry sherry
White pepper to taste
3 Tbs. lemon juice

Combine beef and chicken bouillon and boiling water, stirring to dissolve.
Rub some of the bouillon mixture and the garlic powder under the skin of the chicken.
Spread ginger powder and scallions in cavity of chicken.
Place sherry in large saucepan. Bring to boil.
Add chicken, on its side, and pepper. Simmer, uncovered, 15 minutes.
Turn chicken to other side and simmer 15 minutes more.
Stir in lemon juice and simmer 15 minutes more, or till chicken is tender.
Serve sherry sauce on the side.

Calories per serving: 319   Sodium per serving: 116 mgs.

HONEY CHICKEN WITH FRIED RICE STUFFING

Serves 8

10 Tbs. Soy Sauce Substitute (See Page
   297)
6 Tbs. dry sherry, divided
1½ tsps. sugar
2 Tbs. peanut oil
2 leeks, sliced, including greens
½ can (4 ozs.) water chestnuts, chopped
2 cups cooked rice

¼ cup honey
¼ cup dark molasses or another ¼ cup
   honey
¼ cup lemon juice
1 3-lb. chicken
2 cups water
4 scallions, sliced, including greens
1 Tbs. all-purpose flour

Combine Soy Sauce Substitute, 2 Tbs. sherry, and sugar. Set aside.
Heat oil in wok or large skillet over high heat.
Reduce to medium/low heat. Add leeks and water chestnuts and stir fry 3 minutes.
Add rice and Soy Sauce Substitute mixture. Stir fry 3 minutes more.
Combine remaining sherry with honey, molasses, and lemon juice. Set aside.
Preheat oven to 375°.
Stuff chicken with rice mixture; close neck with skewer.*
Place on side on rack in shallow pan. Add water. Baste with honey mixture. Roast 20
minutes, or till skin browns.

Turn to other side; baste. Roast till brown.
Repeat, turning chicken back side up, then breast side up, basting with pan juices.
Remove rice. Add scallions and toss.
Sprinkle flour into pan juices. Stir to blend. Serve on the side.

Extra rice should be wrapped in foil and placed in oven last 15 minutes of roasting.

Calories per serving: 306	Sodium per serving: 92 mgs.

HOT AND SPICY CHICKEN

Serves 6

½ cup hot water
1 tsp. mustard powder
2 tsps. low sodium beef bouillon
1½ tsps. minced ginger root or dash of
   ginger powder, divided
2 Tbs. plus 1 tsp. sesame oil, divided
Dash of hot pepper flakes
2 scallions, chopped, including greens
1 tsp. white vinegar
½ medium-size onion, chopped

2 chicken breasts, skinned, boned, and
   cut into 1″ chunks
2 whole chicken legs, skinned, boned,
   and cut into 1″ chunks
1½ tsps. paprika
½ lb. snow pea pods, chopped
½ can (4 ozs.) water chestnuts, chopped
1 cup mushrooms, sliced
½ tsp. garlic powder

   Combine hot water, mustard powder, bouillon, ½ tsp. ginger root (or ⅛ tsp. ginger powder), 1 tsp. oil, pepper flakes, scallions, and vinegar. Stir and set aside.
   In wok or large skillet, heat remaining oil over medium/high heat. Add onion and remaining ginger. Stir fry 30 seconds.
   Add chicken and paprika. Stir fry 30 seconds.
   Add pea pods, water chestnuts, mushrooms, and garlic powder. Stir fry 30 seconds.
   Add 2 Tbs. bouillon mixture. Stir fry over medium/low heat 2 minutes.
   Serve over white rice with remaining bouillon mixture as sauce for dunking.

Calories per serving: 278	Sodium per serving: 113 mgs.

SESAME CHICKEN

Serves 6

6 whole chicken legs
¾ cup low sodium Dijon mustard
¾ tsp. garlic powder
¾ cup sesame seed
½ cup lemon juice

1 medium-size onion, minced
½ cup water
1 Tbs. low sodium chicken bouillon
½ cup Sweet and Sour Sauce (See Page
   286)

Preheat oven to 350°.

Line a roasting pan with tin foil. Place chicken in pan. Spoon mustard over chicken. Season with garlic powder and sesame seed.

Pour lemon juice in pan. Sprinkle onion in pan and bake 45 minutes.

Add water to pan. Stir in bouillon. Bake 10 minutes more, basting with pan juices.

Remove chicken to platter. Pour on pan juices.

Serve with Sweet and Sour Sauce and white rice.

Calories per serving: 293   Sodium per serving: 96 mgs.

SWEET AND SOUR CHICKEN

Serves 6

8 pieces chicken (4 half breasts, 4 whole legs)
Black pepper to taste
1½ tsps. garlic powder
1½ Tbs. low sodium beef bouillon
½ cup cider vinegar
½ cup water
2 tsps. mustard powder
2 medium-size onions, cut into chunks

1 can (8 ozs.) pineapple chunks, including liquid
½ cup boiling water
½ bottle (5½ ozs.) low sodium ketchup
¼ cup honey
1 green pepper, cut into chunks
2 tomatoes, cut into wedges
4 low sodium cucumber pickles, cut into ¾" rounds

Preheat oven to 350°.

In large roasting pan, place chicken, skin side up. Season with pepper, garlic powder, and bouillon.

Pour vinegar and water in pan. Sprinkle in mustard powder. Bake 30 minutes.

Add onions and pineapple chunks and their liquid. Bake 10 minutes more.

In bowl, combine boiling water, ketchup, and honey. Stir into roasting pan.

Add remaining ingredients and bake 30 minutes more, turning chicken occasionally. Cut chicken into serving pieces.

Calories per serving: 304   Sodium per serving: 136 mgs.

SWEET AND SOUR DUCK

Serves 8

1 4-lb. duck
4 cloves garlic, slivered
3 cups boiling water, divided
½ cup lemon juice
1 Tbs. unsalted butter or margarine
4 medium-size onions, chopped
½ cup dried apricots
⅔ cup dry white wine

Black pepper to taste
¼ tsp. ground cloves, divided
¼ cup sugar
3 Tbs. cold water
3 peaches, unpeeled, pitted and chopped
3 Tbs. cider vinegar
2 Tbs. low sodium chicken bouillon

Preheat oven to 425°.

Gash duck all over. Insert garlic slivers in gashes.

Place duck on rack in center of roasting pan lined with tin foil. Add ½ cup boiling water to pan. Roast 40 minutes.

Pour off fat. Reduce heat to 350°. Pour ½ cup boiling water over duck. Roast 30 minutes more.

Pour off fat. Pour lemon juice over duck. Roast 1½ hours, or till duck is tender and juices run clear. Baste often.

While duck is cooking, melt butter in medium saucepan. Sauté onions till golden.

Add remaining 2 cups boiling water, apricots, wine, pepper, and cloves. Cover and simmer over low heat 45 minutes.

In small saucepan, combine sugar and cold water. Cook over low heat till sugar caramelizes.

Add sugar and remaining ingredients to wine sauce.

Carve duck. Spoon some of the sauce over the duck. Serve remainder in sauce boat.

Calories per serving: 228   Sodium per serving: 102 mgs.

FRENCH

When we dream of a fine French meal, we also fancy that it is mouth watering, saucy, sumptuous, rich and fattening. And in haute cuisine, the spectacular tastes and rueful results are, more often than not, partners in crime.

Where did it begin—this delectable, sinfully caloric cuisine? Actually, in Italy. It was Catherine de Medici, an Italian noblewoman, who brought to France fragrant spices and sophisticated cooking graces as part of her trousseau when, in 1533, she married the future Henry II. This was the beginning of La Grande Cuisine, but until the French Revolution only the aristocracy enjoyed its pleasures.

After the Bastille, Anton Carême, chef to nobility, brought his skills to the people when he established a restaurant featuring those special dishes formerly savored only on royal tongues. His influence spanned the 18th and 19th centuries. Sauces, for which the French are famous, rose to supreme heights during this period, adorning vegetables, desserts, even masking the sometimes bad taste of meat pungently salted, smoked or marinated in vinegar to preserve it.

Escoffier, the Chef Laureate of the 20th century, did much to refine and advance the delicacies of La Grande Cuisine as we know it today. Indeed, the French regard their cuisine as an art form whose mysteries of taste and texture are to be explored and treasured, nurtured to perfection much as an artist tenders his masterpiece.

Today, thanks to *cuisine minceur* and a new generation of French chefs, greater emphasis is placed on pure ingredients, perfumed with spices, anointed with wines, enhanced by the sweetness of finely chopped fresh vegetables. In this technique, creamy, salted, and fattening sauces are, for the most part, superfluous.

In this chapter, we've adapted this philosophy for those who savor French style food but fear the accompanying pounds. When sauces are used, only a swirl of butter, cream, or flour is used for a final, elegant touch. Otherwise, we've tried to develop recipes that eliminate salt and calories, while retaining the flavor, flair, style and fragrance—that touch of class—that give French foods their special *soupçon.* These plus artful preparation and timing are both the real source and *raison d'être* of French cuisine.

Like most culinary art forms, French food should not be hurried. This doesn't mean it takes a lot of your time. To the contrary, once your meal is started, you're free to do as you please for an hour or so. Time to take a leisurely bath, have a lovely glass of wine. Time to relax and come to the table as casually elegant and tempting as your meal.

So don't think of French food as fancy, fattening, and difficult. While it is fanciful, it's also exciting and can be kind to your figure. If you'll allow, its bounty and *élan* will grace your table, please your senses and flatter you. *A votre santé.*

FLOUNDER AND OYSTER BAKE

Serves 4

¾ lb. flounder fillets
1 pt. oysters, drained, liquid reserved
2 tsps. mustard powder
Coarse black pepper to taste
½ tsp. garlic powder

2½ tsps. low sodium beef bouillon
3 Tbs. lemon juice
1 tomato, cut into 4 slices
¼ cup dry white wine

Preheat oven to 375°.
Place fish in 4 small pieces in large, oven-proof casserole.
Place 3 oysters on half of each piece of fish. Sprinkle with half each of the spices, bouillon, and lemon juice. Top with tomato slices.
Fold fillets over oysters. Sprinkle with remaining spices, bouillon, and lemon juice. Pour oyster liquid and wine around fish.
Cover with tin foil. Bake 15 minutes, or till fish flakes easily.

Calories per serving: 185   Sodium per serving: 170 mgs.

FLOUNDER WITH PARSLEY

Serves 6

6 bunches parsley, divided
3 Tbs. dry white wine
3 Tbs. water
2 Tbs. low sodium beef bouillon, divided
2 cloves garlic, sliced, divided
1 2-lb. flounder, cleaned, head and tail
   intact, or 1½ lbs. flounder fillets

Black pepper to taste
1 Tbs. basil, divided
4 Tbs. lemon juice
1 Tbs. unsalted butter or margarine
1 Tbs. tarragon

Preheat oven to 325°.
Wash parsley and place half on bottom of large, oven-proof casserole. Pour on wine and water.

Sprinkle in 2 tsps. bouillon plus one third of the garlic.

Wash fish. Sprinkle inside with pepper, half the basil, one third of the garlic and 2 tsps. bouillon.

Place fish on parsley bed. Sprinkle on lemon juice, remaining garlic and bouillon.

Dot with butter. Sprinkle with remaining basil and cover with remaining parsley.

Sprinkle tarragon on and around the fish.

Cover tightly and bake 50 minutes.

Test for doneness. Fish should be firm to the fork and opaque. If not done, cover and return to oven for 10 minutes.

Discard all parsley and serve fish with its pan juices.

Calories per serving: 144	Sodium per serving: 110 mgs.

SOLE WITH SAUCE NORMANDE

Serves 6

6 sole fillets (5 ozs. each)
4 Tbs. lemon juice
White pepper to taste
2 tsps. low sodium beef bouillon
2 tsps. low sodium chicken bouillon
3 Tbs. unsalted butter or margarine, divided
½ cup dry white wine
1 medium-size onion, sliced
1 bay leaf

1 tsp. basil
1 tsp. parsley
1 tsp. savory
1 tsp. tarragon
1 pt. oysters, drained, liquid reserved for other use
¼ lb. green seedless grapes
1 cup Sauce Normande (See Page 296)
Dash of nutmeg

Preheat oven to 350°.

Lay fillets in 9″ × 13″ oven-proof casserole in single layer.

Sprinkle with lemon juice, pepper, and beef and chicken bouillon.

Dot with 2 Tbs. butter.

Pour wine over all. Top with onion and herbs.

Bake 20 minutes, or till fish flakes easily. Transfer to platter.

While fish is baking, melt remaining Tbs. butter in skillet. Sauté oysters each side for 30 seconds. Add grapes and cook 1 minute more. Set aside.

In saucepan, heat Sauce Normande. Stir in oysters, grapes, and nutmeg. Pour over fish.

Calories per serving: 316	Sodium per serving: 187 mgs.

STEAMED BAKED FISH AUX HERBES

Serves 4

1 lb. rainbow trout fillets
½ tsp. sage
2 tsps. low sodium chicken bouillon
2 tsps. low sodium beef bouillon
1 tsp. parsley
1 tsp. tarragon
1 tsp. basil
1 Tbs. unsalted butter or margarine

¼ cup dry vermouth
¼ cup brandy
2 leeks, chopped, including greens
1 zucchini, cut into 1″ rounds
1 lb. green beans
10 black peppercorns
2 Tbs. lemon juice

Preheat oven to 375°.
Place fillets in large, oven-proof casserole in one layer.
Sprinkle with sage, chicken and beef bouillon, parsley, tarragon, and basil. Dot with butter.
Pour vermouth and brandy around fish. Scatter the leeks, zucchini, green beans, and peppercorns around the fish. Add lemon juice.
Cover casserole with tin foil. Cut small hole in top.
Bake 20 minutes, or till fish flakes easily.

Calories per serving: 342   Sodium per serving: 19 mgs.

STRIPED BASS AU VIN

Serves 6

1 2½ lb. striped bass, cleaned, head and
   tail intact
2 tsps. low sodium beef bouillon
Black pepper to taste
1 Tbs. unsalted butter or margarine
1 large onion, cut into rings
2 cloves garlic, minced
1½ cups dry white wine

½ cup water
1 Tbs. oil
8 mushrooms, sliced
½ tsp. sage
½ tsp. savory
1 Tbs. all-purpose flour
2 Tbs. heavy cream

Preheat oven to 425°.
Rub fish with bouillon and pepper.
In large skillet, melt butter and sauté onion and garlic till golden.
Add wine and water. Bring to a boil. Reduce heat to low and cook 5 to 7 minutes.
Place fish in 9″ × 13″ oven-proof casserole. Pour wine sauce over it.
Cover loosely with tin foil and bake 25 to 35 minutes, or till fish flakes easily. Remove to warm platter, reserving pan juices.

While fish is cooking, heat oil in skillet. Sauté mushrooms, sage, and savory 3 to 4 minutes.

Sprinkle with flour.

Pour pan juices from fish back into skillet. Cook over low heat 5 minutes. Stir in cream. Bring to a slow boil. Pour over fish.

Calories per serving: 217	Sodium per serving: 12 mgs.

BEEF BOURGUIGNON

Serves 8

1½ lbs. stewing beef, fat trimmed, cut into 1″ chunks
¼ cup all-purpose flour
3 Tbs. oil, divided
Black pepper to taste
1¼ tsps. garlic powder
2 tsps. paprika
2 medium-size onions, chopped
1 can (6 ozs.) low sodium tomato paste
1¼ tsps. sage

1¼ tsps. thyme
1¼ tsps. dried or fresh grated orange peel
1¼ tsps. basil
1 bay leaf
1½ cups boiling water
3 carrots, scraped and quartered
2 cups dry red wine, divided
1 cup mushrooms, sliced
2 Tbs. low sodium beef bouillon

Dredge beef in flour.

Heat 2 Tbs. oil in Dutch oven. Add beef and brown on all sides over medium/low heat. While beef is browning, season with pepper, garlic powder, and paprika. When browned, remove to platter.

To Dutch oven, add onions and remaining tablespoon oil. Cook till golden.

Add tomato paste and fry 1 minute.

Add remaining seasonings, boiling water, and beef. Cover and simmer 45 minutes.

Add carrots and 1 cup wine. Cover and simmer 45 minutes more.

Add remaining wine. Cover and simmer 30 minutes, stirring occasionally.

Add mushrooms and bouillon. Cover and simmer 15 minutes more, or till beef is tender, stirring occasionally.

Serve over noodles that have been cooked al dente.

Calories per serving: 311	Sodium per serving: 90 mgs.

CHICKEN LIVERS AND SQUASH

Serves 4

¾ cup dry red wine
¼ cup dry sherry
1 tsp. plus 1 Tbs. low sodium beef
  bouillon, divided
1 large butternut squash, parboiled,
  peeled, and cut into 1″ chunks
¼ cup golden raisins*

1 Tbs. unsalted butter or margarine
1 medium-size onion, chopped
8 mushrooms, sliced
1 tsp. low sodium chicken bouillon
1 lb. chicken livers
White pepper to taste

Preserved in non-sodium ingredient
  In medium saucepan, bring red wine and sherry to a boil.
  Reduce heat and add 1 tsp. beef bouillon, squash, and raisins. Cover and simmer 5 minutes. Remove from heat.
  In skillet, melt butter. Add onion and mushrooms. Sprinkle with chicken bouillon and cook over low heat, stirring often, till golden.
  Transfer mushrooms and onion to a large, oven-proof casserole.
  Preheat oven to 350°.
  In same skillet, gently sauté chicken livers, sprinkled with the pepper and half the remaining Tbs. beef bouillon.
  Remove livers to casserole. Sprinkle with remaining beef bouillon and cover with squash mixture.
  Cover and bake 45 minutes.

Calories per serving: 306

Sodium per serving: 105 mgs.

FILETS MIGNONS WITH CHOPPED CHICKEN LIVER

Serves 8

1½ lbs. beef bottom round, cut into 4
  filets
2 Tbs. oil
1 Tbs. garlic powder
Black pepper to taste
1 Tbs. unsalted butter or margarine

½ cup Chopped Chicken Liver (See Page
  37)
½ lb. mushrooms, sliced
½ cup sweet sherry or vermouth
1 Tbs. lemon juice
⅓ cup brandy

  Rub filets with oil and sprinkle with garlic powder and pepper. Let stand 20 minutes.
  In skillet, melt butter. Add the Chopped Chicken Liver, mushrooms, and wine, cooking over low heat till smooth.
  While Chopped Chicken Liver mixture is cooking, broil the filets near the heat 4 minutes each side.

Add filets to pâté mixture. Dribble lemon juice on top. Flame with brandy. Slice filets in half. Cover with Chopped Chicken Liver mixture.

Calories per serving: 285	Sodium per serving: 79 mgs.

PORK CHOPS MARSEILLAISE

Serves 8

8 pork chops
White pepper to taste
4 tsps. low sodium chicken bouillon
4 cloves garlic, minced
1 Tbs. unsalted butter or margarine
1 Tbs. all-purpose flour
1 cup Chicken Broth (See Page 45)

2 ozs. low sodium Gouda cheese, chopped
½ cup dry red wine
1 tsp. thyme
2 leeks, chopped, including greens, or 1 medium-size onion, chopped
1 bay leaf

Season pork chops with pepper and chicken bouillon.
In large, ungreased skillet (you may need 2), fry chops till browned on one side. Turn. Add garlic and cook till pork is browned on other side. Transfer to oven-proof casserole.
Preheat oven to 350°.
While chops are frying, melt butter in saucepan. Stir in flour till butter is absorbed.
Stir in Chicken Broth and heat 5 minutes, stirring occasionally.
Add cheese and cook 15 minutes, stirring often.
Pour wine over pork chops, then sprinkle with thyme.
Scatter leeks and bay leaf around pork chops. Then pour on cheese sauce.
Cover and bake 45 minutes.

Calories per serving: 337	Sodium per serving: 92 mgs.

VEAL À LA SUISSE

Serves 8

3 Tbs. unsalted butter or margarine, divided
1 Tbs. shallot, chopped
½ lb. mushrooms, caps chopped, stems sliced
White pepper to taste
¼ cup dry white wine, divided

8 veal scallops pounded thin
2 Tbs. lemon juice
1 tsp. cornstarch
3 tsps. cold water
2 ozs. low sodium Gouda cheese, sliced thin

Preheat oven to broil.
Melt 1 Tbs. butter in small saucepan. Add shallot and cook 1 minute.
Add the mushrooms and pepper. Cook 2 minutes more.

Add half the wine and simmer 3 minutes. Set aside.
In large skillet, melt remaining butter. Add veal and brown 2 minutes over low heat. Turn and brown other side 2 minutes.
Transfer veal to 9″ × 13″ oven-proof casserole, overlapping slices.
Add remaining wine and lemon juice. In bowl, combine cornstarch and cold water. Stir into wine mixture.
Spoon mushroom mixture over veal. Top with cheese.
Broil 4″ from heat, or till cheese melts.

Calories per serving: 315   Sodium per serving: 139 mgs.

VEAL À LA VÉRONIQUE

Serves 8

8 veal scallops
¼ cup all-purpose flour
2 Tbs. low sodium chicken bouillon
1 Tbs. unsalted butter or margarine
1 Tbs. olive oil
1½ cups dry white wine
White pepper to taste
⅛ tsp. nutmeg

⅛ tsp. ground coriander
2 Tbs. parsley
2 Tbs. lemon juice
2 tsps. low sodium beef bouillon
2 cloves garlic, halved
2 bay leaves
½ lb. seedless grapes

In plastic bag, combine veal, flour, and bouillon. Shake to coat veal.
In large skillet, heat butter and oil. Add veal and sauté over medium/high heat till browned on both sides. Transfer to warm platter.
Add all remaining ingredients except grapes. Bring to a boil, scraping particles from bottom of pan. Boil 3 minutes.
Reduce heat. Add grapes and cook 5 minutes more. Add veal and cook over medium heat 3 minutes.
Serve over white rice.

Calories per serving: 280   Sodium per serving: 114 mgs.

CHICKEN DIVAN

Serves 8

4 Tbs. unsalted butter or margarine, divided
4 chicken breasts, halved
1 small onion, minced
1 cup Chicken Broth (See Page 45)

⅓ cup low sodium mayonnaise
⅔ cup milk
2 ozs. low sodium Cheddar cheese, cut into chunks
1 tsp. Curry Powder (see p. 288)
(continued next page)

¼ tsp. nutmeg
2 tsps. low sodium beef bouillon
2 tsps. low sodium chicken bouillon
White pepper to taste

2 Tbs. all-purpose flour
1 bunch broccoli, stalks trimmed,
  separated into flowerets

In large skillet, melt 3 Tbs. butter. Add chicken and onion. Cook over low heat, turning chicken till browned on both sides. Set aside.

Preheat oven to 350°.

In bowl, combine Chicken Broth, mayonnaise, milk, cheese, Curry Powder, nutmeg, beef and chicken bouillon, and pepper.

In saucepan, melt remaining Tbs. butter. Stir in flour. Add Chicken Broth mixture and stir till slightly thickened. (Cheese will not be fully melted.)

In 9″ × 13″ oven-proof casserole, arrange broccoli in a single layer. Place chicken pieces and onion on top.

Pour cheese mixture over all and bake 45 minutes, or till chicken is tender and sauce bubbles.

Calories per serving: 329   Sodium per serving: 110 mgs.

CHICKEN FLAMBÉ

Serves 6

4 Tbs. oil, divided
1 3-lb. roasting chicken
1½ cups water, divided
5 tsps. low sodium chicken bouillon
2 tsps. dried or fresh grated lemon peel
½ cup lemon juice, divided
¼ tsp. black pepper, divided
¼ tsp. white pepper, divided
10 garlic cloves, peeled
1 large tomato, diced

½ tsp. marjoram
2 tsps. oregano
2 tsps. parsley
½ tsp. thyme
1 green pepper, diced
1 red pepper, diced
6 mushrooms, including stems, diced
4 scallions, including greens, diced
¼ cup brandy

Preheat oven to 450°.

In large skillet, heat 2 Tbs. oil.

Add chicken to skillet and sear all sides over medium heat. Remove and place, back side up, on rack in roasting pan. Pour 1 cup water in pan.

Combine bouillon, remaining water, and lemon peel. Insert and spread the mixture under the skin of the chicken. Pour on half the lemon juice. Roast, uncovered, 20 minutes, or till skin is browned. Sprinkle with half the black and white pepper.

Add 1 more Tbs. oil to skillet. Add garlic cloves and diced tomato. Cook over low heat till garlic is golden brown and mushy.

Remove chicken from oven. Turn breast side up. Pour on remaining lemon juice.

Sprinkle with remaining black and white pepper, marjoram, oregano, parsley, and thyme.

Pour on garlic and tomato mixture.

Roast, uncovered, additional 20 minutes, or till skin is browned.

Add last Tbs. oil to skillet. Over medium heat, stir fry the green and red peppers, mushrooms, and scallions till tender-crisp, about 3 minutes.

Remove chicken from oven. Pour on brandy. Ignite.

When flames die down, crown chicken with pepper mixture. Spoon pan juices onto serving platter, surrounding chicken.

Note: If you do not sear the chicken in oil, you can reduce calories to 271 per serving.

Calories per serving: 313	Sodium per serving: 106 mgs.

CHICKEN IN JELLIED LIME JUICE

Serves 4

1 2-lb. chicken
½ cup lime juice, divided
1 Tbs. garlic powder, divided
1 Tbs. unflavored gelatin
2 cups Chicken Broth (See Page 45), divided

2 tsps. low sodium beef bouillon
Coarse black pepper to taste
1 Tbs. low sodium chicken bouillon
Juice of 6 limes

Preheat oven to 475°.

Place chicken on its side on rack in roasting pan. Sprinkle with one third the lime juice, then one third the garlic powder. Roast 10 minutes, or till skin is dark and crackly.

Turn to other side. Sprinkle with one third each lime juice and garlic powder. Roast till skin is dark and crackly.

While chicken is roasting, dissolve gelatin in ½ cup Chicken Broth. Cook over low heat, stirring constantly, 3 minutes. Remove from heat.

Reduce oven to 350°. Turn chicken breast side up. Sprinkle with remaining lime juice and garlic powder. Roast 45 minutes, or till skin is browned and juices run clear.

In second saucepan, combine all remaining ingredients except lime juice and gelatin mixture. Bring to a boil and continue boiling 5 minutes.

Add lime juice and stir in gelatin mixture. Cook over low heat 20 minutes.

Remove chicken to serving platter. Carve and pour on half the lime sauce.

Serve remaining lime sauce on the side.

Calories per serving: 253	Sodium per serving: 112 mgs.

CHICKEN PROVENÇALE

Serves 8

4 Tbs. unsalted butter or margarine,
  divided
Black pepper to taste
4 chicken breasts, halved
1 cup finely chopped onion
2 large, well ripened tomatoes, chopped
  coarse, or 16 cherry tomatoes, cut in
  half

4 cloves garlic, minced
1½ cups dry white wine
3 small zucchini, sliced into ¼" rounds
1 lb. mushrooms, sliced ½" thick
1 Tbs. combination of chives, parsley,
  and tarragon

In large skillet or paella pan, melt half the butter over medium heat. Sprinkle pepper on chicken and fry half the chicken till both sides are browned, about 15 minutes. Remove to platter.

In same skillet, melt remaining butter. Add remaining chicken and fry till both sides are browned. Remove to platter.

Add onion, tomatoes, and garlic to skillet. Cook over low heat 5 minutes, stirring occasionally.

Return chicken to skillet. Add wine. Cover and simmer 30 minutes.

Add zucchini, mushrooms, and herb combination. Cover and simmer 15 minutes more.

Calories per serving: 254   Sodium per serving: 94 mgs.

ROAST CHICKEN À L'ORANGE

Serves 6

1 3-lb. chicken
1 medium-size onion, minced
1 cup orange juice, divided
1 cup dry white wine, divided
4 Tbs. lemon juice, divided
1 tsp. rosemary, crushed
1 tsp. thyme

1 tsp. garlic powder
½ tsp. paprika
Black pepper to taste
¼ cup walnuts, chopped
1 can (8 ozs.) mandarin oranges,
  including liquid

Preheat oven to 400°.
Place chicken, back side up, on rack in roasting pan. Add onion.
Pour half the orange juice and wine in pan.
Sprinkle 2 Tbs. lemon juice over chicken.
Combine all seasonings and sprinkle half over chicken.
Roast 1 hour.

Turn chicken, breast side up. Add remaining orange juice, wine, lemon juice, and seasonings.

Add walnuts to pan.

Roast 30 minutes. Add oranges and their liquid and continue roasting till juices from thigh run clear when pierced with fork.

Skim fat from pan drippings. Serve pan juices on the side.

Calories per serving: 280   Sodium per serving: 94 mgs.

GERMAN

What comes to mind when we think of German food? Traditional specialties such as Sauerbraten, Wiener Schnitzel and the popular staples—cabbage and sauerkraut. Solid. Robust. Substantial.

But neither the foods nor the words fully describe the scope of German fare. Today German cooks do much more than stir in the paprika and spoon on the sour cream. For German cooking is as varied as its regions are different with as many subtleties as French cuisine—though of a different nature.

In the north, for example, fruits are used splendidly, along with vegetables, in preparing the main meal, delicately imparting their juicy flavors to enhance fish, poultry, and especially meats. Some imaginative couplings include raisins with fish, pears with veal, apples with chicken.

Other regions reflect the cosmopolitan flair of neighboring Austria by employing the sweet goodness of butter and cream. Still other areas crown the main dish with a dollop of cereal or porridge.

Despite the differences, there are traditions which distinguish German cuisine from any other. For example, herbs and spices are used sparingly. Instead, German cooks rely on sauces, marinades, fruits, vegetables, and native cheeses to permeate and flavor their foods during cooking.

Thick soups, prodigious in their bounty, and extravagantly lush pastries also favor the German table. In between these courses, pork is served most often, veal following close behind. Beef is readily available, but lamb is served almost not at all.

The fresh waters running through Germany deliver daily gifts of succulent fish, which the Germans usually poach in an aromatic marinade. Chicken is allowed to speak for itself, simply roasted or broiled in its own broth. But other poultry and game birds are more elaborately prepared.

The German meal is truly a sumptuous repast. So when you've the mind and the appetite to heartily gratify your taste, set the horseradish on the table and prepare to feast with gusto.

CARP IN GINGER CREAM

Serves 8

2 medium-size onions
6 cloves
1 carrot, scraped and diced
3 Tbs. parsley
1 Tbs. green peppercorns*
2 Tbs. cider vinegar
2 Tbs. low sodium beef bouillon
1 cup dry red wine

Black pepper to taste
1 cup water
Dash of ginger powder
2 Tbs. lemon juice
2 Tbs. sugar
1 3-lb. carp, head and tail intact
¼ cup heavy cream

Natural green peppercorns, packed in water or vinegar

In Dutch oven, combine first 10 ingredients. Bring to a boil. Reduce heat and simmer 10 minutes.

Stir in ginger, lemon juice, and sugar. Simmer 10 minutes more. Strain. Bring stock to a second boil.

Add carp. Cook over medium heat 20 minutes. Stir in cream.

Remove carp to platter. Cut into serving pieces. Spoon some sauce over carp. Serve remaining sauce on the side.

Calories per serving: 200	Sodium per serving: 85 mgs.

FLOUNDER WITH PICKLES

Serves 8

2 Tbs. oil
10 cloves garlic
1 medium-size onion, minced
½ lb. mushrooms, sliced
Black pepper to taste
½ tsp. mustard powder

2 lbs. flounder fillets
4 low sodium cucumber pickles, chopped
2 Tbs. parsley
1 tsp. dill
2 Tbs. honey
½ cup dry white wine

Preheat oven to 350°.

In skillet, heat oil. Add garlic, onion, and mushrooms. Cook over medium heat 3 minutes, or till garlic is golden. Stir in pepper and mustard.

Place flounder in casserole. Spoon onion mixture and pickles on flounder. Fold in half. Sprinkle with parsley and dill.

Spoon honey over fish. Add wine. Cover and bake 30 minutes.

Calories per serving: 171	Sodium per serving: 99 mgs.

HADDOCK CASSEROLE

Serves 12

3 lbs. haddock, cut into 2″ chunks
⅓ cup lemon juice
6 potatoes, parboiled, peeled, and sliced
3 Tbs. unsalted butter or margarine,
　divided
2 medium-size onions, chopped
Black pepper to taste

2 tsps. dill
2½ tsps. low sodium beef bouillon
¾ cup dry vermouth
¾ cup sour cream*
½ cup low sodium Bread Crumbs (See
　Page 291)
½ tsp. thyme

Preserved in non-sodium ingredient
　Preheat oven to 350°.
　In bowl, combine haddock and lemon juice. Let stand 30 minutes. Drain.
　Place potatoes in 9″ × 13″ oven-proof casserole. Top with haddock.
　In skillet, melt 1 Tbs. butter. Add onions and cook over low heat 5 minutes, stirring occasionally. Spoon over fish. Season with pepper, dill, and bouillon.
　In bowl, blend vermouth and sour cream. Pour on fish mixture.
　In skillet, melt remaining butter. Add Bread Crumbs and stir fry 3 minutes. Spoon on top of casserole. Sprinkle thyme over all. Cover and bake 45 minutes, or till mixture is bubbly.

Calories per serving: 178　　　　　Sodium per serving: 84 mgs.

POACHED COD IN HORSERADISH SAUCE

Serves 8

2 lbs. cod fillets, cut into 1″ chunks
1 cup dry white wine
2 Tbs. low sodium chicken bouillon
2 Tbs. heavy cream
2 medium-size onions, chopped
3 potatoes, parboiled, peeled, and sliced
¼ tsp. mace

¼ tsp. marjoram
Black pepper to taste
1 tsp. dill
1 Tbs. parsley
3 Tbs. White Horseradish (See Page 290)
¼ cup milk

　In large saucepan, combine all ingredients except Horseradish and milk. Bring to a boil. Cover. Reduce heat and simmer 15 minutes, or till fish flakes easily. Transfer fish to platter.
　Bring broth to a boil and continue boiling till liquid is reduced by one third.
　Stir in Horseradish and milk. Cook over medium heat 5 minutes, stirring often. Pour on fish.

Calories per serving: 180　　　　　Sodium per serving: 93 mgs.

SWORDFISH IN CREAM SAUCE

Serves 8

2 lbs. swordfish steaks
1 Tbs. unsalted butter or margarine
1 medium-size onion, minced
8 mushrooms, sliced
4 cloves garlic, minced
2 tomatoes, chopped
2 Tbs. low sodium beef bouillon
1 Tbs. paprika

¼ cup brandy
¼ cup heavy cream
2 tsps. low sodium Dijon mustard
2 tsps. parsley
2 tsps. low sodium ketchup
2 tsps. lemon juice
⅛ tsp. nutmeg

Preheat oven to broil.
Broil swordfish in shallow pan 5 minutes each side.
While fish is broiling, melt butter in skillet. Add onion, mushrooms, and garlic and cook till onion is wilted.
Add tomatoes, bouillon, and paprika. Stir thoroughly to blend.
Stir in remaining ingredients. Top with swordfish. Cover and cook over low heat 10 minutes, basting swordfish occasionally.

Calories per serving: 210   Sodium per serving: 19 mgs.

BOILED BEEF SUPREME

Serves 8

1 2-lb beef brisket
3 Tbs. low sodium beef bouillon
3 cups boiling water
2 Tbs. parsley
10 black peppercorns
2 tsps. green peppercorns*
2 bay leaves

2 medium-size onions, sliced
1 carrot, scraped and cut into 1″ chunks
1 medium-size yellow turnip, chopped
1 Tbs. dill
1 tsp. thyme
¼ cup dry red wine
½ cup Red Horseradish (See Page 290)

Natural green peppercorns, packed in water or vinegar
Rub beef with bouillon. Place in Dutch oven.
Pour water around beef. Bring to a boil and continue boiling 5 minutes.
Add parsley, black and green peppercorns, bay leaves, vegetables, dill, and thyme.
Cover and simmer over low heat 1½ hours.
Uncover beef. Stir in wine. Cover and cook 30 minutes more, or till beef is tender.
Serve with boiled new potatoes and Red Horseradish.

Calories per serving: 487   Sodium per serving: 113 mgs.

BRATWURST

Serves 6

½ lb. ground veal
½ lb. ground pork
½ lb. ground beef
2 Tbs. low sodium beef bouillon
Black pepper to taste

1½ tsps. mustard powder
Dash of ginger powder
½ tsp. mace
¼ tsp. nutmeg
1 egg, lightly beaten

In bowl, combine all ingredients except egg. Grind in blender, a little at a time.
Stir egg into mixture. Blend thoroughly.
Form mixture into small, flat patties about 1″ in diameter.
In large skillet, fry patties in their own fat over low heat till browned on both sides.

Calories per serving: 283   Sodium per serving: 97 mgs.

HORSERADISH STEAK

Serves 8

1 2-lb. sirloin steak, fat trimmed
1 Tbs. low sodium chicken bouillon
1½ tsps. garlic powder
Coarse black pepper to taste
2 Tbs. unsalted butter or margarine

2 medium-size onions, sliced
½ cup sour cream*
2 tsps. Red Horseradish (See Page 290)
2 tsps. parsley
1 Tbs. lemon juice

Preserved in non-sodium ingredient
Sprinkle steak with bouillon, garlic powder, and pepper.
In large skillet, melt butter. Cook steak over high heat till browned on both sides. Transfer to platter.
Add onions to skillet. Stir fry over low heat till onions are wilted, about 5 minutes.
Stir in sour cream, Horseradish and parsley.
Return steak to skillet. Baste with sauce. Cover and cook over low heat 3 minutes.
Spoon lemon juice over steak, and slice very thin.

Calories per serving: 277   Sodium per serving: 88 mgs.

PORK AND SAUERKRAUT

Serves 6

2 medium-size onions
8 cloves
3 Tbs. low sodium beef bouillon
2 carrots, scraped and cut into 2″ chunks
1 1¼-lb. boneless pork loin, fat trimmed
10 black peppercorns
10 juniper berries (optional)

2 cups boiling water
1 cup dry white wine
3 potatoes, parboiled, peeled, and sliced
1½ cups low sodium sauerkraut
1 Tbs. low sodium Dijon mustard
1 Tbs. parsley

Stud each onion with 4 cloves.

Place onions, bouillon, carrots, and pork in Dutch oven.

Add peppercorns, juniper berries, and boiling water. Bring to a boil. Cover. Reduce heat and simmer 1½ hours, turning pork occasionally, adding more water if necessary to keep moist.

Add wine. Cover and simmer 1 hour more.

Add potatoes. Cover with sauerkraut. Cover and simmer 30 minutes, stirring occasionally.

Stir in mustard and parsley. Cook 5 minutes more.

Calories per serving: 411   Sodium per serving: 267 mgs.

SAUERBRATEN

Serves 8

1 2-lb. beef bottom round
1 cup red wine vinegar
½ cup dry red wine
2 medium-size onions, cut into rings
1 carrot, scraped and cut into ½″ rounds
2 Tbs. parsley
Black pepper to taste
2 Tbs. low sodium beef bouillon
⅛ tsp. allspice
4 cloves
8 black peppercorns, crushed
2 bay leaves

2 Tbs. oil
1 medium-size head red cabbage, shredded
¼ cup lemon juice
¼ cup apple juice
¼ cup cider vinegar
¼ cup sugar
Dash of ginger powder
1 Tbs. low sodium chicken bouillon
2 green apples, peeled, cored, and chopped

In large casserole, place roast. Pour on wine vinegar and wine. Scatter onions, carrot, parsley, pepper, beef bouillon, allspice, cloves, peppercorns, and bay leaves around beef. Cover and refrigerate 3 days, turning occasionally.

Remove meat. Pat dry with paper towels. Reserve marinade.

In Dutch oven, heat oil. Add meat and sear on all sides over medium heat.

Add marinade. Bring to a boil. Cover. Reduce heat and simmer 2½ hours, or till meat is tender.

When meat is almost done, place cabbage, lemon juice, apple juice, cider vinegar, sugar, ginger, and chicken bouillon in large saucepan. Cover and cook over medium heat 20 minutes, stirring occasionally.

Add apples and cook 10 minutes more, stirring occasionally.

Remove meat to serving platter. Slice thin. Surround with cabbage mixture.

Bring pan juices to a boil. Boil 5 minutes, stirring often.

Pour some of the gravy over meat and cabbage. Serve remainder on the side.

Calories per serving: 370   Sodium per serving: 126 mgs.

VEAL IN APPLE WINE SAUCE

Serves 8

2 lbs. stewing veal, cut into 1″ chunks
Coarse black pepper to taste
1 cup dry red wine
¾ cup apple juice
¼ tsp. cinnamon

2 apples, peeled, cored, and sliced
1 medium-size onion, cut into rings
2 Tbs. parsley
2 Tbs. sour cream*

Preserved in non-sodium ingredient

Season veal with pepper. In large skillet, cook in ungreased skillet over low heat till all sides are browned. Transfer to platter.

Raise heat to high. Add wine and apple juice. Bring to a boil and continue boiling 2 minutes.

Stir in cinnamon. Add apples, onion, and veal. Cover and cook over low heat 1½ hours, or till veal is tender, adding more wine and apple juice if necessary to keep about 1″ liquid in pan.

Stir in parsley and sour cream. Cook 5 minutes more.

Calories per serving: 261   Sodium per serving: 90 mgs.

WIENER SCHNITZEL

Serves 6

½ cup milk
1 egg, lightly beaten
Black pepper to taste
⅛ tsp. nutmeg
1 tsp. dill
1 tsp. parsley
1 tsp. paprika

2 Tbs. low sodium chicken bouillon
½ cup low sodium Bread Crumbs (See Page 291)
6 veal cutlets
4 Tbs. oil, divided
2 lemons, cut into wedges

In shallow bowl, beat together milk, egg, spices and herbs, and bouillon.

Dip cutlets first in Bread Crumbs, then in egg mixture.

Heat 2 Tbs. oil in large skillet. Fry 3 chops at a time over low heat till browned on both sides.

Repeat above with remaining oil and chops.

Garnish with lemon wedges.

Calories per serving: 309	Sodium per serving: 87 mgs.

APPLE CHICKEN STEW

Serves 6

6 apples, peeled, cored, and sliced
1 medium-size onion, cut into rings
3 chicken breasts, skinned and halved
½ cup dry sherry
¼ cup lemon juice
2 tsps. oregano

½ tsp. rosemary, crushed
¼ tsp. cinnamon
2 Tbs. low sodium chicken bouillon
3 Tbs. sour cream*

Preserved in non-sodium ingredient

Preheat oven to 350°.

In 9" × 13" oven-proof casserole, place apple slices. Cover with onion rings. Top with chicken.

Pour on sherry and lemon juice.

Sprinkle chicken with herbs, cinnamon, and bouillon.

Cover and bake 45 minutes.

Uncover and spoon sour cream on chicken. Bake, covered, 15 minutes more.

Calories per serving: 257	Sodium per serving: 87 mgs.

CHEESE FRIED CHICKEN

Serves 8

2 eggs, lightly beaten
¼ cup water
1 cup low sodium Bread Crumbs (See Page 291)
2 tsps. dill
Black pepper to taste

1 tsp. basil
⅛ tsp. ginger powder
4 ozs. low sodium Gouda cheese, minced
2 tsps. onion powder
4 chicken breasts, halved
¼ cup oil

Preheat oven to 350°.

In shallow bowl, beat together eggs and water. Set aside.

In second bowl, combine Bread Crumbs, dill, pepper, basil, ginger powder, cheese, and onion powder. Stir to blend.

Dip chicken first in egg mixture, then in Bread Crumb mixture.

With a third of the oil, grease a shallow baking pan. Place chicken in pan. Drizzle with remaining oil. Bake 40 minutes, or till chicken is browned and crispy.

Calories per serving: 288   Sodium per serving: 95 mgs.

CHICKEN AND CABBAGE

Serves 6

6 pieces chicken (3 half breasts, 3 whole legs)
¾ cup dry white wine
6 cloves
2 bay leaves
2 Tbs. low sodium chicken bouillon
1 Tbs. unsalted butter or margarine

1 medium-size onion, chopped
½ large head cabbage, chopped
2 tsps. oregano
White pepper to taste
4 peaches, unpeeled, pitted, and chopped
1 Tbs. lemon juice

In Dutch oven, combine first 5 ingredients. Cover and simmer over low heat 1 hour.

In large skillet, melt butter. Add onion and cabbage. Cover and simmer 10 minutes, stirring often.

Stir in oregano and pepper. Add peaches. Stir in lemon juice. Top with chicken and any liquid in Dutch oven. Cover and cook 15 minutes more. Discard cloves.

Calories per serving: 238   Sodium per serving: 98 mgs.

CHICKEN AND VEGETABLE RAGOUT

Serves 4

2 Tbs. unsalted butter or margarine
1 2-lb. chicken, cut into serving pieces
2 tsps. low sodium beef bouillon
¼ lb. mushrooms, sliced
2 Tbs. crushed almonds
1 Tbs. parsley
6 scallions, chopped, including greens

2 cloves garlic, minced
2 Tbs. lemon juice
2 Tbs. low sodium ketchup
2 tsps. paprika
½ cup dry white wine
2 Tbs. brandy
Dash of caraway seed

In large skillet, melt butter. Add chicken and cook over medium/low heat 20 minutes, or till both sides are lightly browned. Transfer to platter. Sprinkle with bouillon.

To skillet, add mushrooms, almonds, parsley, scallions, and garlic. Cook over low heat 5 minutes, stirring occasionally.
Stir in remaining ingredients. Return chicken to skillet.
Cover and cook over low heat 10 minutes.
Serve with noodles.

Calories per serving: 303   Sodium per serving: 106 mgs.

CHICKEN PAPRIKASH

Serves 6

3 Tbs. oil
2 cloves garlic
2 medium-size onions, chopped
6 pieces chicken (3 half breasts, 3 whole legs)
Black pepper to taste
1 tsp. garlic powder
1 can (6 ozs.) low sodium tomato paste

1 Tbs. lemon juice
½ cup dry vermouth or white wine
½ cup water
4 tsps. low sodium chicken bouillon
2 tomatoes, chopped
2 Tbs. paprika
¼ cup sour cream*

Preserved in non-sodium ingredient
In Dutch oven, heat oil. Add garlic, onions, and chicken. Cook over low heat till chicken is browned on all sides.
Discard garlic and stir in pepper, garlic powder, tomato paste, lemon juice, wine, water, bouillon, and tomatoes. Cover and cook over low heat 35 minutes.
Stir in paprika and sour cream. Cook, uncovered, 5 minutes more, stirring often.

Calories per serving: 290   Sodium per serving: 95 mgs.

DILLED LEMON CHICKEN

Serves 4

4 pieces chicken (2 half breasts, 2 whole legs)
2 Tbs. low sodium chicken bouillon, divided
2 Tbs. dill, divided
2 Tbs. dried or fresh grated lemon peel, divided

2 cups Beef Broth (See Page 44)
1 medium-size onion, minced
4 Tbs. sour cream*
1½ tsps. paprika

Preserved in non-sodium ingredient

155

Preheat oven to 375°.

Place chicken in shallow baking pan. Season with half the bouillon, dill, and lemon peel.

Pour Beef Broth around chicken. Scatter onion around chicken. Bake 15 minutes, or till skin is crispy.

Turn chicken. Season with remaining bouillon, dill, and lemon peel. Bake 15 minutes more.

Spoon sour cream over chicken. Sprinkle on paprika. Bake 5 minutes more.

Calories per serving: 217   Sodium per serving: 108 mgs.

GREEK

Greek foods are as tantalizing as their island origins. Spiced with such delicate exotica as cinnamon and nutmeg, pungent with the juice of fresh lemons—Greek cuisine is both subtle and hearty, simple and mysterious.

Certain foods are bountiful on or around the Greek isles. The surrounding Aegean seas offer a variety of fish; olive trees yield the oil indigenous to Greek food; and lemons—whose fragrance and zest permeate the essence of Greek cuisine—ripen throughout the countryside.

Because refrigeration is not commonplace, the Greek table is seasonal, and crops are prepared in myriad ways to avoid waste. Lamb is the favorite meat, perhaps because sure-footed sheep can thrive on the rocky terrain.

Whatever the order of the day, Greek food is usually cooked simply but attended lavishly by home-grown herbs and spices. Its delicate flavor gracefully expresses a timelessness that seems as old and venerable as history itself.

BAKED COD STEW

Serves 8

2 lbs. cod fillets
1 Tbs. oil
1 Tbs. low sodium beef bouillon
Black pepper to taste
2 Tbs. lemon juice
½ cup dry white wine
2 Tbs. unsalted butter or margarine
4 scallions, chopped, including greens

2 carrots, scraped and diced
2 medium-size onions, chopped
2 lbs. green beans, cut into 1" lengths
3 tomatoes, chopped
2 Tbs. raisins*
1 tsp. sugar
1 Tbs. red wine vinegar
1 Tbs. fresh chopped parsley

Preserved in non-sodium ingredient
Preheat oven to 350°.
In oven-proof casserole, arrange fillets. Sprinkle with oil. Season with bouillon and black pepper. Pour lemon juice and wine in casserole. Bake 15 minutes.
While cod is baking, in large skillet, melt butter. Add scallions, carrots, and onions. Cook over very low heat 10 minutes, stirring occasionally.
Stir in green beans, tomatoes, and raisins. Cook 5 minutes more.
Stir in sugar and vinegar. Scrape mixture over fish. Bake 20 minutes more.
Stir in parsley.

Calories per serving: 231   Sodium per serving: 109 mgs.

FRIED FISH ROSEMARY

Serves 8

¼ cup all-purpose flour
Black pepper to taste
1 Tbs. basil
1 Tbs. parsley
1 Tbs. tarragon
⅛ tsp. cinnamon

2 lbs. sole fillets
4 Tbs. olive oil, divided
6 cloves garlic, minced
¼ cup cider vinegar
1 tsp. rosemary, crushed

In plastic bag, combine first six ingredients. Add sole and shake to coat.
In skillet, heat 2 Tbs. oil. Add fillets and cook over low heat till golden.
Add remaining oil. Turn fish and cook till second side is golden. Transfer to platter.
Raise heat to high. Add garlic and cook briefly. Stir in vinegar and rosemary. Cook 2 minutes, stirring often. Spoon over fish.
Serve over pasta or rice.

Calories per serving: 184   Sodium per serving: 93 mgs.

HADDOCK WITH EGG AND LEMON SAUCE

Serves 8

1 Tbs. low sodium beef bouillon
2 lbs. haddock fillets, cut into 2″ chunks
½ cup lemon juice
1 Tbs. garlic powder

¼ cup all-purpose flour
¼ cup oil
2 cups Egg and Lemon Sauce (See Page 288)

In bowl, combine first 4 ingredients. Let stand 30 minutes. Drain.
Coat fish with flour.
In skillet, heat oil. Sauté fish over low heat till lightly browned all over.
Serve with Egg and Lemon Sauce.

Calories per serving: 213   Sodium per serving: 97 mgs.

SEA BASS AND SPINACH

Serves 8

2 Tbs. olive oil
1 sprig watercress, chopped
2 leeks, chopped, including greens
1 lb. spinach, chopped
2 cloves garlic, minced
½ cup low sodium Bread Crumbs (See Page 291)

1½ Tbs. low sodium chicken bouillon
Black pepper to taste
¼ tsp. nutmeg
1 cup milk
2 1-lb. sea bass steaks, cut 1″ thick
2 lemons, cut into wedges

Preheat oven to 350°.
In skillet, heat oil. Add watercress, leeks, spinach, garlic, and Bread Crumbs. Toss to blend. Cover and simmer 10 minutes.
Stir in bouillon, pepper, nutmeg, and milk. Transfer half the spinach mixture to a 9″ square oven-proof casserole.
Place fish on top of spinach mixture. Top with remaining spinach mixture. Cover and bake 45 minutes, or till fish flakes easily.
Garnish with lemon wedges.

Calories per serving: 230   Sodium per serving: 140 mgs.

SQUID AND RICE BAKE

Serves 8

16 squid, cleaned and cut into 1″ chunks
¼ cup lemon juice
1 Tbs. cider vinegar
2 Tbs. olive oil
2 medium-size onions, minced
2 cloves garlic, minced
1 can (16 ozs.) low sodium tomatoes,
  chopped, including liquid
1 Tbs. low sodium beef bouillon
4 Tbs. parsley

White pepper to taste
2 tsps. basil
⅛ tsp. cinnamon
1 cup long grain rice
½ cup dry white wine
1½ cups water
1 Tbs. low sodium chicken bouillon
2 Tbs. crushed almonds
2 lemons, cut into wedges

In bowl, combine first 3 ingredients. Toss to blend. Cover and refrigerate till ready to use.

In large skillet, heat oil. Add onions and garlic and cook over low heat 10 minutes, stirring occasionally.

Stir in tomatoes and their liquid, beef bouillon, parsley, pepper, basil, and cinnamon. Cook 5 minutes more, stirring often.

Stir in squid mixture. Stir in remaining ingredients, except lemon wedges. Bring to a boil. Cover, reduce heat, and simmer 30 minutes, or till liquid is absorbed.

Garnish with lemon wedges.

Calories per serving: 256   Sodium per serving: 22 mgs.

GREEK LAMB ROAST

Serves 10

1 3-lb. leg of lamb
6 cloves garlic, slivered
White pepper to taste
4 tsps. low sodium chicken bouillon,
  divided
4 Tbs. unsalted butter or margarine,
  melted, divided
½ cup lemon juice, divided

1 Tbs. rosemary, crushed
4 potatoes, parboiled, peeled, and sliced
1 cup water
3 Tbs. paprika
1 can (6 ozs.) low sodium tomato paste
2 cups Egg and Lemon Sauce (See Page
  288)

Preheat oven to 325°.
Cut slits in lamb all around and insert slivers of garlic.
Place in shallow roasting pan and rub with pepper and half of the bouillon.
Pour on half the butter. Then pour on half the lemon juice. Sprinkle with rosemary.
Arrange potatoes around lamb. Add water.
Sprinkle all with paprika. Roast, uncovered, 1½ hours.

Add the remaining bouillon to pan.

Pour on remaining butter and spread tomato paste over lamb.

Continue roasting 1 to 1¼ hours, depending on desired doneness, basting with remaining lemon juice.

Serve with Egg and Lemon Sauce.

Calories per serving: 413	Sodium per serving: 132 mgs.

GREEK MEAT LOAF

Serves 8

2 Tbs. olive oil
2 medium-size onions, chopped
1½ lbs. ground beef
Black pepper to taste
1 Tbs. Imitation Worcestershire Sauce (See Page 291), or 1½ tsps. low sodium beef bouillon, plus 1 Tbs. low sodium ketchup

½ cup low sodium Seasoned Bread Crumbs (See Page 291)
2 Tbs. low sodium chicken bouillon
½ cup milk
6 scallions, chopped, including greens
2 tsps. lemon juice
1 Tbs. heavy cream

Preheat oven to 350°.

In skillet, heat oil. Sauté onions till wilted. Transfer to large bowl.

Add all but last 4 ingredients, blending thoroughly. Shape into loaf. Place in casserole and bake 45 minutes.

While loaf is baking, in saucepan, combine milk and scallions. Cook over low heat 10 minutes, stirring often.

Stir in lemon juice and cream. Cook 5 minutes more. Spoon over meat loaf and bake 15 minutes more.

Calories per serving: 318	Sodium per serving: 72 mgs.

GREEK SAUSAGE

Serves 8

1½ lbs. ground pork
½ lb. ground beef
½ cup dry red wine
1 egg
¼ cup low sodium Bread Crumbs (See Page 291)
½ tsp. marjoram
2 Tbs. parsley

1 Tbs. garlic powder
3 Tbs. low sodium beef bouillon
Black pepper to taste
⅜ tsp. ground cumin
⅛ tsp. cinnamon
1 Tbs. unsalted butter or margarine
2 cups Tomato Sauce (See Page 298)
1 cup dry red wine

In large bowl, combine all but last 3 ingredients, blending thoroughly. Roll into small sausages.

In Dutch oven, melt butter. Add sausages and cook over low heat 10 minutes, turning often to brown on all sides.

Pour on Tomato Sauce and 1 cup wine. Cover and simmer 20 minutes.

Calories per serving: 442　　　　Sodium per serving: 112 mgs.

LAMB AND EGGPLANT SKILLET

Serves 8

1 Tbs. olive oil
1½ lbs. stewing lamb, cut into small
　chunks
1 large onion, chopped
3 large cloves garlic, minced
1 small eggplant, peeled and cut into
　1″ chunks
1 carrot, scraped and diced
1 apple, peeled, cored, and diced

1 tsp. brown or white sugar
1 tsp. oregano
1 tsp. mustard powder
¼ tsp. fennel seed
Black pepper to taste
⅓ cup dry white wine
4 tsp. low sodium chicken bouillon
2 ozs. low sodium mozzarella cheese,
　shredded

In large skillet, heat oil. Add lamb, onion, and garlic and cook over medium heat, stirring often, till meat is browned.

Add remaining ingredients, except wine, bouillon, and cheese.

Cover and simmer over low heat till eggplant is tender, but not mushy, about 15 minutes.

Add wine and raise to medium heat, stirring for 1 minute.

Add bouillon and cheese, stirring to blend well. Lower heat, cover, and continue simmering about 5 minutes, or till cheese melts.

Serve accompanied by broiled tomatoes and rice.

Calories per serving: 322　　　　Sodium per serving: 80 mgs.

MOUSSAKA

Serves 12

1 1-lb. eggplant, peeled and chopped
1 medium-size onion, sliced
2 cloves garlic, minced
4 zucchini, chopped
3 Tbs. olive oil
2 Tbs. sweet pepper flakes

2 Tbs. cold water
2 lbs. ground beef
1 Tbs. garlic powder
Dash of hot pepper flakes
4 tsps. low sodium beef bouillon
Black pepper to taste

(continued next page)

1 tsp. basil
1 tsp. oregano
½ tsp. thyme
1 can (6 ozs.) low sodium tomato paste
2 Tbs. unsalted butter or margarine
8 mushrooms, sliced
3 Tbs. all-purpose flour

1 cup boiling water
2 Tbs. low sodium chicken bouillon
¼ lb. low sodium mozzarella cheese, sliced thin
¼ lb. low sodium Gouda cheese, sliced thin
2 Tbs. parsley

In skillet, cook eggplant, onion, garlic, and zucchini in oil, stirring occasionally, 3 minutes. Set aside.

In bowl, combine sweet pepper flakes and cold water. Let stand 10 minutes.

In second skillet, combine beef and garlic powder. Stir to blend. Cook beef in own fat over low heat 10 minutes, stirring occasionally, or till beef loses its pink color. Pour off fat.

Stir in sweet pepper flakes, hot pepper flakes, beef bouillon, pepper, basil, oregano, thyme, and tomato paste. Stir to blend thoroughly.

Stir eggplant mixture into beef mixture. Blend well. Set aside.

Preheat oven to 350°.

In saucepan, melt butter. Add mushrooms and cook over low heat 5 minutes. Stir in flour.

Stir in remaining ingredients and cook over medium/low heat till cheese starts to melt, stirring occasionally.

Spoon half of meat mixture into 9″ square oven-proof casserole. Pour on half the cheese sauce. Repeat with remaining meat mixture and cheese sauce. Cover loosely and bake 30 minutes. Uncover and bake 15 minutes more.

Calories per serving: 377   Sodium per serving: 69 mgs.

PORK STEW

Serves 8

1½ lbs. stewing pork, cut into 1″ chunks
2 medium-size onions, chopped
4 cloves garlic, minced
Black pepper to taste
2 Tbs. lemon juice
2 Tbs. low sodium ketchup

4 leeks, chopped, including greens
1 cup Beef Broth (See Page 44)
Dash of ground cumin
1 Tbs. low sodium chicken bouillon
3 Tbs. parsley

In ungreased skillet, cook pork, onions, and garlic over low heat, turning pork till all sides are lightly browned.

Stir in remaining ingredients. Cover and simmer 30 minutes.

Serve over rice.

Calories per serving: 290   Sodium per serving: 78 mgs.

SPICED BEEF

Serves 8

1 2-lb. sirloin steak, 1″ thick
2 Tbs. dry sherry
¼ cup dry red wine
2 Tbs. low sodium chicken bouillon,
    divided

2 cloves garlic, minced, divided
½ tsp. black pepper, divided
2 tsps. oregano, divided
2 lemons, cut into wedges

Preheat oven to broil.
Place beef in shallow baking pan. Pour on sherry and red wine. Season with half the bouillon, garlic, pepper, and oregano. Broil 6 minutes, close to heat.
Turn beef. Sprinkle with remaining bouillon, garlic, pepper, and oregano. Broil 5 minutes more. Transfer to platter.
Carve beef. Pour on pan juices. Squeeze juice of 2 lemon wedges over beef. Serve remaining wedges as garnish.

Calories per serving: 351   Sodium per serving: 74 mgs.

BRANDIED CHICKEN

Serves 6

4 Tbs. unsalted butter or margarine,
    divided
6 pieces chicken (3 half breasts, 3 whole
    legs)
2 Tbs. low sodium chicken bouillon
White pepper to taste
½ cup dry white wine

3 Tbs. low sodium ketchup
½ cup water
1 Tbs. parsley
1 Tbs. oregano
¼ tsp. cinnamon (optional)
2 Tbs. lemon juice
¼ cup brandy

In large skillet, melt 1 Tbs. butter. Season chicken with bouillon and pepper. Add half the chicken to skillet and cook over low heat till both sides are golden brown. Transfer to 9″ × 13″ oven-proof casserole.
Repeat with remaining butter and chicken. Transfer to casserole.
Preheat oven to 325°.
Add wine, ketchup, water, parsley, oregano, cinnamon, and lemon juice to casserole. Bake 45 minutes.
Pour on brandy and flame.

Calories per serving: 250   Sodium per serving: 84 mgs.

CHICKEN AND ARTICHOKES

Serves 6

5 Tbs. unsalted butter or margarine,
   divided
1 medium-size onion, chopped
4 cloves garlic, minced
6 pieces chicken (3 half breasts, 3 whole
   legs)
1½ Tbs. low sodium chicken bouillon

White pepper to taste
1 cup Chicken Broth (See Page 45)
¼ cup dry white wine
2 tsps. oregano
3 artichokes, stems cut
2 Tbs. lemon juice

In large skillet, melt 1 Tbs. butter. Add onion and garlic and cook over low heat 5 minutes, stirring occasionally. Push to sides of skillet.

Melt remaining butter. Add chicken and brown on all sides over medium/low heat. Transfer chicken mixture to 9″ × 13″ oven-proof casserole. Season with bouillon and pepper.

Pour Chicken Broth and wine over all. Add oregano.

Preheat oven to 350°.

Cut tops and tough outer leaves off artichokes. Halve lengthwise. Discard chokes. Sprinkle with lemon juice and add to casserole.

Cover and bake 45 minutes, or till chicken and artichokes are tender.

Calories per serving: 286   Sodium per serving: 153 mgs.

CHICKEN AVGOLEMONO

Serves 6

3 Tbs. unsalted butter or margarine
6 pieces chicken (3 half breasts, 3 whole
   legs)
3 cloves garlic, minced
Black pepper to taste
1½ cups Chicken Broth (See Page 45)

3 yellow squash, sliced
⅛ tsp. nutmeg
1 Tbs. mint
2 eggs
2 Tbs. lemon juice

In large skillet, melt butter. Add chicken, garlic, and pepper. Cook over medium/low heat 10 minutes, turning chicken to brown on all sides.

Add Chicken Broth, squash, nutmeg, and mint. Cover and simmer 35 minutes.

In bowl, beat together eggs and lemon juice. Pour into saucepan. Slowly beat in 1 cup of pan juices from the skillet and cook over low heat 5 minutes, or till sauce thickens, stirring occasionally.

Transfer chicken to platter. Beat remaining pan juices into avgolemono sauce. Pour sauce over chicken.
Serve with rice.

Calories per serving: 289   Sodium per serving: 126 mgs.

CHICKEN STEW

Serves 6

2 Tbs. unsalted butter or margarine
6 pieces chicken (3 half breasts, 3 whole legs)
1 medium-size onion, chopped
Black pepper to taste
2 cloves garlic, minced
2 Tbs. cider vinegar
1 Tbs. low sodium beef bouillon
1 can (6 ozs.) low sodium tomato paste

1 cup dry white wine
1 cup water
¼ tsp. cinnamon
2 Tbs. low sodium chicken bouillon
2 tomatoes, chopped
2 carrots, scraped and diced
1 lb. green beans, chopped
2 Tbs. lemon juice
Dash of ground cumin (optional)

In Dutch oven, melt butter. Add chicken and onion. Cook over low heat 10 minutes, turning chicken to brown.
Stir in pepper. Add garlic and vinegar. Cook 5 minutes more.
Stir in beef bouillon and tomato paste. Cook 1 minute.
Add wine, water, cinnamon, and chicken bouillon. Cover and simmer 35 minutes.
Add tomatoes and carrots. Cover and simmer 15 minutes more.
Add green beans. Stir in lemon juice. Cover and simmer 15 minutes more. Stir in cumin.
Serve with potatoes.

Calories per serving: 293   Sodium per serving: 101 mgs.

CHICKEN WITH PEAS OREGANO

Serves 6

6 pieces chicken (3 half breasts, 3 whole legs)
Black pepper to taste
¼ tsp. sage
½ tsp. thyme

2 cloves garlic, minced
2 Tbs. lemon juice
1½ cups Chicken Broth (See Page 45)
1 tsp. oregano
1¼ lbs. fresh shelled peas

Preheat oven to broil.
Place chicken on shallow baking sheet. Broil 8 minutes. Turn chicken. Season with pepper, sage, and thyme. Broil 6 minutes more. Transfer to skillet.

Add all remaining ingredients except peas. Cover and simmer 20 minutes. Add peas and simmer 10 minutes more.

Calories per serving: 232   Sodium per serving: 80 mgs.

VINEGAR CHICKEN AND WALNUTS

Serves 6

1 3-lb. chicken
2 cups water, divided
1 Tbs. unsalted butter or margarine
½ tsp. marjoram
2 Tbs. cider vinegar

¼ cup walnuts, chopped
¼ tsp. nutmeg
1 lb. mushrooms, sliced
4 scallions, chopped, including greens
2 Tbs. low sodium chicken bouillon

Preheat oven to 350°.

Place chicken on rack in roasting pan, breast side down. Pour ¾ cup water in pan.

Add butter, marjoram, vinegar, walnuts, nutmeg, mushrooms, and scallions. Roast 35 minutes, or till skin is browned.

Turn chicken, breast side up. Add remaining water to pan. Sprinkle in bouillon. Roast 35 minutes more, or till skin is browned. Transfer to platter and carve.

Serve pan juices on side.

Calories per serving: 285   Sodium per serving: 108 mgs.

INDIAN

When we think of Indian food, we usually think of curry—that subtly sweet yet pungent spice blend so often considered synonymous with the Indian kitchen. However, this erroneous oversimplification of Indian cuisine is as unjust to the Indian artistry as it is limiting to our own expectations.

To be sure, most Indian dishes are prepared with one or more of the herbs and spices found in commercial curry powder. But the proportions are rarely the same, nor is the order in which they are added to a dish. Indeed, the sophistication of Indian cuisine is such that even the amount of cooking time per herb or spice can radically change a meal from sweet to hot and vice versa. The gamut runs from a spark to an explosion of taste just as Chinese food ranges from mild and subtle Cantonese to hot and spicy Szechwan.

The variety doesn't stop there. Although the Hindu religion forbids eating beef, millions of Indians do enjoy it along with veal, pork, and the most popular lamb. Chicken and fish now often appear on the Indian table thanks to the arrival of refrigeration.

But perhaps the two cornerstones of the Indian diet are vegetables and chutney. The former are seasonally plentiful. They are braised, fried, boiled, or pickled in numerous ways, imaginative enough to satisfy and nourish the many Indian vegetarians, as well as other food fanciers.

Puréed vegetables are often blended into one of the myriad chutney accompaniments to every meal. Fruits—all kinds and combinations—are also primary chutney ingredients, prepared with flourish. Chutneys may be sweet or hot, and one or more of each flavor are served at an Indian meal. For chutney is to the Indian table what sauces and relishes are to our own.

Traditionally, Indian cooks grind fresh spices as needed to guarantee a full, fresh flavor. But we want to simplify this cooking adventure for you. We would rather encourage you to try your hand at these foods and experience some marvelous taste sensations. So, we will be using only herbs and spices readily available in your supermarket or health food store. Of course, if an Indian food store is nearby, try the entire range of seasonings.

Indian cuisine is a delicate balance of tastes and textures. It is as colorful and distinctly different—recipe to recipe—as the wonderful kaleidoscopic patterns of Indian silks, carpets, and graphic designs—each one beautiful, each one special, no two quite the same.

INDIAN

HALIBUT IN BROWN SAUCE

Serves 4

2 medium-size onions, chopped
6 cloves garlic, chopped
1 Tbs. chopped ginger root or dash of
  ginger powder
5 Tbs. red wine vinegar
1 Tbs. oil
¼ tsp. cumin seed
½ tsp. fennel seed
2 bay leaves
1 tsp. turmeric

4 Tbs. low sodium chili ketchup
Cayenne pepper to taste
1 Tbs. brown sugar
6 cloves
⅛ tsp. cinnamon
⅛ tsp. mace
1 cup Beef Broth (See Page 44)
1¼ lbs. halibut steaks
2 tsps. low sodium chicken bouillon
1 Tbs. fresh chopped parsley

In blender, grind onions, garlic, ginger, and vinegar to a paste. Set aside.
In large skillet, heat oil. Add cumin and fennel seed.
Stir fry over low heat 1 minute.
Add paste and stir fry 1 minute more.
Add bay leaves and turmeric. Stir fry 1 minute.
Add chili ketchup, cayenne, sugar, cloves, cinnamon, mace, and Beef Broth. Bring to a boil. Cover. Reduce heat and simmer 15 minutes.
Preheat oven to 350°.
Place halibut in oven-proof casserole.
Pour sauce over fish. Sprinkle bouillon on top. Cover and bake 30 minutes, basting occasionally. Discard bay leaves and cloves.
Garnish with parsley.

Calories per serving: 192   Sodium per serving: 101 mgs.

LEMON SWORDFISH

Serves 6

2 Tbs. oil
¼ cup lemon juice
1½ Tbs. chopped ginger root or dash of
  ginger powder
1 medium-size onion, chopped
10 cloves garlic, chopped
2 tsps. turmeric

Coarse black pepper to taste
2 chili peppers, chopped, or dash of hot
  pepper flakes
1½ lbs. swordfish steaks
1 tsp. low sodium beef bouillon
1 tsp. low sodium chicken bouillon
2 lemons, cut into wedges

In blender, combine oil, lemon juice, ginger, onion, garlic, turmeric, pepper, and chili peppers. Grind to a paste.
Place swordfish in a shallow pan and cover with marinade. Cover and refrigerate 3 hours.
Preheat oven to broil.

Place swordfish in broiler. Brush with marinade and sprinkle with half the beef and chicken bouillon. Broil 6 minutes, or until browned.

Turn. Brush with marinade. Sprinkle with remaining bouillon.

Broil 8 minutes longer. Garnish with lemon wedges.

Calories per serving: 205 — Sodium per serving: 8 mgs.

POTATO STUFFED TROUT

Serves 6

1 medium-size onion, chopped
½ tsp. Indian Spice (See Page 291)
1 Tbs. chopped ginger root or dash of ginger powder
2 Tbs. lemon juice
2 Tbs. heavy cream
3 Tbs. oil, divided
1 tsp. mustard powder
1 tsp. dill
1 tsp. low sodium beef bouillon
1 tsp. low sodium chicken bouillon
2 potatoes, boiled, peeled, and mashed
2 1-lb. brook trout boned, heads and tails intact
1 lemon, cut into wedges

In blender, grind onion, Indian Spice, ginger, lemon juice, and cream to a paste. Set aside.

Preheat oven to 350°.

Line a shallow baking pan with tin foil. Grease with 2 Tbs. oil.

Stir paste, mustard powder, dill, and beef and chicken bouillon into potatoes. Blend thoroughly.

Spoon half the potato mixture into each trout.

Place trout in pan. Drizzle with remaining oil. Cover with tin foil and cut hole in center to let steam escape.

Bake 25 minutes. Garnish with lemon wedges.

Calories per serving: 206 — Sodium per serving: 9 mgs.

SALMON IN GINGER AND DILL MARINADE

Serves 4

1½ tsps. chopped ginger root or dash of ginger powder
1 Tbs. lemon juice
1 Tbs. dry sherry
1 Tbs. water
1 Tbs. oil
½ tsp. mustard seed
1 tsp. ground coriander
¼ tsp. ground cumin
1 tsp. Indian Spice (See Page 291)
½ cup water
4 tsps. low sodium chicken bouillon
1 Tbs. dried or 2 bunches fresh dill, chopped
⅛ tsp. nutmeg
1¼ lbs. salmon steak

In blender, grind ginger, lemon juice, sherry, and water to a paste. Set aside.

In skillet, heat oil. Add mustard seed and stir fry over low heat 2 minutes.

Add in the following order: the paste, coriander, cumin, Indian Spice, water, and bouillon. Cook over medium heat 2 minutes.

Add dill. Stir to blend well.

Stir in nutmeg. Add salmon. Cover. Reduce heat and poach 15 to 20 minutes, or till fish flakes easily, adding water, if necessary, to keep fish from sticking.

Calories per serving: 195   Sodium per serving: 97 mgs.

SNAPPER AND PEPPERS

Serves 4

1 Tbs. oil
2 green peppers, chopped
4 cloves garlic, minced
4 cardamom pods
¼ tsp. cinnamon
2 bay leaves
1 lb. red snapper fillets
2 Tbs. lemon juice

¼ tsp. ground coriander
⅛ tsp. cayenne pepper
1 tsp. turmeric
1 can (6 ozs.) low sodium tomato paste
1 carrot, scraped, cut into 1″ rounds and
  boiled tender crisp
1 Tbs. low sodium chicken bouillon

In medium skillet, heat oil. Stir fry green pepper over low heat 5 minutes.

Add garlic, cardamom, cinnamon, and bay leaves. Stir fry 1 minute more.

Preheat oven to broil.

Place fillets in shallow pan. Sprinkle with lemon juice.

To skillet, add coriander, cayenne, turmeric, and tomato paste. Stir fry 1 minute.

Sprinkle carrots around fillets. Sprinkle bouillon on fillets. Pour sauce over all.

Broil fish 6 minutes each side, basting often with sauce.

Remove cardamom pods and bay leaves and serve.

Calories per serving: 209   Sodium per serving: 108 mgs.

BUTTERFLIED LEG OF LAMB

Serves 10

2 medium-size onions, chopped
4 Tbs. chopped ginger root or dash of
  ginger powder
8 cloves garlic, chopped
1 cup lemon juice, divided

¼ cup olive oil
4 Tbs. cider vinegar
1 Tbs. ground coriander
1 Tbs. low sodium beef bouillon
1 tsp. Indian Spice (See Page 291)
(continued next page)

1 tsp. turmeric
½ tsp. cinnamon
½ tsp. mace

½ tsp. nutmeg
16 cloves
1 3-lb. leg of lamb, butterflied*

*Your butcher can do this for you.

In blender, combine onions, ginger, garlic, and 6 Tbs. lemon juice. Grind to a paste. Scrape into large rectangular casserole.
    Add all remaining ingredients except lamb. Blend thoroughly.
    Add lamb. Baste with marinade. Cover and refrigerate overnight.
    Preheat oven to broil.
    Place lamb in baking pan. Broil 12" from heat 25 minutes, basting regularly with marinade.
    Turn lamb and broil 25 minutes more, continuing to baste regularly.

Calories per serving: 322   Sodium per serving: 79 mgs.

GROUND BEEF AND EGGPLANT IN PARSLEY SAUCE

Serves 6

1 cup fresh parsley, loosely packed
2 Tbs. dry red wine
2 Tbs. dry sherry
¼ cup heavy cream
4 Tbs. lemon juice
¼ tsp. ground cumin
3½ tsps. low sodium beef bouillon,
    divided
4 tsps. oil

½ tsp. fennel seed
1 tsp. mustard seed
1½ lbs. eggplant, peeled and chopped
1¼ lbs. ground beef
1 Tbs. garlic powder
⅛ tsp. cayenne pepper
½ tsp. mace
Coarse black pepper to taste
2 Tbs. brandy

In blender, combine parsley, red wine, and sherry. Grind to a paste.
    Scrape paste into bowl. Stir in cream, lemon juice, cumin, and 1 tsp. beef bouillon. Cover and refrigerate.
    In large skillet, heat oil. Add fennel and mustard seed. Stir fry 1 minute.
    Add eggplant and cook over medium heat 2 minutes, stirring often.
    Add beef, garlic powder, and cayenne. Reduce heat and stir fry 5 minutes, or till beef loses its pink color.
    Stir in mace, black pepper, and remaining bouillon. Cook 5 minutes more, stirring often.
    Raise heat to high. When sizzling, pour on brandy and flame.
    Add 3 Tbs. of sauce. Stir to blend.
    Serve remaining sauce on the side as a garnish.

Calories per serving: 367   Sodium per serving: 91 mgs.

CHOPPED BEEF RAGOUT (KHEEMA)

Serves 6

1 Tbs. oil
3 bay leaves
3 cinnamon sticks
8 cloves
3 medium-size onions, chopped
2 Tbs. minced ginger root or dash of
    ginger powder
6 cloves garlic, minced
1 Tbs. ground coriander
1 tsp. cumin seed
2 tsps. turmeric

1 Tbs. heavy cream
1 Tbs. lemon juice
2 Tbs. low sodium ketchup
1¼ lbs. ground beef
1 Tbs. low sodium chicken bouillon
¼ tsp. nutmeg
⅛ tsp. mace
1 tomato, chopped
1 green pepper, chopped
¼ cup water

In a large skillet, heat oil. Add bay leaves, cinnamon, and cloves. Cook over low heat 3 minutes.
   Add onions, ginger, and garlic. Cook 6 minutes, stirring often.
   Add coriander, cumin, and turmeric. Cook 2 minutes, stirring often.
   Stir in cream and lemon juice. Then stir in ketchup and cook 1 minute.
   Add beef. Cook 8 to 10 minutes, stirring often to break up the beef.
   Stir in remaining ingredients. Bring mixture to a boil.
   Cover and simmer 1 hour, stirring occasionally. Discard cinnamon sticks and cloves.

Calories per serving: 325   Sodium per serving: 75 mgs.

LAMB AND RAISINS WITH CARROTS

Serves 6

1 Tbs. oil
1¼ lbs. stewing lamb, cut into 1" chunks
1 Tbs. garlic powder
1 Tbs. paprika
Coarse black pepper to taste
4 medium-size onions, chopped
2 carrots, scraped and sliced thin
1 tsp. turmeric

2 tsps. ground cumin
½ cup water
⅛ tsp. cinnamon
2 Tbs. low sodium ketchup
2 Tbs. golden raisins*
1 orange, unpeeled, cut into 6 wedges
½ cup lemon juice
1 Tbs. low sodium beef bouillon

Preserved in non-sodium ingredient

In Dutch oven, heat oil. Add lamb, garlic powder, paprika, and pepper. Stir fry over low heat till lamb is lightly browned on all sides.
   Add onions, carrots, turmeric, and cumin. Cook over low heat, stirring often, till onions start to brown.

Pour water over all. Cover and simmer 10 minutes, adding more water if necessary to keep moist.

Stir in cinnamon, ketchup, raisins, orange wedges, and lemon juice. Cover and simmer 45 minutes more.

Stir in beef bouillon.

Calories per serving: 356	Sodium per serving: 97 mgs.

MARINATED BEEF ROAST

Serves 12

3 medium-size onions, chopped
1 green pepper, chopped
1 Tbs. chopped ginger root or dash of
  ginger powder
4 cloves garlic, chopped
½ tsp. cumin
2 tsps. mace
2 tsps. turmeric

¼ tsp. cayenne pepper
6 cloves
1½ Tbs. oil, divided
1 cup red wine vinegar
1 3-lb. pot roast (bottom round or rump
  roast)
2 Tbs. low sodium beef bouillon

In blender, place onions, green pepper, ginger, garlic, cumin, mace, turmeric, cayenne, cloves, 1 Tbs. oil, and vinegar. Grind to a paste and set aside.

Gash beef all over. Place in large bowl. Pour paste over beef. Cover and refrigerate at least 6 hours, turning occasionally.

In Dutch oven, heat remaining oil. Sear beef on all sides. Sprinkle with bouillon.

Pour marinade over beef. Cover and simmer 2 hours over low heat, or till beef is tender, turning beef occasionally and adding water, if necessary, to maintain 1″ of liquid.

Calories per serving: 264* *If using rump roast, calories would be 384.*	Sodium per serving: 83 mgs.

PORK AND CABBAGE

Serves 8

8 loin pork chops
2 bay leaves
2 cinnamon sticks
12 black peppercorns
1 cup water
1 tsp. sugar
1 Tbs. oil
½ tsp. cumin seed

1 tsp. fennel seed
2 medium-size onions, sliced
½ large head cabbage, shredded
10 cloves
2 apples, peeled, cored, and chopped
2 tsps. low sodium chicken bouillon
2 Tbs. heavy cream
3 Tbs. lemon juice

In large, ungreased skillet, fry pork chops over very low heat till browned on both sides. Remove to platter.

To same skillet, add bay leaves, cinnamon, and peppercorns. Stir fry 1 minute.

Add water. Stir in sugar. Add pork chops. Bring to a boil. Cover. Reduce heat to low and simmer 45 minutes.

In large saucepan, heat oil. Add cumin and fennel seed. Stir fry 1 minute. Add onions. Stir fry 2 minutes.

Add cabbage. Cook over medium heat 1 minute, stirring often. Add cloves.

Add apple. Reduce heat. Cover and steam 5 minutes.

Stir bouillon into cabbage mixture. Stir fry 15 minutes over medium/low heat. Remove from heat.

When chops are done, stir cabbage mixture, cream, and lemon juice into pork chops. Mix thoroughly. Cover and simmer over low heat 5 minutes more, stirring often.

Remove bay leaves, cinnamon sticks, and cloves.

Calories per serving: 345   Sodium per serving: 97 mgs.

PORK CHOPS IN TOMATO SAUCE

Serves 8

1 medium-size onion, chopped
3 cloves garlic, minced
Dash of ginger powder
1 tsp. fennel seed
2 tsps. turmeric
2 tsps. low sodium beef bouillon

1 can (12 ozs.) low sodium tomato juice
2 Tbs. low sodium chili ketchup
1 tsp. ground coriander
Cayenne pepper to taste
Coarse black pepper to taste
8 loin pork chops

In large casserole, combine all ingredients except pork chops.

Gash chops all around, place in marinade, and thoroughly coat on all sides. Cover and refrigerate overnight.

Preheat oven to broil.

Place chops in shallow pan. Broil close to flame 4 minutes each side.

Pour on half the marinade and remove chops to oven. Reduce heat to 350°. Cover and bake 20 minutes.

Turn chops. Pour on remaining marinade. Cover and bake 15 minutes.

Uncover and bake 15 minutes more.

Calories per serving: 286   Sodium per serving: 92 mgs.

SHISH KEBAB IN WINE MARINADE

Serves 8

2 Tbs. oil
1 large green pepper, cut into 1″ chunks
1 large onion, cut into 1″ cubes
16 medium-size mushroom caps
½ tsp. thyme
½ tsp. ground coriander
12 black peppercorns, crushed

8 bay leaves
½ tsp. garlic powder
½ tsp. mustard powder
1 cup dry red wine
1½ Tbs. white vinegar
1½ lbs. lamb or beef sirloin, cut into
 1″ chunks

In skillet, heat oil. Stir fry green pepper, onion, and mushroom caps about 3 minutes. Remove from heat and cool.
In bowl, combine all herbs and spices, wine, and vinegar. Add vegetables and meat. Marinate 8 hours.
Preheat oven to broil.
Beginning and ending with a mushroom cap, thread meat, green pepper, onion, and mushroom caps on 8 skewers. Reserve marinade.
Broil about 3″ from heat about 7 to 10 minutes to desired doneness, turning and basting often with marinade.
Serve over rice, accompanied by Mushroom Sauce (See Page 293).

Lamb: Calories per serving: 311
Beef Sirloin: Calories per serving: 318

Sodium per serving: 72 mgs.
Sodium per serving: 64 mgs.

SUGAR DUSTED PORK CHOPS

Serves 8

8 loin pork chops
½ large head lettuce, shredded
1 sprig watercress, chopped
5 bay leaves
4 cloves garlic, chopped
½ cup boiling water
4 tsps. low sodium beef bouillon

1 tsp. cider vinegar
2 Tbs. lemon juice
¼ tsp. cinnamon
½ tsp. mace
1 tsp. sugar
2 Tbs. cognac

In large, ungreased skillet, cook pork chops over low heat till browned on both sides. Remove to warm platter.
Add lettuce, watercress, bay leaves, and garlic to skillet. Stir fry 2 minutes.
In bowl, combine boiling water, bouillon, and vinegar. Set aside.
Stir lemon juice, cinnamon, and mace into skillet, blending well.
Return pork chops to skillet. Stir to blend well. Add half the bouillon mixture. Bring to a boil. Cover and reduce to low heat. Simmer 5 minutes.

Add remaining bouillon mixture. Bring to second boil. Reduce heat and cook 5 minutes more, or till liquid has evaporated.

Sprinkle chops with sugar. Turn heat to high. Add cognac and flame.

Calories per serving: 283	Sodium per serving: 94 mgs.

BROILED MARINATED CHICKEN

Serves 6

3 medium-size onions, chopped
6 cloves garlic, chopped
2 chili peppers, chopped
½ tsp. ground cumin
1 Tbs. chopped ginger root or dash of ginger powder
1 tsp. ground coriander
Cayenne pepper to taste
Black pepper to taste
2 Tbs. lemon juice

½ cup cider vinegar
2 Tbs. oil
6 Tbs. warm water
1 tsp. sugar
¼ tsp. cinnamon
1 Tbs. low sodium beef bouillon
6 pieces chicken (3 half breasts, 3 whole legs), skinned
2 Tbs. fresh chopped parsley

In blender, combine all but last 2 ingredients. Grind to a paste.

Place chicken on shallow baking tray. With a fork, pierce chicken all over. Cover with paste. Cover and refrigerate overnight.

Preheat oven to broil.

Broil 15 minutes each side, or till chicken is browned, basting occasionally. Garnish with parsley.

Calories per serving: 218	Sodium per serving: 92 mgs.

CHICKEN IN TOMATO SAUCE

Serves 8

1 medium-size onion, chopped
6 cloves garlic, chopped
2 Tbs. chopped ginger root or dash of ginger powder
2 cups Chicken Broth (See Page 45), divided
2 Tbs. oil
2 cinnamon sticks
2 bay leaves

Dash of hot pepper flakes
4 black peppercorns
8 pieces chicken (4 half breasts, 4 whole legs), skinned
1 tsp. turmeric
1 can (12 ozs.) low sodium tomato juice
3 potatoes, parboiled, peeled, and sliced
1 Tbs. cornstarch

Place onion, garlic, and ginger in blender along with 4 Tbs. Chicken Broth. Grind to a paste. Set aside.

In large skillet, heat oil. Add cinnamon, bay leaves, pepper flakes, peppercorns, and chicken. Fry chicken on both sides over medium heat till browned. Remove to platter.

Add onion paste and turmeric. Stir fry 1 minute.

Add tomato juice and all but 4 Tbs. of remaining Chicken Broth. Bring to a boil. Cover. Reduce heat and simmer 25 minutes.

Add potatoes to skillet. Cover and continue to simmer 25 minutes longer.

Blend cornstarch and remaining 4 Tbs. of Chicken Broth.

Stir cornstarch mixture into skillet. Cook, stirring often, 5 minutes more, or till mixture is thickened.

Calories per serving: 224   Sodium per serving: 87 mgs.

CHICKEN WITH FRIED ONIONS

Serves 8

2 medium-size onions, minced
1 Tbs. minced ginger root or dash of
   ginger powder
3 cloves garlic, chopped
¼ cup water
2 Tbs. oil
2 medium-size onions, cut into rings
8 pieces chicken (4 half breasts, 4 whole
   legs), skinned
1 Tbs. plus 1 cup dry white wine, divided
1 1-lb. eggplant, peeled and chopped
   coarse

1 tsp. cinnamon
2 tsps. turmeric
2 Tbs. lemon juice
2 tsps. sugar
Cayenne pepper to taste
3 potatoes, parboiled, peeled, and cubed
1 red pepper, chopped
1 Tbs. low sodium chicken bouillon
2 Tbs. heavy cream

In blender, grind onions, ginger, garlic, and water to a paste. Set aside.

In large skillet, heat oil. Fry onion rings over very low heat till onions are wilted. Remove to paper towels and drain.

In same skillet, brown chicken on both sides over medium heat. Remove to platter.

Add 1 Tbs. wine and the onion paste. Stir fry over medium heat 5 minutes.

Add eggplant, cinnamon, and turmeric. Stir fry 2 minutes over low heat.

Add lemon juice, sugar, cayenne, and 1 cup wine. Stir to blend.

Add chicken. Bring mixture to a boil. Reduce heat. Add onion rings. Cover and simmer over low heat 30 minutes. Add potatoes and red pepper. Cover and simmer 15 minutes more.

Stir in chicken bouillon and cream, blending thoroughly.

Calories per serving: 289   Sodium per serving: 87 mgs.

CURRIED CHICKEN

Serves 6

1 3-lb. chicken, cut into serving pieces
1 tsp. black pepper, divided
1 Tbs. garlic powder, divided
3 Tbs. mustard powder
6 Tbs. plus ½ cup water, divided
¼ cup lemon juice

¼ cup honey
2 Tbs. Curry Powder (See Page 288)
1 large onion, sliced
3 carrots, scraped, halved lengthwise and
　quartered

Preheat oven to 350°.
Place chicken in roasting pan, skin side down.
Sprinkle half the pepper and garlic powder over chicken.
In bowl, combine mustard powder with 6 Tbs. water. Stir in lemon juice. Stir in honey and Curry Powder.
Pour half the curry mixture over chicken.
Scatter onion and carrots around chicken.
Pour ¼ cup water over vegetables, or enough to cover.
Bake 30 minutes.
Turn chicken. Sprinkle with remaining pepper and garlic. Pour on remaining curry mixture. Add remaining water to pan. Bake 45 minutes more, or till skin is browned and crispy.

Calories per serving: 242　　　　　　　　Sodium per serving: 110 mgs.

OVEN TOASTED CHICKEN

Serves 4

4 cloves garlic, chopped
2 medium-size onions, chopped
1 Tbs. ground coriander
1 chili pepper, minced, or dash of hot
　pepper flakes
¼ cup lemon juice
2 large chicken breasts, skinned, boned,
　and halved

1 egg, lightly beaten
1 cup low sodium Bread Crumbs (See
　Page 291)
¼ cup oil
Coarse black pepper to taste
¼ cup dry sherry, divided
2 Tbs. fresh chopped parsley

In blender, combine garlic, onions, coriander, chili pepper, and lemon juice. Grind to a paste.
With a fork, pierce chicken all over. Place in large bowl and cover with paste. Cover and marinate at least 8 hours, turning occasionally.

179

Lift each chicken piece, coated with marinade, and dip first in egg, then in Bread Crumbs. Let stand 15 minutes.

Preheat oven to 350°.

Coat a shallow pan with 2 Tbs. oil. Lay chicken in pan. Drizzle with remaining oil. Sprinkle with pepper. Bake 15 minutes.

Add a few Tbs. of sherry to the pan. Bake 20 minutes more.

Combine remaining marinade, sherry, and parsley. Serve as a sauce on the side.

Calories per serving: 283   Sodium per serving: 119 mgs.

ITALIAN

Whether northern or southern, Italian food is as American as pizza. Northern food is usually less heavily spiced than southern, cooked in butter rather than olive oil, and delicately flavored with wines and liqueurs. To further emphasize the polarity between northern and southern styles, rice, not pasta, is the preferred side dish or featured as a separate course.

By contrast, the southern variety is robustly seasoned, spiked with garlic and bathed in olive oil. Served with one of many pastas, it is deliciously indulgent.

But in the kitchens of both regions, the fine blending of herbs and spices is the key to good food—prepared with the same relish with which it is eaten and enjoyed. For good food and good times are synonymous—equally savored in the embrace of Italian hospitality.

Sauces are used to complement and enhance, not substitute for, the individual ingredients which are the heart of Italian cuisine. Chicken is ennobled with style and imaginative dash. Fish is as popular as meat thanks to the generosity of the surrounding seas and the loving hands of Italian cooks. And of all the meats, veal reigns as the Italian favorite.

Like so many old world cultures, Italians have adopted as their own foods introduced by other peoples. For example, the tomato, long thought to be an Italian original, was, in fact, brought to them from Mexico. Fish stews derive from the Greeks. And turkey, so popular on today's Italian menu, was the gift of America.

Yet for all the natural goodness in Italian food, we think it's fattening. The thick sauces. The pasta. But it's not these things that make Italian food so wicked. It's the amounts of oil and butter plus the high salt content that really builds up pounds. So we've altered the orthodox preparation by using low sodium ingredients to replace the salt, special spice blends and miserly quantities of oil and butter, if they are used at all.

You'll find most recipes call for searing, broiling, or quick browning in a hot oven before proceeding with a recipe. A slight sidestep—well worth it when you bite into a glorious meal, but not the vainglorious calories. Just try the tomato sauces in this chapter to see how easy it is to rival the best Italian cooking you know.

So *mangia!* Enjoy with all the unabashed exuberance and vitality of Italy. Veal parmigiana will never become you so well.

BAKED OYSTERS OREGANATO

Serves 4

2 pts. oysters, drained, liquid reserved
¼ cup fresh parsley, chopped
4 cloves garlic, minced
¼ cup shredded low sodium Monterey
  Jack cheese
Cayenne pepper to taste
1 tsp. oregano

Black pepper to taste
2 Tbs. warm water
2 Tbs. olive oil
¼ cup low sodium Bread Crumbs (See
  Page 291)
4 Tbs. lemon juice

Preheat oven to 375°.
Divide oysters equally among 4 baking shells.
Combine all other ingredients except oil, Bread Crumbs, and lemon juice. Sprinkle on oysters.
Sprinkle with oil, then Bread Crumbs, then lemon juice.
Bake 8 to 10 minutes.

Calories per serving: 255   Sodium per serving: 94 mgs.

FILLETS IN WHITE WINE

Serves 8

8 small cod, snapper, or salmon fillets
White pepper to taste
2 Tbs. lemon juice
1 tsp. garlic powder
4 tsps. low sodium chicken bouillon
6 scallions, chopped, including greens
¼ cup unsalted butter or margarine,
  melted
¾ cup dry white wine

2 Tbs. fresh chopped parsley
1 tsp. thyme
Cayenne pepper to taste
4 bay leaves, crushed
3 Tbs. unsalted butter or margarine,
  melted
1 Tbs. unsalted butter or margarine
1 Tbs. all-purpose flour
¼ cup heavy cream

Preheat oven to 375°.
Wash and dry fillets. Arrange in buttered oven-proof casserole in single layer.
Sprinkle with pepper, lemon juice, garlic powder, bouillon, scallions, melted butter, wine, parsley, thyme, cayenne, and bay leaves.
Cover with greased paper, facing down. Cover casserole itself and bake 20 minutes.
Remove fillets to warm platter.

Strain juice into saucepan. Add 1 Tbs. butter. Let melt. Add flour and stir till blended. Add cream. Cook, stirring, 4 to 6 minutes.

Pour sauce over fish.

Cod: Calories per serving: 238   Sodium per serving: 111 mgs.
Snapper: Calories per serving: 260   Sodium per serving: 106 mgs.
Salmon: Calories per serving: 296   Sodium per serving: 102 mgs.

OYSTERS MARINARA

Serves 6

1 Tbs. olive oil
3 medium-size onions, chopped fine
6 cloves garlic, minced
3 pts. oysters, drained, liquid reserved
½ cup dry white wine
2 Tbs. low sodium chicken bouillon

½ tsp. basil
½ tsp. thyme
1 Tbs. parsley
White pepper to taste
1 can (6 ozs.) low sodium tomato paste
1 Tbs. unsalted butter or margarine

In skillet, heat oil. Add onions and cook over low heat 10 minutes.

Add garlic and cook 3 minutes more.

Add oysters and cook 30 seconds, turning once.

Add oyster liquid and all remaining ingredients. Cover and cook over low heat 10 minutes.

Serve with toasted low sodium bread.

Calories per serving: 247   Sodium per serving: 165 mgs.

SEA BASS IN TOMATO SAUCE

Serves 8

4 tsps. low sodium chicken bouillon
¼ cup hot water
1 4-lb. sea bass, cleaned, head and tail
   intact
1 Tbs. olive oil
4 cloves garlic, unpeeled
2 cans (16 ozs. each) low sodium
   tomatoes, chopped, including liquid

1 tsp. basil
1 tsp. oregano
1 tsp. garlic powder
Black pepper to taste
Dash of hot pepper flakes
½ cup dry red wine
2 tsps. sugar

Make a paste of the bouillon and hot water. Rub on fish and place in shallow roasting pan.

In saucepan, heat oil. Add garlic. Cook 5 minutes. Mash garlic and discard skins.

Add tomatoes and their liquid, basil, oregano, garlic powder, black pepper, and pepper flakes. Bring to a boil.

Add wine and sugar. Bring to a second boil. Reduce heat and simmer 5 minutes.
Preheat oven to 425°.
Pour sauce over fish. Bake 35 minutes, or till fish flakes easily, basting often.

Calories per serving: 151   Sodium per serving: 101 mgs.

SQUID IN SPICY TOMATO SAUCE

Serves 6

1½ lbs. very small squid
2 Tbs. olive oil
3 large cloves garlic, unpeeled
1 cup Tomato Sauce (See Page 298)

½ cup dry white wine
1 tsp. low sodium beef bouillon
1 tsp. low sodium chicken bouillon
Dash of hot pepper flakes

Skin and clean squid.
Heat oil in large, deep skillet. Add garlic. Cook 5 minutes, or till golden brown. Mash garlic and discard skins.
Add squid and stir fry over medium heat 5 minutes.
Add Tomato Sauce, wine, beef and chicken bouillon, and pepper flakes. Cover and cook over low heat 15 minutes.

Calories per serving: 181   Sodium per serving: 9 mgs.

TUNA WITH GARLIC SAUCE

Serves 6

¼ cup all-purpose flour
Black pepper to taste
½ tsp. savory
4 tsps. low sodium chicken bouillon
½ tsp. rosemary, crushed
1 tsp. sugar
¼ tsp. sage

6 small tuna fillets
3 Tbs. oil
6 cloves garlic, minced
⅓ cup low sodium Bread Crumbs (See Page 291)
2 Tbs. lemon juice
1 lemon, cut into wedges

Combine flour, pepper, savory, bouillon, rosemary, sugar, and sage. Coat fillets with flour mixture.
Heat oil in large skillet. Cook fish over medium/low heat till both sides are browned. Transfer to shallow baking dish.
Preheat oven to broil.

Combine garlic and Bread Crumbs. Sprinkle on fish. Spoon on lemon juice and broil 2 minutes, or till top is browned.

Garnish with lemon wedges.

Calories per serving: 279   Sodium per serving: 60 mgs.

ZUPPA DI PESCE

Serves 10

4 Tbs. olive oil
3 cloves garlic, minced
4 medium-size onions, sliced
2 green peppers, chopped
4 Tbs. sweet pepper flakes
6 Tbs. cold water
2 sprigs watercress
2 leeks, chopped, including greens
½ tsp. allspice
½ tsp. nutmeg
Black pepper to taste
½ tsp. mace
¼ tsp. saffron threads
2 cans (16 ozs. each) low sodium
 tomatoes

1 tsp. basil
1 tsp. tarragon
½ tsp. thyme
½ lb. cod fillets, cut into 2″ chunks
½ lb. haddock fillets, cut into 2″ chunks
½ lb. sea trout fillets, cut into 2″ chunks
½ lb. snapper fillets, cut into 2″ chunks
2 cups dry white wine
1 Tbs. low sodium beef bouillon
2 Tbs. low sodium chicken bouillon
2 pts. oysters, chopped, liquid reserved
4 Tbs. parsley
2 lemons, sliced into rings

In Dutch oven, heat oil. Add first 17 ingredients.

Cook over low heat 10 minutes, stirring often.

Add fish chunks and wine. Cover and cook over medium heat 10 minutes.

Add beef and chicken bouillon and oysters and their liquid Cover and cook 5 minutes over medium heat, stirring frequently. Stir in parsley.

Garnish with lemon rings.

Serve with rice or low sodium toast.

Calories per serving: 304   Sodium per serving: 148 mgs.

BEEF EGGPLANT PARMESAN

Serves 6

5 tsps. low sodium chicken bouillon
¼ cup warm water
2 eggs, lightly beaten
4 Tbs. oil, divided

1 large onion, chopped
3 cloves garlic, minced
½ lb. mushrooms, sliced
½ lb. ground beef

(continued next page)

Black pepper to taste
1 medium-size eggplant, unpeeled, cut
　into ½″ slices
1 cup low sodium Bread Crumbs (See
　Page 291)

2 tomatoes, sliced thin
1 green pepper, chopped
2 cups Tomato Sauce (See Page 298)
3 ozs. low sodium mozzarella cheese,
　sliced thin

Stir bouillon into water to dissolve. Beat briskly into eggs. Set aside.

In large skillet, heat 1 Tbs. oil. Sauté onion, garlic, mushrooms, and beef till meat is browned. Remove, scraping browned particles from pan, and set aside. Stir in black pepper.

Dip eggplant slices first into egg mixture, then into Bread Crumbs. Set aside.

Coat same skillet with remaining oil. Brown eggplant on both sides, adding oil as necessary till all slices are browned.

Drain on paper towels.

Preheat oven to 350°.

Place eggplant in overlapping slices in 9″ × 13″ oven-proof casserole. Add tomatoes and green pepper.

Spoon meat mixture over eggplant. Pour Tomato Sauce over all. Cover with cheese.

Bake 25 to 30 minutes, or till cheese melts.

Calories per serving: 401　　　　　Sodium per serving: 78 mgs.

BEEF WITH SHERRY MUSTARD SAUCE

Serves 8

1 2-lb. bottom round roast, fat trimmed
Black peppercorns
Coarse black pepper to taste
1 tsp. dill
2 Tbs. Tarragon Mustard (See Page 297),
　divided

2 medium-size onions, sliced
2 carrots, scraped and quartered
1½ cups water, divided
1 cup dry sherry or Marsala, divided

Preheat oven to 375°.

Gash beef all over. Insert peppercorns in gashes.

Line a roasting pan with tin foil. Place roast on rack in center of pan. Sprinkle pepper and dill on beef. Spoon on half the mustard.

Scatter onions and carrots in pan. Pour half the water over vegetables.

Roast beef, uncovered, 45 minutes, or till top is browned.

Spoon on remaining mustard.

Pour remaining water and ⅓ cup sherry over vegetables.

Cover pan loosely with tin foil and reduce heat to 350°. Roast 1½ hours.

Pour remaining sherry over beef. Cover and roast 1 hour more, or till beef is fork tender.*

Sliced potatoes may be added during last hour.

Remove beef to warm platter. Surround with vegetables. Spoon on pan juices.
Serve remaining gravy on side, thickened with equal parts of cornstarch and cold water, if desired.

Calories per serving: 269   Sodium per serving: 88 mgs.

HOT PEPPER MEATBALLS

Serves 8

2 lbs. ground beef
1 Tbs. garlic powder
¼ cup low sodium Bread Crumbs (See
  Page 291)
Dash of hot pepper flakes
½ tsp. basil

½ tsp. marjoram
½ tsp. savory
½ tsp. tarragon
½ tsp. thyme
Dash of white pepper
1 Tbs. oil

In bowl, combine all ingredients except oil. Blend thoroughly. Form into small meatballs.
In large skillet, heat oil. Add meatballs and cook over medium/low heat till browned on all sides.
Serve with Tomato Sauce (See Page 298), on Pizza (See Page 77), or in Indian dishes.

Calories per serving: 328   Sodium per serving: 75 mgs.

MARINATED ROAST LAMB

Serves 8

1 3-lb. leg of lamb
4 tsps. low sodium beef bouillon
Black pepper to taste

¾ cup Vinaigrette (See Page 299)
2 Tbs. lemon juice
1 cup dry red wine

Trim fat. Pierce lamb all over. Rub with bouillon and pepper.
Place lamb in roasting pan. Pour Vinaigrette, lemon juice, and wine over roast.
Marinate 24 hours, basting regularly.
Preheat oven to 350°.
Drain lamb, reserving marinade. Roast 15 minutes per lb. for medium rare, adding marinade after 30 minutes of roasting time. Baste often.

Calories per serving: 408   Sodium per serving: 152 mgs.

PORK LORENZO

Serves 8

2 Tbs. unsalted butter or margarine,
  divided
4 medium-size onions, chopped
1 cup mushrooms, chopped
1½ lbs. pork, cut into ½" cubes
½ tsp. rosemary, crushed
½ tsp. mustard powder
¾ tsp. garlic powder

White pepper to taste
1½ Tbs. low sodium chicken bouillon
⅔ cup dry white wine
1 Tbs. all-purpose flour
1 cup Beef Broth (See Page 44)
1 Tbs. low sodium ketchup
1 tsp. cider vinegar

In large skillet, melt 1 Tbs. butter. Sauté onions and mushrooms over low heat till onions are golden, stirring often.

Transfer half the onions to a 9" square oven-proof casserole. Cover with pork.

Sprinkle pork with rosemary, mustard powder, garlic powder, pepper, and bouillon. Cover with remaining onions, then pour wine over all.

Preheat oven to 350°.

In small saucepan, melt remaining butter. Stir in flour. Slowly add the Broth, stirring constantly.

Stir in ketchup and vinegar. Cook over low heat 5 minutes.

Pour Beef Broth mixture over casserole and bake 1½ hours, or till pork is tender.

Calories per serving: 335   Sodium per serving: 78 mgs.

ROUND STEAK IN BRANDY

Serves 6

1 Tbs. olive oil
1 Tbs. unsalted butter or margarine
1 1½-lb. beef bottom round, ½" thick
¼ tsp. rosemary, crushed
¼ tsp. sage
¼ tsp. basil

¼ tsp. dried or fresh grated lemon peel
Black pepper to taste
1 Tbs. low sodium beef bouillon
1 pear, cored, peeled, and sliced
3 Tbs. brandy

In large skillet, heat oil and butter. Add steak. Cook over high heat 2 minutes.

Mix herbs, spices, and bouillon together. Sprinkle over steak. Turn and cook 2 minutes more for medium rare.

Add pear slices. Pour brandy over all. Flame.

Slice steak thin.

Calories per serving: 289   Sodium per serving: 81 mgs.

VEAL MARSALA

Serves 12

4 Tbs. unsalted butter or margarine, divided
12 veal scallops, pounded thin
¾ lb. mushrooms, sliced
2 cloves garlic
2 tsps. low sodium chicken bouillon

Black pepper to taste
¼ tsp. sage
1 tsp. basil
⅔ cup dry Marsala or sherry
1 can (6 ozs.) low sodium tomato paste
1 can (12 ozs.) low sodium tomato juice

In large skillet, melt 2 Tbs. butter. Sauté half the veal over high heat till both sides are golden brown. Transfer to platter.

In same skillet, melt remaining butter. Sauté remaining veal. Transfer to platter.

Add mushrooms and garlic to skillet. Cook over low heat 5 minutes, stirring occasionally. Discard garlic.

Stir in bouillon, pepper, sage, and basil. Stir in Marsala. Cook 5 minutes.

Stir in tomato paste and tomato juice. Cook 10 minutes, or till heated through.

Return veal to skillet. Cook over high heat 2 minutes.

Calories per serving: 260　　　　Sodium per serving: 117 mgs.

VEAL PICCATA

Serves 6

6 veal scallops
¼ cup all-purpose flour
2 tsps. low sodium beef bouillon
2 tsps. low sodium chicken bouillon
½ tsp. oregano
⅛ tsp. sage
⅛ tsp. rosemary, crushed

Coarse black pepper to taste
¼ tsp. mustard powder
1 Tbs. olive oil
2 Tbs. unsalted butter or margarine
3 Tbs. lemon juice
3 Tbs. dry white wine
2 Tbs. fresh chopped parsley

Pound veal very thin.

Combine flour, beef and chicken bouillon, and all herbs and spices except parsley. Coat veal with flour mixture.

In large skillet, heat oil and butter. Brown veal on both sides over medium heat. Remove to warm platter.

Add lemon juice, wine, and parsley to pan. Add veal and coat well. Cook 2 minutes.

Remove veal and scrape lemon sauce on top.

Calories per serving: 271　　　　Sodium per serving: 110 mgs.

BROILED CHICKEN IN HERBED WINE

Serves 4

This dish is uniquely delicious when steak is used instead of chicken.

2 chicken breasts, skinned and halved
½ tsp. black pepper, divided
½ tsp. garlic powder, divided
½ tsp. mustard powder
1 Tbs. low sodium chicken bouillon,
  divided

1 tsp. thyme
2 green peppers, sliced
2 medium-size onions, sliced
¾ cup dry white wine
1 tsp. basil

Preheat oven to broil.
Place chicken, breast side up, in shallow roasting pan. Season with half the pepper and garlic powder. Season with mustard powder, half the bouillon, and the thyme.
Scatter peppers and onions around chicken. Pour wine in pan. Broil 10 minutes.
Turn chicken. Season with remaining spices and bouillon. Broil 5 minutes more.

Calories per serving: 209   Sodium per serving: 93 mgs.

CHICKEN BREASTS IN MUSHROOM SAUCE

Serves 6

3 chicken breasts, skinned, boned, and
  halved
¼ cup all-purpose flour
2 Tbs. olive oil
1 Tbs. unsalted butter or margarine
1 lb. mushrooms, sliced

Black pepper to taste
1 Tbs. low sodium chicken bouillon
⅔ cup dry white wine
1 Tbs. parsley
Dash of marjoram

In bag, combine chicken and flour. Shake to coat.
In large skillet, heat oil and butter. Add chicken and cook over low heat 20 minutes, or till both sides are browned. Transfer to platter. Scrape particles loose.
To skillet, add mushrooms and cook 5 minutes, stirring occasionally.
Stir in remaining ingredients. Return chicken to skillet. Cover and cook 30 minutes, turning occasionally.

Calories per serving: 309   Sodium per serving: 82 mgs.

CHICKEN IN TOMATO SAUCE

Serves 8

8 pieces chicken (4 half breasts, 4 whole legs)
1 can (16 ozs.) low sodium tomatoes, chopped, including liquid
2 cloves garlic, minced
½ cup dry red wine
1 Tbs. parsley

1 tsp. oregano
Black pepper to taste
⅛ tsp. sage
Dash of nutmeg
1 Tbs. olive oil
1 tsp. lemon juice
2 tsps. low sodium chicken bouillon

In large skillet, place chicken. Add remaining ingredients.
Cover and simmer 1½ hours, or till chicken is tender.

Calories per serving: 180   Sodium per serving: 86 mgs.

CHICKEN OR VEAL "PARMESAGNA"

Serves 8

2 eggs, beaten
1 Tbs. low sodium chicken bouillon
¼ tsp. nutmeg
⅓ cup water
4 chicken breasts, halved, or 8 veal chops
1½ cups low sodium Seasoned Bread Crumbs (See Page 296)

¼ cup oil
2 ozs. low sodium mozzarella cheese, sliced thin
2 ozs. low sodium Monterey Jack cheese, minced, divided
2 cups Tomato Sauce (See Page 298)
⅔ cup hot water

In bowl, beat together eggs, bouillon, nutmeg, and water.
Dip each chicken breast or veal chop in egg mixture, then in Seasoned Bread Crumbs.
In large skillet, heat oil. Brown chicken, a few pieces at a time.
Preheat oven to 350°.
Arrange chicken or veal in 9″ × 13″ oven-proof casserole. Top with mozzarella, then half the Monterey Jack cheese.
Pour Tomato Sauce on top. Sprinkle with remaining cheese.
Cover and bake 20 minutes.
Add water to pan. Bake, uncovered, 10 minutes more.

Chicken: Calories per serving: 338   Sodium per serving: 121 mgs.
Veal: Calories per serving: 417   Sodium per serving: 136 mgs.

CHICKEN WITH CHEESE STUFFING

Serves 6

1 3-lb. chicken
2 tsps. garlic powder
Black pepper to taste
5 slices low sodium bread, toasted and
  broken
2 cups water
1 egg
2 medium-size onions, minced
½ tsp. sage
2 tsps. parsley

1 tsp. basil
1 tsp. oregano
2 ozs. low sodium Monterey Jack cheese,
  minced
1 Tbs. low sodium beef bouillon
White pepper to taste
2 Tbs. paprika, divided
2 Tbs. unsalted butter or margarine,
  melted

Season chicken inside and out with garlic powder and black pepper. Set aside.

In bowl, combine bread and water. Let stand 10 minutes.

Stir in egg, onions, sage, parsley, basil, oregano, cheese, bouillon, and white pepper. Blend thoroughly and stuff chicken.

Preheat oven to 450°.

Truss chicken and place, breast side down, on rack in roasting pan. Sprinkle with half the paprika and roast 30 minutes, or till skin is browned. Reduce heat to 350°.

Turn chicken. Sprinkle with remaining paprika and roast 45 minutes more, or till skin is browned and juices run clear.

Spoon on melted butter and roast 5 minutes more.

Calories per serving: 379   Sodium per serving: 123 mgs.

GRILLED CHICKEN ZUCCHINI

Serves 8

2 Tbs. olive oil
2 Tbs. warm water
3 cloves garlic, minced
1 Tbs. brown sugar
1 Tbs. basil
1 Tbs. garlic powder
½ tsp. sage

¼ tsp. dill
Coarse black pepper to taste
Dash of hot pepper flakes
2 tsps. lemon juice
8 whole chicken legs
4 tsps. low sodium chicken bouillon
3 medium zucchini, cut into 1″ rounds

Combine oil, water, garlic, sugar, herbs, black pepper, and pepper flakes in medium saucepan. Simmer over low heat, stirring till sugar is dissolved. Remove from heat and stir in lemon juice.

Place chicken, skin side down, in shallow baking dish.

Cover with marinade. Let stand 20 minutes.

Preheat oven to broil.

Turn chicken skin side up. Sprinkle with bouillon.

Add zucchini to pan and broil 6″ from heat, turning zucchini and chicken once, for 8 to 10 minutes each side, basting occasionally.

Calories per serving: 201	Sodium per serving: 78 mgs.

HOT SPICED DUCK

Serves 8

1 5-lb. duck
2 Tbs. olive oil
2 medium-size onions, minced
3 cloves garlic, minced
6 tsps. low sodium beef bouillon
Black pepper to taste
Dash of hot pepper flakes

1½ Tbs. sweet pepper flakes
3 Tbs. cold water
1 Tbs. green peppercorns*
¾ tsp. rosemary, crushed
¾ tsp. mustard powder
¾ cup dry sherry
2 Tbs. brandy

Natural green peppercorns, packed in water or vinegar

Preheat oven to 425°.

Follow directions for Sweet and Sour Duck (See Page 133).

While duck is roasting, heat oil in medium-size saucepan. Sauté onions and garlic till golden.

Add remaining ingredients except brandy. Simmer over low heat 30 minutes.

Carve duck. Pour some sauce over duck. Add brandy and flame. Serve remaining sauce on the side.

Calories per serving: 307	Sodium per serving: 118 mgs.

JEWISH

More than 4,000 years ago, a Jewish woman named Rebecca learned the skillful art of transforming the tasteless boiled foods of the times into pleasurable experiences, eaten to satisfy the senses as well as hunger. Her magical ingredients were herbs and spices. She passed her knowledge on to her people, and her culinary principles have survived through centuries of Jewish history. These herbs and spices not only gave flavor to the foods, but they turned the plain cooking broths into the first of many savory soups to be prepared by Jewish hands.

Over the next 2,000 years, the Jews adopted and adapted the foods and cooking techniques of those who ruled them. They owe much of their multi-faceted cuisine to the civilizations of Egypt, Persia, Greece, and Rome. Many of these ancient recipes have become meaningful symbols of Jewish history.

For example, at Passover—which celebrates the Jews' escape to freedom from Egypt—a sweet apricot confection is served, learned during their bondage in that land. And the Jewish love for fish also derives from the days when they brought fresh fish from the Nile to the tables of the lords of Egypt.

Purim features light, triangular pastries filled with poppy seeds known as haman-taschen. They take their name from the three-cornered hat worn by Haman, the Prime Minister of Persia who ordered all Jews put to death. They were saved when the Jewish Queen Esther appealed to her husband. Haman was hanged and haman-taschen are among the many delicacies eaten on the Purim celebration of this deliverance. It is this ability to laugh and yet hold fast to their heritage that has so long sustained the Jewish people.

In more recent times, Western Europe also contributed to Jewish cuisine, and the influences of Poland, Hungary, and Czechoslovakia are still very much in evidence. In fact, the fresh waters of these countries spawn carp, used in making the famous specialty, gefilte fish. Probably Poland established the tradition of having chicken take the culinary place of honor at the Sabbath table on Friday nights. From the Mediterranean, particularly Spain, the Sephardic Jews inherited the oriental spice blends and preference for almond flavorings characteristic of this region.

194

Unlike other cultures, until the establishment of the state of Israel, the Jews had no country of their own. Consequently, their foods have no seasonal restrictions, only religious ones. Meat, for example, is usually steamed or braised rather than roasted. That's because the kosher dietary laws prohibit beef consumption until all blood has left the meat. Salt is used to expedite this process. But as a result the beef is dry, and only braising or steaming can produce desirable tenderness. Such cooking methods result in butter soft meat, but on the done side.

Of course, we don't recommend using kosher meat because of the salt. The recipes in this chapter use unkoshered meat, but the final tastes will do any Jewish cook proud. For those of you who do keep kosher homes, but are supposed to have salt free diets, perhaps tradition can be bent for health's sake.

Jewish cooking is a little bit of everything. It's ancient and recent history, many people, many cultures. It will probably change and expand in scope as years go on. But whatever went into the making, when you eat a knish or a brisket or a bagel, you know it's undeniably Jewish. So delve into this chapter and take a bite from the history of the ages.

BAKED HALIBUT

Serves 8

2 lbs. halibut fillets
2 medium-size onions, minced
1 carrot, scraped and cut into ½" rounds
Black pepper to taste
¼ tsp. sage
¼ tsp. thyme
1 tsp. parsley
1 tsp. tarragon

2 tsps. paprika
Dash of marjoram (optional)
1 Tbs. low sodium chicken bouillon
½ cup milk
½ cup water
2 Tbs. lemon juice
1 Tbs. low sodium butter or margarine

Preheat oven to 350°.
Place halibut in 9" × 13" oven-proof casserole. Surround with onions and carrot.
Sprinkle fillets with pepper, herbs, and bouillon.
Pour milk and water around fish. Stir in lemon juice.
Dot fish with butter. Cover with tin foil and bake 20 minutes.
Remove foil and bake 10 minutes more, or till top is browned and fish flakes easily.

Calories per serving: 144   Sodium per serving: 72 mgs.

CREAM PICKLED HERRING

Serves 6

1½ lbs. unsalted herring, cleaned and cut
    into 2″ chunks
2 medium-size onions, sliced into rings
2 Tbs. sour cream*
¾ cup white vinegar
½ tsp. mustard seed

1 bay leaf
12 black peppercorns
1 Tbs. low sodium chicken bouillon
¼ cup dry white wine
2 Tbs. sugar

Preserved in non-sodium ingredients

    Divide herring, onion rings, and sour cream among 2 pint jars.
    In saucepan, combine remaining ingredients. Cook over low heat 5 minutes, stirring to dissolve sugar. Pour over herring.
    Cover jars tightly and refrigerate at least 24 hours.

Calories per serving: 260   Sodium per serving: 25 mgs.

GEFILTE FISH

Serves 8

½ lb. cod
½ lb. haddock
½ lb. carp
½ lb. pike
1 large onion, chopped
White pepper to taste
½ cup matzo meal
1 Tbs. sugar

2 eggs, lightly beaten
3 Tbs. parsley
2 tsps. low sodium chicken bouillon
2 tsps. low sodium beef bouillon
2 cups Fish Stock (See Page 45)
1 carrot, scraped and cut into ¼″ rounds
2 Tbs. unflavored gelatin

    In blender, combine all ingredients except Fish Stock, carrot, and gelatin. Purée till smooth.
    Form fish mixture into small balls and set aside.
    In large saucepan or Dutch oven, combine Fish Stock and carrot. Bring to a boil.
    Reduce heat and drop in fish balls. Cover and simmer over low heat 1½ hours. Uncover and simmer 30 minutes more.
    Transfer fish balls to deep bowl.
    Let stock cool and stir in gelatin till dissolved. Pour over fish balls.
    Cover and refrigerate overnight.

Calories per serving: 194   Sodium per serving: 119 mgs.

HALIBUT IN ALMOND SAUCE

Serves 4

1 lb. halibut steak
4 Tbs. lemon juice
White pepper to taste
2 tsps. low sodium chicken bouillon

2 Tbs. low sodium mayonnaise
2 Tbs. slivered almonds
2 tsps. paprika

In medium bowl, soak fish in lemon juice for 10 minutes.
Preheat oven to broil.
Remove fish to broiling pan.
To bowl, add remaining ingredients except paprika. Blend well. Spoon half over fish.
Sprinkle with paprika. Broil 6" from heat 6 minutes.
Turn fish. Spoon on remaining sauce. Broil 6 minutes more.

Calories per serving: 184   Sodium per serving: 68 mgs.

OVEN FRIED FISH

Serves 8

1 egg
3 Tbs. oil
2 Tbs. low sodium chicken or beef
  bouillon
Coarse black pepper to taste

2 tsps. garlic powder
1 tsp. dill
8 small sole or bluefish fillets
1 cup matzo meal
2 lemons, cut into wedges

Preheat oven to 400°.
In flat bowl, beat egg, oil, bouillon, pepper, garlic powder, and dill.
Dip fillets first in egg mixture, then in matzo meal.
Place fillets in shallow, lightly greased baking dish. Bake 25 minutes without turning.
Garnish with lemon wedges and Tartar Sauce (See Page 297), or Herbed Mayonnaise (See Page 290).

Sole: Calories per serving: 193   Sodium per serving: 129 mgs.
Bluefish: Calories per serving: 247   Sodium per serving: 124 mgs.

PUCKERY GRILLED COD

Serves 6

1 Tbs. oil
6 small (6 ozs. each) cod fillets
2 Tbs. low sodium butter or margarine
1 Tbs. cider vinegar
2 tsps. mustard powder
4 tsps. low sodium beef bouillon

Black pepper to taste
¼ tsp. onion powder
1 tsp. tarragon
½ cup sliced mushrooms
2 Tbs. raisins*
⅔ cup dry vermouth

Preserved in non-sodium ingredient

Preheat oven to broil.
Grease shallow baking pan with oil.
Place fish in baking pan.
Combine butter, vinegar, mustard powder, bouillon, pepper, onion powder, and tarragon. Spread evenly over fish.
Broil 12″ from heat for 10 minutes.
While fish is broiling, combine remaining ingredients in a small saucepan. Bring to a boil. Reduce heat and simmer till fish is done. Serve on the side as a sauce.

Calories per serving: 231   Sodium per serving: 114 mgs.

SALMON CROQUETTES

Serves 4

1 Tbs. low sodium butter or margarine
3 medium-size onions, chopped
2 cans (7¾ ozs. each) low sodium
   salmon
1 egg, lightly beaten
2 Tbs. sour cream*

2 Tbs. lemon juice
½ cup low sodium Seasoned Bread
   Crumbs (See Page 296)
2 tsps. low sodium beef bouillon
3 Tbs. vegetable shortening, divided

Preserved in non-sodium ingredient

In large skillet, melt butter. Sauté onions till golden. Transfer to large bowl.
Add remaining ingredients except shortening to bowl, breaking salmon thoroughly. Mash together. Form into 8 patties.
In same skillet, melt half the shortening. Fry half the patties over low heat till browned on both sides.
Repeat with remaining shortening and patties.

Calories per serving: 311   Sodium per serving: 107 mgs.

BRISKET

Serves 8

1 2-lb. lean beef brisket, fat trimmed
Coarse black pepper to taste
1 tsp. garlic powder
1 Tbs. paprika
1 Tbs. oil
2 small onions, sliced thin
4 cloves garlic, minced
2 bay leaves
2 cups boiling water, divided

2 tsps. mustard powder
1¾ cups dry red wine
4 tsps. low sodium beef bouillon
3 potatoes, parboiled, peeled, and sliced
  thick
½ cup sliced mushrooms
2 Tbs. all-purpose flour (optional)
4 Tbs. cold water (optional)

Season meat with pepper, garlic powder, and paprika.
Heat oil in Dutch oven. Sear meat on all sides over high heat.
Reduce heat to medium. Add onions and fry till golden, stirring often.
Add garlic, bay leaves, and 1 cup boiling water. Cover and cook over low heat 1 hour.
Add remaining boiling water and mustard. Cover and cook 1 hour more.
Add wine, cover and cook 1 hour more.
Stir in bouillon, potatoes, and mushrooms. Cover and cook 45 minutes more.
If desired, combine flour and cold water. Stir into gravy to thicken. Discard bay leaves.

Calories per serving: 404   Sodium per serving: 87 mgs.

FRIED LUNGEN

Makes 5 Cups
(Enough to fill 48 knishes)

3 Tbs. Chicken Fat (See Page 285) or
  unsalted butter or margarine
2 beef lungs, diced
½ lb. beef, diced

3 medium-size onions, diced
3 cloves garlic, minced
1 Tbs. low sodium chicken bouillon
Black pepper to taste

In large skillet, heat Chicken Fat. Add lungs, beef, onions, and garlic. Cook over medium/low heat 10 minutes, stirring occasionally.
Stir in bouillon and pepper.

Calories per recipe: 1451   Sodium per recipe: 525 mgs.
Calories per Tbs.: 36   Sodium per Tbs.: 12 mgs.

LAMB AND EGGPLANT WINE CASSEROLE

Serves 8

2 Tbs. oil
1 2-lb. eggplant, peeled and cubed
1½ lbs. lamb shoulder, cut into 1″ chunks
2 medium-size onions, chopped
2 tomatoes, chopped
½ cup Beef Broth (See Page 44)
3 cloves garlic, minced
1 carrot, grated and chopped
2 tsps. sugar

⅛ tsp. nutmeg
Black pepper to taste
½ tsp. oregano
½ tsp. parsley
½ tsp. mustard powder
½ cup dry vermouth
½ cup dry red wine
4 tsps. low sodium beef bouillon
1 Tbs. lemon juice

In large skillet, heat oil. Sauté eggplant till golden, stirring often. Remove to dish.
Add lamb to skillet and brown on all sides over medium heat. Remove to 9″ square oven-proof casserole.
Preheat oven to 325°.
Add onions to skillet. Cook over low heat till golden, stirring occasionally. Add to casserole.
Add all remaining ingredients except eggplant to casserole. Cover and bake 1½ hours.
Add eggplant, cover and bake 30 minutes more, or till meat is tender.
Serve with parsley potatoes and brown rice.

Calories per serving: 352   Sodium per serving: 81 mgs.

MEAT KNISHES

Makes 24 knishes

2 cups all-purpose flour
2 tsps. low sodium baking powder
1 Tbs. low sodium chicken bouillon

½ cup hot water
½ cup vegetable shortening
2½ cups Fried Lungen (See Page 199)

Sift first 3 ingredients into bowl. Stir in hot water. Cut in shortening.
Form dough into ball. Turn onto lightly floured board. Roll out to ⅛″ thickness.
Preheat oven to 350°.
Cut dough into 2″ squares and place 1 rounded tsp. Fried Lungen on each square.
Fold into triangles and crimp edges together. Pierce lightly with fork.
Place knishes on greased baking sheet and bake 1 hour, or till lightly browned.

Calories per serving: 110   Sodium per serving: 15 mgs.

ROAST LAMB IN ORANGE/WINE SAUCE

Serves 12

1 3-lb. lamb shoulder, gashed all over
5 cloves garlic, slivered
2 tsps. mustard powder
1 tsp. rosemary, crushed
Black pepper to taste
1 Tbs. low sodium chicken bouillon

½ cup orange juice
½ cup brandy
½ cup orange marmalade*
2 tsps. cornstarch
2 Tbs. water

Preserved without pectin or sodium

Preheat oven to 475°.
Insert garlic slivers in gashes. Place roast in pan lined with tin foil. Sprinkle with mustard, rosemary, and pepper. Cover bottom of pan with water.
Bake 10 minutes. Reduce heat to 350° and bake 2 hours (30 minutes per pound; longer if more well done meat is desired).
One hour before lamb is done, sprinkle with bouillon.
In medium saucepan, combine orange juice, brandy, and marmalade. Simmer over low heat till bubbly around the edges.
Combine cornstarch and water, blending well. Stir into orange sauce.
When thickened, spoon over lamb to glaze and continue baking till done.
Serve over noodles or rice.

Calories per serving: 367   Sodium per serving: 89 mgs.

STUFFED CABBAGE

Serves 10
(Makes about 20 rolls)

1 large head cabbage
1½ lbs. ground beef
Black pepper to taste
1 Tbs. garlic powder
1 tsp. parsley
1 tsp. basil
1 tsp. tarragon
1 tsp. thyme
1 tsp. marjoram

2 large onions, sliced into rings
2 cans (12 ozs. each) low sodium tomato
  juice, divided
2 Tbs. cider or red wine vinegar
½ bottle low sodium ketchup
½ cup white or light brown sugar
½ cup lemon juice, divided
4 Tbs. honey, divided

Parboil cabbage in enough water to half cover. Remove and cool.
While cabbage is in pot, knead pepper, garlic powder, and herbs into meat. Set aside.
Line bottom of Dutch oven with onion rings.

Wrap meat in cabbage leaves. (Use about 1 Tbs. meat per cabbage leaf or leaves will open during cooking.)

Stack cabbage rolls on top of onions. Cover with hot water. Simmer, covered, about 1 hour.

Pour off half the water. Add 1 can tomato juice. Cover and cook over low heat 45 minutes.

Add vinegar, second can tomato juice, ketchup, sugar, 4 Tbs. lemon juice, and 2 Tbs. honey.

Cover and continue cooking over low heat 1½ hours.

Add 4 Tbs. lemon juice and 2 Tbs. honey. Cover and cook 30 minutes more. You may add more lemon juice and honey to taste.

Rolls are better if served the next day. To prepare, skim fat off top and reheat.

Cabbage rolls may be frozen up to 3 months.

Calories per serving: 298   Sodium per serving: 74 mgs.

STUFFED PEPPERS

Serves 6

1 lb. ground beef
½ cup cooked rice
2 tsps. garlic powder
1 tsp. low sodium mustard
Coarse black pepper to taste
1½ Tbs. low sodium beef bouillon

1 medium-size onion, minced
6 large green peppers
1 cup water
1 cup Tomato Sauce (See Page 298)
2 Tbs. lemon juice

In large bowl, combine first 7 ingredients.

Cut tops off peppers and remove seeds. Chop tops and set aside.

Preheat oven to 350°.

Stuff peppers with beef mixture. Stand in 9" square oven-proof casserole. Pour water around peppers. Cover and bake 30 minutes.

Add chopped pepper and bake, uncovered, 15 minutes more.

In saucepan, combine Tomato Sauce and lemon juice. Cook over low heat, stirring often, till bubbly. Pour on peppers and bake 5 minutes more.

Calories per serving: 306   Sodium per serving: 89 mgs.

TZIMMES

Serves 10

1½ Tbs. oil
2 lbs. beef chuck, cut into 1″ chunks
½ tsp. coarse black pepper, divided
1½ cups water, divided
1 bunch carrots, scraped and quartered
1 large yellow turnip, parboiled, peeled,
  and quartered
1 Tbs. garlic powder
5 yams, parboiled, peeled, and halved

¼ cup dried apricots
½ cup golden raisins*
6 tsps. low sodium beef bouillon
¼ cup brown sugar, tightly packed
¼ cup honey
2 Tbs. lemon juice
¾ tsp. cinnamon
1 tsp. dried or fresh grated orange peel
¼ tsp. rosemary, crushed

Preserved in non-sodium ingredient

Heat oil in Dutch oven. Sear meat on all sides. Season with half the black pepper. Add ½ cup water. Cover and simmer 30 minutes, or till water is absorbed.

Add another ½ cup water, carrots, turnip, and garlic powder. Cover and simmer 30 minutes more.

Add yams, remaining pepper, fruit, and bouillon. Stir in sugar, remaining water, honey, lemon juice, cinnamon, orange peel, and rosemary. Cover and simmer 1 hour more, or till meat is butter soft, adding more water as necessary and stirring occasionally with wooden spoon.

Calories per serving: 344   Sodium per serving: 101 mgs.

VEAL CHOPS AND MUSHROOMS

Serves 6

1 Tbs. oil
1 Tbs. low sodium butter or margarine
6 boneless veal chops
Coarse black pepper to taste
½ tsp. garlic powder
1 can (6 ozs.) low sodium tomato paste
½ tsp. tarragon

¼ tsp. sage
1 cup Beef Broth (See Page 44)
¾ cup dry vermouth or white wine
¼ tsp. marjoram
4 scallions, chopped, including greens
1 cup small mushrooms, sliced
1 Tbs. parsley

In Dutch oven, heat oil and butter. Season chops with pepper and garlic powder, and brown on both sides over low heat.

Add tomato paste and fry briefly. Transfer to oven-proof casserole.

Add remaining ingredients except mushrooms and parsley. Bring to a boil. Reduce to low heat, cover, and simmer 1 hour, being careful not to let liquid boil, stirring occasionally.

Add mushrooms and heat, uncovered, 20 minutes more.
Stir in parsley. Serve over kasha or noodles.

Calories per serving: 307   Sodium per serving: 123 mgs.

CHICKEN AND FRUITED RICE

Serves 6

2 Tbs. oil
1 medium-size onion, chopped
1 cup long grain rice
Black pepper to taste
3 cloves garlic, minced
¼ tsp. mace
2½ cups Chicken Broth (See Page 45)
2 Tbs. raisins*

¼ cup chopped dried apricots
1 pear, peeled, cored, and chopped
2 Tbs. unsalted butter or margarine
8 mushrooms, sliced
1¼ lbs. leftover chicken, chopped
2 Tbs. brandy
1 Tbs. fresh chopped parsley

Preserved in non-sodium ingredient

In skillet, heat oil. Add onion and cook over low heat 5 minutes, stirring occasionally.
Stir in rice, pepper, garlic, and mace. Cook, stirring constantly, till rice turns golden.
Transfer to 9″ square oven-proof casserole.
Preheat oven to 350°.
Pour on Chicken Broth. Stir in raisins, apricots, and pear.
Cover and bake 20 minutes, or till liquid is absorbed.
While rice is baking, in skillet, melt butter. Add mushrooms and chicken and cook over medium/low heat 5 minutes. Pour on brandy and flame.
Stir chicken mixture into rice. Blend thoroughly. Garnish with parsley.
Serve with zucchini.

Calories per serving: 344   Sodium per serving: 143 mgs.

CHICKEN TOMATO CASSEROLE

Serves 8

4 chicken breasts, halved
1 Tbs. oil
1 medium-size onion, sliced
1 carrot, scraped and cut into ¼″ rounds
3 tomatoes, chopped
2 bay leaves

2 tsps. tarragon
1 Tbs. parsley
1 tsp. dill
¼ tsp. thyme
2 tsps. all-purpose flour
2 Tbs. paprika

(continued next page)

Black pepper to taste
3 cloves garlic, slivered
¾ cup Beef Broth (See Page 44)
1½ tsps. low sodium beef bouillon

¼ cup dry white wine
½ lb. mushrooms, sliced
1 large yellow turnip, peeled and cut into chunks

Place chicken in Dutch oven with enough water to cover. Bring to a boil and continue boiling 10 minutes. Drain. Transfer chicken to platter. Gash all over.

In Dutch oven, heat oil. Add onion and carrot. Cook over low heat 7 minutes, stirring occasionally. Stir in tomatoes. Stir in herbs and flour. Stir to blend.

Rub chicken with paprika and pepper. Insert garlic slivers in gashes in chicken.

Place chicken on top of vegetable mixture. Cook 10 minutes, turning often.

Preheat oven to 325°.

Into deep oven-proof casserole, pour Beef Broth. Stir in bouillon and wine. Add chicken and vegetable mixture. Cover and bake 1 hour, basting occasionally with pan juices.

Add mushrooms and turnip. Cover and bake 45 minutes more.

Calories per serving: 192   Sodium per serving: 96 mgs.

OVEN FRIED CHICKEN AND WINE SAUCE

Serves 8

1 cup cornmeal or matzo meal
2 tsps. dill
2 tsps. paprika
½ tsp. black pepper, divided
4 tsps. low sodium chicken bouillon
1 egg, lightly beaten
3 Tbs. oil, divided
8 pieces chicken (4 half breasts, 4 whole legs)

1 small onion, minced
½ cup dry red wine
1 cup Chicken Broth (See Page 45)
2 Tbs. cornstarch
3 Tbs. cold water
1 Tbs. parsley

In large shallow dish, combine cornmeal, dill, paprika, ¼ tsp. pepper, and bouillon. Set aside.

In a bowl, beat together egg and 2 Tbs. oil. Set aside.

Preheat oven to 475°.

Dip chicken first in egg, then in cornmeal mixture. Transfer to shallow baking pan.

Lower heat to 425° and bake chicken 45 minutes, or till golden brown, turning once.

While chicken is baking, heat remaining oil in medium saucepan. Add onion and cook over medium heat till golden, stirring often.

Add wine, Chicken Broth, and remaining pepper and cook over low heat 10 minutes. Set aside.

Just before serving, bring sauce to a boil. Combine cornstarch and water, reduce heat to low, and stir into sauce.
Stir in parsley.
Serve sauce in gravy boat.

Calories per serving: 287   Sodium per serving: 87 mgs.

STEWED CHICKEN AND VEGETABLES

Serves 6

2 Tbs. Chicken Fat (See Page 285),
  unsalted butter, or margarine, divided
6 pieces chicken (3 half breasts, 3 whole
  legs)
2 cloves garlic, sliced, divided
2 medium-size onions, chopped, divided
1 carrot, scraped and cut into ½″ rounds
1 Tbs. paprika

Black pepper to taste
1 cup water
1 cup Chicken Broth (See Page 45)
2 tsps. dry sherry
2 tomatoes, chopped
2 large zucchini, cut into ¾″ rounds
2 tsps. low sodium chicken bouillon

In a large skillet, melt half the Chicken Fat. Add half the chicken, garlic, and onions and cook over low heat till chicken is browned on all sides. Transfer to platter.
Repeat with remaining Chicken Fat, chicken, garlic, and onions.
Return all chicken, garlic, and onions to skillet. Add remaining ingredients except tomatoes, zucchini, and chicken bouillon. Cover and simmer 30 minutes more.
Stir in remaining ingredients. Cover and simmer 10 minutes more.

Calories per serving: 219   Sodium per serving: 91 mgs.

SUGAR BARBEQUED CHICKEN

Serves 6

3 Tbs. oil, divided
3 chicken breasts, halved
2 medium-size onions, chopped
2 tsps. mustard powder
Black pepper to taste
3 Tbs. lemon juice
¾ cup orange juice

1 Tbs. low sodium beef bouillon
1 tsp. cider vinegar
1 can (6 ozs.) low sodium tomato paste
1½ cups water
3 Tbs. brown sugar
¼ tsp. sage

In large skillet, heat half the oil. Add half the chicken and fry over medium heat till browned on both sides. Transfer to 9″ × 13″ oven-proof casserole.
Repeat with remaining oil and chicken.

Add onions to same skillet. Cook over low heat 10 minutes, stirring occasionally. Preheat oven to 300°.

Stir in remaining ingredients except chicken. Simmer 5 minutes, stirring occasionally. Pour over chicken. Cover and bake 1½ hours.

Calories per serving: 275	Sodium per serving: 93 mgs.

MEXICAN

Mexican food is a unique blending of centuries-old cultures and traditions, starting with the pre-Columbian influence of the Aztecs and Mayans. The Aztecs cultivated corn and created foods still synonymous with Mexico, including tacos, tortillas, tamales, and enchiladas. They also developed other indigenous foods, such as chilies, tomatoes, avocados, beans, papaya, chocolate, and vanilla, which give Mexican specialties their distinguishing spice flavors.

When Cortez conquered Mexico in the 16th century he and his soldiers came bearing gifts as well as arms. They introduced the Mexicans to chicken, livestock, olive oil, wine, potatoes, onions, garlic, cinnamon, cloves, rice, and wheat. All these ingredients are today integral to Mexican cooking. Three centuries later, Maximilian added some of the sophisticated tastes of France and Italy.

Whatever the origin, however many the influences, Mexican cuisine is distinctly Mexican. It is like its people, at once spirited, festive, and colorful. In no other country will you find vegetable patches and market stalls festooned with an outrageous panoply of flowers. Or see such a bursting abundance of earthy goodness.

And spices. Numerous spices are considered synonymous with Mexican food. The cumin seed, which distinguishes chili; achiote to season pastes and color food to a burnt golden hue; cilantro, the Mexican version of parsley; cinnamon, whose sweet flavor often tempers a spicy hot concoction.

Because chilies are so expressly important in Mexican cooking, we'd like to discuss them briefly. There are numerous varieties and most are available fresh, as well as canned. We recommend that you not use the canned products because they contain salt.

There are hot chilies and mild chilies, and the seeds of both are potent. Red chilies are usually mild, dried and sold as anchos. Chilies poblanos are pale red or yellow in color. These mild flavored chilies are often stuffed and when not available, bell peppers are reasonable stand-ins.

In this book, we use only the hot chili peppers because they are easily found in local markets. However, if you live near Mexican or Spanish food stores, by all means, buy some of the fresh chilies and feel free to substitute them for a wider range of flavors.

Chilies aren't the only food commonly used to spark Mexican cooking. In addition, the cool, tart, and refreshing zest of limes often balances the warm spiciness of the chilies.

Herbs, spices, chilies, and limes combine in different ways to enhance meat, fish, or poultry and dazzle the tongue. The results are a habit forming addiction to enticements quite unlike those of any other cuisine.

COD IN RAISIN SAUCE

Serves 6

1½ lbs. cod fillets
1 cup Beef Broth (See Page 44)
1 cup raisins*
½ cup dry white wine
½ cup orange juice

2 tsps. parsley
4 tsps. lemon juice
2 Tbs. low sodium beef bouillon
1 Tbs. cornstarch
3 Tbs. cold water

Preserved in non-sodium ingredient

Preheat oven to 350°.
Place fish in single layer in oven-proof casserole. Set aside.
In bowl, combine remaining ingredients except cornstarch and water. Pour over fish. Bake 25 minutes, or till fish flakes easily. Remove fish.
In small bowl, combine cornstarch and water. Blend thoroughly. Stir into sauce. Return fish to casserole and bake 5 minutes more.

Calories per serving: 218   Sodium per serving: 108 mgs.

FISH EMPANADAS

Serves 12

2 cups plus 1 Tbs. all-purpose flour, divided
1 Tbs. low sodium chicken bouillon
⅔ cup vegetable shortening
1½ Tbs. dry white wine
2 Tbs. water
1½ Tbs. lemon juice
1½ Tbs. oil
2 lbs. cod fillets, chopped
1 medium-size onion, minced

3 cloves garlic, minced
2 Tbs. dry sherry
1½ Tbs. low sodium beef bouillon
Coarse black pepper to taste
¼ tsp. fennel seed
2 chili peppers, chopped, or dash hot pepper flakes
¼ tsp. nutmeg
6 dried apricots,* chopped

Preserved in non-sodium ingredient

Sift 2 cups flour into bowl. Stir in chicken bouillon.
Cut shortening into flour till mixture starts to form a ball.
Add white wine, water, and lemon juice, blending thoroughly into flour mixture.
Shape dough into a ball. Divide in half and roll to ½″ thickness.
Using a salad plate, cut dough into 12 circles 6″ in diameter. Set aside.
In skillet, heat oil. Add fish, onion, and garlic. Stir fry 3 minutes over low heat.
Stir in sherry, beef bouillon, and remaining ingredients. Stir fry 2 minutes more.
Preheat oven to 400°.
Divide fish mixture into 12 sections. Place in center of dough circles. Fold one half over the other to form half moons. Crimp edges together.
Place empanadas on baking sheet and bake 7 minutes, or till lightly browned.

Calories per serving: 267   Sodium per serving: 61 mgs.

PICKLED PERCH

Serves 6

2 Tbs. unsalted butter or margarine
1½ lbs. perch fillets
1 medium-size onion, cut into rings
⅓ cup orange juice
1½ Tbs. low sodium chicken bouillon
1 Tbs. low sodium beef bouillon
1 Tbs. tarragon
¼ cup olive oil

2 Tbs. cider vinegar
2 tsps. low sodium Dijon mustard
2 bay leaves
2 cloves garlic, sliced
1 tsp. ground coriander
⅛ tsp. nutmeg
Black pepper to taste

In large skillet, melt butter. Sauté fillets on both sides till they start to lightly brown, about 2 minutes per side. Transfer to large casserole.
Place onion rings over fillets.
In small bowl, combine remaining ingredients. Blend thoroughly and pour over fillets.
Cover and refrigerate at least 8 hours, basting occasionally. Discard bay leaves.

Calories per serving: 249   Sodium per serving: 99 mgs.

SOLE WITH WINE AND CHEESE

Serves 6

1½ lbs. sole fillets
¼ cup lemon juice
Black pepper to taste
¼ cup dry sherry
¼ cup crushed walnuts

1 Tbs. low sodium chicken bouillon
⅛ tsp. cinnamon
¼ cup heavy cream
3 ozs. low sodium Gouda cheese, sliced

In bowl, combine fish, lemon juice, and pepper. Let stand 20 minutes.
Preheat oven to 400°.
Place fillets in oven-proof casserole in single layer. To the marinade, add sherry, walnuts, bouillon, cinnamon, and cream. Stir well and pour on the fish. Bake 20 minutes.
Place cheese over fish. Bake 10 minutes more, or till cheese starts to bubble.

Calories per serving: 220   Sodium per serving: 103 mgs.

SPICE BAKED SNAPPER

Serves 6

1½ lbs. snapper fillets
½ cup lime juice
1 red pepper, chopped
White pepper to taste
1 tsp. cider vinegar
6 cloves

¼ cup dry white wine
¾ cup Chicken Broth (See Page 45)
2 chili peppers, chopped
1 Tbs. all-purpose flour
2 Tbs. cold water
2 tsps. low sodium chicken bouillon

In large oven-proof casserole, combine fish and lime juice. Let stand 15 minutes.
Preheat oven to 350°.
Scatter red pepper around fish.
Add white pepper, vinegar, cloves, wine, Chicken Broth, and chili peppers. Cover and bake 10 minutes.
Uncover and bake 10 minutes more. Transfer fish to platter.
Combine flour and water, blending thoroughly. Stir into liquid.
Stir in bouillon.
Spoon sauce over fish. Discard cloves.

Calories per serving: 150   Sodium per serving: 88 mgs.

BEEF ENCHILADAS

Serves 6

2 cups Salsa (See Page 295)
3 Tbs. oil, divided
6 Tortillas (See Page 82)
2 medium-size onions, chopped

2 Tbs. low sodium chicken bouillon
1 lb. ground beef round
1 chili pepper, chopped
¼ tsp. cumin seed

Preheat oven to 375°.
In saucepan, simmer Salsa.
While sauce is heating, in large skillet, heat 1 Tbs. oil. Fry Tortillas, two at a time, adding oil as needed, over low heat till soft and supple. Transfer to platter.

To skillet, add onions and bouillon. Stir fry 1 minute. Add beef, chili peppers, and cumin. Stir fry 3 minutes, or till beef has lost its pink color. Add ⅔ cup Salsa, blending thoroughly.

Divide beef mixture among Tortillas. Roll up and place, seam side down, in lightly greased, oven-proof casserole. Bake 30 minutes.

Spoon on remaining sauce.

Calories per serving: 392   Sodium per serving: 83 mgs.

CHILI CON CARNE

Serves 8

1¼ cups kidney beans
9 cups water, divided
1½ lbs. lean ground beef or 1 1½-lb. round steak, sliced into 8 pieces
2 medium-size onions, chopped fine
1 garlic clove, minced
2 tsps. oregano
1 tsp. ground coriander

1 tsp. ground cumin
1 tsp. garlic powder
2 chili peppers, minced
Black pepper to taste
2 cans (12 ozs. each) low sodium tomato juice
2 ozs. low sodium Cheddar cheese, shredded

Rinse beans in cold water.
In Dutch oven, bring beans to boil in 6 cups water and boil 3 minutes.
Remove beans from heat. Cover pan, let stand 1 hour.
Preheat oven to 325°.
In large skillet, cook ground beef till well browned, or sear beef slices on both sides.
Stir beef and next 8 ingredients into beans.
Pour bean mixture into large casserole or roasting pan. Add 1 cup water.
Cover and bake 1 hour. Add 1 more cup water and 1 can tomato juice.
Bake another hour. Add remaining cup of water and can of tomato juice.
Bake another hour.
Sprinkle cheese on top. Moisten with ½ cup water if necessary. Return to oven for 30 minutes.

Ground Beef: Calories per serving: 388   Sodium per serving: 82 mgs.
Round Steak: Calories per serving: 327   Sodium per serving: 82 mgs.

CHORIZO (MEXICAN SAUSAGE)

Serves 8

1 lb. ground pork
1½ Tbs. chili powder
1 Tbs. paprika
½ tsp. coarse black pepper
4 cloves garlic, minced
¼ tsp. cinnamon
1/16 tsp. ground cloves
¼ tsp. ground coriander

⅛ tsp. ginger powder
½ tsp. oregano
½ tsp. ground cumin
Dash of hot pepper flakes
¼ cup cider vinegar
2 Tbs. dry sherry
2 Tbs. brandy

In bowl, combine all ingredients, working mixture with hands to blend thoroughly. Transfer to glass container. Cover tightly. Let stand in cool place or in refrigerator 2 to 3 days.
Form into sausage rolls and fry in ungreased skillet over low heat till browned all over, and till inside loses all pink color.

Calories per serving: 174   Sodium per serving: 43 mgs.

GLAZED PORK

Serves 6

1 Tbs. olive oil
1¼ lbs. pork, cut into 1″ chunks
1 medium-size onion, minced
4 cloves garlic, minced
3 tomatoes, chopped
½ tsp. thyme
½ tsp. cinnamon
½ tsp. oregano

¼ tsp. ground cumin
1 Tbs. mustard powder
1 Tbs. brown sugar
2 Tbs. chopped pecans
¾ cup Chicken Broth (See Page 45)
¼ cup dry sherry
2 tsps. low sodium beef bouillon

In Dutch oven, heat oil. Brown pork on all sides over low heat.
Add onion, garlic, and tomatoes and stir fry 3 minutes.
Add remaining ingredients. Cover and simmer over low heat 1 hour, or till pork is tender.

Calories per serving: 374   Sodium per serving: 77 mgs.

LEMON-LIME STEAK

Serves 6

1 cup boiling water
5 tsps. low sodium beef bouillon
1 tsp. garlic powder
4 cloves
12 mushrooms
2 medium-size onions, cut into chunks
12 cherry tomatoes
3 zucchini, cut into 1" rounds

2 Tbs. cider vinegar
¼ tsp. cumin seed
¼ tsp. fennel seed
1¼ lbs. beef sirloin steak, cut into
   1" chunks
Juice of 1 lemon
Juice of 2 limes
1½ Tbs. all-purpose flour

In large casserole, combine boiling water and bouillon, stirring to blend.
Add all remaining ingredients except flour and lemon and lime juice. Cover and marinate overnight, turning steak and vegetables occasionally.
Preheat oven to broil.
Thread 6 skewers, alternating pieces of beef with vegetables. Pour on lemon and lime juice. Reserve marinade. Place skewers on shallow baking sheet and broil 3 minutes.
Turn skewers and spoon on 2 Tbs. marinade. Broil 3 minutes more.
While beef is broiling, combine flour and marinade in a small saucepan. Cook over medium/low heat, stirring often, till thickened and bubbly.
Spoon half the sauce over skewers and serve remainder on the side.

Calories per serving: 357   Sodium per serving: 88 mgs.

MEXICAN STEW

Serves 8

2 Tbs. oil
1¾ lbs. stewing beef, cut into 1" chunks,
   fat trimmed
2 medium-size onions, chopped
3 cloves garlic, minced
Dash of hot pepper flakes
1 tsp. ground cumin
1 tsp. cinnamon
1 tsp. oregano
1 tsp. turmeric

4 cloves
2 tsps. sugar
1 cup dry white wine
Coarse black pepper to taste
2 cans (12 ozs. each) low sodium tomato
   juice
2 tsps. low sodium beef bouillon
2 cups Chicken Broth (See Page 45)
2 green peppers, chopped
4 potatoes, peeled and cut into 1" chunks

In Dutch oven, heat oil. Sear beef on all sides over medium/high heat. Remove to platter.
Reduce heat to low. Add onions and garlic and cook till onion is wilted.
Return beef to pot. Add all remaining ingredients except Chicken Broth, green peppers, and potatoes. Cover and simmer over low heat 45 minutes, stirring occasionally.

Add Chicken Broth. Cover and simmer 45 minutes more.

Add green peppers and potatoes. Cover and simmer 30 minutes more, or till beef is tender.

Calories per serving: 408	Sodium per serving: 85 mgs.

PICADILLA

Serves 4
(Makes 4 Cups or enough to fill 16 Tortillas, Page 82)

1 Tbs. oil
¼ lb. ground beef
¼ lb. ground pork
1 medium-size onion, chopped
1 green pepper, chopped
3 tomatoes, chopped
3 Tbs. low sodium ketchup
2 cloves garlic, minced
4 Tbs. red wine vinegar

2 tsps. sugar
2 tsps. low sodium chicken bouillon
¼ tsp. ground cumin
Dash of hot pepper flakes
1 Tbs. dried or fresh grated orange peel
2½ Tbs. raisins*
2½ Tbs. crushed walnuts
Coarse black pepper to taste
¼ cup water

Preserved in non-sodium ingredient

In large skillet, heat oil. Sauté meat and onion, breaking meat with fork, till onion is wilted.

Stir in remaining ingredients. Cover and simmer over low heat 35 minutes.

Without Tortillas: (4 Servings)
Calories per serving: 301   Sodium per serving: 59 mgs.
With Tortillas: (16 Servings)
Calories per serving: 156   Sodium per serving: 15 mgs.

PORK IN ORANGE SAUCE

Serves 6

1 lb. pork shoulder, cut into 1" chunks
½ cup dry white wine
¼ cup cider vinegar
¼ cup lemon juice
1 tsp. ground cumin
3 cloves garlic, minced
2 medium-size onions, minced

Black pepper to taste
½ tsp. thyme
2 Tbs. olive oil
1½ cups water
2 cups orange juice, divided
2 Tbs. raisins*
3 zucchini, cut into 1" rounds

Preserved in non-sodium ingredient

In deep bowl, combine first 9 ingredients. Cover and marinate overnight in refrigerator. Drain marinade and reserve. Pat the pork dry.

In large skillet, heat oil. Add pork and cook over medium heat till pork is browned all over. Pour off fat.

Add marinade, water, and half the orange juice. Bring to a boil. Cover. Reduce heat and simmer 30 minutes.

Stir in remaining orange juice, raisins, and zucchini. Cover and simmer 15 minutes more.

Serve over rice.

Calories per serving: 363   Sodium per serving: 63 mgs.

VEAL IN PECAN SAUCE

Serves 6

1¼ lbs. stewing veal, cut into 1" chunks
2 medium-size onions, chopped, divided
2 cloves garlic, minced, divided
1½ Tbs. low sodium chicken bouillon
¾ cup water
¼ cup dry red wine
⅛ tsp. marjoram
½ tsp. oregano

½ tsp. thyme
Coarse black pepper to taste
1 Tbs. unsalted butter or margarine
¼ cup chopped pecans
1 cup Chicken Broth (See Page 45)
2 Tbs. lemon juice
¼ cup heavy cream

In Dutch oven, combine veal, half the onion and garlic, the bouillon, water, wine, herbs, and pepper. Cover and simmer over low heat 1 hour, or till veal is tender.

Drain veal and keep warm, reserving ½ cup of stock.

In medium saucepan, melt butter. Sauté remaining onion and garlic and the pecans till onion is wilted. Set aside.

Add reserved veal stock and Chicken Broth to Dutch oven.

Bring to a boil. Reduce heat and simmer over medium heat 15 minutes.

Remove from heat and stir in lemon juice and cream.

Scrape in onion and nut mixture. Cook over low heat 20 minutes more.

Pour sauce on veal.

Serve over rice.

Calories per serving: 276   Sodium per serving: 103 mgs.

CHICKEN CASSEROLE IN RED WINE SAUCE

Serves 6

1 3-lb. chicken, cut into serving pieces
4 Tbs. lemon juice, divided
1 Tbs. paprika
½ cup walnuts, chopped
2 onions, sliced into rings
3 cloves garlic, minced
1 carrot, scraped and chopped
2 cans (8 ozs. each) low sodium corn
  niblets, drained
¼ tsp. basil
¼ tsp. marjoram
¼ tsp. oregano

¼ tsp. thyme
¼ tsp. rosemary, crushed
Black pepper to taste
2 Tbs. parsley
4 cloves
2 cinnamon sticks
1 tsp. mustard powder
1 tsp. red wine vinegar
1 cup Chicken Broth (See Page 45)
1 cup dry red wine
2 tsps. low sodium chicken bouillon
3 zucchini, cut into 1" rounds

Preheat oven to broil.

Place chicken, skin side up, on shallow baking sheet. Pour on 3 Tbs. lemon juice. Sprinkle with paprika. Broil 6 minutes, or until skin turns brown.

Turn chicken. Pour on remaining lemon juice and broil 5 minutes more. Transfer to large casserole.

Reduce oven temperature to 350°. Surround chicken with onion rings. Add remaining ingredients except zucchini. Cover and bake 50 minutes.

Add zucchini and bake, uncovered, 10 minutes more. Discard cloves and cinnamon. Serve over rice or noodles with sauce on the side.

Calories per serving: 280   Sodium per serving: 114 mgs.

CHICKEN DIABLO

Serves 6

½ cup red wine vinegar
½ cup orange juice
¼ cup oil
½ tsp. cinnamon
2½ tsps. paprika
Black pepper to taste
1 tsp. oregano
2 tsps. parsley
½ tsp. thyme
⅛ tsp. cumin seed

3 chicken breasts, halved
1 large onion, chopped
4 cloves garlic, minced
3 scallions, chopped, including greens
2 chili peppers, minced
2 carrots, scraped and cut into
  ¼" rounds
2 green peppers, sliced
½ cup water
1 cup dry red wine

In large, oven-proof casserole, combine first 10 ingredients. Add chicken, skin side up. Cover and refrigerate 1 hour.

Turn chicken, skin side down. Cover and refrigerate 1 hour more.

Preheat oven to 350°.

In large skillet, combine onion, garlic, scallions, chili peppers, and carrots. Cook over low heat 5 minutes, stirring often.

Stir in green peppers. Add water. Stir to blend. Simmer 5 minutes more. Spoon over chicken in casserole. Pour on wine. Bake 30 minutes.

Turn chicken, skin side up. Bake 30 minutes more, or till skin is browned. Serve with boiled, sliced potatoes.

Calories per serving: 290	Sodium per serving: 103 mgs.

CHICKEN WITH MOLE SAUCE

Serves 6

1 3-lb. chicken
½ cup lime juice, divided
2 Tbs. turmeric, divided
12 cloves
6 black peppercorns
2 cinnamon sticks
1 tsp. oregano
1 tsp. ground coriander
¼ tsp. cumin seed
4 tomatoes, chopped

3 chili peppers, chopped, or dash hot pepper flakes
6 prunes, pitted and chopped
3 cups Chicken Broth (See Page 45), divided
3 Tbs. low sodium peanut butter
1 can (12 ozs.) low sodium tomato juice
1 oz. low sodium bittersweet chocolate (optional)
4 cloves garlic, minced

Preheat oven to 475°.

Place chicken on its side on rack in roasting pan. Pour on ¼ of the lime juice and sprinkle with ¼ of the turmeric. Roast 10 minutes, or till skin is browned.

Turn chicken to other side. Repeat seasoning with lime juice and turmeric. Roast till this side is brown.

Repeat same process with chicken, back side up, and finally, breast side up.

Reduce heat to 350° and roast 30 minutes more, or till juices run clear.

While chicken is roasting, in blender combine cloves peppercorns, cinnamon sticks, oregano, coriander, and cumin. Blend fine. Transfer to medium-size saucepan.

In blender, combine tomatoes, chili peppers, prunes, 1 cup Chicken Broth, and peanut butter. Blend into paste.

Scrape tomato mixture into spice mixture. Add tomato juice, remaining Chicken Broth, chocolate, and garlic. Bring to a boil. Reduce heat and simmer 25 minutes, stirring regularly.

Carve chicken. Spoon on half the sauce and serve remainder on the side.

Calories per serving: 270	Sodium per serving: 117 mgs.

FESTIVAL CHICKEN

Serves 6

6 pieces chicken (3 half breasts, 3 whole
   legs)
1 Tbs. garlic powder
Coarse black pepper to taste
¼ cup water
2 Tbs. low sodium beef bouillon
4 tomatoes, chopped

2 tsps. oregano
½ tsp. fennel seed
¼ tsp. cinnamon
½ tsp. mace
½ cup dried peaches or prunes, chopped
Dash of ground cumin (optional)
2 Tbs. brandy

   Preheat oven to 500°.
   Place chicken, skin side up, in baking pan. Season with garlic powder and pepper.
Pour water around chicken and bake 7 minutes, or till chicken is browned.
   Turn chicken and bake 3 minutes more. Transfer to casserole.
   Reduce oven temperature to 350°.
   Surround chicken with all remaining ingredients except brandy. Cover and bake 45
minutes, or till chicken is tender.
   Pour on brandy. Flame chicken.
   Serve at once with sauce on the side.

With Peaches: Calories per serving: 206	Sodium per serving: 90 mgs.
With Prunes: Calories per serving: 210	Sodium per serving: 89 mgs.

SPICY FRIED CHICKEN MEXICAN

Serves 8

2 Tbs. shredded coconut
½ cup plus 2 Tbs. all-purpose flour,
   divided
1 Tbs. low sodium beef bouillon
¼ tsp. cayenne pepper, divided
Dash of hot pepper flakes
Dash of ginger powder
1 tsp. mustard powder
1 tsp. basil
8 pieces chicken (4 half breasts, 4 whole
   legs)

2 Tbs. olive oil, divided
2 Tbs. unsalted butter or margarine,
   divided
2 medium-size onions, chopped
3 cloves garlic, minced
1 cup Chicken Broth (See Page 45)
2 Tbs. dry white wine
2 Tbs. lemon juice
1 tomato, chopped

   In large plastic bag, combine coconut, ½ cup flour, bouillon, ⅛ tsp. cayenne, the
pepper flakes, ginger, mustard, and basil.
   Add chicken and shake to coat well.

In large skillet, heat half the oil and butter. Add half the chicken, skin side down, and cook over low heat till chicken is browned. Turn and brown other side. Transfer to platter.

Repeat with remaining oil, butter, and chicken. Transfer to platter.

Add onions and garlic to skillet. Cook over low heat till onions are wilted.

Stir in remaining cayenne and flour, blending thoroughly.

Add Chicken Broth, wine, lemon juice, and tomato. Cook 5 minutes, stirring often, till sauce is thickened.

Pour a third of the sauce over chicken. Serve remainder on the side.

Calories per serving: 249	Sodium per serving: 86 mgs.

VERY SHERRY CHICKEN

Serves 6

1 Tbs. oil
2 medium-size onions, chopped
2 cloves garlic, minced
1 3-lb. chicken, cut into serving pieces
1 cup dry sherry
2 tsps. cider vinegar
1 Tbs. low sodium chicken bouillon
2 bay leaves
1 tsp. parsley
1 tsp. green peppercorns* (optional)

⅛ tsp. cinnamon
⅛ tsp. nutmeg
4 tomatoes, chopped
3 scallions, chopped, including greens
6 Tbs. raisins**
1 red pepper, sliced
¼ tsp. marjoram
¼ tsp. oregano
¼ tsp. thyme
8 cloves

Natural green peppercorns, packed in water or vinegar
**Preserved in non-sodium ingredient*

Preheat oven to 350°.

In large skillet, heat oil. Sauté onions and garlic till onions are wilted.

Add chicken pieces and brown over low heat, adding sherry when needed to keep chicken from sticking.

Transfer chicken and onion mixture to large casserole. Stir in remaining ingredients, including sherry.

Cover and bake 1 hour.

Uncover, turn chicken and bake 15 minutes more. Discard cloves.

Serve over rice.

Calories per serving: 240	Sodium per serving: 103 mgs.

SPANISH

Spanish cooking has a fascinating history dating back to the Phoenicians who planted the first vineyards and olive trees. However, some credit the Romans for the latter. It was, indeed, the Roman conquerors who introduced garlic to the Spanish territories. Then the Moors, whose influence spanned eight centuries, brought in a touch of the Orient with such spices as cumin seed, black pepper, nutmeg, peppermint, saffron, cinnamon, and cloves.

Back then, the Spanish were wild for spices and used them with lavish abandon—sometimes as many as twelve flavoring the same dish. In the 18th century, Spain finally began to appreciate some of the bounty Columbus brought back from America, and eventually potatoes, green peppers, and tomatoes established themselves as the foundation of Spanish cuisine. From then on, Spanish cooks learned to rely on the natural flavors of basic ingredients and used spices with loving restraint.

Unlike Mexican food, which commands your attention and with which it is so often confused, Spanish food lies gently on the tongue. The fragrant aroma of olive oil is generic to all Spanish cooking—not just because olive groves are common to Spain, but because heated olive oil brings out the full flavor of food. It especially enhances seafood, still the most popular of all Spanish foods because of Spain's close proximity to the cornucopia of the sea. Garlic is used almost as often, producing a range of tastes from pungent to nutty.

From region to region, the variations of cooking styles are as pronounced as the similarities. Pork is the number one meat because pigs are easy to raise, even in this mountainous country. But seafood is the heart of Spain's culinary art.

In Catalonia, which lies along the Mediterranean coast, fish and game birds are prepared with French touches. Melons and mushrooms also abound in this lush country. When in season, mushrooms are somehow featured in every dish.

The Basque Provinces lure the true gourmand, for nowhere else in Spain is food taken quite so seriously. What's more, the gastronomic societies of this region are exclusively male territory. In fact, as often as not, the lusty Basquais men will cook for the family meals. The Basquais cherish above all quality and freshness. For these reasons they cook only what is in season and prefer to gently simmer foods, pampering their natural sweetness to perfection. Seafood is, of course, particularly remarkable.

Asturias is famous for chorizo and cider, both of which are exported to worldwide acclaim. Castile is the home of Madrid, the geographic and cultural heart of Spain. With no particular specialties of its own, Madrid is the hub for all the regional specialties. Galicia is renowned for shellfish and wonderful vegetables; Aragon and Navarre for their special stews. There are countless regions and cooking styles in Spain.

But the most popularly Spanish of all is Andalusia—the primary source of olive oil and famous Spanish sherry. Andalusia is also the home of the flamenco with its swirling dancers, castanets, and the sweet music of the Spanish guitar. The Moorish influence is also experienced in the food which often hints of fruitiness.

Whatever its origin, Spanish cooking typifies the fiery emotions of its people, held temptingly and tantalizingly in check. Its subtly teasing spiciness is, indeed, the basis of its charm.

BAKED TUNA

Serves 8

2 lbs. tuna steaks
2 Tbs. olive oil
1 medium-size onion, chopped
2 cloves garlic, minced
Dash of ground cumin
½ tsp. thyme
Black pepper to taste

1 Tbs. low sodium beef bouillon
1 cup dry white wine
2 tsps. sugar
1 tsp. dried or fresh grated orange peel
1 Tbs. paprika
2 tomatoes, cut into thin wedges

Preheat oven to 375°.
Moisten tuna with oil. In skillet, fry tuna, onion, and garlic over medium heat 2 minutes, turning tuna once. Transfer to oven-proof casserole.
Season tuna with cumin, thyme, pepper, and bouillon.
In bowl, combine wine, sugar, orange peel, and paprika. Pour around tuna. Bake 40 minutes.
Add tomatoes and bake 20 minutes more.

Calories per serving: 227   Sodium per serving: 50 mgs.

FISH IN SHERRIED TOMATO SAUCE

Serves 8

3 Tbs. unsalted butter or margarine
4 tsps. low sodium chicken bouillon
8 small white onions
2 cloves
6 cloves garlic, minced
1 Tbs. all-purpose flour
¾ cup water
½ cup dry sherry
2 Tbs. lemon juice

2 tsps. low sodium beef bouillon
6 Tbs. low sodium ketchup
1 Tbs. parsley
¼ tsp. basil
¼ tsp. fennel seed
¼ tsp. thyme
Pinch of saffron
2 lbs. fish fillets (1 lb. each cod and
    halibut), cut into 2" chunks

In skillet, melt butter. Stir in chicken bouillon. Add onions and stir fry till glazed.
Stud one of the onions with the cloves.
Add the garlic and fry 2 minutes.
Stir in flour. Slowly add water, stirring constantly.
Stir in remaining ingredients except fish. Simmer, stirring often, 10 minutes.
Add fish and simmer 25 minutes more.

Calories per serving: 185   Sodium per serving: 84 mgs.

FISH PAELLA

Serves 8

2 pts. oysters, including liquid
3 cups water
3 Tbs. low sodium chicken bouillon
Dash of marjoram
Black pepper to taste
Dash of mace
2 Tbs. dry sherry, divided
1 Tbs. olive oil
1½ lbs. halibut, cut into 1" chunks

1 medium-size onion, sliced
4 cloves garlic, minced
2 red peppers, chopped
1 Tbs. cider vinegar
1 bay leaf
¼ tsp. thyme
2 Tbs. lemon juice
1 cup long grain rice
3 Tbs. fresh chopped parsley

In saucepan, combine first 6 ingredients and 1 Tbs. sherry. Cook over medium heat 5 minutes. Set aside.
In large skillet, heat oil. Add halibut, onion, garlic, and peppers. Cook over low heat 5 minutes, stirring often.
Increase heat to high. Stir in vinegar, 1 Tbs. sherry, bay leaf, thyme, and lemon juice.

Reduce heat. Add rice. Stir to blend. Add oyster mixture. Do not stir. Bring to a boil. Reduce heat and cook, uncovered, 15 minutes, or till liquid is absorbed.
Garnish with parsley.

Calories per serving: 281   Sodium per serving: 180 mgs.

HALIBUT, PEPPERS, AND SHERRY

Serves 6

1 Tbs. olive oil
1 medium-size onion, chopped
2 cloves garlic, minced
1/3 cup dry sherry
2 Tbs. lemon juice
1 bay leaf
1½ lbs. halibut fillets

Black pepper to taste
2 tsps. low sodium beef bouillon
1/8 tsp. cinnamon
1 red pepper, chopped
1 green pepper, chopped
1 Tbs. tarragon

In skillet, heat oil. Add onion and garlic and cook over low heat 5 minutes, stirring occasionally. Set aside.
Preheat oven to 350°.
Pour sherry into 9″ × 13″ oven-proof casserole. Stir in lemon juice. Add bay leaf and halibut. Add onion mixture.
Season fish with pepper, bouillon, and cinnamon. Scatter red and green pepper in casserole. Stir in tarragon. Bake 25 minutes, or till fish flakes easily.

Calories per serving: 173   Sodium per serving: 75 mgs.

SALMON IN FENNEL SAUCE

Serves 8

2 lbs. salmon steaks
¼ cup anisette or dry sherry
¼ cup orange juice
1 Tbs. cider vinegar
¼ tsp. fennel seed

¼ tsp. thyme
2 Tbs. olive oil
Dash of ground cumin
1 red pepper, chopped
1 Tbs. low sodium beef bouillon

Place salmon in 9″ square casserole. Add remaining ingredients. Cover and refrigerate overnight, turning salmon occasionally.
Preheat oven to 375°.
Bake, covered, 25 minutes, or till fish flakes easily.

Calories per serving: 171   Sodium per serving: 81 mgs.

SEA BASS AND VEGETABLES

Serves 6

1 Tbs. olive oil
4 cloves garlic, minced
2 chili peppers, minced
1 Tbs. all-purpose flour
2 Tbs. parsley
1½ lbs. sea bass fillets
¼ cup dry sherry

¼ cup boiling water
1 Tbs. low sodium chicken bouillon
3 potatoes, parboiled, peeled, and sliced
1 lb. asparagus, trimmed
1 pt. oysters, chopped, including liquid
2 Tbs. heavy cream

Preheat oven to 350°.
In skillet, heat oil. Add garlic and chili peppers and cook over low heat till garlic is golden. Stir in flour and parsley.
Add sea bass and cook 5 minutes, turning fish once. Transfer to 9″ × 13″ oven-proof casserole.
Add sherry and boiling water. Sprinkle in bouillon.
Add potatoes to casserole and bake 20 minutes.
Add asparagus and bake 10 minutes more.
Add oysters and their liquid. Bake 3 minutes. Stir in cream.

Calories per serving: 274	Sodium per serving: 135 mgs.

SOLE WITH CREAMED SPINACH

Serves 6

1 lb. spinach, chopped
⅛ tsp. nutmeg
2 tsps. low sodium chicken bouillon
2 Tbs. heavy cream
1½ lbs. sole fillets

Black pepper to taste
1 tsp. mint
½ cup dry white wine
3 peaches, pitted and sliced
1 Tbs. brandy

In saucepan, combine spinach with enough water to cover. Cook over medium heat 10 minutes, or till spinach is limp. Drain thoroughly.
In blender, combine spinach, nutmeg, bouillon, and cream. Purée. Set aside.
Preheat oven to 375°.
In 9″ × 13″ oven-proof casserole, place sole. Season with pepper and mint. Top with spinach purée.
Pour wine around fish. Add peaches. Cover and bake 15 minutes, or till fish flakes easily. Sprinkle with brandy.

Calories per serving: 168	Sodium per serving: 149 mgs.

SWORDFISH IN LEMON VINEGAR

Serves 8

2 lbs. swordfish steaks, ½" thick
¼ cup lemon juice
4 Tbs. cider vinegar
2 Tbs. oil
2 Tbs. warm water
3 cloves garlic, minced
½ medium-size onion, minced
Black pepper to taste

Dash of cayenne pepper
1 Tbs. sugar
1 Tbs. parsley
¼ cup dry white wine
1 Tbs. tarragon
1½ Tbs. low sodium chicken bouillon,
  divided

In large casserole, place swordfish.

In bowl, combine all remaining ingredients except bouillon. Blend well and pour over swordfish. Cover and refrigerate 4 hours.

Preheat oven to broil.

Remove fish from marinade and place in shallow baking pan. Season with half the bouillon and broil 4 minutes. Baste with marinade.

Turn fish. Season with remaining bouillon and broil 3 minutes more. Baste with marinade and serve remainder on the side.

Calories per serving: 189   Sodium per serving: 6 mgs.

BEEF IN CITRUS SAUCE

Serves 6

1 cup dry white wine
1 lemon, quartered
1 orange, quartered
2 cloves
2 bay leaves

3 cloves garlic, sliced
1¼ lbs. beef sirloin, cut into 1" chunks
Black pepper to taste
1 Tbs. low sodium beef bouillon

In saucepan, combine first 6 ingredients. Simmer 10 minutes. Set aside.

Season sirloin with pepper and bouillon. In skillet, sear beef on all sides till browned. Remove to platter.

Bring wine sauce to a boil. Boil 5 minutes. Discard lemon, orange, cloves, and bay leaves. Pour sauce over beef.

Calories per serving: 328   Sodium per serving: 69 mgs.

MOORISH LAMB

Serves 8

1 Tbs. olive oil
1½ lbs. stewing lamb, cut into 2″ chunks
2 medium-size onions, diced
3 cloves garlic, minced
2 green peppers, chopped
1 can (16 ozs.) low sodium tomatoes
¼ cup dry white wine
¼ tsp. cinnamon
1 Tbs. low sodium beef bouillon
1 Tbs. low sodium chicken bouillon
2 bay leaves
Black pepper to taste

2 Tbs. unsalted butter or margarine
¼ tsp. fennel seed
½ tsp. basil
½ tsp. mustard powder
½ tsp. mace
½ tsp. marjoram
½ tsp. savory
½ tsp. parsley
½ tsp. thyme
½ cup low sodium Bread Crumbs (See Page 291)
1 Tbs. lemon juice

In large skillet, heat oil and sauté lamb till brown on all sides.

Add onions, garlic, and green peppers. Cook over medium/low heat, stirring till onions are golden.

Add tomatoes. Bring to a boil.

Add wine and simmer 5 minutes.

Add cinnamon, beef and chicken bouillon, bay leaves, and pepper. Cook, uncovered, over medium heat 15 minutes.

While lamb is cooking, melt butter in small saucepan. Stir in all remaining ingredients except lemon juice. Cook, stirring, till butter is absorbed.

Stir in lemon juice.

Top lamb with bread crumb mixture. Discard bay leaves.

Calories per serving: 346   Sodium per serving: 94 mgs.

PORK CHOPS WITH TOMATO SAUCE

Serves 6

2 cloves garlic, chopped
1 Tbs. olive oil
1 Tbs. water
1 Tbs. paprika
⅛ tsp. ground cloves
⅛ tsp. ground cumin
6 pork chops

1 medium-size onion, minced
1 tomato, chopped
1 Tbs. parsley
1 cup water
2 Tbs. cider vinegar
2 tsps. low sodium chicken bouillon
1 Tbs. brandy (optional)

In blender, combine first 6 ingredients. Purée to a paste. Spread mixture over pork chops and let stand 30 minutes. Scrape off paste and reserve.

In ungreased skillet, cook pork chops over low heat 15 minutes, or till both sides are browned. Transfer to platter.

Add onion to skillet and cook over low heat 5 minutes.

Stir in tomato and reserved paste. Cook 3 minutes more, stirring often.

Stir in parsley, water, vinegar, and bouillon. Bring to a boil. Reduce heat.

Return pork chops to skillet. Cover and simmer 20 minutes, or till chops are tender.

Pour on brandy and flame.

Calories per serving: 305	Sodium per serving: 85 mgs.

SPANISH BEEF STEW

Serves 8

1½ lbs. stewing beef, cut into 1″ chunks, fat trimmed
1 Tbs. olive oil
2 medium-size onions, chopped
4 cloves garlic, minced
3 tomatoes, chopped
2 Tbs. brandy
¾ cup dry white wine
1 Tbs. low sodium chicken bouillon
2 tsps. paprika

Black pepper to taste
2 Tbs. all-purpose flour
2 cups boiling water
1½ Tbs. low sodium beef bouillon
4 potatoes, peeled and cubed
1 Tbs. parsley
½ tsp. thyme
⅛ tsp. cinnamon
1 Tbs. cider vinegar
2 cloves

In ungreased Dutch oven, sear beef till browned all over. Transfer to platter.

Heat oil in Dutch oven. Add onions and garlic and cook over low heat 5 minutes, stirring often.

Add tomatoes and cook 3 minutes more. Stir in brandy, wine, chicken bouillon, paprika, and black pepper. Cook 5 minutes.

Sprinkle in flour. Return beef to Dutch oven and add remaining ingredients. Cover and simmer 1½ hours, or till beef is fork tender. Discard cloves.

Calories per serving: 250	Sodium per serving: 70 mgs.

VEAL STEAKS TOLEDO

Serves 4

4 veal chops
2 Tbs. olive oil
1 cup dry white wine
4 tsps. low sodium beef bouillon
2 Tbs. lemon juice
¼ tsp. cinnamon

¼ tsp. oregano
¼ tsp. thyme
¼ tsp. marjoram
Black pepper to taste
2 cloves garlic, minced

Pierce the chops several times with a fork.

Combine remaining ingredients. Pour over chops, making sure the marinade goes into the punched holes. Let stand 1 hour at room temperature.

Preheat oven to broil.

Broil chops 4″ from heat till crispy brown, approximately 10 minutes, basting occasionally with marinade.

Turn and repeat. Discard remaining marinade.

Calories per serving: 295	Sodium per serving: 116 mgs.

VEAL WITH ALMONDS

Serves 8

8 veal scallops
2 Tbs. all-purpose flour
3 Tbs. olive oil, divided
1 Tbs. unsalted butter or margarine
2 medium-size onions, chopped
½ cup dry sherry
1 cup boiling water

1 tsp. basil
½ tsp. thyme
1 tsp. dried or fresh grated lemon peel
1 Tbs. parsley
¾ tsp. garlic powder
Black pepper to taste
¼ cup almonds, chopped

Pound scallops with mallet or saucer till paper thin. Dust with flour.

In large skillet, heat half the oil. Sauté half the scallops till golden brown on both sides. Transfer to platter.

Repeat with remaining oil and scallopini. Transfer to platter.

Add butter to skillet and melt. Add onions and cook over low heat 7 minutes, stirring occasionally. Transfer to 9″ × 13″ oven-proof casserole.

Preheat oven to 375°.

Lay scallops on top of onions, overlapping if necessary. Pour on sherry and water. Add remaining ingredients, except almonds, and bake 5 minutes.

Sprinkle on almonds. Cover and bake 20 minutes more.

Calories per serving: 351	Sodium per serving: 133 mgs.

CHICKEN ESPAGNOL

Serves 4

¼ cup all-purpose flour
1 Tbs. low sodium beef bouillon
1 Tbs. low sodium chicken bouillon
2 chicken breasts, boned and halved
1 carrot, peeled and quartered

4 leeks, chopped into 2″ rounds, including greens
1½ cups water
2 Tbs. lemon juice
1 Tbs. olive oil

(continued next page)

1 Tbs. unsalted butter or margarine
4 cloves garlic, sliced
Black pepper to taste

2 tsps. parsley
1 tsp. cornstarch
½ cup dry white wine

Combine flour and beef and chicken bouillon in bag. Add chicken and shake to coat. Set aside.

In medium saucepan, cook carrot and leeks in water and lemon juice over medium/high heat 7 minutes. Remove vegetables to plate, reserving stock.

While vegetables are cooking, in large skillet, heat oil and butter and sauté chicken breasts on both sides till golden.

Place chicken skin side up, in 9″ × 13″ oven-proof casserole. Surround with vegetables. Add garlic and sprinkle chicken with pepper and parsley.

Preheat oven to 350°.

Stir cornstarch into reserved vegetable stock and boil down to ½ cup, scraping brown bits from sides of pan. Pour over chicken along with wine.

Bake covered, 20 minutes. Uncover and bake 5 minutes more.

Calories per serving: 317   Sodium per serving: 104 mgs.

CHICKEN PAELLA

Serves 12

1 Tbs. olive oil
6 pieces chicken (3 half breasts, 3 whole
    legs), skinned, boned, and cut into
    1″ chunks
1 large onion, thinly sliced
1 carrot, scraped and cut into ½″ rounds
½ cup dry white wine or vermouth
2 large cloves garlic, minced
4 cups boiling water or Chicken Broth
    (See Page 45)
5 Tbs. low sodium chicken bouillon
½ tsp. sage
1 tsp. dill
1 tsp. ground coriander
2 tsps. oregano

2 tsps. paprika
2 tsps. saffron threads
½ tsp. thyme
2 bay leaves
Black pepper to taste
1 can (12 ozs.) low sodium tomato juice
1 can (16 ozs.) low sodium tomatoes,
    chopped, including liquid
2 cups whole grain rice
2½ lbs. green beans, chopped into
    1″ lengths
1 green pepper, sliced
2 pts. oysters, including liquid
2 lemons, cut into wedges

Heat oil in large skillet or paella pan. Brown chicken on both sides.

Add onion and all except last 4 ingredients. Cover and simmer slowly 15 minutes. Bring to boil.

Stir in rice and green beans, mixing thoroughly into the liquid. Boil, uncovered, 5 minutes. Do not stir.

Add green pepper and mix into the rice.

Add oysters and their liquid.

Add additional water or Chicken Broth if rice is dry. Reduce heat and cook, uncovered, 10 minutes more. Discard bay leaves.

Garnish with lemon wedges.

Calories per serving: 504   Sodium per serving: 176 mgs.

CHICKEN WITH ALMOND SAUCE

Serves 4

2 chicken breasts, boned and halved
½ cup lemon juice, divided
1 Tbs. olive oil
2 medium-size onions, chopped
2 Tbs. coarsely chopped almonds
2 Tbs. all-purpose flour
½ cup dry red wine
½ cup water

2 Tbs. heavy cream
4 tsps. low sodium chicken bouillon
Black pepper to taste
1 tsp. garlic powder
⅛ tsp. mace
1 tsp. parsley
¼ tsp. thyme

Preheat oven to 350°.

Place chicken in roasting pan, skin side down. Pour on half the lemon juice and bake, covered, 20 minutes.

In saucepan, heat oil. Sauté onions till golden. Add almonds and sauté 2 minutes.

Stir in flour to blend well. Slowly add wine, water, and cream, stirring constantly.

Stir in bouillon, spices, and herbs. Cook over low heat 5 minutes. Set aside.

Turn chicken, skin side up. Cover with remaining lemon juice and bake, uncovered, 20 minutes more, or till browned on top.

Cover with almond sauce and bake 10 minutes, uncovered, or till sauce is bubbly.

Serve over white rice.

Calories per serving: 292   Sodium per serving: 91 mgs.

FRIED CHICKEN IN WINE SAUCE

Serves 8

8 pieces chicken (4 half breasts, 4 whole
  legs)
¼ cup all-purpose flour
4 Tbs. olive oil, divided
2 medium-size onions, minced
4 cloves garlic, minced
⅛ tsp. cinnamon

6 cloves
1 Tbs. paprika
Black pepper to taste
½ can (3 ozs.) low sodium tomato paste
1 Tbs. low sodium chicken bouillon
1½ cups dry white wine

231

In bag, combine chicken and flour. Shake to coat well.

In large skillet, heat 2 Tbs. oil. Fry 4 chicken pieces over medium/low heat till browned on both sides. Transfer to platter.

Repeat with remaining oil and chicken. Transfer to platter.

To skillet, add onions and garlic. Sauté over low heat 5 minutes, stirring occasionally, or till garlic is golden.

Stir in cinnamon, cloves, paprika, pepper, and tomato paste. Fry 1 minute.

Preheat oven to 350°.

Stir bouillon and wine into onion mixture in skillet. Simmer 5 minutes. Pour into large casserole. Add chicken. Cover and bake 20 minutes.

Calories per serving: 274   Sodium per serving: 84 mgs.

ROCK CORNISH HENS IN COGNAC

Serves 8

¼ cup water
¼ cup cider vinegar, divided
4 small Rock Cornish hens
4 Tbs. olive oil
Coarse black pepper to taste
8 tsps. low sodium beef bouillon
2 carrots, scraped and quartered
16 small white onions
4 small tomatoes, halved

10 cloves garlic
2 tsps. all-purpose flour
¼ cup slivered almonds
2 Tbs. plus ¼ cup cognac, divided
¼ cup dry white wine
1 Tbs. unsalted butter or margarine
½ tsp. mustard powder
⅛ tsp. cinnamon
½ tsp. rosemary, crushed

Preheat oven to 400°.

Combine water and all but 2 Tbs. vinegar. Wash cavities of hens with the mixture.

Rub outside of hens with oil. Season with pepper and beef bouillon.

Place hens in lightly oiled roasting pan. Scatter carrots, onions, and tomatoes in pan. Roast 25 minutes.

While hens are roasting, place garlic on tin foil in oven for 5 minutes. Mash with flour, almonds, and 2 Tbs. cognac till pasty. Set aside.

Pour ¼ cup cognac and wine over hens and continue roasting till hens are browned and tender, about 20 minutes more. Remove hens and vegetables to oven-proof casserole.

Pour pan juices into saucepan. Add garlic/almond paste, butter, remaining 2 Tbs. vinegar, mustard, cinnamon, and rosemary. Bring to a slow boil and cook 5 minutes.

Pour over hens and bake 10 more minutes, basting often.

Split each hen in half. Serve with vegetables and gravy on the side.

Calories per serving: 315   Sodium per serving: 112 mgs.

SHERRY BROILED CHICKEN

Serves 6

1 cup dry sherry
½ tsp. ground coriander
1 Tbs. lemon juice
1 Tbs. paprika
½ tsp. ground cumin
2 cloves garlic, minced
1 Tbs. honey
1 medium-size onion, minced

1 Tbs. parsley
1 tsp. almond extract
6 pieces chicken (3 half breasts, 3 whole legs)
2 Tbs. low sodium chicken bouillon
2 Tbs. cold water
1 tsp. cornstarch
2 lemons, cut into wedges

In casserole, combine first 10 ingredients. Add chicken. Cover and refrigerate overnight. Remove chicken. Reserve marinade.

Preheat oven to broil.

Season chicken with bouillon and broil 6 minutes on each side, or till skin is crispy, basting each side with some of the marinade.

In saucepan, simmer remaining marinade 5 minutes.

In bowl, combine cold water and cornstarch. Stir into marinade. Cook until thickened. Pour over chicken.

Garnish with lemon wedges.

Calories per serving: 207   Sodium per serving: 85 mgs.

VEGETABLES

Vegetables are not those things your mother made you eat when you were a child. You know by now they are pretty good. Steamed, baked, boiled, broiled, fried, saucy, or plain—vegetables are versatile, slimming, nutritious, and delicious.

If you're interested in sodium no-noes, beware of the following: celery (126 mgs. raw, 88 mgs. cooked); spinach (71 mgs. raw, 50 mgs. cooked); watercress (52 mgs. raw); beets (43 mgs. cooked); carrots (43 mgs. raw, 33 mgs. cooked); white turnips (34 mgs. cooked); and artichokes (30 mgs. cooked)—all per 3½ oz. serving. These foods should be eaten sparingly if at all and avoided completely if your doctor so advises.

Otherwise, indulge and enjoy vegetables to your heart's content because they're among the healthiest of foods: low in sodium and fat while providing nourishing amounts of carbohydrate, protein, and important minerals. To put it plainly, you can gorge yourself on vegetables and stay thin and healthy.

Now for the different methods of preparation:

To steam: If you don't have one, buy yourself a vegetable steamer. They're available for as little as $2.00. Place the steamer in a pot that will allow it to open as wide as necessary. Fill the pot with water that just starts to creep through the steamer, and bring to a boil. Add vegetables. Cover. Reduce heat to simmer and steam till vegetables are tender crisp. Add boiling water, if necessary, to prevent complete evaporation.

If you want to steam two or more vegetables together, layer them with the one requiring the longest time on the bottom. Common sense and your own experience will guide you.

To add a special zing to vegetables when steaming (or boiling for that matter), add a tablespoon or two of lemon juice, wine, brandy, or any juice or liqueur to the water. This little addition will subtly permeate the vegetables and result in a light, delectable flavor.

However you steam, when the vegetables are done, drain, then serve piping hot —plain, with a little unsalted butter or nestled in your favorite sauce.

To boil: Boiling is convenient and can produce lovely to look at, lovely to taste vegetables. Just remember: Don't overboil. For not only will the vegetables be limp, pale, truly unappetizing, but they'll have lost their fresh, full flavor and most of their nutritional value.

Instead, in a saucepan, bring to a boil just enough water to cover the vegetables. Slip them in and continue boiling till tender crisp—usually no more than ten to twelve minutes for fresh, less if frozen.

To fry: Vegetables contain considerable amounts of natural juices which they release during cooking. If you use these juices to aid the cooking process, and cook over low heat, you'll need far less oil or butter than most recipes require. Indeed, with this method, you'll be braising the vegetables at first, then stir frying over higher heat to absorb excess moisture.

Stir frying, traditional to Chinese cooking, is a terrific all-purpose frying technique. Simply add a tablespoon of butter or oil to a skillet. Add the vegetables and stir fry till vegetables are thoroughly coated and tender crisp.

Either way, you'll seal in natural flavor and goodness and produce perfect vegetables, slightly crunchy and delectably rich in texture as well as taste.

If frying a variety of vegetables, fry first those requiring the longest cooking time and add the others in succeeding order. And if you want to stir a sauce directly into the vegetables, add it before the vegetables are completely cooked, raise to high heat, and continue stirring till sauce is bubbly.

Deep frying should be a once-in-a-while pleasure because there is no way to escape the necessary but calorie heavy oil so rarely worth the tradeoff. But at least oil has no sodium, so if you do have an uncontrollable and unconscionable urge, at least use a deep fryer to avoid saturating the foods in grease.

The trick is to plunge in the foods you're going to fry after the oil starts to crackle and spit. Fry quickly over high heat. When browned, remove the food at once and drain thoroughly on paper toweling. Sprinkle with low sodium bouillon, pepper, whatever other seasonings you'd like, toss to blend well and serve immediately.

To broil: Easy. Broil near the heat—with or without marinade—until vegetables are crunchy and lightly browned.

To bake: Baked is really a misnomer because most vegetables are covered and allowed to oven steam in their own juices. Thus, they require very little additional liquid and emerge bubbly and tender. The secret is not to leave them in the oven longer than directed.

Potatoes are the exception to this rule. If they're wrapped in tin foil and steamed, they'll be slightly mealy in texture and taste. The best baked potatoes are simply slit down the center to allow steam to escape and baked in a moderate oven till fork tender.

We've been talking about fresh vegetables. For it's really just as easy, and takes as little time, to chop a stalk of broccoli as it is to open a frozen carton or a can. Fresh vegetables have richer flavor, better texture, and more nutritional value than either frozen or canned. And you can still freeze what you don't want for later use in soups and casseroles.

It's also important to note that, per serving, fresh vegetables are often cheaper than the frozen variety. But if, for whatever reason, frozen is your choice, read the labels carefully before you buy. Many frozen vegetables—peas, for one—contain sodium preservatives and should be avoided.

As for canned vegetables, don't use them unless they're marked low sodium and provide a complete ingredient listing. Aside from the overcooked taste, regular canned vegetables are loaded with salt which is bad for your figure and your health.

While there's no denying that canned vegetables—low sodium or not—can't compare with fresh or frozen for eating pleasure and health goodness, the low sodium brands are quite good, especially for casseroles or cold salads.

Whatever your pleasure—fresh, frozen, or canned—eat plenty of vegetables. They not only taste terrific, but they are terrific for your health and your looks.

American

Though not particularly stylized as American, vegetables in the United States are becoming an increasingly important part of the American meal. In summer, even big city residents can find the freshest offerings from neighboring farms. And all year round, if shoppers find fresh produce too expensive, they can choose from a complete variety of frozen products available—thanks to this country's advanced processing and refrigeration.

American cooks have long since passed the basics of boiling, frying, and baking, often artfully using spices, flavorings, and sauces to enhance not only the vegetable, but to accent the meal as well.

BAKED DILL TOMATOES

Serves 4

4 medium tomatoes, cored, pulp removed
  and reserved*
2 tsps. dill

Dash of black pepper
½ tsp. oregano
1 tsp. oil

*Do not pierce tomato shells.

Preheat oven to 350°.
In bowl, combine pulp, dill, pepper, oregano, and oil. Lightly stuff mixture into tomatoes.
Loosely wrap each tomato in tin foil. Bake 15 minutes. Uncover and bake 10 minutes more.

Calories per serving: 36   Sodium per serving: 3 mgs.

BAKED STUFFED ACORN SQUASH

Serves 4

2 small acorn squash, halved and seeded
½ tsp. nutmeg, divided
1 large leek, chopped fine, including
  greens
6 water chestnuts, chopped

1 Tbs. unsalted butter or margarine
Black pepper to taste
½ can (4 ozs.) whole berry cranberry
  sauce

Preheat oven to 350°.
Sprinkle squash cavities with ⅛ tsp. nutmeg each and bake 30 minutes.
In small skillet, sauté leek and water chestnuts in butter seasoned with pepper till leek
is golden brown.
Combine cranberry sauce with leek mixture.
Remove squash from oven and stuff cavities with cranberry mixture.
Cover and return squash to oven for another 15 minutes.

Calories per serving: 194   Sodium per serving: 9 mgs.

BRUSSELS SPROUTS AND MUSHROOMS

Serves 4

1 lb. Brussels sprouts
2 Tbs. unsalted butter or margarine
1 small onion, chopped
¼ lb. mushrooms, sliced

1 Tbs. lemon juice
¼ tsp. garlic powder
Black pepper to taste
⅛ tsp. caraway seed (optional)

Soak sprouts for 10 minutes in cold water. Rinse and drain.
Drop into boiling water. Lower heat and simmer 10 minutes. Drain and cover. Remove
from heat.
Melt butter in skillet. Sauté onion and mushrooms 5 minutes.
Add the lemon juice, seasonings, and sprouts. Stir thoroughly.

Calories per serving: 121   Sodium per serving: 21 mgs.

CABBAGE WITH CHEESE SAUCE

Serves 10

1 large head cabbage
4 cups water
1½ Tbs. unsalted butter or margarine
2½ Tbs. all-purpose flour
2 cups Chicken Broth (See Page 45)
1 tsp. lemon juice
¼ tsp. nutmeg
1 Tbs. onion powder

Black pepper to taste
4 ozs. low sodium Cheddar cheese,
   minced
1 leek, chopped, including greens
   (optional)
1 sprig watercress, chopped (optional)
1½ Tbs. oil

Cut cabbage into 10 wedges. Soak 10 minutes in cold water to cover. Drain.
Bring 4 cups water to boil. Add the cabbage and cook over medium heat 10 minutes, or till tender crisp. Drain. Set aside.
While cabbage is cooking, in medium-size saucepan, melt butter. Slowly stir in flour until well blended.
Slowly stir in broth. Add lemon juice, nutmeg, onion powder, and pepper.
Fold the cheese into the broth mixture. Simmer, stirring occasionally, until cheese melts.
While cheese mixture is cooking, sauté leek and watercress in oil. Add to cheese mixture along with cabbage. Cook 5 minutes more.

Calories per serving: 125	Sodium per serving: 26 mgs.

FRUITED CARROTS

Serves 8

4 large carrots, scraped
1 apple, peeled and cored
1 medium-size onion, sliced into rings
1 tsp. dried or fresh grated orange peel
1 tsp. dried or fresh grated lemon peel
Dash of minced ginger root or powder

Dash of black pepper
¼ tsp. cinnamon
Water to cover
¼ cup apple or pineapple juice
2 canned peach halves, chopped
2 Tbs. peach preserves*

Preserved without pectin or sodium

Cut carrots in half lengthwise and cut each half lengthwise into quarters.
Cut apple in half lengthwise and slice each half crosswise into thin sections.
Place onion rings on bottom of Dutch oven.
Add carrots, apples, seasonings, and water to cover.
Simmer on stove in covered pot 1 hour, or till carrots are tender, adding water as

necessary to maintain about 1″ liquid in pan during first 30 minutes. During last half hour, add juice.

Five minutes before serving, stir in peaches and preserves, blending thoroughly.

Calories per serving: 50   Sodium per serving: 22 mgs.

RHUBARB COMPOTE

Serves 8

1 lb. rhubarb, peeled and cut into
  2″ slices
½ cup brown sugar, loosely packed
½ tsp. nutmeg
½ tsp. aniseed

1 Tbs. dried or fresh grated lemon peel
1 Tbs. dried or fresh grated orange peel
1 pt. blueberries
1 cup water

Combine all ingredients in medium-size saucepan. Simmer, covered, 20 to 25 minutes, or until rhubarb is tender.

Serve hot as meat accompaniment or cold as dessert.

Calories per serving: 88   Sodium per serving: 5 mgs.

VEGETABLE MEDLEY

Serves 6

1 large onion, cut into wedges
1 large yellow squash or zucchini, cut into
  ½″ wedges
2 medium tomatoes, cut into wedges
1 tsp. garlic powder
Black pepper to taste

1 Tbs. dill
2 Tbs. warm water
2 Tbs. oil
2 Tbs. dry white wine
4 tsps. low sodium beef bouillon
3 ozs. low sodium cheese*

A combination of Gouda, Cheddar, and Mozzarella is delicious

Preheat oven to 350°.
Lay onion in a small casserole, covering entire bottom.
Layer squash and tomatoes on top. Sprinkle with garlic powder, pepper, and dill.
In bowl, combine water, oil, and wine. Pour over vegetable mixture.
Bake, uncovered, 30 minutes, or till mixture starts to bubble.

Add bouillon and cheese. Bake 10 minutes longer, or till cheese melts. Toss to blend all ingredients.

Calories per serving: 184
Omitting oil: calories per serving: 142

Sodium per serving: 20 mgs.

ZUCCHINI ROSEMARY

Serves 8

2 Tbs. oil
4 medium zucchini, halved lengthwise,
  each half cut into 4 wedges

1 tsp. rosemary, crushed
1½ Tbs. sugar
2½ Tbs. cider vinegar

In large skillet, heat oil.
Add zucchini and fry over medium heat until slightly brown.
Turn and fry other side. Lower heat.
Sprinkle zucchini with rosemary and sugar.
Add vinegar, and stir fry till sugar is dissolved and ingredients are thoroughly mixed.

Calories per serving: 54

Sodium per serving: 2 mgs.

Chinese

When you want to give vegetables a Chinese flavor, stir fry them in a small amount of oil, then stir in low sodium bouillon and sugar to taste.

BROCCOLI WITH SESAME SEED

Serves 6

2 Tbs. sesame or peanut oil
2 Tbs. sesame seed
2 stalks broccoli, separated into flowerets,
  stalks peeled and cut into ½" rounds

1 clove garlic, minced
½ tsp. low sodium beef bouillon
2 tomatoes, sliced into wedges
Dash of hot pepper flakes

In large skillet, heat oil. Add sesame seed and stir fry 30 seconds.
Add broccoli, garlic, and bouillon. Stir fry 30 seconds more.
Add tomatoes and pepper flakes. Stir fry 1 minute more.

Calories per serving: 86

Sodium per serving: 6 mgs.

CHINESE VEGETABLES

Serves 6

2 Tbs. sesame oil
1 large onion, sliced thin
2 cloves garlic, minced
½ tsp. minced ginger root, or dash of
　ginger powder
Black pepper to taste
½ tsp. mustard powder
¼ green pepper, chopped
¼ red pepper, chopped

2 Tbs. dry sherry
4 mushrooms, sliced
½ can (4 ozs.) water chestnuts, sliced
2 stalks broccoli, broken into flowerets,
　stalks peeled and cut into ½" rounds
1 cup boiling water
4½ tsps. low sodium chicken bouillon
1 Tbs. cornstarch
¼ cup cold water

In wok, heat oil. Add onion, garlic, ginger, pepper, and mustard powder. Stir fry over medium low heat 2 minutes.

Add green and red pepper. Stir fry 30 seconds.

Stir in sherry. Then add mushrooms, water chestnuts, and broccoli. Toss to blend. Stir fry 30 seconds.

In bowl, combine boiling water and bouillon. Add to vegetables. Raise heat to high and cook till bubbly.

In bowl, combine cornstarch and cold water. Stir into vegetable mixture and cook till mixture starts to thicken.

Calories per serving: 96　　　　Sodium per serving: 21 mgs.

DRY FRIED GREEN BEANS

Serves 6

4 Tbs. oil
1½ lbs. green beans, parboiled and
　drained while firm
1 medium-size onion, minced
2 tsps. low sodium beef bouillon

½ tsp. mustard powder
Dash of hot pepper flakes
1 tsp. sugar
2 Tbs. dry sherry

In wok or skillet, heat oil. Add all ingredients except sugar and sherry. Cook over high heat, stirring constantly, 5 minutes, or till beans are lightly browned.

Stir in sugar and sherry. Toss to blend.

Calories per serving: 131　　　　Sodium per serving: 10 mgs.

STIR FRIED ASPARAGUS

Serves 4

2 Tbs. oil
1 lb. asparagus, ends trimmed, cut into
  2″ pieces
1 tsp. low sodium chicken bouillon

¾ tsp. sugar
1½ tsps. dry sherry
1 tsp. lemon juice

In wok or large skillet, heat oil. Add asparagus and stir fry 3 minutes.
Stir in bouillon and sugar. Stir fry 1 minute more. Stir in sherry and lemon juice. Stir fry
1 minute more.

Calories per serving: 86

Sodium per serving: 3 mgs.

French

The French treat their vegetables with the same care as they do the rest of the
meal. Vegetables are featured as separate side dish accompaniments to the main
meal, as hors d'oeuvres and garnishes, in soups, salads, and aspics.

ARTICHOKES VINAIGRETTE

Serves 6

6 artichokes, stems cut
¼ cup lemon juice

½ cup Vinaigrette Dressing (See Page
  299)

In large saucepan, place artichokes in enough water to cover.
Add lemon juice.
Boil 45 minutes. Drain. If artichokes have flopped on their sides, be sure to turn them
while boiling.
Cool. Remove spiny center leaves and the chokes.
In well formed by removal of chokes, spoon 2 Tbs. dressing. Refrigerate overnight.
Serve with extra dressing.

Calories per serving: 145

Sodium per serving: 170 mgs.

ASPARAGUS WITH LEMON CRUMBED TOPPING

Serves 4

1 lb. asparagus, ends trimmed
1 Tbs. unsalted butter or margarine

¼ cup Seasoned Bread Crumbs (See
  Page 296)
2 Tbs. lemon juice

Cook asparagus in boiling water until tender/crisp, about 10 minutes. Drain. Transfer to platter.

While asparagus is cooking, melt butter in small skillet. Add Seasoned Bread Crumbs and stir fry over low heat till slightly browned.

Add lemon juice and cook over medium heat 1 minute. Sprinkle on asparagus.

Calories per serving: 61   Sodium per serving: 4 mgs.

BRAISED CUCUMBERS

Serves 8

1 Tbs. lemon juice
4 cucumbers, peeled and cut into
  1″ rounds
2 Tbs. unsalted butter or margarine

Dash of cayenne pepper
1 tsp. sugar
2 tsps. tarragon

In saucepan, combine lemon juice and cucumbers with enough boiling water to cover. Boil 5 minutes. Drain.

In skillet, melt butter. Add cucumbers and sauté, turning often, till cucumbers are golden on both sides. Stir in remaining ingredients.

Calories per serving: 47   Sodium per serving: 9 mgs.

MUSHROOM CAPS IN CREAM SAUCE

Serves 4

2 Tbs. unsalted butter or margarine
1 lb. mushrooms, stems removed
3 shallots, minced
Black pepper to taste

1 tsp. low sodium chicken bouillon
1 Tbs. all-purpose flour
¼ cup heavy cream
2 tsps. fresh chopped chives (optional)

In large skillet, melt butter. Add mushrooms and shallots and sauté over medium heat 2 minutes, turning mushrooms occasionally. Stir in pepper, bouillon, and flour.

243

Reduce heat to low. Stir in cream, blending thoroughly.
Garnish with chives.

Calories per serving: 154   Sodium per serving: 27 mgs.

German

Vegetables in the German tradition are usually simply boiled and buttered or floated in a cream-based sauce.

ASPARAGUS WITH NUT BUTTER

Serves 8

2 lbs. asparagus, ends trimmed
2 Tbs. unsalted butter or margarine,
   softened
2 Tbs. lemon juice
½ tsp. sugar

2 Tbs. slivered almonds
2 tsps. low sodium chicken bouillon
2 Tbs. chopped pecans
1 tsp. sesame seed

Lay asparagus in large skillet. Cover with boiling water and simmer 10 minutes, or till tender/crisp. Drain.
In saucepan, combine remaining ingredients except sesame seed. Heat till butter melts. Toss with asparagus.
Sprinkle sesame seed over all.

Calories per serving: 72   Sodium per serving: 4 mgs.

CHRISTMAS CABBAGE

Serves 10

1 large head red cabbage
1 Tbs. unsalted butter or margarine
1 Tbs. sugar
White pepper to taste
½ tsp. nutmeg
1 large onion, chopped

2 cups hot water
2 apples, cored and sliced
4 cloves
1 Tbs. cider vinegar
4 Tbs. raspberry, currant, or cherry jelly*

Preserved without pectin or sodium

Slice cabbage and soak 10 minutes in enough cold water to cover.

In large saucepan, melt butter. Add cabbage, sugar, pepper, nutmeg, and onion. Simmer 20 minutes.

Add hot water, apples, cloves, and vinegar. Cover and cook over low heat till tender, about 30 minutes. Discard cloves.

Stir in jelly.

Calories per serving: 74   Sodium per serving: 27 mgs.

LIMA BEANS IN SOUR CREAM

Serves 8

1 cup dried lima beans
4 cups water
1 Tbs. unsalted butter or margarine
1 medium-size onion, chopped
4 mushrooms, sliced

1 Tbs. all-purpose flour
2 Tbs. lemon juice
1 Tbs. low sodium beef bouillon
½ cup water
½ cup sour cream*

Preserved in non-sodium ingredient

Soak beans in water overnight. Cook, in water in which they were soaked, over low heat 1½ hours, or till tender.

When beans are almost done, in large skillet, melt butter. Sauté onion and mushrooms over low heat 5 minutes.

Stir in flour, then stir in lemon juice, bouillon, and water.

Drain beans. Stir into onion mixture. Stir in sour cream and cook 2 minutes.

Calories per serving: 130   Sodium per serving: 15 mgs.

SAUERKRAUT CHEESE CASSEROLE

Serves 8

4 potatoes, parboiled, peeled, and sliced
Black pepper to taste
2 tsps. low sodium chicken bouillon
¾ cup boiling water
½ tsp. onion powder

¼ tsp. mustard powder
3 ozs. low sodium Cheddar cheese, minced
1½ cups low sodium sauerkraut

Preheat oven to 350°.

Place potatoes in 9″ square oven-proof casserole. Sprinkle with pepper.

In bowl, combine bouillon, boiling water, and onion and mustard powder. Pour over potatoes. Sprinkle with cheese.

Top with sauerkraut and bake 20 minutes. Raise heat to 375° and bake 5 minutes more.

Calories per serving: 100   Sodium per serving: 17 mgs.

Greek

Vegetables are plentiful and popular in Greece. They are often found in main dishes or as part of a rice or pasta specialty. As a side dish, they are most often boiled, steamed, or braised, bathed in an olive oil and lemon sauce or cooked in a tomato base.

BAKED STUFFED AVOCADO

Serves 4

2 Tbs. unsalted butter or margarine, divided
1 leek, chopped, including greens
2 Tbs. all-purpose flour
½ cup Chicken Broth (See Page 45)
White pepper to taste
6 mushrooms, chopped
2 Tbs. dry white wine

¾ lb. any of the following: chicken, turkey, tuna, or salmon, cooked and cut into chunks
2 large, ripe avocados
4 Tbs. Vinaigrette Dressing (See Page 299), divided
2 ozs. low sodium Gouda cheese, sliced
1 tsp. paprika

Melt 1 Tbs. butter in medium saucepan. Sauté leek and reserve.

Melt remaining butter. Stir in flour till thoroughly blended.

Add Chicken Broth, pepper, mushrooms, wine, and leek. Stir till mixture thickens slightly, about 7 minutes.

Preheat oven to 375°.

Fold chicken or fish into broth mixture. Heat 3 minutes more, stirring constantly. Remove from heat.

Scoop out enough avocado to make full boat for filling. Reserve pulp. Coat boats with ½ Tbs. each Vinaigrette Dressing.

Stir avocado pulp into broth mixture. Spoon mixture into avocado boats. Top with slices of cheese, then sprinkle with paprika and remaining Vinaigrette.

Bake 10 minutes, or till cheese is completely melted.
Serve as main course with salad.

Chicken: Calories per serving: 411	Sodium per serving: 78 mgs.
Turkey: Calories per serving: 406	Sodium per serving: 78 mgs.
Tuna: Calories per serving: 348	Sodium per serving: 64 mgs.
Salmon: Calories per serving: 380	Sodium per serving: 80 mgs.

HERBED CAULIFLOWER

Serves 8

1 head cauliflower, separated into
  flowerets
3 Tbs. olive oil
3 Tbs. lemon juice
1 tsp. basil

¼ tsp. savory
1 Tbs. low sodium chicken bouillon
1 Tbs. parsley
¼ tsp. nutmeg
1 tsp. dried or fresh grated orange peel

In large saucepan, combine cauliflower with enough water to cover. Bring to a boil. Boil 15 minutes, or till cauliflower is tender/crisp. Drain. Transfer to bowl.

In small bowl, beat together remaining ingredients. Pour dressing over cauliflower, blending well.

Calories per serving: 59	Sodium per serving: 10 mgs.

MINTED CARROTS

Serves 8

6 carrots, scraped and cut into 1″ rounds
2 Tbs. unsalted butter or margarine
Black pepper to taste

1 Tbs. mint
1 tsp. Grand Marnier

In medium-size saucepan, place carrots, butter, and pepper. Cover tightly and steam over very low heat till tender when pierced with a fork, about 15 minutes, adding a small amount of water if necessary to keep from burning.

Toss with mint and Grand Marnier. Heat through 1 minute more.

Calories per serving: 53	Sodium per serving: 31 mgs.

SPINACH-RICE COMBINATION

Serves 8

1 Tbs. olive oil
2 leeks, chopped, including greens
2 cloves garlic, minced
¾ cup long grain rice
1½ lbs. spinach
1½ cups Beef Broth (See Page 44)

Black pepper to taste
¼ cup walnuts, crushed
2 tsps. low sodium beef bouillon
⅛ tsp. sage
2 lemons, cut into wedges

In large skillet, heat oil. Add leeks and garlic and cook over low heat 7 minutes, or till leeks are tender, stirring occasionally.

Stir in remaining ingredients except lemon wedges. Cover and simmer 20 minutes, or till liquid is absorbed.

Garnish with lemon wedges.

Calories per serving: 142   Sodium per serving: 73 mgs.

STUFFED TOMATOES

Serves 6

6 large tomatoes
1 Tbs. olive oil
1 medium-size onion, chopped
Black pepper to taste
3 Tbs. parsley
3 Tbs. lemon juice
1 Tbs. low sodium chicken bouillon

¼ cup walnuts, chopped
1 cup cooked rice
1 cup Beef Broth (See Page 44)
2 Tbs. dry red wine
2 tsps. cornstarch
6 Tbs. cold water

Cut ½″ top off tomatoes. Discard. Scoop out pulp and place in bowl. Chop. Set aside.

In skillet, heat oil. Add onion and pepper. Cook over low heat till onion is wilted. Stir in parsley, lemon juice, bouillon, walnuts, rice, and tomato pulp. Stir to blend. Cover and simmer 5 minutes.

Spoon rice mixture into tomatoes. Return to skillet. Pour Beef Broth all around. Cover and simmer 5 minutes. Transfer tomatoes to platter.

Stir wine into Beef Broth.

In bowl, combine cornstarch and cold water. Stir into Beef Broth and cook till mixture thickens. Pour over tomatoes.

Serve with lamb chops, broiled chicken, or hamburgers.

Calories per serving: 143   Sodium per serving: 11 mgs.

Indian

Many Indians thrive on vegetarian diets. Not only does the Indian climate provide an abundance and variety of vegetables, but the cooking techniques and seasonings turn vegetables into substantial and satisfying substitutes for meat.

Formerly, braising or steaming were the standard methods for vegetable preparation. Today, vegetables are generally cooked to a sauce-like consistency to allow full absorption of the spices—by no means tender crisp, but delicious all the same.

CURRY STUFFED SQUASH

Serves 4

2 large acorn squash, split in half
  lengthwise and seeded
1 Tbs. oil
¾ lb. ground beef
4 chili peppers, chopped
½ tsp. turmeric

¼ tsp. ground cumin
Black pepper to taste
1 medium-size onion, minced
1½ tsps. garlic powder
2 tsps. low sodium beef bouillon
Dash of ginger powder

Preheat oven to 350°.
Bake squash 30 minutes.
In skillet, heat oil. Cook meat over low heat 5 minutes, or till it loses its pink color, stirring often.
Add remaining ingredients to skillet. Cook over medium heat 2 minutes, stirring to blend well.
Spoon meat mixture into squash cavities. Cover with tin foil and bake 20 minutes more, or till squash is fork tender.
Serve as main dish with salad.

Calories per serving: 360   Sodium per serving: 64 mgs.

PEAS AND ONIONS

Serves 6

2 Tbs. unsalted butter or margarine
1½ lbs. fresh shelled peas
1 tsp. turmeric
Dash of ground cumin
Dash of ginger powder
½ tsp. ground coriander

Dash of cayenne pepper
1½ tsps. low sodium chicken bouillon
2 medium-size onions, cut into rings
3 Tbs. water
½ tsp. mustard powder

In skillet, melt butter. Add peas, turmeric, cumin, ginger, and coriander. Stir fry 5 minutes over very low heat.
Stir in cayenne and bouillon. Top with onions.
In bowl, blend water and mustard. Spoon on top of onions. Cover and simmer 5 minutes, or till peas are tender.
Toss to blend.

Calories per serving: 145   Sodium per serving: 7 mgs.

SPICE ROASTED EGGPLANT

Serves 8
(Makes 2 Cups)

1 2-lb. eggplant
½ tsp. cinnamon
½ tsp. ground cumin
Cayenne pepper to taste
¼ cup heavy cream

4 Tbs. lemon juice
1 Tbs. low sodium chicken bouillon
2 medium-size onions, minced
⅓ cup low sodium chili ketchup
1½ Tbs. mint

Preheat oven to broil.
Place eggplant on pan and broil close to heat, turning often, till scorched all around.
Run under cold water, peel, and remove stem.
Mash pulp in medium bowl. Stir in remaining ingredients. Blend thoroughly.
Cover and refrigerate up to 1 week.
Serve as side dish, relish for meats, or as an hors d'oeuvre dip.

Calories per serving: 60   Sodium per serving: 16 mgs.

Italian

In Italy, vegetables are purchased daily, chosen for their unblemished perfection. Small size is generally preferred as promising the most tender results.

Italians love their vegetables and prepare them in every way imaginable: in soups, with pasta, breaded, fried, braised, baked, stuffed. They are often featured before the main course so their flavors can be savored fully. But the simpler variations are often served as side dish accompaniments.

SPINACH WITH CHEESE SAUCE

Serves 8

2 lbs. spinach, chopped
1 Tbs. low sodium chicken bouillon
¼ tsp. garlic powder
2 Tbs. unsalted butter or margarine, melted

2 ozs. low sodium Gouda cheese, chopped
¼ cup milk

In saucepan, combine spinach with enough water to cover. Bring to a boil. Boil 5 minutes. Drain.

In blender, purée spinach with remaining ingredients. Return to saucepan. Simmer 5 minutes, stirring often, or till heated through.

Calories per serving: 81   Sodium per serving: 90 mgs.

STIR FRIED BROCCOLI

Serves 8

2 Tbs. oil
1 head broccoli, separated into flowerets, stalks cut into 1″ rounds

10 cloves garlic, minced
8 mushrooms, sliced (optional)
8 water chestnuts, sliced in half (optional)

Heat oil in large skillet. Add broccoli and garlic. Stir fry over medium heat 3 minutes, or till garlic is browned.

Stir in mushrooms and water chestnuts. Stir fry additional 2 minutes.

Serve over pasta shells cooked al dente.*

*Do not add salt to boiling water.

Without Mushrooms and Water Chestnuts:
Calories per serving: 72   Sodium per serving: 10 mgs.
With Mushrooms and Water Chestnuts:
Calories per serving: 82   Sodium per serving: 15 mgs.

ZUCCHINI AND EGGPLANT CASSEROLE

Serves 8

2 Tbs. olive oil
1 large onion, chopped
2 cloves garlic, chopped
1 green pepper, chopped
2 medium-size zucchini, chopped
1 medium-size eggplant, unpeeled,
  chopped
2 tomatoes, chopped
¼ tsp. basil

¼ tsp. oregano
¼ cup Vinaigrette Dressing (See Page
  299)
Black pepper to taste
1 can (12 ozs.) low sodium tomato juice
2 Tbs. low sodium ketchup
2 tsps. lemon juice
½ tsp. parsley

Heat oil in Dutch oven. Sauté onion, garlic, and green pepper about 4 minutes.
Stir in remaining ingredients. Simmer, stirring occasionally till mixture thickens and vegetables are soft, about 20 minutes.

Calories per serving: 92   Sodium per serving: 12 mgs.

Jewish

Vegetables in the Jewish tradition generally reflect their origin—both geographic and cultural. They range from the simply prepared offerings of Russian and Polish derivation to the more exotic delicacies of Spanish and Israeli influence.

But one thing is certain. Vegetables are always served and enjoyed as part of the main meal.

CREAMED CORN

Serves 4

2 cans (8 ozs. each) low sodium corn
  niblets, including liquid
½ cup boiling water
1 Tbs. low sodium chicken bouillon

⅛ tsp. mace
Black pepper to taste
1 tsp. tarragon
4 Tbs. heavy cream

In saucepan, combine all ingredients except cream. Cook over low heat 10 minutes.
Stir in cream. Cook 2 minutes more, stirring constantly.

Calories per serving: 127   Sodium per serving: 14 mgs.

HONEYED CARROTS

Serves 8

1 lb. carrots, scraped and cut into
  1″ rounds
1 cup water
2 Tbs. cornstarch

¼ cup cold water
¼ cup honey
Dash of ginger
1 Tbs. dried or fresh grated orange peel

   In saucepan, combine carrots and 1 cup water. Cover and simmer 20 minutes.
   In bowl, combine cornstarch and cold water. Stir into carrots. Add remaining
ingredients. Cook over low heat 10 minutes more.

Calories per serving: 51   Sodium per serving: 28 mgs.

MUSHROOMS AND LEEKS

Serves 4

2 Tbs. unsalted butter or margarine
2 leeks, chopped, including greens
8 mushrooms, sliced
2 cloves garlic, minced
Black pepper to taste

2 tsps. low sodium chicken bouillon
⅛ tsp. nutmeg
1 Tbs. dry sherry
1 tsp. lemon juice

   In skillet, melt butter. Add leeks and cook over low heat 2 minutes, stirring
occasionally.
   Stir in mushrooms, garlic, pepper, and bouillon. Cook 2 minutes more, stirring
occasionally.
   Stir in remaining ingredients. Cook 2 minutes more, stirring often.

Calories per serving: 79   Sodium per serving: 13 mgs.

Mexican

Mexicans like their vegetables as part of a potpourri—in combination with each other, with cheese or fruit. They are generally served before rather than with the main course, unless they are blended into a stew.

CORN AND CHEESE BAKE

Serves 6

3 cans (8 ozs. each) low sodium corn
 niblets, including liquid
2 medium-size onions, minced
2 tsps. mustard powder
1 chili pepper, chopped

1 Tbs. dry sherry
1 Tbs. low sodium chicken bouillon
2 ozs. low sodium Cheddar cheese,
 chopped fine
1½ tsps. paprika

Preheat oven to 325°.
Combine first 6 ingredients in oven-proof casserole. Cover and bake 10 minutes. Uncover and bake 5 minutes more.
Top casserole with cheese, then paprika. Bake 5 minutes more, or till cheese is completely melted.

Calories per serving: 127	Sodium per serving: 14 mgs.

PEAS AND ALMONDS

Serves 6

1 Tbs. olive oil
2 Tbs. sliced almonds
6 scallions, chopped, including greens
1 lb. fresh shelled peas

1½ cups boiling water
1 tsp. sugar
Black pepper to taste
1 Tbs. low sodium chicken bouillon

In saucepan, heat oil. Add almonds and cook over medium/low heat 5 minutes. Stir in scallions and cook 2 minutes more.
Add peas, water, and sugar. Cover and cook over medium heat 15 minutes, or till peas are tender. Drain. Transfer to bowl. Stir in pepper and bouillon, blending thoroughly.

Calories per serving: 107	Sodium per serving: 6 mgs.

Spanish

Vegetables do not usually accompany the main meal, unless they are an integral part of it. Instead, they are served as a first course or as the entire entree.

BRAISED LIMA BEANS

Serves 8

1 Tbs. olive oil
2 Tbs. unsalted butter or margarine
6 Tbs. water
1 medium-size onion, minced
1½ lbs. fresh shelled lima beans

1 Tbs. low sodium chicken bouillon
1 tsp. oregano
Dash of black pepper
Dash of cayenne pepper

In skillet, heat oil, butter, and water. Add onion and beans. Cover and simmer 15 minutes, or till beans are tender.
Stir in remaining ingredients.

Calories per serving: 155	Sodium per serving: 8 mgs.

FRIED CAULIFLOWER

Serves 6

½ cup water
1 small onion, minced
4 Tbs. cider vinegar
1 tsp. sugar
4 tsps. low sodium beef bouillon
1 head cauliflower, separated into
  flowerets
¼ cup all-purpose flour

2 eggs, beaten
2 Tbs. lemon juice
½ cup low sodium Bread Crumbs (See
  Page 291)
White pepper to taste
¾ tsp. garlic powder
¾ tsp. nutmeg
½ cup olive oil

In large bowl, combine water, onion, vinegar, sugar, and bouillon. Marinate flowerets 45 minutes. Drain.
In second bowl, put flour. Stir in eggs. Then stir in lemon juice. Set aside.
In large flat dish, combine Bread Crumbs and remaining ingredients except oil. Blend well.

Heat a third of the oil in large skillet.

Dip flowerets in batter, then in crumbs. Fry till brown on all sides, adding more oil as necessary.

Calories per serving: 142   Sodium per serving: 39 mgs.

GREEN BEANS AND PEPPERS

Serves 6

1 Tbs. olive oil
4 cloves garlic, minced
1 red pepper, chopped
1 Tbs. lemon juice
1½ lbs. green beans, chopped, steamed,
  and drained

½ tsp. sugar
Dash of nutmeg
Dash of cayenne pepper
1½ Tbs. low sodium chicken bouillon
1 Tbs. parsley

In skillet, heat oil. Add garlic and cook over low heat 5 minutes, stirring often.

Add remaining ingredients. Stir to blend. Cook over low heat 5 minutes, stirring occasionally.

Calories per serving: 75   Sodium per serving: 13 mgs.

POTATOES, PASTA, RICE, BEANS, AND STUFFING

What do potatoes, pasta, beans, and rice have in common? They're all starches, carbohydrates. Carbohydrates—that food group so much and so unfairly maligned. Let's destroy the first myth: Carbohydrates are not fattening. A calorie is a calorie is a calorie. Your body can't tell one kind from another. It only knows when it has too many and passes the word on to you.

Carbohydrates are good for you. They feed the brain and nerve tissues, and you should include them in your daily diet unless your doctor advises against it for specific medical reasons. In fact, the average diet should contain more carbohydrates than either of the other key nutrients, proteins and fats. That is, 45 to 50% carbohydrates, no more than 12 to 20% protein, and a maximum of 35% fats.

When you deprive the body of carbohydrates—or any basic food group—the body starts to flush out fluid, sometimes to such excess that you run the risk of becoming malnourished, overworking and damaging your kidneys, and putting unnatural stress on your heart. That's why so many of the popular food diets warn you not to follow them for more than two weeks. And that's why 95% of all people who lose weight on such diets regain it in a matter of months. But by eliminating (or reducing) salt, and properly balancing what you eat, your body automatically controls and depletes excess water safely, till a natural fluid balance is achieved and fat melts away to reveal the real, slim you.

We hope by now your intellectual aversion to starches is gone. For there's no denying how good they are. Which would you rather have: a baked potato, three-quarters of a cup of baked beans, rice, or spaghetti, or four tablespoons of cottage cheese? Tell the truth because they all have the same number of calories.

No matter how you prepare them, with whatever ingredients you choose, they taste delicious. All you have to do is decide what will taste best with your main meal and be best for you. Just remember, the idea is to enjoy only one starch at a time. That's why if you want Potatoes au Gratin (page 265), have them, by all means, but not with Spaghetti and Meatballs (page 275).

257

One important thing to note: Never add salt to any cooking liquid during preparation.

Now that you have the idea, never again do you have to deny yourself the pleasure of pan roasted potatoes, Saffron Rice (See Page 266), or Refried Beans (See Page 279). You can even tell yourself that you're doing something good for your body and know you're not rationalizing.

American

Americans love potatoes, any shape, any style, anyhow. But old-fashioned baked beans or a savory rice, while served less often, frequently find their way to the American table.

BAKED BEANS

Serves 14

1 lb. navy or pinto beans
6 cups water
1 medium-size onion, minced
¾ cup molasses

¾ cup low sodium ketchup
¾ cup sugar
2 tsps. dry mustard powder

Soak beans in water 4 to 5 hours or overnight.
Bring beans to a boil in water in which they were soaked. Simmer over medium heat till almost tender.
Drain, reserving liquid.
Preheat oven to 250°.
Place beans and remaining ingredients in 2-quart casserole.
Stir in 1 cup reserved liquid, adding enough to cover beans.
Cover and bake till beans are tender, 3½ to 4 hours, adding more liquid when necessary to keep sauce from drying up.

Calories per serving: 194   Sodium per serving: 32 mgs.

BREAD STUFFING

Serves 10
(Makes enough to loosely stuff a 4- to 5-lb. bird)

2 Tbs. unsalted butter or margarine
3 medium-size onions, chopped
Black pepper to taste
1½ tsps. thyme
½ Tbs. sage

1¼ cups warm water
2 Tbs. low sodium chicken bouillon
12 slices low sodium bread, toasted and
    cubed
¼ cup raisins*

*Preserved in non-sodium ingredient

In skillet, melt butter. Add onions, pepper, thyme, and sage. Sauté till onions turn dark golden brown.
   Add water and bouillon to bread cubes, stirring to thoroughly moisten. Stir in raisins.
   Makes enough to loosely stuff a 4- to 5-lb. bird. Or wrap loosely in tin foil and bake at 350° 45 minutes.
   Serve with fish or fowl.

Calories per serving: 182   Sodium per serving: 25 mgs.

CHEESE STUFFED POTATOES

Serves 6

3 baking potatoes, gashed down the
    center
1½ tsps. dill
2 tsps. parsley
Black pepper to taste
2 Tbs. sweet pepper flakes

¼ cup water
2 tsps. low sodium chicken bouillon
2 ozs. low sodium Cheddar cheese, diced
½ tsp. mustard powder (optional)
1 Tbs. paprika

Preheat oven to 350°.
   Bake potatoes till tender. Remove from oven. Split in half. Leaving skins intact, scoop out potatoes and mash in bowl.
   Stir in dill, parsley, and pepper, blending well.
   In bowl, combine pepper flakes and water. Let stand 10 minutes. Stir in bouillon.
   Stir pepper flakes mixture into mashed potatoes. Stir in cheese and mustard powder. Stuff mixture into shells.
   Sprinkle paprika on potato halves. Place on shallow baking sheet and bake at 350° 20 minutes, or till browned on top.

Calories per serving: 98   Sodium per serving: 7 mgs.

OYSTER-RICE DRESSING

Serves 10

2 cups water or Chicken Broth (See Page 45)
1½ cups long grain rice
2 pts. oysters, drained, liquid reserved
8 tsps. low sodium chicken bouillon
1½ Tbs. unsalted butter or margarine, divided
1 Tbs. oil

2 leeks or 2 small onions, chopped
⅛ tsp. nutmeg
½ tsp. dried or fresh grated orange peel
¼ tsp. rosemary, crushed
2 tsps. tarragon
½ tsp. garlic powder, divided
¼ tsp. black pepper, divided
3 Tbs. lemon juice

In medium-size saucepan, combine water, rice, and oyster liquid. Bring to a boil and continue to boil 2 minutes.

Reduce heat to low. Cover pan and simmer 5 minutes.

After 5 minutes, stir in bouillon. Cover and simmer 10 minutes more, or till liquid is absorbed. Set aside.

While rice is cooking, melt ½ Tbs. butter and 1 Tbs. oil in medium-size skillet. Add leeks and cook over low heat 5 minutes, stirring occasionally.

Add nutmeg, orange peel, rosemary, tarragon, and half the garlic powder and pepper. Stir well and continue to fry till leeks are golden. Remove and stir into rice mixture.

Preheat oven to 350°.

Using same skillet, melt remaining Tbs. butter. Add oysters. Sprinkle with remaining garlic powder and pepper and fry over high heat for 30 seconds. Chop.

Add lemon juice and fry 30 seconds more.

Remove from heat and stir into rice mixture.

Turn mixture into 2-quart oven-proof casserole. Cover and bake till heated through, about 30 minutes.

With Water: Calories per serving: 197   Sodium per serving: 69 mgs.
With Chicken Broth: Calories per serving: 208   Sodium per serving: 73 mgs.

POTATO SALAD

Serves 8

3 potatoes, parboiled, peeled, and cubed
6 Tbs. low sodium mayonnaise
4½ Tbs. white vinegar
2½ tsps. sugar
1 small onion, minced
½ green pepper, chopped

½ red pepper, chopped
Black pepper to taste
⅛ tsp. garlic powder
⅛ tsp. mustard powder
2 Tbs. fresh chopped parsley

In bowl, combine all ingredients. Toss to blend thoroughly. Cover and refrigerate at least 6 hours before serving to allow flavors to blend.

Calories per serving: 121	Sodium per serving: 9 mgs.

Chinese

Although rice is a staple long associated with Chinese food, in China, it is common in the southern regions. There, rice is usually served boiled to accompany a main meal.

In the north, where the climate is unfavorable for growing rice, wheat is the primary meal supplement. From the northern regions come the delectable buns, dumplings, lo mein, and crunchy fried noodles so loved as Chinese specialties.

While potatoes and beans are not part of the Chinese diet, bean curd (tofu) is found all over China, and indeed is a source of protein for most of the Orient.

BEAN CURD SPECIALTY

Serves 8

4 Tbs. oil
4 squares bean curd, sliced
2 Tbs. low sodium beef bouillon
1 Tbs. dry sherry
½ tsp. sugar
4 mushrooms, sliced

1 tomato, chopped
1 clove garlic, minced
Dash of ginger powder
1 green pepper, chopped
2 peaches, pitted and chopped

In wok or skillet, heat oil. Add bean curd and stir fry till lightly browned. Transfer to bowl.

To wok, add remaining ingredients except peaches. Stir fry 2 minutes.

Add peaches and bean curd. Stir fry 1 minute more.

Calories per serving: 108	Sodium per serving: 16 mgs.

LO MEIN WITH PORK SHREDS

Serves 8

½ lb. lo mein noodles or vermicelli,
 cooked al dente*
1 Tbs. sesame oil
1 medium-size onion, minced
½ lb. snow pea pods, chopped
1 lb. fresh bean sprouts
1 Tbs. red wine vinegar
¼ medium-size head cabbage, shredded

1 Tbs. dry sherry
¼ lb. roast pork, cut into shreds
1 tsp. sugar
½ cup boiling water
¼ tsp. mustard powder
1½ Tbs. low sodium beef bouillon
Dash of ginger powder

Do not add salt to boiling water.

Place noodles in casserole. Place in oven to keep warm.
In wok or large skillet, heat oil. Add onion and pea pods. Stir fry 1 minute over medium heat.
Stir in bean sprouts, vinegar, and cabbage. Stir fry 2 minutes over low heat.
Push cabbage mixture to side. Add sherry and pork. Stir fry 1 minute.
Add boiling water, mustard, bouillon, and ginger. Cook over medium heat 5 minutes.
Remove noodles from oven. Combine with pork mixture. Toss to blend.

Calories per serving: 216   Sodium per serving: 28 mgs.

NOODLES IN HOT PEANUT SAUCE

Serves 8

1 cup Beef Broth (See Page 44)
1 star anise
Coarse black pepper to taste
1 Tbs. Chili Oil (See Page 286)
1 tsp. minced ginger root or dash of
 ginger powder
3 cloves garlic, minced

1 Tbs. dry sherry
2 scallions, chopped, including greens
Dash of hot pepper flakes
2 Tbs. sesame seed
2 tsps. peanuts, crushed
½ lb. vermicelli

In saucepan, combine all ingredients except vermicelli. Simmer 20 minutes.
In second saucepan, cook vermicelli al dente.* Drain. Transfer to bowl.
Pour sauce over vermicelli. Toss to blend well.

Do not add salt to boiling water.

Calories per serving: 140   Sodium per serving: 6 mgs.

VEGETABLE FRIED RICE

Serves 10

You may add ¼ lb. leftover pork or chicken, chopped, when frying vegetables.

4 Tbs. sesame oil, divided
2 large onions, diced
2 cloves garlic, minced
Black pepper to taste
Dash of ginger powder
¼ tsp. mustard powder
½ lb. snow pea pods, chopped
1 can (8 ozs.) water chestnuts, chopped
½ green pepper, chopped

½ red pepper, chopped
½ lb. fresh bean sprouts
1 zucchini, chopped
3 cups cooked rice, chilled
1 Tbs. cider vinegar
½ cup boiling water
3 Tbs. low sodium beef bouillon
2 eggs, lightly beaten
4 scallions, chopped, including greens

In wok or large skillet, heat 2 Tbs. oil. Add onions and garlic and cook over low heat 7 minutes, stirring occasionally. Stir in black pepper, ginger, and mustard.

Stir in pea pods, water chestnuts, green pepper, red pepper, and bean sprouts. Stir fry 2 minutes.

Push vegetables to sides. Add zucchini and stir fry 1 minute. Push to the side.

Add remaining 2 Tbs. oil and the rice. Stir fry 2 minutes. Add vinegar. Stir fry 1 minute more.

In bowl, combine boiling water and bouillon. Stir into rice mixture and blend in vegetables. Cook over high heat 2 minutes, stirring constantly.

Push mixture to sides. Add eggs. When eggs start to set, break up with fork and blend into rice mixture.

Stir in scallions and stir fry 2 minutes more.

Plain: Calories per serving: 201
Pork: Calories per serving: 232
Chicken: Calories per serving: 222

Sodium per serving: 33 mgs.
Sodium per serving: 41 mgs.
Sodium per serving: 41 mgs.

French

Potatoes are a favorite vegetable in France. They are savored fried, creamed, sauced, boiled, and baked with that soupçon of French to distinguish them. Rice and beans, while less common in French cuisine, nonetheless are prepared with the same flair, the former most often found in soufflés and desserts, the latter, rounding out a stew or cassoulet. But pasta is most often reserved for garnishing.

BROWN RICE AND WALNUTS

Serves 10

1 Tbs. unsalted butter or margarine
6 mushrooms, chopped
½ medium-size onion, minced
Black pepper to taste
¼ cup walnuts, crushed

1⅔ cups long grain rice
3⅔ cups boiling water
¼ cup dry sherry
3 Tbs. low sodium beef bouillon

In saucepan, melt butter. Add mushrooms and onion. Cook over low heat 5 minutes, stirring occasionally.
Stir in pepper, walnuts, and rice.
In bowl, combine remaining ingredients. Add to rice mixture. Bring to a boil. Cover. Reduce heat and simmer till liquid is absorbed.

Calories per serving: 161   Sodium per serving: 17 mgs.

DUCHESS POTATOES WITH ONION

Serves 8

4 large potatoes, parboiled, peeled, and
  chopped
1 medium-size onion, minced
2 Tbs. unsalted butter or margarine
1 Tbs. low sodium chicken bouillon

White pepper to taste
⅛ tsp. nutmeg
2 eggs
2 tsps. paprika

Force potatoes and onion through a food mill. Cream in remaining ingredients except paprika.
Preheat oven to broil.
Pipe potato mixture through a pastry tube into a pie plate. Sprinkle with paprika. Run under the broiler till top is browned and crispy.

Calories per serving: 99   Sodium per serving: 19 mgs.

KIDNEY BEANS IN BURGUNDY

Serves 14

1 lb. kidney beans
1 Tbs. olive oil
1 medium-size onion, minced
2 cloves garlic, minced
2 cups water
2 cups red Burgundy wine

1 tsp. thyme
Black pepper to taste
2 Tbs. parsley
8 small white onions, peeled
2 carrots, scraped and cut into 1″ pieces
2 Tbs. low sodium beef bouillon

In large bowl, combine beans with water to cover. Soak overnight. Drain. Set aside.
In Dutch oven, heat oil. Add onion and garlic. Cook over low heat 5 minutes.
Add beans and all remaining ingredients except onions, carrots, and bouillon. Cover and simmer 1½ hours.
Add remaining ingredients. Stir to blend. Cover and simmer 1½ hours more, adding additional water or wine if necessary to keep beans from sticking.

Calories per serving: 168   Sodium per serving: 14 mgs.

POTATOES AU GRATIN

Serves 8

6 medium potatoes, boiled till easily
   pierced by fork but not mashing soft
1 Tbs. unsalted butter or margarine
1 Tbs. all-purpose flour
1½ cups water
½ cup heavy cream or milk

8 tsps. low sodium chicken bouillon
½ tsp. onion powder
Black pepper to taste
4 ozs. low sodium Cheddar cheese,
   cubed
1 tsp. paprika

Peel potatoes and cut in cubes. Place in 9″ square oven-proof casserole.
In medium-size saucepan, melt butter. Stir in flour till butter is absorbed.
Add water, cream, and bouillon. Cook over low heat, stirring constantly, till thickened.
Preheat oven to 350°.
Stir into cream sauce the onion powder, pepper, and cheese. Heat, stirring occasionally, till cheese is dissolved. Pour over potatoes.
Sprinkle top with paprika and bake till bubbling and brown on top, about 3 minutes.

With Cream: Calories per serving: 210   Sodium per serving: 15 mgs.
With Milk: Calories per serving: 167   Sodium per serving: 22 mgs.

SAFFRON RICE

Serves 8

1 Tbs. unsalted butter or margarine
1 medium-size onion, minced
1 clove garlic, minced
1¼ cups long grain rice
2½ cups Chicken Broth (See Page 45)
¼ tsp. saffron threads

⅛ tsp. thyme
2 tsps. tarragon
White pepper to taste
2 ozs. low sodium Monterey Jack cheese, minced

In saucepan, melt butter. Add onion and garlic and cook over low heat 7 minutes, stirring occasionally.

Stir in rice, coating thoroughly. Add Chicken Broth, saffron, thyme, tarragon, and pepper. Cover and simmer over low heat 20 minutes, or till liquid is absorbed.

Add cheese. Toss to blend. Cover and let stand 5 minutes.

Calories per serving: 174   Sodium per serving: 15 mgs.

German

Potatoes are almost as popular in Germany as sauerkraut and cabbage. They are, in fact, prepared in every way imaginable: mashed, boiled, creamed; in dumplings, pancakes, salads—served hot or cold.

Beans and rice are not traditional offerings at the German table, although the latter is often served, baked with fruit, for dessert.

But spatzle, very similar to Italian pasta in taste and texture, is so hearty it often suffices as the main meal when prepared in combination with vegetables. Noodles are an integral part of such German specialties as goulash, as well as being featured, usually in combination with another ingredient, as a relished side dish.

CARAWAY CREAM POTATOES

Serves 6

2 cups boiling water
4 potatoes, peeled
2 bay leaves
2 tsps. low sodium beef bouillon
1 tsp. low sodium chicken bouillon

2 Tbs. cider vinegar
1 Tbs. parsley
½ cup sour cream*
1 tsp. caraway seed

*Preserved in non-sodium ingredient

In saucepan, combine first 3 ingredients. Boil till potatoes are tender. Drain, and discard bay leaves. Transfer potatoes to bowl and slice.
Stir in remaining ingredients, blending well.

Calories per serving: 94   Sodium per serving: 16 mgs.

NOODLES AND CABBAGE

Serves 8

1 medium-size head cabbage, shredded
4 cups water
½ cup dried apricots, chopped
2 Tbs. cider vinegar

1½ Tbs. sugar
1 Tbs. low sodium beef bouillon
2 Tbs. parsley
½ lb. noodles, cooked al dente*

Do not add salt to boiling water.

In saucepan, combine cabbage and water. Bring to a boil. Cover. Reduce heat and simmer 10 minutes. Add apricots. Cover and simmer 10 minutes more. Drain.
Stir in vinegar, sugar, bouillon, and parsley. Transfer to bowl. Add noodles. Toss to blend thoroughly.

Calories per serving: 152   Sodium per serving: 22 mgs.

POTATOES WITH HORSERADISH

Serves 6

6 potatoes, parboiled, peeled, and
   mashed
1 Tbs. unsalted butter or margarine
Black pepper to taste
¼ cup milk

1½ Tbs. sour cream*
1 Tbs. White Horseradish (See Page 290)
2 tsps. dill
1 Tbs. parsley
⅛ tsp. mustard powder

Preserved in non-sodium ingredient

In bowl, beat together all ingredients, blending thoroughly.

Calories per serving: 136   Sodium per serving: 16 mgs.

SOUR POTATOES

Serves 6

3 potatoes, parboiled, peeled, and sliced
2 bay leaves
¼ tsp. thyme
1 cup boiling water
1 Tbs. low sodium chicken bouillon

Black pepper to taste
1 Tbs. cider vinegar
2 Tbs. heavy cream
1 lemon, cut into wedges

Preheat oven to 375°.
Place potatoes in 9″ pie plate, overlapping if necessary. Add bay leaves.
In bowl, combine thyme, boiling water, bouillon, pepper, and vinegar. Pour over potatoes. Cover and bake 15 minutes. Stir in cream. Discard bay leaves.
Garnish with lemon wedges.

Calories per serving: 75   Sodium per serving: 8 mgs.

Greek

Potatoes and pasta are popular in Greece, often as part of a main dish, or in combination with other vegetables. Rice is clearly the favorite side dish, but it, too, is generally prepared with a cheese or vegetable mixture.

MACARONI WITH NUTMEG

Serves 8

½ lb. low sodium cottage cheese
4 tsps. low sodium chicken bouillon
Black pepper to taste
¹⁄₁₆ tsp. nutmeg

¼ cup heavy cream
¾ lb. macaroni, cooked al dente*
2 ozs. low sodium Monterey Jack cheese, minced fine

Do not add salt to boiling water.

In bowl, combine cottage cheese, bouillon, pepper, and nutmeg, blending thoroughly. Beat in the cream.
Toss with the macaroni and cheese.

Calories per serving: 240   Sodium per serving: 17 mgs.

POTATO AND SPINACH CASSEROLE

Serves 8

4 potatoes, parboiled, peeled, and sliced
¼ tsp. black pepper, divided
¼ tsp. mustard powder, divided
2 tsps. cider vinegar, divided
1 lb. spinach, chopped

1½ cups water
1 Tbs. lemon juice
¼ tsp. cinnamon
1 Tbs. low sodium chicken bouillon, divided

Place half the potatoes in oven-proof casserole. Sprinkle with half the pepper, mustard, and vinegar.

In saucepan, combine spinach and water. Bring to a boil. Cover. Reduce heat and simmer 10 minutes. Drain.

Preheat oven to 350°.

In bowl, combine spinach, lemon juice, and cinnamon, blending thoroughly. Spoon half the spinach mixture over potatoes. Sprinkle with half the bouillon.

Add remaining potatoes. Sprinkle with remaining pepper, mustard, and vinegar. Top with remaining spinach mixture, then bouillon. Cover and bake 30 minutes.

Calories per serving: 67   Sodium per serving: 45 mgs.

POTATOES IN TOMATO SAUCE

Serves 4

1 Tbs. unsalted butter or margarine
3 potatoes, parboiled, peeled, and cubed
2 tsps. low sodium beef bouillon
2 Tbs. lemon juice

1 can (16 ozs.) low sodium tomatoes, chopped, including liquid
Black pepper to taste

In large skillet, melt butter. Add potatoes and cook over low heat 10 minutes, stirring often. Stir in bouillon and lemon juice.

Add tomatoes. Bring to a boil. Reduce heat. Stir in pepper and cook over medium heat 10 minutes.

Calories per serving: 128   Sodium per serving: 30 mgs.

RICE AND CUCUMBERS

Serves 6

1½ tsps. dried or fresh grated orange
  peel
1 cup long grain rice
2 cups Chicken Broth (See Page 45)

1 tsp. green peppercorns*, crushed
1 cucumber, scraped and diced
1 Tbs. low sodium beef bouillon

Natural green peppercorns, packed in water or vinegar

In saucepan, combine first 4 ingredients. Bring to a boil. Cover. Reduce heat and simmer 15 minutes, or till liquid is absorbed.
Stir in cucumber and bouillon. Cover. Let stand 5 minutes.

Calories per serving: 149   Sodium per serving: 19 mgs.

Indian

In India, rice nourishes well over half of the population. It is no wonder, then, that it is an integral part of Indian cooking. Rice is prized throughout India and preferred, far and away, to potatoes and pasta. It is served boiled, steamed, baked; with spices, vegetables, and broths; sweet for dessert or as a main course pilau—to the Indian what paella is to the Spanish.

Dals are lentils, eaten daily in most Indian homes. Like rice, they often serve as main dishes for the poor, varied by the method of cooking, as well as by the different spices and vegetables that flavor them.

Pasta is generally unknown in India. But potatoes are wonderfully prepared, sparked with herbs and spices unfamiliar to the American palate, but quickly savored for their tantalizing flavors, ranging from hot and spicy to sweet and sour.

CURRIED RICE

Serves 8

1¼ cups long grain rice
2½ cups water
12 prunes, pitted and chopped
¼ tsp. Curry Powder (See Page 288)
Dash of ginger powder

⅛ tsp. dried or fresh grated orange peel
Dash of white pepper
1 tsp. turmeric
2 Tbs. low sodium chicken bouillon
3 scallions, chopped, including greens

270

Put rice and water in medium-size saucepan. Bring to a boil. Reduce heat to simmer. Cover and cook for 10 minutes.

Add prunes, seasonings, and bouillon. Stir thoroughly. Cover and cook till water is absorbed.

Stir in scallions.

Calories per serving: 127	Sodium per serving: 10 mgs.

DRY POTATOES

Serves 6

2 Tbs. oil, divided
1 tsp. fennel seed
½ tsp. cumin seed
1 tsp. mustard seed
¼ tsp. fenugreek (optional)
Dash of hot pepper flakes

6 potatoes, boiled, well cooled, peeled,
  and cubed
6 Tbs. lemon juice
1 Tbs. low sodium beef bouillon
1 Tbs. turmeric

In wok or skillet, heat 2 tsps. oil. Add as follows: fennel, cumin, mustard seed, and fenugreek. Stir fry briefly.

Add pepper flakes and remaining oil.

Add potatoes and stir 1 minute.

Add lemon juice. Raise heat to high and stir fry till liquid is almost absorbed.

Stir in bouillon and turmeric. Stir fry 1 minute more.

Calories per serving: 145	Sodium per serving: 10 mgs.

LENTILS IN CHILI CREAM

Serves 6

1 cup lentils
2 quarts water
1 Tbs. cider vinegar
1 tsp. chopped ginger root or dash of
  ginger powder

2 bay leaves
2 tomatoes, chopped
1 carrot, scraped and cut into 1″ rounds
½ cup milk
½ tsp. chili powder*

Prepared without salt

In saucepan, combine lentils and water. Soak overnight. Add vinegar, ginger, and bay leaves. Simmer 2½ hours, or till lentils are tender. Drain. Discard ginger and bay leaves.

Add remaining ingredients. Stir to blend. Cover and simmer over low heat 30 minutes.

Calories per serving: 134	Sodium per serving: 22 mgs.

SWEET RICE WITH CARROTS

Serves 10

2 Tbs. unsalted butter or margarine
2 carrots, scraped and grated
1 medium-size onion, minced
2 Tbs. sugar
3 cups Chicken Broth (See Page 45)
2 tsps. low sodium chicken bouillon
1/16 tsp. allspice

1/4 tsp. mace
1/8 tsp. cinnamon
1/8 tsp. nutmeg
1½ cups long grain rice
1 tsp. dried or fresh grated orange peel
1 Tbs. shredded coconut

In skillet, melt butter. Add carrots and onion and cook over low heat 10 minutes, stirring occasionally. Set aside.

In saucepan, melt sugar. When it starts to brown, stir in remaining ingredients, including vegetable mixture. Bring to a boil. Cover. Reduce heat and simmer 15 minutes, or till liquid is absorbed. Toss to blend. Cover and let stand 5 minutes.

Calories per serving: 174   Sodium per serving: 19 mgs.

Italian

Although Italians take a proprietary pride in pasta, they serve it to whet rather than satisfy the appetite. Accordingly, pasta is usually eaten before the main meal in smaller quantities than arrive on the American plate.

Pasta is best served al dente and hot from the pot, well drained but not rinsed.

Rice is especially popular in the northern regions and was once the express privilege of the rich. Today it is traditionally served as a separate course or as a risotto —a rice main dish studded with numerous varieties of meat, fish, or poultry and simmered to succulence with Italian herbs.

Potatoes are not the staple in Italy they are in America. Beans are found most often in the thick, hearty Italian soups.

POTATOES STUFFED WITH LIVERS

Serves 8

A wonderful side dish with chicken or fish.

4 large potatoes, baked
1 Tbs. unsalted butter or margarine
2 cloves garlic, minced

½ lb. mushrooms, sliced
Black pepper to taste
2 Tbs. parsley

(continued next page)

¼ lb. chicken livers, chopped
2 tsps. low sodium chicken bouillon
Dash of cayenne pepper

⅛ tsp. nutmeg
2 Tbs. dry red wine

Scoop potato from shells, being careful not to break shells. In bowl, mash potatoes. Set aside.

In skillet, melt butter. Add garlic and mushrooms. Cook over low heat 5 minutes, stirring occasionally. Stir in black pepper and parsley. Cook 1 minute more. Add to potatoes.

In same skillet, cook chicken livers over low heat till they lose their pink color. Stir in bouillon, cayenne, nutmeg, and wine. Add to potato mixture. Stir to blend well.

Preheat oven to 350°.

Stuff potato shells with potato mixture. Place shells on baking sheet and bake 20 minutes, or till heated through.

Calories per serving: 91   Sodium per serving: 28 mgs.

RAVIOLI

Serves 6
(Makes 24 Ravioli)

4 cups all-purpose flour
2 tsps. low sodium beef bouillon

3 eggs
4 Tbs. cold lemon juice

Sift flour into bowl.

Stir in bouillon.

Make a well in the center. Add the eggs and lemon juice. Blend till ball of dough forms.

Turn onto lightly floured board and knead till very elastic, flouring surface and hands occasionally.

Cover with bowl. Let stand 20 minutes.

Divide dough in half. Roll to ⅛" thickness. Cut into 2" strips.

Place teaspoonsful of Ravioli Filling (See Page 274) along center of half the strips. Cover with remaining strips and press edges together.

Cut into 2" squares. Seal edges. Let stand 2 hours before cooking.

To cook, drop into deep boiling water to which 1 tsp. garlic powder and 2 Tbs. lemon juice have been added. Cook 7 to 8 minutes or till ravioli float to the top.

Serve as main dish with Tomato Sauce (See Page 298).

Calories per serving: 322*   Sodium per serving: 35*
Does not include Ravioli Filling

RAVIOLI FILLING

Serves 6
(Makes enough to fill 24 Ravioli)

¾ lb. beef, veal, lamb, pork, or chicken, chopped
1 small onion, minced
1 Tbs. unsalted butter or margarine
½ tsp. garlic powder
Black pepper to taste
½ tsp. oregano for beef and chicken;

¼ tsp. rosemary, crushed, for veal, lamb, or pork.
2 Tbs. low sodium Monterey Jack cheese, minced fine
¼ cup low sodium Bread Crumbs (See Page 291)
¼ tsp. nutmeg

Sauté meat and onion in butter for 3 minutes. Add all seasonings except nutmeg. Stir fry 2 minutes more.

Let cool. Add cheese, Bread Crumbs, and nutmeg.

Fill Ravioli. Follow directions for cooking Ravioli. Serve with Tomato Sauce (See Page 298).

Beef: Calories per serving: 195	Sodium per serving: 41 mgs.
Veal: Calories per serving: 122	Sodium per serving: 56 mgs.
Lamb: Calories per serving: 179	Sodium per serving: 47 mgs.
Pork: Calories per serving: 196	Sodium per serving: 44 mgs.
Chicken: Calories per serving: 114	Sodium per serving: 41 mgs.

RISOTTO

Serves 10

2 Tbs. unsalted butter or margarine
1 large onion, sliced thin
¼ cup dry white wine
1½ cups long grain rice
3 cups Beef Broth (See Page 44)
1 Tbs. low sodium ketchup
4 tsps. low sodium beef bouillon
1 Tbs. dry red wine
2 ozs. low sodium Gouda cheese, chopped

2 ozs. low sodium Cheddar cheese, chopped
2 Tbs. tarragon
3 Tbs. chives
½ tsp. turmeric
White pepper to taste
3 Tbs. heavy cream

In large skillet, melt butter. Sauté onion till golden.

Add white wine and cook over medium heat 7 minutes.

Add rice and cook, stirring occasionally, till rice starts to brown.

While rice is cooking, bring Beef Broth to a boil.

POTATOES

Add ketchup, bouillon, and red wine to broth. Blend well.
Add broth and cheese to rice. Cover and cook 20 minutes, or till liquid is absorbed.
Stir in tarragon, chives, turmeric, pepper, and cream.

Calories per serving: 214   Sodium per serving: 28 mgs.

SPAGHETTI AND MEATBALLS

Serves 8

1½ lbs. ground beef round
1½ Tbs. garlic powder
Black pepper to taste
2 tsps. basil
1½ Tbs. low sodium beef bouillon

½ tsp. marjoram
4 cups Tomato Sauce (See Page 298)
1 can (6 ozs.) low sodium tomato paste
1 lb. spaghetti, cooked al dente*

Do not add salt to boiling water.

In bowl, combine first 6 ingredients, blending thoroughly. Form into 16 meatballs.
In ungreased Dutch oven, cook meatballs over low heat 10 minutes, or till browned all over. Drain off fat.
Add Tomato Sauce. Cover and simmer 15 minutes. Add tomato paste. Stir to blend. Cover and simmer 15 minutes more, or till mixture is bubbly, stirring occasionally.
In bowl, combine spaghetti, meatballs, and sauce. Toss to blend, and serve as main dish.

Calories per serving: 467   Sodium per serving: 91 mgs.

SPAGHETTI WITH OYSTER SAUCE

Serves 4

1 Tbs. olive oil
6 cloves garlic, minced
Black pepper to taste
½ tsp. basil
½ tsp. oregano
1 Tbs. parsley

2 pts. oysters, drained and chopped, liquid reserved
¼ cup boiling water
1 tsp. low sodium chicken bouillon
½ lb. spaghetti, cooked al dente*

Do not add salt to boiling water.

In saucepan, heat oil. Add garlic and cook over low heat 10 minutes, or till garlic is golden brown, stirring occasionally.
Stir in all remaining ingredients except spaghetti. Cover and cook over low heat 10 minutes, stirring occasionally. Stir in reserved oyster liquid.

In bowl, combine spaghetti and oyster mixture, tossing to blend.
Serve as main dish with Baked Dill Tomatoes (See Page 236) and salad.

Calories per serving: 383   Sodium per serving: 152 mgs.

Jewish

When one thinks of potatoes in the Jewish tradition, Potato Latkes (See Page 277) come wonderfully to mind. Jewish cooking is, after all, very much meat and potato basics.

But, of course, from their Austrian and German ancestry, Jews inherited a love for noodles and other pastas. Their enjoyment of rice is inherited as well, perhaps from the Sephardic Jews.

In any case, one thing is sure: Jewish people love their potatoes, their pasta, their rice, and their beans. Not to mention stuffings.

CHEESE NOODLE PUDDING

Serves 16

½ lb. medium-size noodles, cooked al
  dente*
1½ lbs. low sodium cottage cheese
⅔ cup sour cream**
½ cup unsalted butter or margarine,
  melted
¼ cup sugar
3 eggs, beaten

2 tsps. low sodium chicken bouillon
½ cup raisins** (optional)
½ tsp. cinnamon
¼ tsp. dried or fresh grated orange peel
1 tsp. vanilla extract
1 can (8 ozs.) peaches or crushed
  pineapple, drained

*Do not add salt to boiling water.
**Preserved in non-sodium ingredient

Preheat oven to 350°.
Grease a 9″ square oven-proof casserole.
In large bowl, combine all ingredients. Blend well.
Pour mixture into casserole. Bake 1 hour, or till firm and golden on top.

With Raisins: Calories per serving: 183   Sodium per serving: 34 mgs.
Without Raisins: Calories per serving: 170   Sodium per serving: 32 mgs.

POTATO LATKES

Serves 10

4 large potatoes, peeled and grated fine
2 medium-size onions, peeled and grated
 fine
1 egg
Coarse black pepper to taste

¼ tsp. garlic powder
2 Tbs. matzo meal
2 Tbs. low sodium chicken bouillon
¾ tsp. low sodium baking powder
4 Tbs. oil, divided

In medium bowl, combine all ingredients except oil, blending well.
In large skillet, heat 2 Tbs. oil. Drop potato mixture by full tablespoons into skillet.
Brown both sides over medium heat, adding more oil as necessary.
Drain on paper towels.
Serve with sour cream or apple sauce.

Calories per serving: 119	Sodium per serving: 13 mgs.

RICE, LEEKS, AND RAISINS

Serves 8

1 Tbs. unsalted butter or margarine
3 leeks, chopped, including greens
1½ cups brown rice
3¾ cups water

3 Tbs. low sodium beef bouillon
¼ cup raisins*
Black pepper to taste

Preserved in non-sodium ingredient

In saucepan, melt butter. Add leeks and sauté 5 minutes, stirring occasionally.
Stir in remaining ingredients. Bring to a boil. Cover. Reduce heat and simmer 25
minutes, or till liquid is absorbed.

Calories per serving: 171	Sodium per serving: 24 mgs.

SWEET POTATO STUFFING

Serves 8
(Makes enough to stuff a 5-lb. bird)

6 baked yams
½ cup long grain rice
1 green apple, peeled, cored, and
 chopped

1 tsp. cinnamon
1 tsp. sage
1 tsp. tarragon
1 tsp. parsley

Coarse black pepper to taste
3 Tbs. lemon juice
½ tsp. dried or fresh grated lemon peel

½ tsp. dried or fresh grated orange peel
¼ cup chopped walnuts (optional)

Cool potatoes, then scoop out pulp and mash.
Stir in remaining ingredients, blending thoroughly.
Lightly stuff chicken, duck, or turkey.

With walnuts:
Calories per serving: 177
Without walnuts:
Calories per serving: 152

Sodium per serving: 2 mgs.

Sodium per serving: 1 mg.

Mexican

Of all the foods of Mexico, beans are given their due here as in no other country. They are served at every meal, in every fashion. And if, as some claim, there are 100 varieties of beans, you'll find them, at one time or another, in the Mexican home. Often, they are also between meal snacks, particularly the refried beans.

Rice is eaten almost as often as a side dish, along with beans; as an arroz (Mexico's answer to Spain's paella); cooked with vegetables, fruits, or just served plain or spiced with Mexican flavors.

Potatoes and pasta are somewhat afterthoughts in Mexican fare, but when served, hold the aromatic promise of those spicy and succulent tastes that signal Mexican foods as both unique and memorable.

ORANGE RICE

Serves 6

¾ cup long grain rice
1½ cups water
5 tsps. low sodium chicken bouillon
2 scallions, minced
¼ red pepper, chopped
¼ green pepper, chopped

¼ lb. mushrooms, chopped
Black pepper to taste
⅛ tsp. garlic powder
1 tsp. tarragon
1 tangerine, peeled and sectioned

Bring rice and water to a boil. Boil 5 minutes.
Reduce to simmer. Cover and cook 10 minutes.
Add bouillon and stir to blend well. Cook 3 minutes more, or till liquid is almost absorbed.
Add vegetables, seasonings, and tangerine sections. Mix, cover and let stand 5 minutes.

Calories per serving: 142

Sodium per serving: 16 mgs.

PARSLEY NOODLES WITH AVOCADO

Serves 8

½ lb. noodles, cooked al dente*
½ lb. low sodium cottage cheese
1 Tbs. sugar
1 Tbs. lemon juice
1 medium-size onion, minced
Dash of ground cumin

White pepper to taste
2 Tbs. parsley
1 egg, lightly beaten
1 avocado, peeled and sliced
2 tsps. paprika

Do not add salt to boiling water.

Preheat oven to 350°.
In 9″ square oven-proof casserole, combine first 8 ingredients. Toss to blend. Stir in egg and bake 20 minutes.
Top with avocado. Sprinkle with paprika. Bake 10 minutes more.

Calories per serving: 189	Sodium per serving: 23 mgs.

REFRIED BEANS

Serves 14

1 lb. red beans
8 cups water
5 Tbs. oil, divided
2 medium-size onions, chopped
4 cloves garlic, chopped
3½ Tbs. dry sherry

2 tsps. mustard powder
1 Tbs. low sodium beef bouillon
3½ Tbs. low sodium chicken bouillon
4 ozs. low sodium Cheddar cheese,
  chopped fine

Combine beans and water. Soak overnight.
Bring beans to a boil. Cover. Reduce heat and simmer over low heat till beans are soft, stirring occasionally. Add more water, if necessary, to keep beans from sticking.
Drain beans. Reserve liquid.
In large skillet, heat 1 Tbs. oil. Add onions and garlic, cooking over low heat 5 minutes. Add 1 Tbs. oil and a quarter of the beans and mash well.
Keep adding oil and beans till both are used, mashing beans thoroughly. Add reserved liquid as needed to keep beans from sticking.
Stir in sherry, mustard powder, and beef and chicken bouillon. Continue to fry, stirring often, till mixture is thick and dry.
Top with cheese.

Calories per serving: 202	Sodium per serving: 10 mgs.

RICE AND OKRA

Serves 8

3 Tbs. olive oil
1¼ cups long grain rice
1 medium-size onion, minced
2 cloves garlic, minced
1 Tbs. dry sherry
¼ tsp. cinnamon

1½ lbs. fresh okra, chopped
1 cup Salsa (See Page 295)
1 tsp. paprika
1 Tbs. parsley
2 cups boiling water
1½ Tbs. low sodium chicken bouillon

In skillet, heat oil. Stir in rice, onion, and garlic and cook over low heat till all are golden brown, stirring constantly. Stir in sherry and cinnamon.
Stir in okra and cook 2 minutes more, stirring occasionally.
Add Salsa, paprika, and parsley. Stir to blend, and cook 5 minutes.
In bowl, combine boiling water and bouillon. Pour over rice mixture. Cover and simmer 20 minutes, or till liquid is absorbed.

Calories per serving: 207   Sodium per serving: 17 mgs.

Spanish

For the Spanish, rice is the basis for the one dish meal—paella—which can contain any variety of meat, fish, or poultry, plus vegetables, your imagination can conjure. And by itself, rice is the preferred accompaniment to the Spanish meal.
Potatoes, especially if fried, are sometimes served with the main meal, but are generally reserved for casseroles and stews.
As for beans and pasta, they are prepared for specific dishes, but are definitely not the answer to a Spanish cook's fancy.

EGG CRUSTED RICE

Serves 6

1 Tbs. olive oil
1 Tbs. unsalted butter or margarine
1½ lbs. chicken livers, chopped
1 medium-size onion, chopped
1 red pepper, chopped
1 green pepper, chopped
1 leek, chopped, including greens

1¾ cups water
¼ cup dry white wine
¼ cup dry sherry
1 cup fresh shelled peas
1 bay leaf
¼ tsp. ground cumin
1 tsp. parsley

¼ tsp. sage
⅛ tsp. nutmeg
Black pepper to taste

1 cup long grain rice
8 tsps. low sodium chicken bouillon
2 eggs, beaten

In large skillet, heat oil and butter. Sauté chicken livers and onion 3 minutes, turning livers to brown all over.

Add red and green pepper and leek. Sauté 1 minute more.

Add water. Bring to a boil. Continue boiling 5 minutes.

Reduce heat. Cover and simmer 10 minutes.

Stir in white wine, sherry, and all remaining ingredients except eggs. Cover and simmer till liquid is absorbed.

Preheat oven to 400°.

Transfer rice mixture to lightly greased, 9″ square oven-proof casserole.

Spread eggs over surface of rice. Bake, uncovered, till crust forms, about 6 minutes. Serves as main dish with salad.

Calories per serving: 415   Sodium per serving: 131 mgs.

POTATOES AND ALMONDS

Serves 6

3 Tbs. olive oil, divided
2 medium-size onions, sliced, divided
3 potatoes, peeled and sliced, divided

Black pepper to taste
2 tsps. low sodium chicken bouillon
3 Tbs. slivered almonds

In large skillet, heat half the oil. Add half the onions and half the potatoes. Cook over low heat 10 minutes, turning to brown potatoes on both sides. Transfer to deep serving dish.

Repeat with remaining oil, onions, and potatoes. Transfer to serving dish. Season with pepper and bouillon. Toss to blend.

Add almonds to skillet and cook 2 minutes, stirring often. Add to potatoes and onions. Toss to blend.

Calories per serving: 150   Sodium per serving: 7 mgs.

RICE WITH CHICKEN AND SEAFOOD

Serves 8

1 Tbs. olive oil
2 chicken breasts, skinned, boned, and
    cut into 1″ chunks
4 cloves garlic, minced

½ lb. squid, cut into 1″ chunks
2 tomatoes, chopped
Dash of mace
White pepper to taste

⅛ tsp. rosemary, crushed
1 tsp. oregano
1 Tbs. paprika
1 red pepper, chopped
1 lb. green beans, chopped
1½ cups long grain rice

4 cups boiling water
4½ Tbs. low sodium chicken bouillon
½ cup dry white wine
1 Tbs. dry sherry
1 pt. oysters, including liquid

In large saucepan, heat oil. Add chicken, garlic, and squid. Cook over medium heat 1 minute, stirring constantly.

Reduce to low heat. Add all but last 2 ingredients.

Bring to a boil. Cover. Reduce heat and simmer 20 minutes, or till liquid is absorbed.

Stir in sherry and oysters and their liquid. Cover and simmer 5 minutes more, or till liquid is absorbed.

Serve as main dish with salad.

Calories per serving: 337	Sodium per serving: 94 mgs.

SPANISH RICE

Serves 8

2 Tbs. unsalted butter or margarine
1 large onion, chopped
2 cloves garlic, minced
1¼ cups long grain rice
½ tsp. saffron threads
2 chili peppers, chopped
1 Tbs. sweet pepper flakes

Black pepper to taste
3 cups boiling water
6 Tbs. low sodium chicken bouillon
4 large ripe tomatoes, chopped
1 green or red pepper, chopped
1 tsp. basil
1 tsp. fresh chopped parsley

Melt butter in large saucepan and sauté onion and garlic till onion is golden and wilted. Stir in rice and sauté till grains are transparent.

Add saffron, chili peppers, pepper flakes, black pepper, boiling water, bouillon, and tomatoes. Cover and simmer 15 minutes.

Add green pepper and basil. Cover again and simmer 5 to 10 minutes more, or till liquid is absorbed.

Sprinkle parsley on top.

Calories per serving: 190	Sodium per serving: 24 mgs.

SAUCES, RELISHES, AND CONDIMENTS

Sauces. The final, exquisite touch to many foods. The essential accompaniment to many others. What would spaghetti be without tomato sauce? Asparagus without bearnaise? Lamb without chutney?

Desirable? Yes. Fattening and unhealthful? Not necessarily. Sauces and relishes don't have to be made with multi-tablespoons of butter or cups of cream. They certainly don't need salt to taste properly seasoned. They can be fit for a king or queen of a slim and healthy nature.

The recipes in this chapter prove that. Indeed, a sauce can be simply the final touch, not the final blow. Use one to accent one of your own standbys and discover a new one. Or use them to add a new taste experience to your repertoire.

A sauce or relish can set a dish apart, providing the special dash that adds style and grace to the humblest of foods.

APRICOT-PEAR SAUCE

Makes 2 Cups

2 cups water
1¾ cups sugar
2 tsps. lemon juice
1 tsp. vanilla extract
½ tsp. almond extract
3 pears, peeled, cored, and quartered

1 can (16 ozs.) apricot halves, including
  liquid
¼ cup orange juice
⅛ tsp. nutmeg
½ tsp. dried or fresh grated orange peel
2 tsps. cornstarch

Combine water, sugar, lemon juice, and vanilla and almond extract in medium-size saucepan. Cook over medium heat, stirring, till sugar is dissolved.
　Add pears. Bring to a boil. Reduce heat. Cover and simmer 30 minutes. Set aside.
　Place apricots and remaining ingredients in blender. Purée till smooth.
　Pour apricot mixture into second saucepan. Cook over medium heat, stirring constantly, till thickened.
　Add pear mixture. Cook 5 minutes over medium heat, stirring constantly.
　Use in preparing or as an accompaniment to lamb, chicken, or veal dishes. Or serve either warm or chilled as dessert sauce.

Calories per recipe: 2064
Calories per Tbs.: 65

Sodium per recipe: 104 mgs.
Sodium per Tbs.: 3 mgs.

AU GRATIN SAUCE

Makes 4 Cups

1 Tbs. unsalted butter or margarine
1 Tbs. all-purpose flour
4 cups boiling water
5 Tbs. low sodium chicken bouillon
4 ozs. low sodium Cheddar cheese,
  minced

Black pepper to taste
½ tsp. mustard powder
¼ tsp. onion powder
¼ cup heavy cream

In saucepan, melt butter. Stir in flour. Add boiling water. Stir in chicken bouillon. Cook over medium heat 5 minutes, stirring often.
　Stir in all remaining ingredients except cream. Simmer 30 minutes, stirring occasionally.
　Stir in cream and simmer 20 minutes more, stirring occasionally.
　Use as sauce for vegetables and meats and in Potatoes Au Gratin (See Page 265).

Calories per recipe: 993
Calories per Tbs.: 16

Sodium per recipe: 121 mgs.
Sodium per Tbs.: 2 mgs.

CHERRY GLAZE

Makes 3 Cups

2 cans (8 ozs. each) pitted cherries,
  including liquid
½ cup sugar
6 cloves
⅛ tsp. allspice
1 tsp. dried or fresh grated orange peel
¼ tsp. cinnamon

3 Tbs. lemon juice
3 tsps. low sodium beef bouillon
½ cup dry white wine
½ cup boiling water
4 tsps. low sodium chicken bouillon
2 Tbs. all-purpose flour

Combine all ingredients except flour in saucepan. Bring to a slow boil, stirring often.
Remove from heat. Stir in flour.
Cook over low heat, stirring to thicken, 10 minutes. Discard cloves.
Use as glaze for chicken, veal, or pork.

Calories per recipe: 1048
Calories per Tbs.: 22

Sodium per recipe: 85 mgs.
Sodium per Tbs.: 2 mgs.

CHICKEN FAT

Makes 1 Cup

1 cup chicken fat
1 medium-size onion, minced

1 cup water

In saucepan, combine all ingredients. Cook over very low heat till fat melts and
browned pieces of fat are left.
Remove browned pieces and either discard or use in meat gravy. Let liquid in pan cool
thoroughly. Then pour into freezer containers. May be frozen up to six months or
refrigerated up to two months.

Calories per recipe: 2734
Calories per Tbs.: 114

Sodium per recipe: 10 mgs.
Sodium per Tbs.: trace

CHICKEN GRAVY

Makes 2 Cups

2 cups Chicken Broth (See Page 45)
1 Tbs. low sodium chicken bouillon
3 Tbs. dry vermouth
White pepper to taste

¼ tsp. sage
1 Tbs. cornstarch
2 Tbs. cold water

In saucepan, combine first 5 ingredients. Cook over low heat 10 minutes, stirring occasionally.

In bowl, combine cornstarch and cold water. Stir into gravy. Cook 2 minutes, or till gravy starts to thicken.

Serve with chicken or sweet white fish such as flounder. Chicken Gravy is also good with pork.

Calories per recipe: 191	Sodium per recipe: 56 mgs.
Calories per Tbs.: 6	Sodium per Tbs.: 2 mgs.

CHILI OIL

Makes 1 Cup

1 cup peanut oil   1 tsp. crushed hot pepper flakes

Heat oil in skillet till very hot but not smoking.
Remove from heat and let stand 1 minute.
Add pepper flakes. Stir to blend.
Cool and place in jar. Store, covered, in refrigerator up to 6 months.

Calories per recipe: 1927	Sodium per recipe: 4 mgs.
Calories per Tbs.: 120	Sodium per Tbs.: Trace

CHINESE SWEET AND SOUR SAUCE

Makes 2 Cups

½ medium-size onion, minced
4 peaches, unpeeled, pitted and chopped
3 red plums, pitted and chopped
¼ cup dried apricots, chopped, or ¼ cup
  raisins*

2 cups water
¼ cup white or cider vinegar
6 Tbs. sugar
1/16 tsp. garlic powder
Black pepper to taste

Preserved in non-sodium ingredient

In medium-size saucepan, combine all ingredients. Bring to a boil. Reduce heat and simmer 2 hours, or till liquid is almost absorbed.

Purée mixture in blender. Pour into jars and seal tightly. Store in refrigerator up to 2 weeks. Or pour into freezer containers and freeze up to 6 months.

With Apricots: Calories per recipe: 916	Sodium per recipe: 67 mgs.
With Raisins: Calories per Tbs.: 28	Sodium per Tbs.: 2 mgs.

COCONUT MILK

Makes 4 Cups

4½ cups shredded coconut

4½ cups boiling water

In medium-size bowl, place coconut. Cover with boiling water. Cool to room temperature.

Strain through cheesecloth. Discard coconut. Pour liquid into container and cover tightly.

Cover and store up to 3 days.

Calories per recipe: 3557	Sodium per recipe: trace
Calories per Tbs.: 56	Sodium per Tbs.: trace

CRANBERRY APPLE SAUCE

Serves 16 (Makes 4 Cups)

2 cups fresh cranberries
½ cup sugar
½ cup water
¼ tsp. cinnamon

¼ tsp. dried or fresh grated lemon peel
½ tsp. dried or fresh grated orange peel
1 cup apple sauce

Combine all ingredients except apple sauce in large saucepan. Bring to a boil and continue boiling till berries start to pop.

Reduce heat and cook over low heat 7 to 10 minutes, stirring often.

Remove from heat and stir in apple sauce.

Serve warm or chilled.

Calories per serving: 44	Sodium per serving: 3 mgs.
Calories per recipe: 695	Sodium per recipe: 44 mgs.

CREAMY MUSTARD DRESSING

Makes ¾ Cup

¼ cup low sodium mayonnaise
¼ cup heavy cream
1½ Tbs. cider vinegar
3½ Tbs. lemon juice

1 Tbs. low sodium Dijon mustard
¼ tsp. garlic powder
1½ Tbs. tarragon

In blender, combine all ingredients. Purée briefly. Chill 1 hour.
Serve over meat, fish, or vegetables.

Calories per recipe: 842	Sodium per recipe: 138 mgs.
Calories per Tbs.: 70	Sodium per Tbs.: 12 mgs.

CURRY POWDER

Makes 2 Ounces

Some commercially prepared curry powders contain salt. If yours does, try the following:

8 tsps. turmeric
4 tsps. ground cumin
½ tsp. cinnamon

Cayenne pepper to taste
Dash of ginger powder
¼ tsp. ground cloves

In bowl, combine all ingredients. Stir to blend thoroughly.
Pour into spice jar. Cover and store in cool, dark place.

Calories per recipe: 100	Sodium per recipe: 14 mgs.

EGG AND LEMON SAUCE

Makes 2 Cups

3 eggs, lightly beaten
1 Tbs. cornstarch
⅓ cup lemon juice
2 cups boiling water

Black pepper to taste
½ tsp. onion powder
2½ Tbs. low sodium chicken bouillon

In bowl, beat together eggs, cornstarch, and lemon juice. Set aside.
In saucepan, combine remaining ingredients. Cook over medium heat 10 minutes, stirring often.
Gradually whisk bouillon mixture into egg mixture.
Serve over fish, meat, poultry, or vegetables, especially with Greek dishes.

Calories per recipe: 352	Sodium per recipe: 177 mgs.
Calories per Tbs.: 11	Sodium per Tbs.: 6 mgs.

FIVE SPICE POWDER

Makes ¼ Cup

2 Tbs. black peppercorns
2 Tbs. fennel seed
10 whole star anise or 2 tsps. aniseed

4 cinnamon sticks, broken into small
  pieces
30 cloves

In blender, combine all ingredients. Grind thoroughly.
Store in tightly covered jar in cool, dry place.

Calories per recipe: 108	Sodium per recipe: 13 mgs.

GOOD AND HOT BARBEQUE SAUCE

Makes 2¼ Cups

1 can (12 ozs.) low sodium tomato juice
4 Tbs. low sodium chili ketchup
2 Tbs. red wine vinegar
2 Tbs. Imitation Worcestershire Sauce
  (See Page 291)
1 medium-size onion, minced
½ cup water
2 chili peppers, minced, or dash of hot
  pepper flakes

2 Tbs. mustard powder
1 Tbs. sugar
1 Tbs. molasses
2 tsps. paprika
Black pepper to taste
⅜ tsp. cinnamon

In saucepan, combine all ingredients. Simmer over very low heat, stirring occasionally,
till sauce starts to bubble around the edges.
  Use with chicken, pork, or beef.

Calories per recipe: 257	Sodium per recipe: 142 mgs.
Calories per Tbs.: 11	Sodium per Tbs.: 6 mgs.

GREEN SAUCE

Makes 1 Cup

1 Tbs. plus ¼ cup oil, divided
1 medium-size onion, minced
½ cup fresh parsley, chopped
¼ cup dry white wine or sherry

¼ cup water
2 Tbs. lemon juice
Cayenne pepper to taste
5 tsps. low sodium chicken bouillon

In small pan, sauté onion in 1 Tbs. oil till golden.
  Add remaining ingredients except remaining ¼ cup oil. Simmer 6 minutes.

289

Pour into blender. Blend, streaming in remaining oil till smooth and creamy.
Serve over fish or fowl.

Calories per recipe: 786	Sodium per recipe: 88 mgs.
Calories per Tbs.: 33	Sodium per Tbs.: 4 mgs.

HERBED MAYONNAISE

Makes 1½ Cups

1 cup low sodium mayonnaise
2 Tbs. chives
2 Tbs. parsley
2 Tbs. tarragon
1 sprig watercress, chopped
2 tsps. dry sherry

1 Tbs. cider vinegar
1 tsp. dill
1 tsp. mustard powder
White pepper to taste
1 Tbs. lemon juice

In blender, combine all ingredients. Purée. Place in jar. Cover tightly and chill 1 hour.
Serve with vegetables, chicken, or fish.

Calories per recipe: 1608	Sodium per recipe: 68 mgs.
Calories per Tbs.: 67	Sodium per Tbs.: 3 mgs.

HORSERADISH

Makes ¾ Cup

½ lb. horseradish root, peeled and
   chopped fine
⅓ cup white vinegar
½ cup cooked chopped beets (optional)

2 Tbs. sugar
Black pepper to taste
1 Tbs. low sodium chicken bouillon

Combine all ingredients in blender. Purée.
Store in sterilized jars, covered tightly, up to 6 weeks, or in regular covered jar, up to 3
weeks in refrigerator.

White: (Plain)
Calories per recipe: 350   Sodium per recipe: 61 mgs.
Calories per Tbs.: 29   Sodium per Tbs.: 5 mgs.
Red: (With Beets)
Calories per recipe: 387   Sodium per recipe: 110 mgs.
Calories per Tbs.: 32   Sodium per Tbs.: 9 mgs.

IMITATION WORCESTERSHIRE SAUCE

Makes 1½ Cups

1½ cups boiling water
2 Tbs. low sodium beef bouillon
2 tsps. low sodium ketchup
½ tsp. red wine vinegar
1 tsp. molasses
1 tsp. sugar

⅛ tsp. onion powder
⅛ tsp. garlic powder
⅛ tsp. dried or fresh orange peel
1 shallot, minced
Dash of allspice

Combine all ingredients. Blend thoroughly and place in pint jar. Cover tightly and refrigerate up to 3 months.

Calories per recipe: 105	Sodium per recipe: 65 mgs.
Calories per Tbs.: 4	Sodium per Tbs.: 3 mgs.

INDIAN SPICE BLEND *(Garam Masala)*

Makes ½ Cup

30 cardamom pods
½ cup black peppercorns
¼ cup cumin seed

3 cinnamon sticks
6 whole cloves
1 tsp. ground coriander

Place first 5 ingredients in blender or food processor. Blend thoroughly.
Stir in coriander, blending well.
Place in jar. Cover tightly and store in cupboard.
Use as flavoring in meat or vegetable dishes, or experiment with fish or fowl recipes for an Indian touch.

Calories per recipe: 235	Sodium per recipe: 41 mgs.

LOW SODIUM BREAD CRUMBS

Makes 1½ Cups

6 slices low sodium bread (or enough to make 1½ cups), toasted

On board, crush bread with rolling pin. Place in jar. Cover tightly and store in cool, dry place. Will keep indefinitely.

Calories per recipe: 325	Sodium per recipe: 35 mgs.
Calories per Tbs.: 16	Sodium per Tbs.: 2 mgs.

MINTED FRUIT CHUTNEY

Makes 3 Cups

1 medium-size onion, chopped
1½ cups dried apricots, chopped
1 banana, peeled and chopped
1 green apple, cored and chopped
1 orange, peeled, seeded, and chopped
1¾ cups water
¼ cup lemon juice

2 Tbs. sugar
¾ cup cider vinegar
⅓ cup fresh mint, chopped, or 1 Tbs.,
    dried
½ tsp. cinnamon
2 Tbs. turmeric
½ cup raisins*

Preserved in non-sodium ingredient

In large saucepan, combine first 8 ingredients. Simmer over low heat 30 minutes, stirring occasionally.
In second saucepan, combine all remaining ingredients. Cook 5 minutes, stirring often.
Stir raisin mixture into apricot mixture, blending thoroughly. Let cool.
Spoon chutney into pint jars. Cover tightly and store in refrigerator up to 2 months.

Calories per recipe: 1729	Sodium per recipe: 164 mgs.
Calories per Tbs.: 36	Sodium per Tbs.: 3 mgs.

MORNAY SAUCE

Makes 2 Cups

3 Tbs. unsalted butter or margarine
4 Tbs. all-purpose flour
1 cup milk
1 cup boiling water
2 Tbs. low sodium chicken bouillon
2 ozs. low sodium Gouda cheese, minced

2 Tbs. brandy
3½ Tbs. lemon juice
Black pepper to taste
⅛ tsp. nutmeg
Dash of cayenne pepper
1 egg yolk

In saucepan, melt butter. Stir in flour to blend. Add milk, boiling water, and bouillon, stirring with whisk over medium/low heat till thickened.
Stir in remaining ingredients except egg yolk. Cook 10 minutes, stirring often, or till cheese is melted.
Remove from heat. Beat in egg yolk.

Calories per recipe: 991	Sodium per recipe: 201 mgs.
Calories per Tbs.: 31	Sodium per Tbs.: 6 mgs.

MUSHROOM SAUCE

Makes 1 Cup

8 mushrooms, sliced
2 Tbs. unsalted butter or margarine
2 Tbs. low sodium beef bouillon
1 cup boiling water

Black pepper to taste
1 Tbs. cornstarch, dissolved in 2 Tbs.
  cold water

In skillet, sauté mushrooms in butter till lightly browned.
In saucepan, blend bouillon into boiling water. Stir in pepper. Stir in cornstarch and mushrooms.
Simmer till thickened, stirring occasionally. Serve on shish kebab, chicken, or any broiled meat.

Calories per recipe: 127
Calories per Tbs.: 8

Sodium per recipe: 76 mgs.
Calories per Tbs.: 5 mgs.

OIL FREE MAYONNAISE

Makes 1 Cup

1 Tbs. unflavored gelatin
¼ cup water
4 Tbs. white vinegar
3 egg yolks

1 tsp. mustard powder
1 Tbs. lemon juice
White pepper to taste
1 Tbs. tarragon

In saucepan, dissolve gelatin in water, heating slowly.
Add vinegar and bring to a boil over very low heat.
In blender, whirl egg yolks, mustard, and lemon juice.
When vinegar mixture is boiled, add to egg mixture in a steady stream and continue to blend 5 minutes.
Transfer to mixing bowl and beat in remaining ingredients with a whisk. Pour into chilled pint container and store immediately in refrigerator.
Let set overnight before using. Keeps 4 to 6 weeks.

Calories per recipe: 196
Calories per Tbs.: 12

Sodium per recipe: 105 mgs.
Sodium per Tbs.: 7 mgs.

ORANGE-CARROT RELISH

Makes 4 Cups

16 carrots, peeled and grated
¼ cup orange juice
3½ tsps. dried or fresh grated orange
  peel
3½ cups water

1 Tbs. cider vinegar
4 tsps. low sodium chicken bouillon
1 small onion, minced
¼ cup lemon juice
4 cups sugar

In medium-size saucepan, combine all ingredients except lemon juice and sugar. Heat to boiling. Cover. Reduce heat and simmer 15 minutes.
Stir in lemon juice and sugar. Heat to boiling. Boil, uncovered, over medium heat, stirring constantly, 20 minutes.
Spoon to within ⅛″ of top of jars. Cover tightly.
Keeps 3 weeks in refrigerator.
Serve as meat, fish, or poultry condiment.

Calories per recipe: 3616
Calories per Tbs.: 57

Sodium per recipe: 788 mgs.
Sodium per Tbs.: 12 mgs.

PIQUANT SPICE SAUCE

Makes ¾ Cup

¼ cup low sodium mayonnaise
1 tsp. sugar
1 tsp. lemon juice
1 Tbs. parsley
5 walnuts, chopped fine
1 apple, cored and chopped fine

½ chili pepper, seeded and chopped fine
Black pepper to taste
2 low sodium cucumber pickle slices,
  chopped
1 low sodium dill pickle, chopped
1 Tbs. low sodium chili ketchup

Combine all ingredients in small saucepan. Cover loosely and cook over extremely low heat, stirring occasionally, till sauce is hot throughout.
Serve with fish, fowl, squash, or tomatoes.

Calories per recipe: 974
Calories per Tbs.: 81

Sodium per recipe: 37 mgs.
Sodium per Tbs.: 3 mgs.

RUSSIAN DRESSING

Makes 1 Cup

¾ cup low sodium mayonnaise
½ medium-size onion, minced
4 Tbs. low sodium chili ketchup

3 Tbs. lemon juice
4 low sodium cucumber pickles, minced
1/16 tsp. garlic powder

In bowl, blend all ingredients. Cover and chill 1 hour. Cover tightly and store in refrigerator up to 3 months.
Serve with salads, chicken, or fish.

Calories per recipe: 1309
Calories per Tbs.: 82

Sodium per recipe: 116 mgs.
Sodium per Tbs.: 7 mgs.

SALSA

Makes 3½ Cups

2 lbs. very ripe tomatoes or 1 can
   (16 ozs.) low sodium tomatoes
2 large onions, chopped
1 chili pepper, minced
½ green pepper, chopped
2 tsps. low sodium beef bouillon

2 tsps. low sodium chicken bouillon
Black pepper to taste
3 large cloves garlic, minced
½ tsp. ground coriander
1½ tsps. basil
2 Tbs. red wine vinegar

If using fresh tomatoes, core but do not peel. Cut into small cubes.
Combine with other ingredients. Blend well.
Serve hot or cold, not more than 1 hour after preparing, with pork, beef, or chicken.

Fresh Tomatoes:
Calories per recipe: 404
Calories per Tbs.: 14
Canned Tomatoes:
Calories per recipe: 299
Calories per Tbs.: 11

Sodium per recipe: 98 mgs.
Sodium per Tbs.: 4 mgs.

Sodium per recipe: 71 mgs.
Sodium per Tbs.: 3 mgs.

SAUCE NORMANDE

Makes 2 Cups

3 Tbs. unsalted butter or margarine
½ lb. mushrooms, sliced
3 Tbs. all-purpose flour
1 cup Easy Fish Stock (See Page 45)
½ cup dry vermouth

2 egg yolks, lightly beaten
1 Tbs. heavy cream
1 Tbs. lemon juice
White pepper to taste

In saucepan, melt butter and sauté mushrooms, stirring occasionally, about 3 minutes.
Remove from heat and stir in flour.
Add fish stock and vermouth. Cook over medium heat, stirring constantly, till mixture starts to boil. Reduce heat and simmer 2 minutes.
In medium-size bowl, combine egg yolks, cream, lemon juice, and white pepper. Mix well.
Stir a little of the mushroom mixture into the egg mixture. Pour back into mushroom mixture. Simmer till mixture thickens slightly.
Use as base or accompanying sauce for any mild-flavored fish, such as flounder.

Calories per recipe: 971
Calories per Tbs.: 30

Sodium per recipe: 280 mgs.
Sodium per Tbs.: 9 mgs.

SEASONED BREAD CRUMBS

Makes 1½ Cups

1½ cups Low Sodium Bread Crumbs
    (See Page 291)
1 Tbs. dill
½ tsps. garlic powder
½ tsp. marjoram

¼ tsp. sage
Black pepper to taste
2 tsps. tarragon
2 tsps. basil

In bowl, combine all ingredients. Stir well to blend.
Place in jar. Cover tightly and store in cool, dry place. Keeps indefinitely.

Calories per recipe: 340
Calories per Tbs.: 17

Sodium per recipe: 40 mgs.
Sodium per Tbs.: 2 mgs.

SOY SAUCE SUBSTITUTE

Makes 1 Cup

1 cup boiling water
2 rounded Tbs. low sodium beef bouillon
½ tsp. sesame oil

1 tsp. white vinegar
Dash of mustard powder
Dash of black pepper

In bowl, combine first 2 ingredients, stirring to dissolve bouillon.
Stir in remaining ingredients.
Use as dip or in recipes calling for soy sauce.
Store in refrigerator up to 6 months in tightly covered jar. Stir thoroughly and let come to room temperature before using.

Calories per recipe: 93
Calories per Tbs.: 4

Sodium per recipe: 60 mgs.
Sodium per Tbs.: 3 mgs.

TARRAGON MUSTARD

Makes 1 Cup

7¼ ozs. low sodium mustard, preferably
   Dijon style
2 Tbs. dry white wine
2 Tbs. white vinegar

Black pepper to taste
Dash of hot pepper flakes (optional)
1 Tbs. tarragon
Dash of garlic powder

In bowl, blend all ingredients thoroughly. Pour into small jar.
Chill till ready for use. Store in refrigerator up to 6 months.

Calories per recipe: 129
Calories per Tbs.: 8

Sodium per recipe: 38 mgs.
Sodium per Tbs.: 2 mgs.

TARTAR SAUCE

Makes ¾ Cup

½ cup low sodium mayonnaise
1½ Tbs. lemon juice
4 low sodium cucumber pickles, chopped
4 low sodium dill pickles, chopped
2 Tbs. low sodium dill pickle juice

½ medium-size onion, minced
1 Tbs. parsley
White pepper to taste
1 hard boiled egg, chopped

In blender, combine all ingredients. Purée. Transfer to jar and cover tightly. Chill overnight. Store in refrigerator up to 2 months
Serve with fish or chicken.

Calories per recipe: 963	Sodium per recipe: 134 mgs.
Calories per Tbs.: 80	Sodium per Tbs.: 11 mgs.

TOMATO ASPIC

Makes 1½ Cups

¾ cup hot water
2 tsps. low sodium beef bouillon
½ tsp. thyme
1 tsp. low sodium ketchup

2 Tbs. unflavored gelatin
½ cup cold water
½ cup low sodium tomato juice

In saucepan, combine hot water, bouillon, thyme, and ketchup. Cook over low heat 7 to 8 minutes. Remove from heat.
In bowl, dissolve gelatin in cold water. Stir into bouillon mixture till completely dissolved. Add tomato juice, and stir to blend thoroughly.

Calories per recipe: 82	Sodium per recipe: 34 mgs.

TOMATO SAUCE

Makes 2¾ Quarts

2 Tbs. olive oil
3 medium-size onions, chopped
12 cloves garlic, minced
2 cans (6 ozs. each) low sodium tomato paste
4 bay leaves
Black pepper to taste
1 Tbs. basil
1 Tbs. oregano

8 tomatoes, chopped fine, or 2 cans (16 ozs. each) low sodium tomatoes, chopped, including liquid
2 cups water
2 cans (12 ozs. each) low sodium tomato juice
1 tsp. sugar
1 Tbs. low sodium chicken bouillon

In Dutch oven, heat oil. Add onions and garlic. Simmer over very low heat 20 minutes, stirring occasionally, till onions are wilted and golden.
Add tomato paste and fry briefly.
Stir in bay leaves, pepper, basil, and oregano. Add tomatoes, water, and 1 can tomato juice. Cover and simmer 1½ hours, stirring occasionally.
Stir in remaining tomato juice and sugar. Cover and simmer 30 minutes more.
Stir in bouillon. Cover and simmer 10 minutes more. Discard bay leaves.

If desired, you may add the following 30 minutes before sauce is done: 1 green pepper, chopped, and 12 mushrooms, chopped.

Store in freezer up to 6 months. If you plan to use green pepper and mushrooms, add when reheating.

Fresh Tomatoes:
Calories per recipe: 1399   Sodium per recipe: 339 mgs.
Calories per Tbs.: 8   Sodium per Tbs.: 2 mgs.
Canned Tomatoes:
Calories per recipe: 1399   Sodium per recipe: 475 mgs.
Calories per Tbs.: 8   Sodium per Tbs.: 3 mgs.

VINAIGRETTE DRESSING

Makes 2 Cups

⅔ cup oil
⅔ cup hot water
⅔ cup red wine vinegar
1½ tsps. sugar
1 tsp. onion powder
1 tsp. oregano
1 tsp. basil

1½ tsps. mustard powder
2 cloves garlic, sliced
Black pepper to taste
¼ tsp. rosemary, crushed (optional)
¼ tsp. thyme (optional)
1 tsp. tarragon
2 Tbs. sweet pepper flakes

In jar, combine all ingredients. Cover and shake vigorously to blend.
Store in refrigerator up to 6 months.

Calories per recipe: 1307   Sodium per recipe: 50 mgs.
Calories per Tbs.: 41   Sodium per Tbs.: 2 mgs.

EGGS

If all good things come in small packages, eggs are certainly a case in point. They're perfect little jewels of proteins and minerals.

We all know the virtues of eggs. They are not only high in protein, but low in calories and economical to boot. In America, however, eggs are rarely enjoyed for their sweet wholesome selves, except at breakfast. Yet eggs can offer a harried cook an easy, fast, and imaginative dinner for one or several. That's why so many of the dishes in this chapter are suggested as such.

Eggs are far more than accents for ham and toast. Serve them with Salsa (See Page 295) for a touch of Mexican exuberance. Or float them on a bed of rice or spinach for a baked, sophisticated casserole.

Just one note of caution: eggs contain about 55 mgs. of sodium apiece. So if you're on a specific low sodium diet, don't use up all your sodium allowance on eggs at the expense of other nutritionally valuable foods. Other than that, enjoy them for the delicious, nutritious slenderizers they are.

American

Breakfast food—sunnyside up or scrambled. First and foremost, that's how Americans think of eggs. But although primarily relegated to the breakfast table, eggs are being enjoyed in more ways than ever before. Americans are discovering the delights of omelets. Even poached eggs are no longer a rarity.

In this land where a bucket of chicken to go is the enthusiastic answer to last minute meals, its humbler beginning—the egg—is coming into its own.

EGGS AND ASPARAGUS WITH CHEESE SAUCE

Serves 4

6 eggs, lightly beaten
1 tsp. low sodium chicken bouillon
Black pepper to taste
2 Tbs. unsalted butter or margarine

18 asparagus spears, ends trimmed, boiled tender crisp*
1 cup Au Gratin Sauce (See Page 284), divided

In bowl, beat together first 3 ingredients.
In skillet, melt butter. Pour in egg mixture and cook over low heat till eggs are set. Preheat oven to broil.
Lay asparagus on eggs in pinwheel fashion. Spoon on ¼ cup Au Gratin Sauce. Run under broiler 5 minutes.
While eggs are baking, bring remaining Au Gratin Sauce to a slow boil. Serve on side.
Serve eggs as main dish on toasted low sodium bread with potato and salad.

Do not add salt to boiling water.

Calories per serving: 162	Sodium per serving: 64 mgs.

EGG SALAD

Serves 6

10 hard boiled eggs
5 Tbs. low sodium mayonnaise
5 scallions, chopped, including greens

1 Tbs. dill
Coarse black pepper to taste
1½ tsps. low sodium Dijon mustard

In bowl, mash eggs. Add mayonnaise and blend thoroughly.
Stir in remaining ingredients, blending well.

301

Cover and chill 1 hour.
Serve as main dish with potatoes and green beans.

Calories per serving: 210   Sodium per serving: 104 mgs.

OMELET EXTRAORDINAIRE

Serves 4

4 Tbs. unsalted butter or margarine,
  divided
1 large onion, chopped
½ red or green pepper, chopped
4 mushrooms, sliced
5 eggs
2 Tbs. water
½ tsp. low sodium chicken bouillon

Black pepper to taste
Dash of sweet pepper flakes
2 tsps. chives
1 oz. low sodium Gouda or Monterey
  Jack cheese, chopped
1 oz. low sodium Cheddar cheese,
  chopped

In large skillet, melt 2 Tbs. butter. Add onion. Sauté 3 minutes.
  Add green pepper and mushrooms. Sauté 3 minutes more. Spread vegetables evenly over skillet.
  Beat eggs, water, bouillon, and black pepper. Add remaining butter to skillet.
  When butter is melted, pour eggs over vegetables. Cook over low heat 3 minutes.
  Sprinkle pepper flakes, chives, and Gouda and cheddar cheese over egg mixture. Cook till egg loses runny appearance.
  Preheat oven to broil.
  Slip omelet under broiler for 1½ minutes to set it and complete melting of cheese.
  Serve as main dish with lemon, boiled red potatoes, and asparagus.

Calories per serving: 242   Sodium per serving: 85 mgs.

OYSTER OMELET

Serves 4

3 Tbs. unsalted butter or margarine,
  divided
1 medium-size onion, chopped
Black pepper to taste
1 pt. oysters, drained and cut in half,
  liquid reserved

¼ tsp. garlic powder
1 Tbs. lemon juice
4 eggs, lightly beaten
¾ tsp. low sodium chicken bouillon

In skillet, melt 1 Tbs. butter. Add onion and cook over low heat 5 minutes. Transfer to bowl. Sprinkle with pepper. Set aside.
  Add oysters to skillet. Sprinkle with garlic powder. Cook over low heat 10 seconds.

Turn oysters. Add lemon juice and cook 10 seconds more. Transfer to platter.
In bowl, beat together onion, eggs, bouillon, and oyster liquid.
In same skillet, melt remaining butter. Pour in egg mixture and cook over low heat till almost set.
Preheat oven to broil.
Scrape oysters on top of eggs and run under broiler 30 seconds.
Serve as main dish.

Calories per serving: 227   Sodium per serving: 132 mgs.

Chinese

In China, eggs are highly regarded as fertility symbols—the white signifying male and the yolk female. They are examples of Yin and Yang, containing all the positive and negative forces of life.

The Chinese also prize eggs for their nutritional value—they provide protein for those too poor to buy the meat or fish that usually supplies this vitally important nutrient. Eggs are exploited to their fullest potential by Chinese cooks, appearing in soups and main dishes and served as specialties unto themselves.

PORK OMELETS WITH CABBAGE

Serves 6

4 mushrooms, sliced
½ medium-size head cabbage, shredded
1 can (8 ozs.) bamboo shoots, drained and chopped
1 lb. fresh bean sprouts, chopped
6 eggs, well beaten
¼ lb. ground pork
1 tsp. cornstarch
1 Tbs. low sodium beef bouillon

1 tsp. cider vinegar
1 Tbs. dry sherry
2 scallions, chopped, including greens
4 Tbs. sesame or peanut oil, divided
½ cup boiling water
1 Tbs. low sodium chicken bouillon
1 Tbs. dry sherry
½ tsp. sugar

In bowl, combine first 4 ingredients. Toss to blend.
In second bowl, beat together eggs, pork, cornstarch, beef bouillon, vinegar, sherry, and scallions.
In skillet, heat 1 Tbs. oil. Add half of egg mixture, 1 Tbs. at a time, to form 6 miniature patties in the skillet.
Cook over low heat 2 minutes. Fold in half and cook 1 minute more. Transfer to platter.

Repeat with 1 Tbs. oil and remaining egg mixture.
In bowl, combine boiling water and bouillon.
Add remaining 2 Tbs. oil to skillet. When hot, add cabbage mixture and stir fry 2 minutes over medium heat.
Stir in sherry. Add bouillon mixture. Stir in sugar. Blend thoroughly.
Place miniature omelets on top of cabbage. Cover and cook 5 minutes.
Serve as main dish.

Calories per serving: 353	Sodium per serving: 93 mgs.

SHERRIED EGGS AND OYSTERS

Serves 4

1 pt. oysters, drained, liquid reserved for
   other use
Dash of ginger powder
Black pepper to taste
⅛ tsp. garlic powder
2 Tbs. lemon juice
1 medium-size onion, minced

2 Tbs. oil
4 eggs, lightly beaten
½ tsp. low sodium chicken bouillon
1 tsp. low sodium beef bouillon
1 Tbs. dry sherry
2 scallions, chopped, including greens

Heat large skillet. Add oysters. Sprinkle with ginger, pepper, and garlic powder. Add lemon juice and fry over low heat 20 seconds. Transfer to platter.
Add oil. Add onion and stir fry over low heat 1 minute.
In bowl, beat together eggs, chicken and beef bouillon, and sherry. Pour into skillet and cook over low heat till eggs start to set.
Preheat oven to broil.
Spoon scallions and oysters over eggs. Run under broiler to set completely.
Serve as main dish with vegetables and rice.

Calories per serving: 217	Sodium per serving: 125 mgs.

SPICED HARD BOILED EGGS

Serves 4

1 medium-size onion, minced
4 cloves garlic, chopped
Dash of hot pepper flakes
½ tsp. sugar
1 Tbs. low sodium beef bouillon
2 tsps. dried or fresh grated lemon peel
1 cup oil
8 hard boiled eggs

3 stalks broccoli, broken into flowerets,
   stalks peeled and cut into ½″ rounds
8 mushrooms, sliced
¼ cup boiling water
1 Tbs. low sodium beef bouillon
½ tsp. cider vinegar
2 tsps. lemon juice
2 scallions, chopped, including greens

In blender, combine first 6 ingredients. Grind to a paste. Set aside.

In wok or large skillet, heat oil. When bubbly, add eggs and fry 1 minute. Transfer to platter.

Pour off all but 2 Tbs. of oil. Reduce heat to medium/low. Add broccoli, mushrooms, and onion paste. Stir fry 1 minute.

In bowl, combine remaining ingredients. Stir into vegetable mixture and stir fry briefly. Spoon vegetables around eggs.

Serve as main dish with Vegetable Fried Rice (See Page 263).

Calories per serving: 306   Sodium per serving: 133 mgs.

French

In the backyard of every French village home is a chicken coop, valued as much for the eggs produced there as for the chickens themselves. For eggs are necessary to the art of French cuisine.

Not only do eggs puff up soufflés and thicken sauces, but as omelets—plain or adorned with meat, seafood, or vegetables—they are savored for lunch or dinner.

CHICKEN OMELET

Serves 6

2 Tbs. unsalted butter or margarine
6 eggs, lightly beaten
2 Tbs. heavy cream
2 Tbs. water
Black pepper to taste

¼ lb. leftover chicken, chopped
1½ tsps. low sodium chicken bouillon
2 tsps. tarragon
1 tomato, chopped
1 scallion, minced, including greens

In skillet, melt butter.

In bowl, beat together eggs, cream, water, and pepper. Pour into skillet and cook over low heat 7 minutes, or till eggs start to set.

In a bowl, combine remaining ingredients. When eggs are almost set, spoon chicken mixture on top of eggs. Cook 3 minutes more. Then run under broiler for 2 minutes to lightly brown top.

Calories per serving: 167   Sodium per serving: 71 mgs.

JELLY RUM OMELET

Serves 4

5 eggs, lightly beaten
Black pepper to taste
2½ tsps. low sodium chicken bouillon
½ cup water

¼ cup heavy cream
1½ Tbs. unsalted butter or margarine
3 Tbs. cherry preserves*
¼ cup rum

Preserved without pectin or sodium

In bowl, beat together first 5 ingredients.
In skillet, melt butter. Pour egg mixture into pan and cook over low heat till eggs start to set. Run under broiler till lightly brown on top.
Spoon preserves on top of omelet. Fold in half. Transfer to platter.
In same skillet, heat rum. Pour over omelet.

Calories per serving: 233   Sodium per serving: 89 mgs.

SHIRRED EGGS WITH TARRAGON BLACK BUTTER

Serves 4

4 tsps. plus 4 Tbs. unsalted butter or
  margarine, divided
4 eggs
1 tsp. low sodium chicken bouillon

Black pepper to taste
½ tsp. green peppercorns,* crushed
2 tsps. tarragon

Natural green peppercorns, packed in water or vinegar

Preheat oven to 350°.
In each of 4 baking cups, melt 1 tsp. butter. Break eggs into cups. Season with bouillon and pepper. Bake 10 minutes, or till eggs are set.
While eggs are baking, melt 4 Tbs. butter in saucepan. Stir in peppercorns and tarragon. Cook, stirring often, till butter darkens. Spoon over eggs.

Calories per serving: 211   Sodium per serving: 67 mgs.

German

Germans are unconventional where eggs are concerned. They serve them on hash, stuff them for hors d'oeuvres, and use them in innumerable other ways. But they prefer the continental breakfast of juice, sweet roll, and coffee, and use eggs most often as casual accents preceding or during the main meal.

DILLED EGGS

Serves 6

8 eggs
2 Tbs. dill
1 tsp. red wine vinegar
1 tsp. dry sherry
Dash of allspice
Black pepper to taste

Dash of nutmeg
½ tsp. mustard powder
1 tsp. lemon juice
2 Tbs. heavy cream
2 tsps. low sodium beef bouillon
3 Tbs. unsalted butter or margarine

In bowl, beat together all ingredients except butter.
In skillet, melt butter. Pour in egg mixture and stir over medium heat till eggs are set.

Calories per serving: 171   Sodium per serving: 82 mgs.

ROAST BEEF OMELET

Serves 6

¼ lb. leftover beef, chopped
1 medium-size onion, minced
1½ tsps. Horseradish (See Page 290),
   White or Red
Black pepper to taste
2½ tsps. low sodium beef bouillon
1 potato, parboiled, peeled, and chopped

¼ tsp. thyme
½ tsp. mustard powder
4 Tbs. unsalted butter or margarine,
   divided
6 eggs, lightly beaten
4 Tbs. water

In blender, combine first 8 ingredients. Grind coarse. Set aside.
In large skillet, melt 1 Tbs. butter. Add meat mixture and stir fry 2 minutes over medium/low heat. Transfer to platter.
In same skillet, melt remaining butter.
In bowl, beat together eggs and water. Pour into skillet and cook over low heat / minutes, or till eggs start to set.

Spoon beef mixture on top of eggs and cook 3 minutes more. Then run under broiler to completely set.

Serve as main dish with salad, vegetable, and sour cream.

Calories per serving: 213   Sodium per serving: 76 mgs.

SOUR CREAM OMELET

Serves 4

3 Tbs. unsalted butter or margarine, divided
1 medium-size onion, minced
Black pepper to taste
1½ tsps. low sodium chicken bouillon

5 eggs, lightly beaten
4 Tbs. water
1 Tbs. chives
1 Tbs. parsley
2 Tbs. sour cream*

Preserved in non-sodium ingredient

In skillet, melt 1 Tbs. butter. Add onion. Sprinkle with pepper and cook over low heat 5 minutes, stirring occasionally. Stir in bouillon.

Add remaining butter to skillet.

In bowl, beat together eggs, water, chives, and parsley. Pour into skillet and cook over low heat till eggs are set. Run under broiler till top is lightly browned.

Spoon sour cream on top of eggs. Fold in half.

Calories per serving: 170   Sodium per serving: 79 mgs.

Greek

Greeks, of course, enjoy eggs but rarely for themselves. Instead, they honor eggs in their famous avgolemono sauce and in many other main meal recipes, as well. The following, however, are a few favorites from the Greek breakfast table.

GREEK CHEESE OMELET

Serves 4

2 Tbs. unsalted butter or margarine, divided
¼ lb. cod fillet, chopped

⅛ tsp. garlic powder
⅛ tsp. marjoram
White pepper to taste

(continued next page)

2 tsps. low sodium beef bouillon
4 eggs
2 Tbs. water
1 tsp. oregano
1 tsp. tarragon

¼ tsp. thyme
½ tsp. dill
2 ozs. low sodium Gouda cheese,
  chopped

In skillet, melt 1 Tbs. butter. Add fish, garlic powder, marjoram, pepper, and bouillon. Cook over low heat 5 minutes, stirring often. Add remaining Tbs. butter.

In bowl, beat together remaining ingredients except cheese. Pour into skillet. Cook over low heat 5 minutes.

Sprinkle cheese on top. Cook till cheese melts and eggs are set.

Serve as main dish with salad and potato.

Calories per serving: 201   Sodium per serving: 88 mgs.

SCRAMBLED EGGS AND RICE

Serves 6

2 tomatoes, cut into wedges
Black pepper to taste
1 Tbs. low sodium beef bouillon
1 tsp. sugar
¼ cup low sodium Bread Crumbs (See
  Page 291)
2 Tbs. oil

2 Tbs. unsalted butter or margarine
2 medium-size onions, minced
6 eggs
Dash of nutmeg
½ tsp. dill
Dash of cayenne pepper
½ cup cooked rice

Sprinkle tomatoes with black pepper, bouillon, and sugar. Roll in Bread Crumbs. Set aside.

In skillet, heat oil. Add tomato wedges and cook over low heat till browned on both sides. Transfer to platter.

In second skillet, melt butter. Add onions and cook over low heat 5 minutes, stirring occasionally.

In bowl, beat together eggs, nutmeg, dill, cayenne, and rice. Pour into skillet and cook over low heat till set, stirring occasionally. Transfer to platter. Surround with tomato wedges.

Calories per serving: 205   Sodium per serving: 68 mgs.

Indian

Eggs don't play a dominant role in Indian cuisine. Understandable, since poultry was not readily available in India until a few years ago. But though the selections are consequently few, they are unmistakably Indian.

EGGS IN CREAMED TOMATO SAUCE

Serves 4

2 Tbs. oil, divided
1 Tbs. unsalted butter or margarine
1 medium-size onion, chopped
2 cloves garlic, minced
½ tsp. Curry Powder (See Page 288)

6 eggs, lightly beaten
1½ tsps. low sodium chicken bouillon
½ cup milk
2 Tbs. low sodium tomato paste

In skillet, heat 1 Tbs. oil and butter. Add onion and garlic and cook over low heat 5 minutes, stirring occasionally.
In bowl, beat together Curry Powder, eggs, and bouillon.
Heat remaining oil in skillet. Pour in egg mixture and cook over low heat till eggs start to set.
While eggs are cooking, in saucepan, combine milk and tomato paste. Simmer 10 minutes, stirring constantly.
Preheat oven to broil.
When eggs are set, pour on tomato sauce and run under broiler 5 minutes.
Serve as main dish with green beans and rice.

Calories per serving: 237   Sodium per serving: 104 mgs.

INDIAN SCRAMBLED EGGS

Serves 4

3 Tbs. unsalted butter or margarine, divided
1 medium-size onion, chopped
⅛ tsp. ground cumin
1 tomato, chopped
⅛ tsp. nutmeg

1 chili pepper, minced, or dash of hot pepper flakes
1 green pepper, chopped
4 eggs, lightly beaten
1½ tsps. low sodium beef bouillon

In skillet, melt 2 Tbs. butter. Add onion and cook over low heat 5 minutes, stirring occasionally.
Stir in cumin, tomato, nutmeg, chili pepper, and green pepper. Cook 2 minutes more.
In bowl, beat together eggs and bouillon.

Melt remaining butter in skillet.
Pour in eggs and stir fry over medium/low heat till eggs are set.

Calories per serving: 186   Sodium per serving: 75 mgs.

SWEET SPICED EGGS

Serves 6

2 medium-size onions, chopped
1 tsp. minced ginger root or dash of
   ginger powder
4 cloves garlic, minced
4 Tbs. water
2 Tbs. oil
2 medium-size onions, sliced into rings
⅛ tsp. cinnamon

4 cloves
6 hard boiled eggs, peeled
1 bay leaf
½ tsp. ground coriander
Dash of ground cumin
1 Tbs. turmeric
Dash of cayenne pepper
½ can (3 ozs.) low sodium tomato paste

In blender, combine first 4 ingredients. Grind to a paste. Set aside.
In skillet, heat oil. Add onion rings and cook over low heat 5 minutes, stirring occasionally.
Stir in reserved paste and all remaining ingredients except tomato paste. Cook over low heat 10 minutes, turning eggs to brown on both sides.
Stir in tomato paste and cook 5 minutes more, stirring often.

Calories per serving: 154   Sodium per serving: 66 mgs.

Italian

Italians forego eggs for breakfast, preferring to enjoy them for lunch or dinner. Usually a frittata is their choice—the Italian version of an omelet that has been browned on both sides and served flat, cut in wedges. A sauce, salad, and garnishes are the standard accompaniments, resulting in an altogether satisfying meal.

EGGS AND HERBED ONION PIE

Serves 8

4 Tbs. olive oil
2 Tbs. unsalted butter or margarine
4 medium-size onions, chopped

3 cloves garlic, minced
1 cup fresh parsley, chopped
¼ cup fresh basil, chopped

(continued next page)

½ head romaine lettuce, chopped
1 bunch arugula, chopped
½ tsp. nutmeg

Black pepper to taste
1½ Tbs. low sodium chicken bouillon
8 eggs, beaten

In skillet, heat oil and butter. Add onions and garlic and cook over low heat 10 minutes, stirring occasionally.
Preheat oven to 350°.
Stir in parsley, basil, romaine, and arugula. Sprinkle with nutmeg and pepper. Stir to blend. Cook 5 minutes more. Transfer to 9″ pie plate.
In bowl, beat together bouillon and eggs. Stir into lettuce mixture. Bake 30 minutes, or till eggs are set and top is lightly browned.
Serve as main dish with potato and salad, or cut in 16 wedges and serve as hors d'oeuvres.

Calories per serving: 195   Sodium per serving: 64 mgs.

POACHED EGGS WITH ZUCCHINI

Serves 4

2 Tbs. olive oil
1 medium-size onion, chopped
1 clove garlic, minced
Black pepper to taste
2 zucchini, chopped
1½ tsps. low sodium chicken bouillon

½ can (8 ozs.) low sodium tomato sauce
½ tsp. oregano
¼ tsp. thyme
4 eggs
1 tsp. low sodium beef bouillon

In large skillet, heat oil. Add onion and garlic and cook over low heat 5 minutes, stirring occasionally. Sprinkle with pepper.
Add zucchini. Sprinkle with chicken bouillon and cook 5 minutes, stirring occasionally.
Pour in tomato sauce. Stir in oregano and thyme and simmer 10 minutes.
Break eggs carefully on top of tomato sauce. Cover and poach 2 to 3 minutes. Sprinkle with beef bouillon.
Serve as main dish with salad and pasta.

Calories per serving: 186   Sodium per serving: 66 mgs.

SPINACH, EGGS, AND PORK

Serves 6

1 lb. spinach, chopped
2 tsps. low sodium beef bouillon
Black pepper to taste

¼ cup dry sherry
¼ tsp. nutmeg
1½ cups water

(continued next page)

312

2 Tbs. heavy cream
6 ozs. leftover pork or chicken, chopped
 fine

2 Tbs. unsalted butter or margarine
6 eggs
2 tsps. low sodium chicken bouillon

In saucepan, combine first 6 ingredients. Bring to a boil. Cover. Reduce heat and simmer 15 minutes, or till spinach is tender. Drain thoroughly and purée in blender.
 Preheat oven to 375°.
 In bowl, combine spinach, cream, and pork. Blend well.
 Melt 1 tsp. butter in each of 6 baking bowls. Divide spinach mixture among bowls.
 Break 1 egg in each of the bowls. Sprinkle with chicken bouillon and bake 7 minutes, or till eggs are cooked through.
 Serve as main dish with salad and rice.

Pork: Calories per serving: 244
Chicken: Calories per serving: 211

Sodium per serving: 137 mgs.
Sodium per serving: 136 mgs.

Jewish

Whether or not they keep kosher homes, Jewish cooks pay special attention to dairy dishes. So does everyone who has ever savored cheese blintzes with sour cream or omelets whipped to frothy light perfection with milk or cream.

APPLE AND APRICOT OMELET

Serves 4

¾ cup water
1 apple, peeled, cored, and chopped
¼ cup dried apricots, chopped
¼ tsp. cinnamon
4 eggs, lightly beaten

1 Tbs. heavy cream
Black pepper to taste
1 tsp. low sodium chicken bouillon
2 Tbs. unsalted butter or margarine

In small saucepan, combine water, apple, apricots, and cinnamon. Cook over medium/low heat till liquid is absorbed, stirring occasionally.
 In bowl, beat together eggs, cream, pepper, and bouillon.
 In large skillet, melt butter. Pour in egg mixture and cook over medium heat, till bottom sets, letting egg run under edges.
 Preheat oven to broil.
 Top eggs with fruit mixture. Run under broiler 30 seconds to set.
 Serve as main dish with salad, broccoli, and noodles.

Calories per serving: 198

Sodium per serving: 64 mgs.

BAKED EGGS WITH TUNA

Serves 8

1 cup milk
2 Tbs. unsalted butter or margarine
¼ cup all-purpose flour
1 tsp. mustard powder
White pepper to taste
½ lb. low sodium cottage cheese
3 scallions, chopped, including greens

1½ Tbs. low sodium chicken bouillon
2 zucchini, chopped
1 tsp. oregano
2 cans (6½ ozs. each) low sodium tuna
8 eggs
3 Tbs. Imitation Worcestershire Sauce
  (See Page 291)

In saucepan, heat milk. Pour into 9″ × 13″ oven-proof casserole.
In same saucepan, melt butter. Stir in flour, mustard powder, pepper, cheese, scallions, and bouillon. Cook 2 minutes, stirring briefly.
Preheat oven to 350°.
Stir zucchini, oregano, and tuna into saucepan. Stir mixture into milk in casserole.
Break eggs on top of casserole. Sprinkle with Imitation Worcestershire Sauce. Bake 20 minutes, or till eggs are set.
Serve as main dish with Potato and Spinach Casserole (See Page 269).

Calories per serving: 235   Sodium per serving: 109 mgs.

Mexican

Mexicans do not breakfast. They brunch on a festive and hearty meal which always includes eggs and a variety of foods which could include refried beans, avocado, fruits, or anything that strikes their buoyant fancy.

BAKED EGGS IN RICE CUPS

Serves 6

3 Tbs. unsalted butter or margarine
2 medium-size onions, minced
½ cup long grain rice
¼ tsp. ground coriander
½ tsp. oregano
½ tsp. garlic powder
⅛ tsp. nutmeg

¼ tsp. ground cumin
2 cups Beef Broth (See Page 44)
1 Tbs. low sodium beef bouillon
6 eggs
3 ozs. low sodium Monterey Jack or
  Cheddar cheese, minced fine

Preheat oven to 350°.
In skillet, melt butter. Sauté onions till transparent.
Stir in rice and cook 3 minutes, stirring to coat well.
Add all remaining ingredients except eggs and cheese. Cook 3 minutes over low heat, stirring to blend.
Pour rice mixture into lightly greased oven-proof casserole. Bake, covered, 40 minutes, or till liquid is absorbed.
Make 6 depressions in rice. Break eggs into depressions. Bake, uncovered, 8 minutes.
Top each egg with some of the cheese. Bake 3 minutes more.
Serve as main dish with salad and vegetable.

Monterey Jack: Calories per serving: 269	Sodium per serving: 84 mgs.
Cheddar: Calories per serving: 274	Sodium per serving: 80 mgs.

EGGS AND SALMON

Serves 6

1 can (7¾ ozs.) low sodium salmon
1 tsp. black peppercorns, crushed
1 Tbs. low sodium beef bouillon
2 Tbs. lemon juice
2 low sodium dill pickles, minced
5 Tbs. unsalted butter or margarine, divided

1 medium-size onion, chopped
8 eggs, lightly beaten
Black pepper to taste
2 scallions, minced, including greens
2 tsps. fresh chopped dill

In bowl, combine first 5 ingredients. Stir to blend thoroughly. Cover and refrigerate 30 minutes.
In skillet, melt 1 Tbs. butter. Add onion and cook over low heat 5 minutes, stirring occasionally. Stir into salmon mixture.
In 2 skillets, melt equal amounts of remaining butter. Pour half the eggs into each skillet and cook over low heat 2 minutes. Sprinkle with pepper. Cook 2 minutes more.
Spoon salmon mixture over eggs. Cook 2 minutes more.
Preheat oven to broil.
Sprinkle eggs with scallions and dill. Run under broiler 2 minutes to set eggs.
Serve as main dish with salad and potatoes.

Calories per serving: 250	Sodium per serving: 112 mgs.

RANCH STYLE EGGS

Serves 4

4 Tortillas (See Page 82)
3 Tbs. unsalted butter or margarine,
    divided
2 medium-size onions, minced
2 cloves garlic
1 green pepper, chopped
2 tomatoes, chopped

1 chili pepper, chopped, or dash of hot
    pepper flakes
4 eggs
½ head romaine lettuce, shredded
4 ozs. low sodium Monterey Jack or
    Cheddar cheese, minced fine

Preheat oven to 350°.
Place Tortillas on tin foil. Heat in oven 3 minutes, or till crisp, but not brittle.
In large skillet, melt 1 Tbs. butter. Sauté onions, garlic, and green pepper till onions are wilted, stirring often.
Add tomatoes and chili peppers. Cook 2 minutes.
Remove vegetables to bowl.
Melt remaining butter. Break eggs into skillet and fry till whites are firm.
For each serving, place 1 Tortilla on a plate. Top with lettuce, then egg.
Scrape vegetable mixture on top of eggs. Sprinkle with cheese.
Serve as main dish with salad.

Monterey Jack: Calories per serving: 394   Sodium per serving: 96 mgs.
Cheddar: Calories per serving: 404   Sodium per serving: 89 mgs.

SUNRISE EGGS

Serves 4

1½ Tbs. unsalted butter or margarine
1 medium-size onion, chopped
4 eggs, lightly beaten
1 Tbs. low sodium relish or 2 low sodium
    cucumber pickles, minced
1½ tsps. low sodium chicken bouillon

Dash of hot pepper flakes
¼ lb. low sodium cottage cheese
Dash of cinnamon
3 Tbs. Salsa (See Page 295), or low
    sodium ketchup

In large skillet, melt ½ Tbs. butter. Cook onion over low heat till wilted.
In bowl, beat eggs, relish, bouillon, and pepper flakes.
Melt remaining butter. Add egg mixture to onions in skillet and cook over low heat, stirring with fork parallel to pan, till eggs are set.
Preheat oven to broil.
Spoon cottage cheese over eggs. Sprinkle with cinnamon.

Run under broiler till cheese starts to bubble.
Spoon on Salsa or ketchup. Place under broiler 30 seconds more.

Calories per serving: 160   Sodium per serving: 77 mgs.

Spanish

If a prize were awarded for imaginative cooking, the Spanish would take first place for their way with eggs. In Spain, eggs are jellied, stuffed, deep fried, baked, simmered, grilled—served hot or cold for breakfast, lunch, or dinner. Whether they serve them fancy or as a simple omelet (tortilla in Spanish), the Spanish do love their eggs.

EGGPLANT OMELET

Serves 4

3 Tbs. olive oil, divided
1 medium-size onion, chopped
1 small eggplant, peeled and chopped
2 tsps. low sodium chicken bouillon

Black pepper to taste
1 tsp. oregano
4 eggs, lightly beaten

In skillet, heat 1 Tbs. oil. Add onion and eggplant and cook over low heat 5 minutes, stirring often.
Stir in bouillon, pepper, and oregano. Blend thoroughly. Transfer mixture to bowl.
Add remaining oil to skillet. Pour eggs into eggplant mixture. When oil is hot, add egg and eggplant mixture and fry over medium/low heat till bottom is brown.
Preheat oven to broil.
Run omelet under broiler to set top.

Calories per serving: 174   Sodium per serving: 61 mgs.

EGGS AND SPINACH WITH ALMONDS

Serves 8

3 cloves garlic, chopped
4 saffron threads
1 clove
3 black peppercorns
⅛ tsp. ground cumin
1 Tbs. olive oil
¼ cup almonds, ground

1 lb. spinach, cooked and chopped
1 cup Chicken Broth (See Page 45),
   divided
¼ tsp. nutmeg
8 eggs
1 Tbs. dry sherry
2 tsps. paprika

In blender, combine garlic, saffron, clove, peppercorns, and cumin. Grind to a paste. Set aside.

In skillet, heat oil. Add almonds and cook over medium heat 1 minute.

Stir in garlic paste, spinach, and 2 Tbs. Chicken Broth. Stir to blend.

Preheat oven to 400°.

In blender, combine spinach mixture, remaining Chicken Broth, and nutmeg. Purée. Spoon into 9" square oven-proof casserole.

Break eggs on top of spinach mixture. Sprinkle with sherry and paprika. Bake till eggs are set.

Calories per serving: 137	Sodium per serving: 87 mgs.

SPANISH OMELET

Serves 4

2 Tbs. olive oil
½ green pepper, chopped
½ red pepper, chopped
1 large tomato, chopped coarse
1 large onion, chopped
2 cloves garlic, minced
Cayenne pepper to taste
½ tsp. basil
5 eggs

½ tsp. turmeric
2 Tbs. water
Dash of white pepper
2 tsps. low sodium chicken bouillon
2 Tbs. unsalted butter or margarine
¼ cup leftover pork or beef, chopped fine
   (optional)
½ cup Salsa (See Page 295)

In large skillet, heat oil. Sauté green and red pepper, tomato, onion, and garlic 5 minutes.

Add cayenne and basil to vegetables.

While vegetables are cooking, beat eggs, turmeric, water, white pepper, and bouillon in large bowl.

Add butter to skillet. When melted, add pork or beef, if desired, and eggs and cook over low heat till eggs are beginning to set on top. Lift sides of eggs from time to time to let mixture flow into pan.

Preheat oven to broil.

While eggs are cooking, heat Salsa in saucepan over low heat.

When eggs are loosely firm, run under the broiler 1 to 2 minutes to set top.

Spoon 3 Tbs. Salsa over omelet and fold.

Serve as main dish with remaining Salsa on the side.

Pork: Calories per serving: 295	Sodium per serving: 116 mgs.
Beef: Calories per serving: 295	Sodium per serving: 114 mgs.
Without Beef or Pork:	
Calories per serving: 260	Sodium per serving: 105 mgs.

DESSERTS

Dessert. The very word is plump with calories. Fattening. And in this age of physical fitness, not so much fun any more. But not all is lost. Lots of desserts can be sumptuous, scrumptious and not pound-filled culprits.

Pears poached in wine and topped with cream are so elegant and sensuous you'll swear they are no-no's. Not so. Have them, by all means. Or treat your taste buds and figure to some homemade ice cream. Made with a little cream and lots of fruit, it's delicious, refreshing, and slenderizing. Even candy and chocolate can be okay. Try some of the dietetic, low sodium brands. They're creamy, rich tasting, but so low in sodium and moderate calorically, you'll actually be getting away with murder—not to mention less fat. What's more, your dentist will be as happy as you because dietetic and low sodium sweets are usually sugar free.

But what about the other kind, the real desserts, you say. Chocolate mousse, rice pudding, crêpes suzettes? Well, let's not kid each other. Finding alternatives to salt can compensate only partially for the nutritional imbalance of fat and sugar overdose found in many after dinner delectables. Oh, but what's a chocolate mousse without the cream? There's no answer necessary and only one solution. When you crave a luscious dessert, have one or two lovely tablespoons—just enough to satisfy your hunger rather than your appetite and round out a meal without rounding you out as well.

So while you're savoring what might seem to be bewitchingly fattening fancies, just relax. If you're smart, they can look as good on you as they taste going down.

American

Often it seems as though Americans eat their lunch or dinner just to get to the dessert. It's a kind of reward. But today that treat is as apt to be a piece of fruit as it is a rich pudding or dish of ice cream. That's because physical fitness has been jogging from coast to coast, the body beautiful becoming more important than the stomach sublime.

Not to imply that Americans no longer indulge in desserts. They enjoy them with as much zest as ever. Only now, they plan them to better complement the main meal.

AMBROSIA

Serves 16

¼ cup orange juice
¼ cup brandy
¼ cup confectioners sugar
8 oranges, peeled and sectioned
2 pts. strawberries, hulled
1 medium-size pineapple, peeled and cut
   into 1" chunks

½ cup freshly grated or shredded
   coconut
1 lb. seedless grapes
3 bananas
4 apples

In large bowl, combine juice, brandy, and sugar.
Add oranges, strawberries, pineapple, and coconut.
Chill overnight.
Two hours before serving, scatter grapes throughout.
Just before serving, peel and cut bananas into ½" rounds and core and slice unpeeled apples. Stir into mixture.

Calories per serving: 135   Sodium per serving: 5 mgs.

FUDGE

Makes 36 Squares

1 cup milk
2 cups plus 1 Tbs. sugar
2 ozs. low sodium bittersweet chocolate

1 oz. low sodium milk chocolate
2 Tbs. unsalted butter or margarine
1 tsp. vanilla extract

In saucepan, bring milk to a slow boil, stirring often. Remove from heat.
Stir in sugar and bittersweet and milk chocolate. Bring to a boil. Cover. Reduce heat and simmer 2 minutes. Uncover and simmer till mixture is bubbly. Remove from heat. Let cool 20 minutes.

Cream in butter. Stir in vanilla and beat vigorously till mixture is like thick syrup. Pour into buttered 9″ square pan. Let stand till firm. Then cut into small squares and let harden completely.

Calories per square: 67	Sodium per square: 7 mgs.
Calories per recipe: 2396	Sodium per recipe: 252 mgs.

MINTED COFFEE CUSTARD

Serves 6

2 Tbs. crème de menthe
1 cup strong black coffee
1½ ozs. low sodium bittersweet chocolate
1 cup milk

4 Tbs. sugar
2 eggs
1 tsp. nutmeg

Preheat oven to 325°.
In blender, combine first 2 ingredients. Add remaining ingredients except nutmeg, and blend briefly. Sprinkle with nutmeg. Pour mixture into 6 individual baking cups.
Place cups in pan containing 1″ hot water and bake 1 hour, or till knife inserted in center comes out clean.

Calories per serving: 115	Sodium per serving: 40 mgs.
Calories per serving: 89	Sodium per serving: 5 mgs.

RUM RAISIN ICE CREAM

Serves 12

2 Tbs. raisins*
3 Tbs. rum
3 eggs, separated

¾ cup sugar
1 tsp. vanilla extract
1 cup heavy cream

Preserved in non-sodium ingredient

Soak raisins in rum 2 hours.
In bowl, combine egg yolks and rum mixture.
In second bowl, beat egg whites, then beat in sugar, a little at a time.
Beat raisin mixture into egg white mixture. Add vanilla. Beat thoroughly.
In bowl, beat cream till firm. Fold into raisin mixture. Pour into freezer tray. Cover and freeze.

Calories per serving: 141	Sodium per serving: 24 mgs.

SPICED RHUBARB

Serves 6

1 lb. rhubarb, cut into 2″ lengths
Water to cover
1 tsp. cardamom seed
½ tsp. cinnamon
Black pepper to taste

2 tsps. honey
½ cup almonds, chopped
1 tsp. cornstarch
1 Tbs. cold water

Place first 7 ingredients in medium-size saucepan. Cover and cook over medium/low heat till mixture has consistency of loose jelly.

Stir in cornstarch mixed with cold water to thicken.

Can be served as dessert or as a condiment with lamb, veal, or fowl.

Calories per serving: 96   Sodium per serving: 3 mgs.

Chinese

Soup is the usual dessert in China. Sweets are usually reserved for between courses to clear the palate, much the same purpose sherbet serves at a continental banquet. However, since most cultures prefer to end a meal on a sweet note, the recipes in this section will more than fulfill that desire.

ALMOND FRUIT GELATIN

Serves 12

2 pkges. unflavored gelatin
2 cups water, divided
1 cup milk
1 Tbs. almond extract
1 can (16 ozs.) pineapple chunks, drained
  and chopped, liquid reserved

½ can (8 ozs.) lychee nuts, drained and
  chopped, liquid reserved
2 Tbs. sugar

In saucepan, combine gelatin and ½ cup water. Stir to dissolve. Stir in remaining water and bring to a boil, stirring to completely dissolve gelatin.

Stir in milk and almond extract. Pour into 9″ square casserole. Refrigerate till gelatin is completely chilled, about 30 minutes.

Fold in pineapple chunks and lychee nuts. Refrigerate 3 hours, or till set.

In saucepan, combine pineapple and lychee liquid with sugar. Cook over medium heat 10 minutes. Cool. Pour over gelatin. Chill.

Calories per serving: 91   Sodium per serving: 11 mgs.

KUMQUATS WITH COCONUT

Serves 4

1 can (16 ozs.) kumquats, including liquid
¼ tsp. ginger powder
2 Tbs. lime juice

¼ cup heavy cream
2 Tbs. shredded coconut

In bowl, combine first 4 ingredients. Stir to blend. Cover and chill 2 hours. Garnish with coconut.

Calories per serving: 149   Sodium per serving: 12 mgs.

French

Although it is not unique to France, the French are devotees of the hot—or, more exactly, warm—dessert. Particular among these are glorious crêpes, flaming fruits, and soufflés. Crowned with fruit, vanilla, or hard sauce, these warm confections are a balm to the spirit as well as delectable to the tongue.

APRICOT CRÊPES FLAMBÉ

Serves 4

4 eggs, separated
1 tsp. low sodium chicken bouillon
2 Tbs. unsalted butter or margarine
1 can (8 ozs.) apricots, drained and
   chopped, liquid reserved

3 Tbs. brandy
1 Tbs. sugar
¼ tsp. nutmeg

In bowl, beat together egg yolks and bouillon. Set aside.

In second bowl, beat egg whites till stiff. Fold into yolk mixture.

In skillet, melt butter. Pour in egg mixture and cook over low heat till eggs are almost set.

Preheat oven to broil.

Spoon chopped apricots on top of eggs. Run under broiler to brown top.
Roll up crêpe and pour on brandy. Flame. Transfer to serving dish.
In same skillet, combine sugar and apricot liquid. Cook over medium heat, stirring to dissolve sugar. Pour over crêpes. Sprinkle with nutmeg.

Calories per serving: 191   Sodium per serving: 60 mgs.

CHOCOLATE MOUSSE

Serves 10

1 cup milk
1 cup water
¼ cup sugar
4 ozs. low sodium bittersweet chocolate
4 eggs, separated

½ cup heavy cream
1 tsp. vanilla extract
2 Tbs. dry sherry
1 tsp. dried or fresh grated orange peel

In saucepan, combine first 4 ingredients. Bring to a slow boil, stirring often.
In bowl, beat egg yolks and combine with a quarter of the milk mixture. Return egg yolk mixture to saucepan. Cook over low heat till it starts to thicken. Place saucepan in bowl of ice to cool.
In another bowl, beat cream till firm.
In a third bowl, beat egg whites till stiff. Fold into whipped cream. Fold in remaining ingredients.
Fold cream mixture into chocolate mixture. Spoon into 10 small cups and chill at least 1 hour.

Calories per serving: 155   Sodium per serving: 39 mgs.

FAKE APPLE TART

Serves 12

2 Tbs. unsalted butter or margarine
6 green apples, peeled, cored, and sliced
  thin
½ cup dried apricots
2 Tbs. lemon juice

1 tsp. dried or fresh grated lemon peel
¼ cup brown sugar, firmly packed
¼ cup orange juice
¼ cup granulated sugar
¼ cup honey

Preheat oven to 450°.
Butter a 9″ square oven-proof casserole.
Arrange half the apple slices on bottom of casserole. Layer apricots on top and then the remaining apples, sprinkling each layer with lemon juice, lemon peel, and brown sugar.
Pour orange juice over all and bake, covered with tin foil, 45 minutes, or till apples are tender.

Fifteen minutes before apples are done, combine granulated sugar and honey in small saucepan. Cook over medium heat till sugar begins to caramelize.

Pour sugar/honey mixture over apple mixture. Set aside for 30 minutes before serving.

Calories per serving: 119	Sodium per serving: 6 mgs.

PEARS VANILLA

Serves 12

6 pears, peeled, halved, and cored
1½ cups water
3 Tbs. sugar

2 tsps. vanilla extract
1 tsp. fresh chopped mint
1 recipe Watermelon Ice (See Page 331)

Preheat oven to 325°.

Place pears, cut side down, in 9" × 13" oven-proof casserole.

In saucepan, combine water, sugar, and vanilla. Cook over very low heat, stirring to dissolve sugar. Pour over pears.

Sprinkle pears with mint. Cover and bake 40 minutes, or till pears are tender.

Place on individual plates and top with Watermelon Ice.

Calories per serving: 111	Sodium per serving: 6 mgs.

German

The Germans so love and appreciate the sweet freshness of fruit, they often serve it throughout the meal as well as for dessert. However, their love of good food often turns to a light pudding, custard, soufflé, or even pancakes (with fruit sauce, of course) to finish their meal.

APPLES AND PEACHES IN WINE CREAM

Serves 10

8 peaches, unpeeled, pitted, and sliced
2 Tbs. lemon juice
1 Tbs. brandy
4 apples, peeled, cored, and sliced
½ tsp. nutmeg
½ cup apple juice

½ cup orange juice
½ cup dry or sweet sherry
2 Tbs. sugar
1 Tbs. cornstarch
¼ cup heavy cream

In saucepan, combine all ingredients except cream. Cook over low heat 25 minutes, stirring occasionally. Cool. Cover and chill 2 hours.

Just before serving, stir in cream.

Calories per serving: 131   Sodium per serving: 6 mgs.

COTTAGE CHEESE SOUFFLÉ

Serves 12

6 eggs, separated
¼ cup sugar
3 Tbs. unsalted butter or margarine,
    softened, divided
¾ lb. low sodium cottage cheese, drained

2 Tbs. all-purpose flour
1 tsp. cinnamon
¼ cup walnuts, chopped
¼ cup dried apricots, chopped
2 tsps. dried or fresh grated lemon peel

Preheat oven to 325°.

In bowl, beat egg whites till stiff.

In second bowl, beat egg yolks. Beat in sugar, then 2 Tbs. butter, then cheese.

Stir in all remaining ingredients except 1 Tbs. butter.

With remaining Tbs. butter, grease a 5″ × 9″ cake pan. Pour in soufflé mixture. Cover loosely with tin foil and place in large casserole containing 1″ hot water. Bake 1 hour, or till top is firm.

Calories per serving: 134   Sodium per serving: 41 mgs.

RUM FRUIT

Serves 12

3 pears, peeled, cored, and sliced
6 peaches, peeled, pitted, and sliced
1 cup peach nectar
1 pt. strawberries, hulled
½ cup apple juice

2 tsps. lemon juice
1 tsp. cinnamon
1 lime, cut into wedges
½ cup rum

In saucepan, combine all ingredients except rum. Cook over low heat 20 minutes, stirring occasionally. Stir in rum.

Pour into bowl. Cover and chill 2 hours.

Calories per serving: 103   Sodium per serving: 3 mgs.

Greek

Like so many others, the Greeks favor light desserts such as mild custards and puddings and, most preferably, the sweetness of ripe, fresh fruits.

BAKED FRUIT WITH JAM

Serves 4

1 can (16 ozs.) apricot halves, including
   liquid
4 Tbs. cherry or strawberry preserves*
¼ cup orange juice

¼ cup apple juice
2 Tbs. lemon juice
2 Tbs. dry or sweet sherry
2 Tbs. shredded coconut

Preserved without pectin or sodium

Preheat oven to 350°.
Place apricots, cut side up, and their liquid in 9″ square oven-proof casserole.
In saucepan, combine all remaining ingredients except coconut. Cook over low heat 5 minutes, stirring often. Pour over apricots.
Sprinkle coconut over all. Cover and bake 10 minutes.

Calories per serving: 159   Sodium per serving: 6 mgs.

COCONUT DROPS

Serves 18

3 eggs, separated
⅔ cup sugar
1 cup shredded coconut

¼ cup raisins*
1 tsp. almond extract
½ tsp. nutmeg

Preserved in non-sodium ingredient

In bowl, beat egg yolks till creamy. Gradually beat in sugar. Then beat in coconut, raisins, almond extract, and nutmeg.
Preheat oven to 325°.
In second bowl, beat egg whites till stiff. Fold into yolk mixture. Drop by teaspoonfuls onto greased baking sheet. Bake 20 minutes, or till golden brown.

Calories per serving: 75   Sodium per serving: 12 mgs.

LEMON ICE

Serves 8

2 cups water
1 cup sugar

1 Tbs. dried or fresh grated lemon peel
1 cup lemon juice

In saucepan, combine water and sugar. Bring to a boil, stirring constantly, till sugar is dissolved.

Remove from heat. Stir in remaining ingredients. Pour into freezer tray or 8 small freezer containers. Freeze till set.

Calories per serving: 103   Sodium per serving: 7 mgs.

Indian

Fruit is the decided Indian favorite for ending a meal. A close second, however, is Indian ice cream, made from boiled down milk. In fact, milk reduced almost to a paste is the base for most sweets, including halva and puddings.

BANANAS IN COCONUT CREAM

Serves 8

2 Tbs. butter
4 bananas, peeled and halved lengthwise
3 Tbs. sugar

4 Tbs. dry sherry, divided
½ cup heavy cream
¼ cup shredded coconut

In large skillet, melt butter. Place bananas, cut side down, in skillet and cook over low heat till they start to brown.

Sprinkle on sugar and 2 Tbs. sherry. Cook till sugar starts to caramelize. Transfer bananas and caramelized sugar to serving dish.

In bowl, beat cream and remaining sherry. Spoon over bananas. Top with coconut. Chill 3 to 4 hours.

Calories per serving: 168   Sodium per serving: 23 mgs.

CARROT HALVA

Serves 12

2 lbs. carrots, scraped and grated
2½ cups water
1½ cups milk
3 cardamom pods

¼ cup sugar
4 Tbs. oil
2 Tbs. raisins*
½ tsp. nutmeg

Preserved in non-sodium ingredient

    In Dutch oven, combine first 4 ingredients. Bring to a boil. Reduce heat and simmer 30 minutes, or till liquid is almost absorbed.
    Stir in sugar and oil and simmer 30 minutes more, stirring occasionally.
    Stir in raisins and nutmeg. Cook 2 minutes more, stirring often. Remove from heat. Remove and discard cardamom pods. Serve hot or cold.

Calories per serving: 111   Sodium per serving: 52 mgs.

INDIAN ICE CREAM

Serves 8

6 cups milk
4 cardamom pods
2 Tbs. sugar

1 tsp. vanilla extract
1 Tbs. chopped almonds
2 Tbs. raisins*

Preserved in non-sodium ingredient

    In saucepan, bring milk to a very slow boil. Let it bubble, but not boil over, till milk is reduced by two thirds, about 1¼ hours. Stir occasionally.
    When milk is reduced, crush the cardamom pods; discard shells and add seeds to milk. Stir to blend.
    Stir in remaining ingredients and let mixture cool. Pour into 8 small containers, cover with tin foil, and place in freezer.
    Stir mixture every 30 minutes. When it becomes too hard to stir, let freeze solid.
    When ready to serve, loosen ice cream from sides of containers by running a warm knife around the inside edges.

Calories per serving: 148   Sodium per serving: 88 mgs.

Italian

Desserts in Italy generally take the form of fruit, cheese, or nuts. Of the latter, almonds are a decided favorite and flavor many of the refreshing subtleties, including ice cream, that grace the end of a meal.

COCONUT PEARS

Serves 8

4 pears, peeled, halved, and cored
2 Tbs. shredded coconut
2 Tbs. raisins*

¾ cup sweet vermouth
1 tsp. cinnamon

Preserved in non-sodium ingredient

Preheat oven to 325°.
Place pears, cut side up, in 9″ × 13″ oven-proof casserole. Sprinkle coconut and raisins in hollows of pears.
Pour vermouth around pears.
Sprinkle pears with cinnamon. Cover and bake 40 minutes, or till pears are tender but firm.
Place pears on individual plates. Spoon pan juices over all.

Calories per serving: 98	Sodium per serving: 4 mgs.

STRAWBERRY ICE CREAM

Serves 8

2 pts. strawberries, hulled and chopped,
    divided
¼ cup orange juice

1 Tbs. lemon juice
¼ cup sugar
½ cup heavy cream

In blender, purée 1½ pints of the strawberries. Set aside.
In saucepan, combine orange juice, lemon juice, and sugar. Cook over low heat 10 minutes, or till mixture starts to bubble, stirring often. Let cool.
In bowl, combine sugar mixture and puréed berries.
In another bowl, beat cream till whipped. Fold into berry mixture. Fold in remaining chopped berries. Pour into 8 small freezer containers and freeze till firm.

Note: Two cups of any fruit and one-fourth cup of any fruit juice can be substituted in this recipe.

Calories per serving: 122	Sodium per serving: 8 mgs.

WATERMELON ICE

Serves 12

1 medium-size watermelon (approximately
  6 lbs.), seeded, pulp chopped
2 Tbs. cornstarch

1 tsp. vanilla extract
⅓ cup sugar
2 Tbs. lemon juice

In blender, purée watermelon. Set aside.
In saucepan, combine remaining ingredients. Cook over low heat, stirring frequently.
Add watermelon mixture and cook 3 minutes more, stirring often. Let stand 5 minutes.
Beat vigorously and pour into 12 small freezer containers. Freeze till solid. Serve with
fresh fruit.

Calories per serving: 49   Sodium per serving: 3 mgs.

Jewish

When you smell a pot of tayglach boiling on the stove, perfuming the air with honey,
you'd never believe that desserts don't have a prominent place in Jewish cuisine.
Well, in general, it's true. The Jews do enjoy fresh fruit after a meal, or an occasional
pudding, but otherwise hold out for pastry or simply opt for a steaming pot of coffee
or tea.

ALMOND FRUIT PUDDING

Serves 10

2 eggs
¼ cup sugar
¼ cup brandy
¾ cup water
¾ cup heavy cream
4 tsps. low sodium chicken bouillon
1 tsp. almond extract

1 tsp. lemon extract
1 tsp. vanilla extract
1 can (12 ozs.) mandarin oranges,
  drained
1 can (8 ozs.) peach or pineapple slices,
  drained and chopped
¼ cup almonds, chopped

In medium-size saucepan, beat eggs. Stir in sugar, brandy, water, cream, and bouillon.
Cook over medium heat 5 minutes, or till mixture starts to thicken. Set aside and cool 5
minutes.
Stir in remaining ingredients. Spoon into dessert dishes. Chill overnight.

Calories per serving: 154   Sodium per serving: 27 mgs.

BAKED APPLES

Serves 6

6 large apples, cored
2 Tbs. sugar
2 tsps. cinnamon

2 Tbs. raisins*
1 cup apple juice
1 Tbs. dry or sweet sherry

Preserved in non-sodium ingredient

Preheat oven to 350°.
Place apples in shallow baking dish. Sprinkle with sugar and cinnamon.
Spoon 1 tsp. raisins into each apple cavity. Pour apple juice in dish. Bake 45 minutes, or till apples are fork tender.
Stir sherry into dish. Spoon pan juices over apples.

Calories per serving: 129   Sodium per serving: 10 mgs.

KISSEL

Serves 8

1 pt. raspberries
1 pt. strawberries, hulled
2½ cups cranberry juice

3½ Tbs. cornstarch
3½ Tbs. water
3 Tbs. sugar

In blender, purée berries.
Add cranberry juice and blend. Pour into saucepan. Blend in cornstarch and water. Cook over low heat, stirring constantly, till mixture bubbles and thickens.
Stir in sugar. Pour into 8 individual cups. Chill in refrigerator till icy cold.

Calories per serving: 121   Sodium per serving: 4 mgs.

TAYGLACH

Serves 25

4 eggs
2 cups all-purpose flour
1½ Tbs. oil
½ cup walnuts, chopped

1 cup honey
¾ cup cold water
1 cup sugar
Dash of ginger powder

In large bowl, combine first 4 ingredients. Stir thoroughly till dough is formed.
Turn dough onto lightly floured board and break off walnut-size pieces. Roll out each piece to ½″ diameter and twist into pretzel shape. Set aside.

In Dutch oven, bring honey, cold water, sugar, and ginger to a boil. Drop in tayglach, one by one, and boil slowly 20 minutes. (Do not stir.)
Stir to blend and cook 20 minutes more.

Calories per serving: 112　　　　　　　　Sodium per serving: 12 mgs.

Mexican

Although their cuisines are radically different in style and flavor, there is one thing, other than language, the Mexicans have in common with their Spanish cousins. They prefer light, fruit based desserts or creamy flans as the finishing touch to a meal. Everyday dessert favorites also include rice and bread puddings filled with nuts and fruits and enhanced by wines and spices.

BANANAS AND RUM SAUCE

Serves 12

2 Tbs. unsalted butter or margarine
6 bananas, peeled and split lengthwise
1 orange, peeled and sectioned

¼ cup rum
2 tsps. brown sugar

In large skillet, melt butter. Place bananas cut side down and cook over low heat 1 minute.
Add orange sections. Cook 3 minutes more, turning oranges occasionally.
Pour in rum and flame.
Stir in brown sugar.

Calories per serving: 87　　　　　　　　Sodium per serving: 7 mgs.

FRUIT AND HONEY COMPOTE

Serves 12

1 banana, peeled and cut into 1″ rounds
2 apples, peeled, cored and sliced
1 pear, cored and sliced
3 peaches, unpeeled, pitted, and
　quartered
2 oranges, peeled and sectioned
1 grapefruit, peeled and sectioned

1 cup seedless grapes
½ cup orange juice
¼ cup honey
4 Tbs. lime juice
4 cloves
½ tsp. allspice

In large bowl, combine fruit. Toss to mix well and set aside.
In saucepan combine remaining ingredients. Cook over low heat 5 minutes, stirring constantly.
Pour honey mixture over fruit. Stir to blend thoroughly.
Cover and refrigerate 4 hours.

Calories per serving: 102   Sodium per serving: 3 mgs.

ORANGES WITH MINT SAUCE

Serves 6

4 oranges, peeled and sectioned
2 Tbs. fresh chopped orange peel
2 Tbs. sugar
1 Tbs. mint

1 tsp. almond extract
¼ cup rum
⅛ tsp. nutmeg

In bowl, combine all ingredients. Toss to blend well. Cover and refrigerate 4 hours.

Calories per serving: 85   Sodium per serving: 4 mgs.

Spanish

Desserts are simple affairs in Spain, usually whatever fruits are in season. Native grown oranges are a favorite, but all fruits are relished for their sweet refreshment —often showered with wine or wrapped in ice cream, another Spanish favorite.

Fruits are particularly enjoyed for their lightness, so welcome after a hearty meal. But as often as not, the Spanish also indulge in the famous custard they call flan.

BAKED APPLES WITH CHEESE

Serves 12

6 large apples, halved and cored
1 Tbs. cinnamon
2 Tbs. raisins*

¼ cup dry sherry
6 ozs. low sodium Gouda cheese, sliced thin

*Preserved in non-sodium ingredient

Preheat oven to 350°.

Place apples, cut side up, in shallow baking pan. Sprinkle with cinnamon, then raisins. Pour sherry in pan. Cover with tin foil and bake 45 minutes, or till apples are tender, adding water to pan, if necessary, to prevent sticking.

Place a slice of cheese on each apple half. Bake 5 minutes more, or till cheese melts.

Calories per serving: 101   Sodium per serving: 9 mgs.

CARAMEL CUSTARD (FLAN)

Serves 12

1½ cups sugar, divided
4 cups milk
2 cinnamon sticks
1 tsp. dried or fresh grated lemon peel

1 tsp. dried or fresh grated orange peel
4 eggs
½ tsp. vanilla extract

In saucepan, combine 1 cup sugar, the milk, cinnamon, and lemon and orange peel. Simmer 5 minutes. Let cool. Discard cinnamon.

While milk mixture is cooking, in small saucepan, melt remaining sugar over very low heat. Do not allow to burn. Spoon a small amount into 12 individual custard molds.

Preheat oven to 450°.

In bowl, blend eggs, vanilla, and milk mixture. Skim off any foam. Pour mixture into molds. Place molds in pan with water that comes two thirds up the sides of the molds. Bake 40 minutes, or till custard is lightly browned and firm, adding cold water to pan, if necessary, to prevent boiling.

Calories per serving: 174   Sodium per serving: 63 mgs.

HONEYED FRUIT

Serves 8

4 oranges, peeled and chopped
4 peaches, unpeeled, pitted, and sliced
½ honeydew melon, cut into chunks

¼ tsp. cinnamon
3 Tbs. honey
¼ cup brandy

In bowl, combine all ingredients. Cover and chill 4 hours.

Calories per serving: 107   Sodium per serving: 12 mgs.

CAKES, PIES, AND PASTRIES

There's no use pretending cakes, pies, and pastries aren't fattening. They are. It's not the salt in this case, for it's minimal, but the disproportionately high content of sugars and fats. But take heart. There's no reason you can't enjoy these luxuries, or we wouldn't have devoted a whole chapter to them.

Just remember, common sense is really your best friend. A small slice is better than none at all. What's more, if you've had a rich main meal, opt for one of the light desserts offered in the preceding chapter. Save the cakes to celebrate the perfect end to a simpler dish like broiled chicken or fish. But to ensure guilt-free pleasure, prepare or buy your favorite sweet without salt.

Now that we've discussed the facts, let's wander through the fantasy of pastryland. There's no sweeter satisfaction than lifting your own warm spicy Banana Bread (page 337) from the oven or offering a tray of delectable Almond Crescents (page 347) to your guests. Your friends will marvel at your skill, and you don't have to tell them how truly easy it is.

It is easy, you know. Cakes, pies, and pastries have fewer ingredients to worry about than any main dish you could prepare. But there's such mystery attached to them that we think they're difficult. The only hard part is knowing your own oven because baking time is critically important. If you know that, you've mastered the art. As for the time involved, generally you won't spend more than a half hour assembling and preparing a cake. Pastries take a little longer since you have to roll the dough. But most doughs can be wrapped and refrigerated overnight and rolled out the next day.

So make a fruit cake for the holidays or some pastries for that special occasion. Your pride will heighten your pleasure. And if you don't feel like making your own, you can choose from a wonderful selection of low sodium cookies and cakes on the market. Cookies average 30 calories and 5 mgs. sodium apiece; cakes, 80 calories and 10 mgs. sodium per slice. You see, sweets can be just that.

You don't have to deny yourself that creamy pie ever again. As we promised at the beginning of this book, you can have everything you want as long as you know what you're doing. So bring on the Walnut Cake (page 334). If you know what to do, and how, you can have your cake and eat it, too. And we hope you've enjoyed your meal.

American

"As American as apple pie" is more than an expression. It's a way of life. No occasion is so insignificant that it doesn't warrant some pastry adornment. Cakes are so much enjoyed that every holiday has its own specialty. Mincemeat pie is Thanksgiving; rum fruit cake, Christmas; and so on.

Americans are as openly enthusiastic about cakes as they are about baseball.

BANANA BREAD

Serves 18

1 cup all-purpose flour
⅔ cup sugar
1 Tbs. low sodium baking powder
½ cup vegetable shortening
2 bananas, peeled and mashed
2 eggs

1 tsp. dried or fresh grated lemon peel
1 tsp. orange extract
¼ tsp. cinnamon
¼ tsp. ginger powder
½ cup raisins*
¼ cup chopped walnuts (optional)

Preserved in non-sodium ingredient

Preheat oven to 350°.
In bowl, combine first 3 ingredients, blending thoroughly.
Blend in shortening, mashing with fork. Beat in bananas and eggs.
Stir in lemon peel, orange extract, cinnamon, ginger, raisins, and nuts. Pour batter into greased 5" × 9" loaf pan and bake 45 minutes, or till toothpick inserted in center comes out clean.
Serve hot or cold.

With Walnuts: Calories per serving: 143
Without Walnuts: Calories per serving: 132

Sodium per serving: 11 mgs.
Sodium per serving: 11 mgs.

BASIC PIE CRUST

Pastry for 1 two-crust pie

2½ cups all-purpose flour
¾ cup unsalted butter, margarine, or
  vegetable shortening

4 Tbs. ice water

In large bowl, sift flour. Make a well in the center. To it, add butter and blend into flour till crumbly.

Add water and form dough to pastry consistency, adding more water, if needed, till pastry sticks together. Form into ball. Roll in waxed paper and refrigerate 1 hour.

Divide dough in half. Turn each half onto lightly floured board. Roll out with floured rolling pin till dough is stretched enough to overlap a 9″ pie plate.

Fold dough in half and ease into pie plate. Fill shell and ease second circle of dough over pie plate. When top half is in place, crimp both halves together. Pierce top dough with fork.

Bake according to directions.

Calories per recipe: 2262	Sodium per recipe: 71 mgs.

DEVIL'S FOOD CAKE

Serves 24

1¾ cups cake flour
4½ tsps. low sodium baking powder
½ tsp. cinnamon
1½ tsps. low sodium beef bouillon
1 tsp. dried or fresh grated orange peel
2½ ozs. low sodium bittersweet chocolate
5 Tbs. orange juice
2 cups sugar, divided
½ cup unsalted butter or margarine

3 eggs, separated
⅔ cup milk
1 tsp. vanilla extract
2 egg whites
¼ tsp. nutmeg
2 Tbs. Grand Marnier
1 tsp. almond extract
1 Tbs. lemon juice

In bowl, sift together first 5 ingredients. Set aside.

Over simmering water, melt chocolate in saucepan. Stir in orange juice. Set aside. Preheat oven to 350°.

In second bowl, cream together 1½ cups of the sugar, butter, and eggs, beating till smooth. Stir in chocolate mixture.

Alternately stir flour mixture and milk into chocolate mixture. Stir in vanilla. Pour batter into greased 9″ cake pan. Bake 35 minutes, or till toothpick inserted in center comes out clean.

While cake is baking, in saucepan, combine egg whites, remaining ½ cup sugar, nutmeg, and Grand Marnier. Place over pan of simmering water and stir briskly with whisk till mixture is stiff. Remove from heat.

Stir in almond extract and lemon juice, blending thoroughly.

When cake is cooled, spread with icing.

Calories per serving: 165	Sodium per serving: 21 mgs.

FRUIT CAKE

Serves 36

Wonderful treat for holidays, and keeps several months in refrigerator if tightly wrapped.

2 cups all-purpose flour
1 tsp. cinnamon
1 tsp. nutmeg
1 tsp. allspice
½ tsp. ground cloves
1 cup raisins*
½ cup dried apricots, chopped
½ cup dates, pitted and chopped
½ cup figs, chopped
½ cup almonds, chopped

1⅓ cups brown sugar, tightly packed
1 cup unsalted butter or margarine
4 eggs
2 Tbs. orange juice
¼ cup apricot nectar
1 tsp. vanilla extract
1 tsp. dried or fresh grated orange peel
1 Tbs. lemon juice
4 Tbs. rum

Preserved in non-sodium ingredient

In large bowl, sift together first 5 ingredients. Stir in all fruits and almonds.
Preheat oven to 275°.
In second bowl, cream together sugar and butter till mixture is smooth. Beat in eggs.
Beat remaining ingredients into sugar mixture alternately with flour mixture.
Pour batter into two 5" × 9" loaf pans lined with tin foil, and place on middle rack in oven.
Place a shallow pan filled with water under the fruit cakes and bake 1½ hours, or till knife inserted in center comes out clean.

Calories per serving: 138   Sodium per serving: 14 mgs.

HONEY CAKE

Serves 36

1½ cups all-purpose flour, sifted
3 eggs
¾ cup sugar
1 cup strong tea (made with 3 tea bags)
1 cup honey
4½ tsps. low sodium baking powder
3 Tbs. Grand Marnier
½ tsp. cinnamon

½ tsp. ginger powder
½ tsp. nutmeg
1 Tbs. dried or fresh grated lemon peel
1 Tbs. dried or fresh grated orange peel
1 tsp. lemon juice
½ cup raisins*
½ cup walnuts, chopped (optional)

Preserved in non-sodium ingredient

Preheat oven to 350°.
In large bowl, combine all ingredients. Pour into 9″ square oven-proof casserole, blending thoroughly. Bake 45 minutes, or till toothpick inserted in center comes out clean.

With Walnuts: Calories per serving: 86	Sodium per serving: 8 mgs.
Without Walnuts: Calories per serving: 75	Sodium per serving: 8 mgs.

LEMON BARS

Serves 24 (Makes 2 Dozen)

¾ cup sugar
3 Tbs. unsalted butter or margarine
1 egg
3 Tbs. milk

1 tsp. vanilla extract
2 Tbs. lemon juice
1¼ cups all-purpose flour
1½ tsps. low sodium baking powder

Preheat oven to 375°.
In bowl, cream together sugar and butter. Beat in egg, milk, vanilla, and lemon juice.
In second bowl, combine flour and baking powder. Blend into sugar mixture.
Spread mixture in a greased shallow baking pan, about 9″ square. Bake 15 minutes, or till lightly browned. Let cool and cut into small bars about 1½″ × 2¼″.

Calories per serving: 46	Sodium per serving: 6 mgs.

RICE PUDDING

Serves 12

2 cups cooked rice
½ cup sugar
2 cups milk
4 tsps. low sodium chicken bouillon
1 tsp. vanilla extract

1 tsp. orange extract
¼ cup water
½ cup golden raisins*
½ tsp. cinnamon

Preserved in non-sodium ingredient

Preheat oven to 325°.
Combine rice, sugar, and milk in a 9″ × 13″ oven-proof casserole. Bake 1½ hours, stirring occasionally.
Stir in bouillon, vanilla, orange extract, and water. Stir in raisins and cinnamon. Bake, uncovered, 45 minutes, or till golden crust forms on top.
Serve with fresh fruit and heavy cream.

Calories per serving: 104	Sodium per serving: 33 mgs.

SPICED APPLE PIE

Serves 20

Basic Pie Crust (See Page 337)
6 green apples, peeled, cored, and sliced
  thin
¼ cup sugar
1 tsp. cinnamon
1 tsp. dried or fresh grated orange peel

3 Tbs. dry or sweet sherry
½ tsp. allspice
¼ tsp. ground cloves
2 Tbs. lemon juice
2 Tbs. milk

Prepare Basic Pie Crust for two-crust pie according to directions. Line a 9″ pie plate with half the pastry.
Preheat oven to 400°.
Place apples in pie shell, overlapping at the edges. Sprinkle with remaining ingredients except milk.
Cover with second half of the pastry and crimp edges together.
Pierce top crust. Brush with milk. Bake 10 minutes. Reduce heat to 350° and bake 40 minutes, or till crust is golden brown.

Calories per serving: 146   Sodium per serving: 6 mgs.
Note: Without the top crust, calories are reduced to 89; sodium to 4 mgs.

STRAWBERRY RHUBARB PIE

Serves 20

1 pt. strawberries, hulled and halved
1 lb. rhubarb, peeled and chopped
⅔ cup sugar
1 tsp. cinnamon

2 tsps. lemon juice
⅓ cup all-purpose flour
Basic Pie Crust (See Page 337)
2 Tbs. milk

In bowl, combine all ingredients, except pie crust and milk. Blend thoroughly. Let stand 1 hour.
Preheat oven to 400°.
Prepare Basic Pie Crust for two-crust pie according to directions. Line a 9″ pie plate with half the pastry. Fill with fruit mixture.
Cover with second half of the pastry. Pierce with fork. Brush with milk. Place on baking sheet to catch escaping juices and bake 15 minutes.
Reduce heat to 375° and bake 20 minutes more, or till crust is evenly golden brown.

Calories per serving: 158   Sodium per serving: 7 mgs.
Note: Without the top crust, calories are reduced to 101; sodium to 5 mgs.

Chinese

Rice is often used to make pastry confections in the Orient. Buns are another reasonable substitute for pastries. Plain, of course, they are served as breads. Stuffed with jellies or fruits, they are delectable bites.

ALMOND COOKIES

Serves 30

1 cup almonds, ground
1 cup rice flour or sifted all-purpose flour
½ cup brown sugar, tightly packed
¼ tsp. nutmeg

6 Tbs. unsalted butter or margarine
1 tsp. almond extract
1 Tbs. cold water

Preheat oven to 350°.
In bowl, place ground almonds. Sift in flour and sugar. Stir in nutmeg.
Cream in butter, using fingers, if necessary, to blend in thoroughly. Stir in almond extract and cold water.
Break off tablespoons of dough. Flatten slightly on greased baking tray, leaving 1″ between pieces. Bake 20 minutes, or till cookies are lightly browned.

Calories per serving: 71   Sodium per serving: 7 mgs.

SESAME SEED COOKIES

Serves 35

⅓ cup oil
3 Tbs. hot water
2 cups all-purpose flour
1⅛ Tbs. low sodium baking powder
½ cup sugar

1 egg, lightly beaten
2 Tbs. cold water
1 Tbs. honey
½ cup sesame seed
35 dates, pitted

In bowl, beat together oil and hot water. Set aside.
In second bowl, sift together flour, baking powder, and sugar. Make a well in the center. Stir in oil mixture, egg, cold water, and honey, working mixture till dough is formed.
Preheat oven to 375°.
Turn dough onto lightly floured surface and roll to ⅛″ thickness. Cut into 2½″ circles and place, 1″ apart, on lightly greased baking sheet.
Sprinkle on sesame seed. Top each piece with 1 date. Bake 10 minutes, or till cookies are golden brown.

Calories per serving: 92   Sodium per serving: 3 mgs.

STEAMED FRUIT SPONGE BALLS

Serves 16

2 eggs, separated
½ cup powdered sugar
⅔ cup all-purpose flour, sifted
1 tsp. orange extract

⅜ tsp. low sodium baking powder
10 prunes, pitted and chopped
½ cup dried apricots, chopped
¾ cup water

In bowl, beat egg whites till stiff. Beat in egg yolks, sugar, flour, orange extract, and baking powder. Blend thoroughly.
Divide dough among 16 small greased oven-proof cups. Make slight depressions in dough.
In saucepan, combine remaining ingredients. Simmer over medium heat 15 minutes, or till fruit is soft. Purée in blender.
Spoon fruit mixture into depressions in dough. Place cups on rack in large pan filled with water to just below the rack. Cover. Bring to a boil. Steam over low heat 15 minutes, or till set.

Calories per serving: 65   Sodium per serving: 10 mgs.

French

Pastry making is a fine and honorable art in France. The work requires deft hands and a light touch to bring forth the flaky pastries, filled with cream, brimming with fruits, or adorned with a delicate frosting.
The pastry chef is highly regarded and rightly so. Not everyone could produce such delicious and intricately elegant creations.

BUTTER ALMOND CAKE

Serves 36

¼ cup unsalted butter or margarine,
   melted
6 eggs
1 cup sugar, divided
2 Tbs. rum

2 Tbs. dried or fresh grated orange peel
1 tsp. vanilla extract
1 cup almonds, ground
½ tsp. nutmeg
1 cup cake flour

343

In bowl, place butter. Set in warm place.

In saucepan, combine eggs and ⅔ cup sugar. Set over pan of boiling water and stir till smooth and creamy.

With whisk, stir in rum, orange peel, vanilla, and remaining sugar. Whisk till smooth and creamy.

Preheat oven to 350°.

In bowl, combine almonds, nutmeg, and flour, blending thoroughly. Stir into egg mixture. Fold in melted butter.

Pour batter into 2 greased and floured 9″ cake pans. Bake 40 minutes, or till toothpick inserted in center comes out clean.

Calories per serving: 79	Sodium per serving: 12 mgs.

WALNUT CAKE

Serves 40

2½ cups walnuts
1½ cups sugar, divided
2 tsps. cinnamon
1 tsp. nutmeg
1½ cups all-purpose flour
1½ cups unsalted butter or margarine,
  softened

6 eggs
1 tsp. vanilla extract
2 tsps. dried or fresh grated orange peel
Basic Pie Crust (See Page 337)

In blender, grind walnuts with ½ cup sugar, cinnamon, and nutmeg. Transfer to bowl. Stir in flour. Set aside.

In bowl, cream together butter and remaining sugar. Beat in eggs, vanilla, and orange peel.

Blend walnut and butter mixtures.

Prepare Basic Pie Crust for two-crust pie according to directions. Line two 9″ pie plates with pastry.

Preheat oven to 350°.

Divide walnut mixture between pie plates. Bake 10 minutes. Reduce heat to 300° and bake 30 minutes more, or till set and brown on top.

Calories per serving: 212	Sodium per serving: 16 mgs.

German

Germans revel in their pastries. Luxuriant with whipped cream, succulent with honey, pastries are part of the fiber of their social life—the cake of the coffee and cake enjoyed late mornings and afternoons when people gather to exchange pleasantries.

The results of the German enthusiasm for their pastry cooks' art include the famous Black Forest cake, marzipan, and linzer torte. No wonder the Germans never serve cakes for dessert. They wisely savor them in their own good time.

CINNAMON COFFEE CAKE

Serves 28

1 pkg. active dry yeast
⅔ cup warm water
⅓ cup milk
3 cups all-purpose flour, divided
⅔ cup raisins*
½ cup sugar

⅔ cup unsalted butter or margarine
3 eggs
1 Tbs. brandy
1 Tbs. dried or fresh grated lemon peel
3 Tbs. cinnamon
2 Tbs. powdered sugar

Preserved in non-sodium ingredient

In bowl, combine yeast and warm water. Stir in milk. Beat in half the flour. Cover and let rise in warm place 1 hour.

In bowl, place raisins with just enough water to cover. Set aside.

In second bowl, cream together sugar and butter till smooth. Beat in eggs, then brandy.

Beat yeast mixture into sugar mixture. Beat in remaining flour. Then beat in lemon peel and cinnamon.

Drain raisins and stir into dough.

Place dough in greased ring mold. Cover and let rise in warm place 1¼ hours.

Preheat oven to 350°.

Sprinkle dough with powdered sugar and bake 45 minutes, or till top is golden and firm.

Calories per serving: 117   Sodium per serving: 13 mgs.

LINZER TORTE

Serves 24

1 cup unsalted butter or margarine,
  softened
1 cup sugar
1 egg
1 Tbs. lemon juice
2 Tbs. milk
1½ cups all-purpose flour

⅔ cup almonds, crushed
¼ tsp. cinnamon
1 tsp. dried or fresh grated orange peel
⅛ tsp. ground cloves
Dash of allspice
1 cup raspberry jam*
3 apples, peeled, cored, and chopped

Preserved without pectin or sodium

In bowl, beat together butter and sugar till mixture is creamy.
Beat in egg, lemon juice, and milk.
Gradually stir in flour, almonds, cinnamon, orange peel, cloves, and allspice. Beat till dough is formed and elastic in consistency. Cover and refrigerate 1 hour.
Preheat oven to 325°.
Turn dough onto lightly floured board and roll to ¼" thickness. Line a pie plate and trim away excess, leaving ¼" overhanging the rim of the plate.
Spoon raspberry jam over dough. Cover with apples.
Gather and roll remaining dough. Cut into 1" strips and make a lattice over the filling. Crimp edge of torte and bake 1 hour, or till crust is golden.

Calories per serving: 186	Sodium per serving: 10 mgs.

SPICED CHEESE CAKE

Serves 20

1½ cups crushed low sodium crackers
1½ cups sugar, divided
1½ tsps. cinnamon
6 Tbs. unsalted butter or margarine,
  melted
4 eggs

2 Tbs. lemon juice
3 Tbs. orange juice (optional)
6 Tbs. all-purpose flour
1 Tbs. dried or fresh grated orange peel
1½ lbs. low sodium cottage cheese,
  drained

Preheat oven to 350°.
Butter a large cake pan.
In bowl, combine crushed crackers, ½ cup sugar, cinnamon, and melted butter. Spread over bottom and sides of cake pan, pressing to form a crust. Bake 10 minutes. Let cool.

In bowl, beat eggs till light and lemony. Beat in remaining sugar, lemon juice, orange juice, and flour. Beat until smooth.

Beat in orange peel and cottage cheese till mixture is creamy. Pour into cooled crust and bake at 350° 1 hour, or till mixture is set.

Calories per serving: 126	Sodium per serving: 47 mgs.

Greek

If baklava were Greece's only pastry legacy, it would be enough. Nothing is more luscious than the warm, flaky crust, dripping with honey and nuts. But sweets are always on hand for the smallest social occasion. They are representatives of Greek hospitality and do their job well.

ALMOND CRESCENTS

Serves 30 (Makes 60 Crescents)

1 cup unsalted butter or margarine
3 Tbs. powdered sugar
1 egg yolk
1½ tsps. almond extract

2 Tbs. ground almonds
2 cups all-purpose flour
1 cup powdered sugar

Preheat oven to 325°.

In bowl, combine first 5 ingredients, beating till creamy.

Stir in flour, blending thoroughly. Break off small pieces of dough and shape into half moons with fingers. Place on lightly greased baking sheet and bake 35 minutes, or till crescents are golden brown. Let cool. Sprinkle with powdered sugar.

Calories per serving: 98	Sodium per serving: 4 mgs.

BAKLAVA

Serves 48

¾ cup sugar
¾ cup water
1 Tbs. dried or fresh grated lemon peel
6 cloves
2 cinnamon sticks

1 cup honey
2 Tbs. brandy
2 Tbs. lemon juice
2 tsps. dried or fresh grated orange peel
2 cups walnuts, chopped

(continued next page)

1 cup almonds, chopped
⅓ cup sugar
2 tsps. cinnamon
½ tsp. nutmeg

1 tsp. almond extract
½ cup unsalted butter or margarine,
    melted, divided
Strudel Dough (See Page 354)

In saucepan, combine first 5 ingredients. Bring to a boil and boil till thickened slightly.
Add honey, brandy, lemon juice, and orange peel. Heat 5 minutes, stirring to blend. Let cool. Discard cinnamon sticks. Set aside.
Preheat oven to 300°.
Place chopped nuts on shallow baking sheet. Toast 5 minutes, or till browned. Set aside.
In bowl, blend together sugar, cinnamon, nutmeg, and almond extract. Add toasted nuts. Stir to blend. Set aside.
Brush a shallow baking sheet with butter. Then brush Strudel Dough with butter.
Spread Strudel Dough with rows of nut mixture 2″ apart. Roll dough up and over filling. Cut rows apart and crimp together. Brush with remaining butter.
Cut baklava to fit baking sheet. Bake at 325° 1 hour, or till dough is golden brown. Let cool slightly and cut on the diagonal.
Pour cooled honey mixture over baklava.

Calories per serving: 126   Sodium per serving: 4 mgs.

LICORICE BARS

Serves 40

¼ cup unsalted butter or margarine
¼ cup oil
¾ cup sugar
1 egg
4½ tsps. low sodium baking powder

1 tsp. aniseed
1 tsp. vanilla extract
6 Tbs. lemon juice
2¾ cups all-purpose flour, sifted

In bowl, beat vigorously the butter, oil, and sugar till blended smooth.
Beat in egg. Then stir in baking powder, aniseed, vanilla, and lemon juice.
Add flour, a little at a time, blending in thoroughly to form dough.
Preheat oven to 375°.
Grease 2 cookie sheets.
Divide dough into 4 sections. Shape each section into narrow rolls, 2″ wide. Place on cookie sheets, well spaced. Bake 20 minutes, or till golden brown. Turn and bake 5 minutes more.
Cut rolls into 2″ lengths. Store in covered container.

Calories per serving: 68   Sodium per serving: 4 mgs.

Indian

Though they do love sweets, Indians rarely indulge in cakes and pastries as they are thought of in other countries. Far preferable to them are their sweet and lovely milk-based desserts.

COCONUT SQUARES

Serves 36

1 cup granulated sugar
1½ cups water
1 cup all-purpose flour
1½ cups shredded coconut
2 eggs, beaten
1 Tbs. lemon juice
1 tsp. vanilla extract

1 cup brown sugar, tightly packed
1 tsp. aniseed
1 cup Coconut Milk (See Page 287)
⅛ tsp. mace
⅛ tsp. ground cloves
1 Tbs. dried or fresh grated orange peel

In saucepan, combine first 2 ingredients. Cook over medium heat, stirring constantly, till sugar is dissolved and mixture is syrupy. Stir in flour, blending thoroughly. Set aside.

In skillet, cook coconut till lightly toasted. Stir in eggs, lemon juice, vanilla, brown sugar, and aniseed.

Stir in Coconut Milk. Stir in syrup mixture. Stir in remaining ingredients. Cook over low heat 10 minutes, stirring occasionally. Pour into buttered 9″ square casserole and let cool. Cut into 36 small squares.

Calories per serving: 83	Sodium per serving: 10 mgs.

PANCAKES IN BANANA SYRUP

Serves 16

1¼ cups all-purpose flour
¾ cup milk
½ cup heavy cream
1 cup sugar
1 banana, peeled and mashed
¾ cup water

1 tsp. lemon juice
4 Tbs. orange juice
½ tsp. nutmeg
3 cardamom pods, crushed fine
4 Tbs. oil, divided

In bowl, combine first 3 ingredients, beating with a whisk. Cover and refrigerate overnight.

In saucepan, combine all remaining ingredients except oil. Bring to a slow boil. Reduce heat and simmer 5 minutes, stirring till sugar is dissolved. Pour into large bowl.

In large skillet, heat 1 Tbs. oil. Drop 2 individual heaping Tbs. of batter onto skillet. Cook over low heat till both sides are browned. Transfer to syrup mixture.

Repeat with remaining oil and batter.

Transfer pancakes to serving platter and cut each pancake in half.

Calories per serving: 154   Sodium per serving: 11 mgs.

Italian

The Italians believe you can't improve on perfection. That's why they rarely end a meal with anything more elaborate than a piece of fruit, a slice of cheese, and a bowl of nuts.

That's not to say cakes and other pastries are not highly regarded. Quite the contrary. Italy is credited with fathering the pastry arts in the 13th century, and Italian cooks present the results of their delicate art with great flourish at holidays and special family occasions, or as lovely between meal snacks.

CHERRY ROLLS

Serves 30 (Makes 5 Dozen)

1 egg
¾ lb. low sodium cottage cheese, drained
½ cup sugar
½ cup unsalted butter or margarine
2 tsps. dried or fresh grated lemon peel

1 tsp. vanilla extract
2 cups all-purpose flour
1½ cups cherry preserves*
1 Tbs. cinnamon

*Preserved without pectin or sodium

In bowl, cream together egg, cottage cheese, sugar, butter, lemon peel, and vanilla.

Gradually stir in flour, blending till dough is formed. Shape into ball. Cover with waxed paper and refrigerate 1 hour.

Preheat oven to 375°.

Turn dough onto lightly floured board. Roll to ⅛" thickness. Cut into 2" triangles.

Place 1 tsp. of cherry preserves on each triangle. Fold ends up and over filling. Place, seam side down, on greased baking sheets, 1″ apart.

Sprinkle with cinnamon and bake 10 minutes, or till cookies are golden brown.

Calories per serving: 111	Sodium per serving: 10 mgs.

FRUIT AND BUTTER CAKE

Serves 30

½ cup unsalted butter or margarine, softened
1 cup sugar
2 eggs
1 tsp. vanilla extract
2½ cups all-purpose flour, divided
½ tsp. nutmeg

3¾ tsps. low sodium baking powder
⅓ cup milk
⅓ cup orange juice
1 cup blueberries
3 peaches, peeled, pitted and chopped
1 cup strawberries, hulled and chopped

Preheat oven to 350°.
In bowl, cream together butter and sugar. Beat in eggs and vanilla.
Gradually beat in half the flour. Stir in nutmeg and baking powder.
Stir in milk and orange juice. Stir in remaining flour.
Fold in all fruits, blending well. Pour batter into greased 9″ square casserole and bake 1 hour, or till top is golden and toothpick inserted in center comes out clean.

Calories per serving: 105	Sodium per serving: 9 mgs.

LADY FINGERS

Serves 20 (Makes 40)

1 egg yolk
1 cup powdered sugar
2 eggs

½ tsp. vanilla extract
1 tsp. lemon extract
1 cup cake flour

Preheat oven to 350°.
In bowl, beat together all ingredients except flour.
Gradually beat in flour.
Through a pastry tube, squeeze dough onto baking tray lined with waxed paper, into strips ¾″ × 3″. Bake 10 minutes, or till lightly browned.

Calories per serving: 54	Sodium per serving: 8 mgs.

Jewish

No Jewish home would be worthy of the name if it didn't contain a platter of cookies or cakes with which to greet visitors or bolster a family's spirits.

Sponge cake, mandel bread, strudel, and coffee cake, all these and more are tasty examples of Jewish hospitality.

HAMANTASCHEN DOUGH

Serves 16

⅔ cup vegetable shortening
½ cup sugar
1 egg
1 tsp. dried or fresh grated orange peel

3 Tbs. water
1 tsp. vanilla extract
2 cups all-purpose flour, sifted

In bowl, cream together shortening and sugar. Cream in egg till mixture is smooth.

Stir in orange peel, water, and vanilla. Then stir in flour till dough forms. Cover and chill overnight.

Turn dough onto lightly floured board. Roll to ⅛″ thickness. Cut into 2″ discs.

Fill as desired and bake per directions for Prune Filled Hamantaschen. (See page 353.)

Calories per serving: 155*
*Does not include filling

Sodium per serving: 6 mgs.*

MANDEL BREAD

Serves 24

3 eggs
½ cup sugar
2 tsps. dried or fresh grated lemon peel
1 tsp. lemon juice
1 Tbs. low sodium baking powder

½ tsp. almond extract
½ tsp. vanilla extract
1½ cups all-purpose flour
¼ cup slivered almonds

Preheat oven to 350°.

In bowl, beat together first 7 ingredients. Sift in flour. Stir in nuts.

Form dough into long oval loaf. Place loaf on greased and floured baking sheet. Bake 40 minutes, or till lightly browned.

Let cool. Cut into ½″ slices and bake at 250° 10 minutes more.

Calories per serving: 59

Sodium per serving: 9 mgs.

PRUNE FILLED HAMANTASCHEN

Serves 16

1½ cups prunes, chopped
¼ cup raisins*
1 tsp. dried or fresh grated lemon peel
1 Tbs. lemon juice

2 Tbs. sugar
1½ cups water
Hamantaschen Dough (See Page 352)

Preserved in non-sodium ingredient

In saucepan, combine all ingredients except Hamantaschen Dough. Bring to a boil and continue boiling 15 minutes, stirring occasionally. Drain off excess liquid and chop fine.
Preheat oven to 350°.
Place 1 tsp. of prune filling on each dough disc. Cover with second disc and crimp together to form triangle shape.
Place cakes on lightly greased baking sheet 1″ apart. Brush tops with water or milk and bake 30 minutes, or till tops are golden brown.

| Calories per serving: 205 | Sodium per serving: 11 mgs. |

SPONGE CAKE

Serves 18

5 eggs, separated
3 Tbs. lemon juice
2 tsps. vanilla extract

1 cup sugar
1 cup all-purpose flour

Preheat oven to 300°.
In bowl, beat egg yolks. Beat in lemon juice and vanilla.
In second bowl, beat egg whites till stiff. Gradually beat in sugar.
Fold egg white mixture into egg yolk mixture.
Sift ¼ cup flour into egg mixture. Fold in till smooth. Repeat till all flour is used.
Pour batter into lightly floured ring mold. Bake 30 minutes. Increase heat to 350° and bake 15 minutes more, or till top is golden and springs back to the touch.
Invert cake; remove from pan when cool.

| Calories per serving: 86 | Sodium per serving: 19 mgs. |

STRUDEL DOUGH

2 cups all-purpose flour, sifted
2 Tbs. oil
1 egg

½ cup warm water
2 tsps. low sodium beef bouillon

In bowl, place flour. Make a well in the center and drop in oil, egg, water, and bouillon. Stir till dough is formed.

Turn dough onto lightly floured board and knead till dough is elastic. Cover with bowl and let stand 45 minutes.

Turn dough onto lightly floured cloth and roll to ⅛" thickness. Brush with a little additional oil. Then, with hands, work dough underneath and, moving from the center to the outer edges, coax as thin as possible.

Fill as desired and bake per directions for Strudel with Apple Filling (See below).

Calories per recipe: 1178   Sodium per recipe: 93 mgs.

STRUDEL WITH APPLE FILLING

Serves 20

6 green apples, peeled, cored, thinly
   sliced, and chopped
½ cup raisins*, chopped
⅓ cup sugar
½ cup low sodium Bread Crumbs (See
   Page 000)

1 tsp. cinnamon
⅛ tsp. nutmeg
1 tsp. dried or fresh grated orange peel
1 tsp. dried or fresh grated lemon peel
¼ cup oil
Strudel Dough (See above)

Preserved in non-sodium ingredient

Preheat oven to 375°.

In bowl, combine all ingredients except Strudel Dough. Stir to blend thoroughly. Set aside.

Spread filling on strudel dough in rows, 2" apart. Roll dough up and over each row of filling. Cut to separate into individual rolls.

Cut rolls to fit a greased baking sheet, leaving ample space between rolls. Bake 40 minutes, or till top is browned and crisp.

Calories per serving: 135   Sodium per serving: 7 mgs.

Mexican

The streets of Mexico are filled with pastry shops, offering tantalizing companions to pleasure your walk. But pastries reach their deserved heights of appreciation on holidays and special occasions.

MINIATURE PUFF PASTRIES

Serves 24

1 pkge. active dry yeast
2 Tbs. warm water
2⅔ cups all-purpose flour, divided
½ cup brown sugar, tightly packed
½ cup unsalted butter or margarine,
    softened, divided

¼ cup milk
1 tsp. vanilla extract
2 Tbs. orange juice

In bowl, combine yeast and warm water, stirring to dissolve. Stir in ½ cup flour. Cover and let stand in warm place 15 minutes, or till double in bulk.

In second bowl, blend remaining flour and sugar. Make a well in the center. In it, place half the butter, the milk, vanilla, orange juice, and yeast mixture. Beat till dough forms. Cover and let stand in warm place 4 hours.

Beat in remaining butter, blending thoroughly.

Divide dough into 24 portions and shape into balls. Place on lightly greased baking sheet and let stand in warm place 1 hour, or till double in bulk.

Preheat oven to 400°.

Bake 20 minutes, or till lightly golden.

Calories per serving: 100	Sodium per serving: 5 mgs.

ORANGE SAND TARTS

Serves 40
(Makes 80 Tarts)

6 Tbs. unsalted butter or margarine
1¼ cups sugar
2 eggs
1 Tbs. dried or fresh grated orange peel

2 Tbs. orange juice
3¼ cups all-purpose flour
1½ tsps. low sodium baking powder
1 egg white

In bowl, cream together butter and sugar. Beat in eggs, orange peel, and orange juice.

Sift flour and baking powder into butter mixture, blending thoroughly. Cover and refrigerate 1 hour.

Preheat oven to 400°.

Turn dough onto lightly floured board and roll to ¼″ thickness. Cut into small rounds and place on greased baking sheet, 1″ apart. Brush with egg white and bake 8 minutes, or till tops are golden.

Calories per serving: 78	Sodium per serving: 6 mgs.

PECAN COOKIES

Serves 15

1 egg white
⅔ cup powdered sugar
⅛ tsp. ground cloves
1 tsp. almond extract

½ tsp. vanilla extract
½ cup pecans, crushed fine
½ cup dried apricots, minced
2 Tbs. all-purpose flour

Preheat oven to 350°.
In bowl, beat egg white till stiff. Beat in sugar. Beat in remaining ingredients.
Form mixture into walnut size balls. Place on baking sheet, 2″ apart. Bake 10 minutes, or till cookies are lightly browned.

Calories per serving: 62	Sodium per serving: 4 mgs.

Spanish

The Spanish so love cakes, they reserve these sweet morsels for late afternoon snacks. This simple repast, eaten with coffee or tea, satisfies their hunger between the hearty noonday meal and late night supper.

Doughs are made with olive oil rather than butter and, when made at home, are usually fried, a preference cultivated before private residences had ovens. But, in whatever form, generally one or more spices are used to heighten the taste of the treats.

CHICK PEA CAKE

Serves 20

¾ lb. dried chick peas*
6 egg yolks
¼ tsp. cinnamon
¼ tsp. nutmeg
1 Tbs. dried or fresh grated orange peel
1½ cups sugar

5 egg whites
⅓ cup heavy cream
1 Tbs. lemon juice
3 Tbs. low sodium Bread Crumbs (See
   Page 291), toasted

Do not substitute canned chick peas.

In saucepan, combine chick peas with enough water to cover. Let stand 6 hours. Bring to a boil. Reduce heat and simmer 1½ hours, or till skins burst and peas are tender. Drain. Remove skins. Spread peas on cloth and let dry overnight.

Preheat oven to 350°.

In blender, grind peas to a paste. Set aside.

In bowl, beat together egg yolks, cinnamon, nutmeg, orange peel, and sugar till mixture is thick and creamy.

In second bowl, beat egg whites till stiff. Fold into egg yolk mixture. Stir in chick pea paste. Fold in cream and lemon juice.

Sprinkle Bread Crumbs in a buttered 9" square casserole.

Spoon in batter. Bake 1 hour, or till set. Let cool. Turn onto platter.

Calories per serving: 159   Sodium per serving: 26 mgs.

SHERRY CAKE

Serves 16

6 eggs, separated
1 cup sugar, divided
1⅔ cups all-purpose flour
½ tsp. ginger powder

½ tsp. nutmeg
1 tsp. cinnamon
1¾ cups sweet sherry

Preheat oven to 375°.

In bowl, beat egg yolks and ⅔ cup sugar till mixture is smooth and creamy.

Beat in flour. Then beat in ginger, nutmeg, and cinnamon. Beat in egg whites till mixture is stiff.

Pour batter into lightly greased 9" square casserole. Bake 30 minutes, or till top is golden and springs back to the touch. Cool. Cut into 16 squares.

While cake is cooling, melt remaining sugar in saucepan over low heat till sugar is caramelized.

Stir in sherry and cook over low heat 10 minutes.

Dip cake squares in sherry. Let dry before serving.

Calories per serving: 140   Sodium per serving: 25 mgs.

HOW TO APPROACH DIET AND MAINTENANCE

Variety is one of the key elements in good nutrition. Balance is another. Common sense should be a third. Thus, if you're planning a saucy main meal, spirited with wine, cream, or low sodium cheese, serve vegetables that are neither as fancy nor as rich. The converse is also true.

The foods in this book tend toward the fanciful to illustrate how imagination and daring can produce exotic, taste-rich meals without salt. But we hope you'll also discover that salt taste can be produced without salt and its negative effects. What's more, herbs and spices, wine, vinegar, lemon juice, and numerous other alternatives—with or without low sodium helpers—will make your meals wonderfully memorable. All you have to do is stock your kitchen properly to make your meals work for you, not against you.

The menus on the next few pages will prove the point. You'll see how easy it is to plan meals you can look forward to, how delightfully easy it is to be healthy and slim without depriving yourself.

The first thing to realize is that diet is not a temporary phase. Good and proper diet is a lifetime habit like brushing your teeth or taking a shower. But don't think of diet as a bad word, a punishment for overeating. Substitute the words good eating and enrichment for diet, and you have the concept.

Good diet basics are necessary whatever your salt or calorie restrictions and whatever your particular problem. Interestingly, many people believe good diet means lots of protein and little or no fats and carbohydrates. Not true. Protein is a versatile body builder, but too much puts pressure and strain on the heart and kidneys. In fact, according to Dr. David Kritchersky, a biochemical nutritionist who is associate director of the Wistar Institute of Anatomy and Biology in Philadelphia, a 1950's study pointed to animal protein as "the best correlation with heart disease." Excess protein could even cause aging by increasing the metabolic rate, thereby shortening the life span of some cells.

Fad diets high in protein force water, not fat, loss by imposing excess pressure on the kidneys. So of the 10 or 15 pounds you might lose over the recommended two week period, very little is real fat. Indeed, any diet that virtually eliminates a key food element will produce similar results. That's why 95% of all who lose weight on such diets gain it back again in a matter of weeks.

Low sodium diets, on the other hand, do not force water loss. They simply prevent water from accumulating in the body, allowing it to stabilize and come down to what is normal body weight for each individual.

Lengthy high protein diets and the high fats which are automatically part of them cause ketosis—the accumulation of toxic acids in the blood. This toxicity can damage vital life organs and could ultimately cause death. In other words, too much of a good thing, even so good a thing as protein, is no good at all. Protein is only one of the essential nutrients in a balanced diet. Actually, men and women alike should not have more than 20% protein in their daily diets.

Carbohydrates, the mislabelled enemies of dieters, are in truth the body's source of glucose which supplies the brain with energy. Without glucose, the brain could die. Without carbohydrates, our bodies would start feeding off their own protein and fat, preventing these nutrients from doing their proper jobs and resulting in malnutrition. Indeed, fats can't metabolize properly without the help of complex carbohydrates.

Athletes, perhaps the most health conscious among us, know the value of carbohydrates. Before a competition, they are far more likely to eat cereal, toast, and fruit than the fabled 16-ounce steak. The stored carbohydrate energy will provide greater endurance over a longer period of time than an equal amount of protein. A *New York Times* article on August 22, 1979, pointed out that "the well-conditioned mature athlete needs no more protein than sedentary people of similar size." On a percentage basis, carbohydrates are the most important food element in your diet and should make up 45% of the total. Please remember we are talking about breads, potatoes, fibrous foods, generally, plus fruits and vegetables—complex carbohydrates—not about refined sugars.

Fats, too, are necessary for health and weight control. They transport other nutrients through the body and are a source of concentrated energy. We're not suggesting you gobble extra fats such as butter and mayonnaise; these should be eaten in moderation. But natural fat, found in meat and even in vegetables, is good for you in proper amounts. To wit, approximately 35% of your daily diet should be fat, and will be automatically if your diet is well balanced.

All menus and dietary information in this book have been nutritionist approved and are based on daily food requirements. Before you try our sample starter program, we'd like to share guidelines to help you in planning meals to suit your own lifestyle. The rules for good health and diet are really a matter of common sense and they are quite liberal. You don't have to eat three meals a day. Several mini-meals might be more satisfying. Or you might prefer to save most of your calories and sodium for one big meal, supplemented by snacks throughout the day.

Plan your meals according to your day. Contrary to popular belief, you can even eat your big meal late at night. Half the pleasure is being able to eat when you want to, when you feel free to relax and enjoy a meal. As long as you don't exceed your calorie and sodium limits, enjoy them whenever and however you please.

If you want to maintain your weight, multiply it by 13.5 to determine your daily calorie requirements. For example, a woman weighing 105 pounds needs 1400 calories for weight maintenance. One thousand mgs. of sodium, and certainly no more than 1500, would help ensure that goal without fluctuation. A man weighing 155 pounds needs 2000 calories to maintain his weight, with sodium not exceeding 2000 mgs.

Thirty-five hundred calories more or less in your diet will result in a one pound gain or loss. Thus, on a 1200 calorie diet, the woman cited above would lose one pound every 2½ weeks; the man, one pound in 4 or 5 days. Following is a 1200 calorie master diet plan:

1200 Calorie Diet
Master Plan

Food	Basic Nutrient
1 pint milk	Protein
1 egg	Protein
5 ozs. meat, fish, poultry, or low sodium cheese*	Protein/Fat
3 to 4 vegetable servings (4 ozs. each), including	
1 green or yellow variety for vitamins C and A**	Carbohydrates
3 fruit servings (4 ozs. each or 3 whole), including	
1 citrus for vitamin C	Carbohydrates
1 serving low sodium bread or cereal	Carbohydrates
3 tsps. oil or unsalted butter or margarine	Fat

*Limit beef, lamb, or pork to 3 times a week. Eat poultry, fish, or veal the rest of the time.
**See chapter on vegetables to see which high sodium items you should avoid.

To increase your calorie intake to 1500, add 1 potato, 2 servings bread, and 2 tsps. butter, margarine, or oil. To go down to 1000 calories, substitute skim milk for whole. To reach 800 calories, substitute skim milk for whole, eliminate 1 fruit, ½ slice of bread, and the 3 tsps. butter, margarine, or oil. In other words, adjust your fats and carbohydrates; leave the protein alone.

You can also exchange basics from the same food group. For example, you may replace the egg with 1 oz. of meat, fish, poultry, or cheese. Substitute 1 potato for the slice of bread, or 1 oz. of oil or unsalted butter or margarine for an equal amount of meat. Likewise, you may change fruits and vegetables as long as you remember to include those containing vitamins C and A.

After trying the following diet and menu plans, if you want additional help in developing a personal diet program, or if you need help obtaining low sodium products, write to the author, Merle Schell, c/o Healthy Kitchens, Inc., 225 East 57th Street, Apartment 15K, New York, New York 10022.

But right now, turn the page and discover how much fun, sheer enjoyment, and beautiful rewards a good diet can bring.

THREE WEEK DIET PLAN

The following diet plan has been devised as follows:

1. For three weeks, because it often takes that long for your body to adjust to a diet and start to show real weight loss.
2. For 1200 calories, because this is an average prescribed program. To raise or lower your caloric intake, consult the preceding pages on How to Approach Diet and Maintenance.
3. For 500 mgs. sodium, because such a diet is considered very restricted. We wanted to show you how much you could eat and how easy it is to live within these so-called limits.

If your restrictions aren't so stringent, check the Food Summary Guides or the Tables of Nutritional Values for possibilities. For example, a slice of commercial bread will add 200 mgs. sodium to your total, but only slightly more calories than low sodium bread. A small serving of mussels will tack on 289 mgs. If you're allowed, go to it. If you have no medical restrictions, still try to stay below 1500 mgs. sodium. It's really easy.

For those on diets allowing only 250 mgs. sodium per day, you are not alone. I, for one, am among you, but can enjoy all the foods in this book and have a balanced diet within my limits. How? One of two ways: eating more of the vegetables and less of the meat, fish, or poultry in a main dish. Or by eating two very simple meals and saving my goodies for a one-meal splurge of the day. Either way you do it, you'll never be hungry. I promise. And you'll have one big advantage no one else will—if your diet is balanced, you'll never, never have to worry about calories.

If you wish to have a cocktail, exchange it with a cake, dessert, or some other food that contains refined sugar. For example, if you drink your coffee black, you save 45 calories per day. Just keep in mind the following:

- A half glass (4 ozs.) of wine has approximately   85 calories
- A jigger of brandy or liqueur has approximately   59 calories
- A jigger of hard liquor has approximately   99 calories
- All liquor contains approximately 4 mgs. sodium per 4 ounces.

Note: You may switch breakfast with lunch, lunch with dinner if it better suits your schedule. In addition, an easier way to plan lunches is to have a smaller portion of your previous night's dinner plus a small salad with dressing, a piece of fruit, and coffee.

Week One

Monday

Breakfast

	Cal.	Sod. Mgs.
½ glass grapefruit juice	51	2
1 egg, boiled	72	55
1 slice low sodium toast	110	11
1 pat unsalted butter or margarine	36	2
1 tsp. jam or jelly	18	2
½ tsp. low sodium chicken bouillon	6	3
Coffee or tea	-	-
1 tsp. sugar (opt.)	15	1
2 tsps. milk (opt.)	6	2
	314	78

Lunch

	Page	Cal.	Sod. Mgs.
Borscht	57	50	45
Pickled Fish Salad	102	165	72
Apple		80	2
Coffee or tea		-	-
1 tsp. sugar (opt.)		15	1
2 tsps. sugar (opt.)		6	2
		316	122

Dinner

	Page	Cal.	Sod. Mgs.
Roast Chicken à L'Orange	144	280	94
Brown Rice and Walnuts	264	161	17
Braised Cucumbers	243	47	9
Rum Fruit	326	103	3
Coffee or tea		-	-
1 tsp. sugar (opt.)		15	1
2 tsps. milk (opt.)		6	2
		612	129
Total		1242	329

Tuesday

Breakfast

	Cal.	Sod. Mgs.
1 cup fresh fruit	86	3
2 tbs. low sodium cottage cheese	25	10
1 slice low sodium toast	110	11
1 tsp. chives	-	-
½ tsp. low sodium chicken bouillon	6	3
Coffee or tea	-	-
1 tsp. sugar (opt.)	15	1
2 tsps. milk (opt.)	6	2
	249	30

Lunch

	Page	Cal.	Sod. Mgs.
Sour Cream Omelet	308	194	80
Honeyed Carrots	253	51	28
Pear		100	4
Coffee or tea		-	-
1 tsp. sugar (opt.)		15	1
2 tsps. milk (opt.)		6	2
		385	123

Dinner

	Page	Cal.	Sod. Mgs.
Flounder with Pickles	147	171	99
Sour Potatoes	268	75	8
Asparagus with Lemon Crumbed Topping	243	61	4
Almond Cookies	342	71	7
Coffee or tea		-	-
1 tsp. sugar (opt.)		15	1
2 tsps. milk (opt.)		6	2
		399	121
Total		1014	266

Wednesday

Breakfast

	Cal.	Sod. Mgs.
½ glass orange juice	56	2
2 low sodium toast crackers	60	4
1 oz. low sodium cheddar cheese or	113	5
1 hard or soft boiled egg	72	55
½ tomato, sliced, or broiled with herbs	13	2
Coffee or tea	-	-
1 tsp. sugar (opt.)	15	1
2 tsps. milk (opt.)	6	2
	263	16
	222	66

Lunch

	Page	Cal.	Sod. Mgs.
Chicken, Raisin, and Almond Salad	99	268	17
1 cup lettuce		10	9
Banana		101	2
Coffee or tea		-	-
1 tsp. sugar (opt.)		15	2
2 tsps. milk (opt.)		6	2
		400	31

Dinner

	Page	Cal.	Sod. Mgs.
London Broil with Spice Sauce	110	186	88
Baked potato		100	5
Spice Roasted Eggplant	250	60	16
Pears Vanilla	325	111	6
Coffee or tea		-	-
1 tsp. sugar (opt.)		15	1
2 tsps. milk (opt.)		6	2
		478	118
Total		1141	165

Thursday

Breakfast	Cal.	Sod. Mgs.
1 cup fresh fruit	86	3
1 slice low sodium toast	110	11
1 pat unsalted butter or margarine	36	2
½ tsp. low sodium chicken bouillon	6	3
Coffee or tea	-	-
1 tsp. sugar (opt.)	15	1
2 tsps. milk (opt.)	6	2
	259	22

Lunch	Page	Cal.	Sod. Mgs.
Golden Mushroom Soup	46	95	24
Avocado with Minced Fish	93	298	28
Coffee or tea		-	-
1 tsp. sugar (opt.)		15	1
2 tsps. milk (opt.)		6	2
		414	55

Dinner	Page	Cal.	Sod. Mgs.
Chicken in Tomato Sauce	177	180	86
Macaroni with Nutmeg	268	214	17
Steamed or boiled broccoli (4 ozs.)		36	10
Fresh strawberries and pineapples (1½ cups)		114	6
Coffee or tea		-	-
1 tsp. sugar (opt.)		15	1
2 tsps. milk (opt.)		6	2
		565	122
Total		1238	199

Friday

Breakfast	Cal.	Sod. Mgs.
½ melon, topped with	58	14
2 tbs. low sodium cottage cheese	25	10
2 low sodium toast crackers	60	4
Coffee or tea	-	-
1 tsp. sugar (opt.)	15	1
2 tsps. milk (opt.)	6	2
	164	41

Lunch	Page	Cal.	Sod. Mgs.
Minestrone	56	86	25
Can of low sodium sardines		77	70
Lettuce, tomato, and cucumber salad (1 cup)		44	17
2 tsps. oil		84	-
2 Tbs. vinegar		2	2
½ melon		58	24
Coffee or tea		-	-
1 tsp. sugar (opt.)		15	1
2 tsps. milk (opt.)		6	2
		372	141

Dinner	Page	Cal.	Sod. Mgs.
Herbed Lamb Chops	110	296	86
Duchess Potatoes with Onions	264	99	19
Zucchini Rosemary	240	54	2
Baked Apple	332	129	10
Coffee or tea		-	-
1 tsp. sugar (opt.)		15	1
2 tsps. milk (opt.)		6	2
		599	120
Total		1135	302

Saturday

Breakfast	Cal.	Sod. Mgs.
½ glass grapefruit juice	51	2
1 egg, boiled	72	55
1 slice low sodium toast	110	11
1 pat unsalted butter or margarine	36	2
1 tsp. jam or jelly	18	2
1 tsp. low sodium chicken bouillon	6	3
Coffee or tea	-	-
1 tsp. sugar (opt.)	15	1
2 tsps. milk (opt.)	6	2
	314	78

Lunch	Page	Cal.	Sod. Mgs.
Chicken, Raisin, and Almond Salad	99	268	59
Steamed or boiled cauliflower (4 ozs.)		31	9
Slice of low sodium honey cake		80	10
Coffee or tea		-	-
1 tsp. sugar (opt.)		15	1
2 tsps. milk (opt.)		6	2
		400	81

Dinner	Page	Cal.	Sod. Mgs.
Salmon in Fennel Sauce	224	171	81
Orange Rice	278	142	16
Spinach with Cheese Sauce	251	81	90
Coconut Drops	327	75	12
Coffee or tea		-	-
1 tsp. sugar (opt.)		15	1
2 tsps. milk (opt.)		6	2
		490	202
Total		1204	361

Sunday

Brunch	Page	Cal.	Sod. Mgs.
Chicken Broth	45	37	13
Cauliflower and Pork Salad, plus egg, hard boiled	90	358	105
Baked Dill Tomatoes	236	36	3
1 low sodium toast cracker		30	2
Orange		65	2
Coffee or tea		-	-
1 tsp. sugar (opt.)		15	1
2 tsps. milk (opt.)		6	2
		547	128

Dinner	Page	Cal.	Sod. Mgs.
Lemon Lime Steak	214	357	88
Saffron Rice	266	174	15
Honeyed Fruit	335	107	12
Coffee or tea		-	-
1 tsp. sugar (opt.)		15	1
2 tsps. milk (opt.)		6	2
		659	118
Total		1206	246

Week Two

Monday

Breakfast		Cal.	Sod. Mgs.
½ glass orange juice		56	3
½ cup low sodium cottage cheese, mixed with herbs, spices and:		100	40
½ zucchini, chopped		20	1
¼ green pepper, chopped		9	3
2 scallions, chopped		14	3
2 low sodium toast crackers		60	4
Coffee or tea		-	-
1 tsp. sugar (opt.)		15	1
2 tsps. milk (opt.)		6	2
		280	57

Lunch	Page	Cal.	Sod. Mgs.
Greek Cheese Omelet*	308	201	88
Fruit Soup	52	112	5
Coffee or tea		-	-
1 tsp. sugar (opt.)		15	1
2 tsps. milk		6	2
* Includes fish			
		334	96

Dinner	Page	Cal.	Sod. Mgs.
Mixed Greens Salad	102	124	11
Country Chicken*	114	250	99
Sherry Cake	357	140	25
Coffee or tea		-	-
1 tsp. sugar (opt.)		15	1
2 tsps. milk (opt.)		6	2
* Includes vegetables and potato			
		535	138
Total		1149	291

Tuesday

Breakfast		Cal.	Sod. Mgs.
1 cup fresh fruit		86	3
Coffee or tea		-	-
1 tsp. sugar (opt.)		15	1
2 tsps. milk (opt.)		6	2
		107	6

Lunch	Page	Cal.	Sod. Mgs.
Brown Bagged Chicken	113	188	97
Steamed green beans		32	2
Lettuce, tomato, and cucumber salad		44	17
1 tbs. low sodium mayonnaise		100	4
2 tbs. vinegar		2	2
½ cup canned plums		57	3
Coffee or tea		-	-
1 tsp. sugar (opt.)		15	1
2 tsps. milk (opt.)		6	2
		544	126

Dinner	Page	Cal.	Sod. Mgs.
Pork Chops in Tomato Sauce	175	286	92
Potato and Spinach Casserole	269	67	45
Honeyed Carrots	253	51	28
Oranges with Mint Sauce	334	85	4
Coffee or tea		-	-
1 tsp. sugar (opt.)		15	1
2 tsps. milk (opt.)		6	2
		510	172
Total		1161	305

Wednesday

Breakfast		Cal.	Sod. Mgs.
½ glass grapefruit juice		51	2
½ onion, minced		19	2
1 egg beaten, both cooked in		72	55
2 tsps. unsalted butter or margarine		68	3
2 low sodium toast crackers		60	4
Coffee or tea		-	-
1 tsp. sugar (opt.)		15	1
2 tsps. milk (opt.)		6	2
		291	69

Lunch	Page	Cal.	Sod. Mgs.
½ can (3¼ oz.) low sodium salmon		141	64
Honey Beet Salad	99	85	33
½ melon		58	24
Coffee or tea		-	-
1 tsp. sugar (opt.)		15	2
2 tsps. milk (opt.)		6	2
		305	124

Dinner	Page	Cal.	Sod. Mgs.
Beef with Sherry Mustard Sauce	186	269	88
Potatoes in Tomato Sauce	269	128	30
Butter Almond Cake	343	79	12
Coffee or tea		-	-
1 tsp. sugar (opt.)		15	1
2 tsps. milk (opt.)		6	2
		497	133
Total		1093	327

THREE WEEK DIET PLAN

Thursday

Breakfast		Cal.	Sod. Mgs.
1 cup fresh fruit			
topped with			
½ cup low sodium cottage cheese		100	40
Coffee or tea		-	-
1 tsp. sugar (opt.)		15	1
2 tsps. milk (opt.)		6	2
		207	46

Lunch	Page	Cal.	Sod. Mgs.
Simply Luscious Oyster Stew	47	185	97
Creamy Cucumber Salad	91	56	11
Banana		101	2
Coffee or tea		-	-
1 tsp. sugar (opt.)		15	1
2 tsps. milk (opt.)		6	2
		363	113

Dinner	Page	Cal.	Sod. Mgs.
Broiled Chicken in Herbed Wine	190	209	93
Rice, Leeks, and Raisins	277	171	24
Steamed or boiled broccoli (4 ozs.)		36	10
Fruit and Honey Compote	333	102	3
Coffee or tea		-	-
1 tsp. sugar (opt.)		15	1
2 tsps. milk (opt.)		6	2
		539	133
Total			
		1009	292

Friday

Breakfast		Cal.	Sod. Mgs.
½ cup grapefruit sections		80	2
½ cup low sodium cottage cheese, mixed with herbs spices and:		100	40
¼ green pepper, chopped		9	3
½ cucumber, chopped		13	5
2 scallions, chopped		14	3
½ tomato, chopped		13	2
2 low sodium toast crackers		60	4
Coffee or tea		-	-
1 tsp. sugar (opt.)		15	1
2 tsps. milk (opt.)		6	2
		310	62

Lunch	Page	Cal.	Sod. Mgs.
Apple and Apricot Omelet	313	198	64
Steamed or boiled asparagus (4 spears)		20	2
Slice of low sodium honey cake		20	2
Coffee or tea		-	-
1 tsp. sugar (opt.)		15	1
2 tsps. milk (opt.)		6	2
		319	79

Dinner	Page	Cal.	Sod. Mgs.
Oriental Fried Fish	121	217	76
Boiled white rice (½ cup)		112	10
Chinese Vegetables	241	96	21
Butter Almond Cake	343	79	21
Coffee or tea		-	-
1 tsp. sugar (opt.)		15	1
2 tsps. milk (opt.)		6	2
		525	122
Total			
		1154	263

Saturday

Breakfast		Cal.	Sod. Mgs.
½ glass orange juice		56	3
1 oz. low sodium cheddar cheese		113	5
2 low sodium toast crackers		60	4
1 tomato, broiled, plus herbs		25	3
Coffee or tea		-	-
1 tsp. sugar (opt.)		15	1
2 tsps. milk (opt.)		6	2
		275	18

Lunch	Page	Cal.	Sod. Mgs.
Zucchini, sliced		39	4
Chicken Salad	87	161	54
½ cup pineapple chunks		95	2
Coffee or tea		-	-
1 tsp. sugar (opt.)		15	1
2 tsps. milk (opt.)		6	2
		316	63

Dinner	Page	Cal.	Sod. Mgs.
Veal Veronique	141	280	114
Boiled noodles (2 ozs.)		210	3
Fresh Strawberries (1 cup)		55	3
Coffee or tea		-	-
1 tsp. sugar (opt.)		15	1
2 tsps. milk (opt.)		6	2
		566	123
Total			
		1157	204

Sunday

Breakfast		Cal.	Sod. Mgs.
½ glass grapefruit juice		51	2
1 egg, boiled		72	55
1 slice low sodium toast		110	11
1 pat unsalted butter or margarine		36	2
1 tsp. jam or jelly		18	2
½ tsp. low sodium chicken bouillon		6	3
Coffee or tea		-	-
1 tsp. sugar (opt.)		15	1
2 tsps. milk (opt.)		6	2
		314	78

Lunch	Page	Cal.	Sod. Mgs.
Fish in Mayonnaise Sauce*	106	154	95
Molded Cucumber Salad	100	86	5
Coffee or tea		-	-
1 tsp. sugar (opt.)		15	1
2 tsps. milk (opt.)		6	2
*Use flounder			
		261	98

Dinner	Page	Cal.	Sod. Mgs.
Festival Chicken	219	210	89
Curried Rice	270	127	10
Broccoli with Sesame Seeds	240	86	6
Cinnamon Coffee Cake	345	117	13
Coffee or tea		-	-
1 tsp. sugar (opt.)		15	1
2 tsps. milk (opt.)		6	2
		561	121
Total			
		1136	297

Week Three

Monday

Breakfast		Cal.	Sod. Mgs.
½ melon, topped with		58	24
2 Tbs. low sodium cottage cheese		25	10
2 low sodium toast crackers		60	4
Coffee or tea		-	-
1 tsp. sugar (opt.)		15	1
2 tsps. milk (opt.)		6	2
		164	41

Lunch	Page	Cal.	Sod. Mgs.
Indian Scrambled Eggs	310	186	75
Mixed Greens Salad	102	124	11
Pear		100	4
Coffee or tea		-	-
1 tsp. sugar (opt.)		15	1
2 tsps. milk (opt.)		6	2
		431	93

Dinner	Page	Cal.	Sod. Mgs.
Baked Cod Stew	158	231	109
Caraway Cream Potatoes	266	94	16
Baked Stuffed Acorn Squash	237	194	9
Bananas and Rum Sauce	333	87	7
Coffee or tea		-	-
1 tsp. sugar (opt.)		15	1
2 tsps. milk (opt.)		6	2
		627	144
Total		1222	278

Tuesday

Breakfast		Cal.	Sod. Mgs.
½ glass orange juice		56	3
1 egg, boiled		72	55
1 slice low sodium toast		110	11
1 pat unsalted butter or margarine		36	2
1 tsp. jam or jelly		18	2
½ tsp. low sodium chicken bouillon		6	3
Coffee or tea		-	-
1 tsp. sugar (opt.)		15	1
2 tsps. milk (opt.)		6	2
		319	79

Lunch	Page	Cal.	Sod. Mgs.
Salad Nicoise (without the hard-boiled eggs)	90	234	62
½ melon		58	24
Coffee or tea		-	-
1 tsp. sugar (opt.)		15	1
2 tsps. milk (opt.)		6	2
		313	89

Dinner	Page	Cal.	Sod. Mgs.
Veal in Apple Wine Sauce	152	261	90
Saffron Rice	266	174	15
Herbed Cauliflower	247	59	10
Honey Cake	339	86	8
Coffee or tea		-	-
1 tsp. sugar (opt.)		15	1
2 tsps. milk (opt.)		6	2
		601	126
Total		1233	294

Wednesday

Breakfast		Cal.	Sod. Mgs.
½ glass grapefruit juice		51	2
2 low sodium toast crackers		60	4
1 oz. low sodium cottage cheese		50	20
1 tomato, broiled, plus herbs		25	3
Coffee or tea		-	-
1 tsp. sugar (opt.)		15	1
2 tsps. milk (opt.)		6	2
		217	32

Lunch	Page	Cal.	Sod. Mgs.
Eggplant Omelet	317	174	61
Lettuce, tomato and beansprout salad		55	12
1 Tbs. low sodium mayonnaise		100	4
2 Tbs. vinegar		2	2
Apple		80	2
Coffee or tea		-	-
1 tsp. sugar (opt.)		15	2
2 tsps. milk (opt.)		6	2
		432	84

Dinner	Page	Cal.	Sod. Mgs.
Curried Chicken	179	242	110
Corn on the cob		70	1
1 pat unsalted butter or margarine		36	2
Rum Fruit	326	103	3
Coffee or tea		-	-
1 tsp. sugar (opt.)		15	1
2 tsps. milk (opt.)		6	2
		472	119
Total		1121	235

Thursday

Breakfast

	Cal.	Sod. Mgs.
1 cup fresh fruit	86	3
½ cup low sodium cottage cheese	100	40
Coffee or tea	-	-
1 tsp. sugar (opt.)	15	1
2 tsps. milk (opt.)	6	2
	207	46

Lunch

	Page	Cal.	Sod. Mgs.
Chicken with Peas Oregano	166	232	80
Watercress Salad	91	106	28
Almond Fruit Gelatin	322	91	11
Coffee or tea		-	-
1 tsp. sugar (opt.)		15	1
2 tsps. milk (opt.)		6	2
		450	122

Dinner

	Page	Cal.	Sod. Mgs.
Beef and Pea Pods	124	343	66
Boiled white rice (½ cup)		112	10
Kissel	332	121	4
Coffee or tea		-	-
1 tsp. sugar (opt.)		15	1
2 tsps. milk (opt.)		6	2
		597	83
Total		1254	251

Friday

Breakfast

	Cal.	Sod. Mgs.
½ glass orange juice	56	3
1 egg, poached, plus herbs	72	55
2 low sodium toast crackers	60	4
1 pat unsalted butter or margarine	36	2
Coffee or tea	-	-
1 tsp. sugar (opt.)	15	1
2 tsps. milk (opt.)	6	2
	245	67

Lunch

	Page	Cal.	Sod. Mgs.
Fruit Salad (without the hard-boiled eggs)	101	225	22
Almond Cookies	342	71	7
Coffee or tea		-	-
1 tsp. sugar (opt.)		15	1
2 tsps. milk (opt.)		6	2
		317	32

Dinner

	Page	Cal.	Sod. Mgs.
Carrot Salad	86	130	25
Sea Bass and Vegetables*	225	274	135
Fruit and Butter Cake	351	105	9
Coffee or tea		-	-
1 tsp. sugar (opt.)		15	1
2 tsps. milk (opt.)		6	2
*includes potato		530	172
Total		1092	271

Saturday

Breakfast

	Cal.	Sod. Mgs.
½ glass grapefruit juice	51	2
1 egg, boiled	72	55
1 slice low sodium toast	110	11
1 pat unsalted butter or margarine	36	2
1 tsp. jam or jelly	18	2
1 tsp. low sodium chicken bouillon	6	3
Coffee or tea	-	-
1 tsp. sugar (opt.)	15	1
2 tsps. milk (opt.)	6	2
	314	78

Lunch

	Page	Cal.	Sod. Mgs.
Madrilene	50	81	32
Creamy Cucumber Salad	91	56	11
Baked Apple with Cheese	334	101	9
Coffee or tea		-	-
1 tsp. sugar (opt.)		15	1
2 tsps. milk (opt.)		6	2
		259	55

Dinner

	Page	Cal.	Sod. Mgs.
Stewed Chicken and Vegetables	206	219	91
Potatoes and Almonds	281	150	7
Apples and Peaches in Wine Cream	325	131	6
Coffee or tea		-	-
1 tsp. sugar (opt.)		15	1
2 tsps. milk (opt.)		6	2
		521	107
Total		1094	240

Sunday

Brunch

	Page	Cal.	Sod. Mgs.
½ glass grapefruit juice		51	2
Eggs and Salmon	315	250	112
2 low sodium toast crackers		60	4
1 pat unsalted butter or margarine		36	2
Green Beans and Peppers	256	75	13
Honey Cake	339	86	8
Coffee or tea		-	-
1 tsp. sugar (opt.)		15	1
2 tsps. milk (opt.)		6	2
		579	144

Dinner

	Page	Cal.	Sod. Mgs.
Round Steak in Brandy	188	289	91
Rice and Cucumbers	270	149	19
Rhubarb Compote	239	88	5
Fresh strawberries (1 cup)		55	3
Coffee or tea		-	-
1 tsp. sugar (opt.)		15	1
2 tsps. milk (opt.)		6	2
		602	121
Total		1181	265

TABLES OF NUTRITIONAL VALUES

The minerals sodium and potassium counterbalance each other and work together to ensure proper kidney function and the elimination of excess body fluid. Therefore, people on doctor-recommended low sodium diets must be careful not to deplete their potassium.

No need to worry. It's all easier than you think. Sodium reduction is accomplished through dietary control. The advice in this book will enable you to be your body's best friend in this regard. Potassium is maintained at healthy levels with doctor-prescribed potassium supplements or, more often, by including potassium rich foods in daily meal planning. Among these are: bananas, any dried fruit, cantaloupes, avocados, and potatoes. Indeed, a properly balanced food program will automatically provide all the daily potassium you need.

However, because of its important relationship to sodium, potassium may be of special interest to some of you. For that reason, the following tables include nutritional values for potassium as well as for sodium, and calorie counts for many of the most often used foods. When appropriate and possible, comparisons are made between salted and unsalted items.

Raw values are used unless otherwise indicated, all based on 100 gram (3½ oz.) weights. The following symbols are used:

N/A	denotes not available
N/T	denotes not traceable, therefore read as zero
Dash (—)	denotes not applicable

We have divided the food groups as follows:

Food Group	Page(s)	Food Group	Page(s)
Baked Goods	369–370	Meat	379–380
Beverages, Alcoholic	370	Nuts	381
Beverages, Non-Alcoholic	371–372	Poultry	382
Condiments	372–373	Soups	383
Dairy	374	Vegetables	284–287
Fish and Shellfish	375–376	Miscellaneous	388
Fruit	377–379		

Table Of Nutritional Values
Per 100 Grams (3½ Ozs.)
Baked Goods

Food Item	Calories	Potassium Mgs.	Unsalted Sodium Mgs.	Salted Sodium Mgs.
Breads				
French	290	90	—	580
Raisin	262	233	—	365
Rye, Dark	241	454	—	569
Rye, Light	243	145	—	557
White	269	85	—	507
Whole Wheat	243	273	—	527
Low Sodium*	262	N/A	40	—
Bread Crumbs				
Regular, Commercial	392	152	—	736
Low Sodium**	270	N/A	18	—
Breakfast Cereals, Dried				
Corn Flakes, Regular	386	120	—	1,005
Corn Flakes, Low Sodium	385	N/A	10	—
Rice Flakes, Regular	390	180	—	987
Rice Flakes, Low Sodium	385	N/A	10	—
Cakes***				
Regular				
Low Sodium				

Cookies****
  Regular
  Low Sodium

*Averages for all kinds of low sodium breads.
**Not available commercially. Based on recipe page 291
***Commercial cakes average 200 mgs. sodium or more per 3½ ozs. versus low sodium brands which average 10 mgs. sodium.
****Commercial cookies average 150 mgs. sodium or more per 3½ ozs. versus low sodium brands which average 10 mgs. sodium.

Table Of Nutritional Values
Per 100 Grams (3½ Ozs.)
Beverages, Alcoholic

Food Item	Calories	Potassium Mgs.	Unsalted Sodium Mgs.	Salted Sodium Mgs.
Beer*	42	25	7	N/A
Bourbon	231	2	1	—
Brandy and Liqueurs	137	2	1	—
Gin	231	2	1	—
Rum	231	2	1	—
Rye	231	2	1	—
Scotch	231	2	1	—
Vodka	231	2	1	—
Whiskey	231	2	1	—
Wine	85	2	1	—

*Most beers are made with salt. It's best to avoid them.

Table Of Nutritional Values
Per 100 Grams (3½ Ozs.)
(Beverages, Non-alcoholic)

Food Item	Calories	Potassium Mgs.	Unsalted Sodium Mgs.	Salted Sodium Mgs.
Apple Juice	47	101	1	—
Apricot Nectar	57	151	1	—
Carbonated Sodas	46	N/A	—	N/A*
Carbonated Sodas, Low Calorie	16	N/A	—	N/A*
Coconut Milk	22	147	25	—
Cola	39	N/A	4**	—
Club Soda, Regular	39	N/A	—	N/A*
Club Soda, Low Sodium	31	N/A	6	—
Ginger Ale	31	N/A	4***	—
Grapefruit Juice	41	162	1	—
Grape Juice	45	116	2	—
Lemon Juice, Bottled	23	141	1	—
Lime Juice, Bottled	26	104	1	—
Orange Juice				
Unsweetened	48	199	1	—
Sweetened	52	199	1	—
Frozen, Diluted	45	186	—	N/A*
Orange and Grapefruit Juice				
Unsweetened	43	184	1	—
Sweetened	50	184	1	—
Peach Nectar	48	78	1	—
Pear Nectar	52	39	1	—
Pineapple Juice				
Unsweetened	55	149	1	—
Prune Juice	77	235	2	—
Tomato Juice				
Regular	19	227	—	200
Low Sodium	19	227	3	—

Food Item	Calories	Potassium Mgs.	Unsalted Sodium Mgs.	Salted Sodium Mgs.
Vegetable Juice				
Regular	17	221	—	200
Low Sodium	15	N/A	30	—

*These beverages generally contain sodium. Unless you know for sure, avoid such drinks.
**Applies to Coca-Cola only.
***Applies to Canada Dry only.

Table Of Nutritional Values
Per 100 Grams (3½ Ozs.)
Condiments

Food Item	Calories	Potassium Mgs.	Unsalted Sodium Mgs.	Salted Sodium Mgs.
Applesauce				
Sweetened	91	65	2	—
Unsweetened	41	78	2	—
Chocolate*				
Baking	505	830	4	—
Bittersweet	477	615	3	**
Milk	520	384	3	94
Chocolate Syrup	330	284	—	89
Cocoa				
Regular Powder	295	800	—	525
Carob Powder	180	N/T	N/T	—
Horseradish	87	564	8	96
Jams***	272	88	12	—
Jellies***	273	75	17	—
Marmalade***	257	33	14	—
Mayonnaise				
Regular	718	34	—	597
Low Sodium	718	30	28	—
Molasses				
Light	252	917	15	—
Medium	232	1,063	37	—
Blackstrap	213	2,927	96	—

TABLES OF NUTRITIONAL VALUES

Food Item	Calories	Potassium Mgs.	Unsalted Sodium Mgs.	Salted Sodium Mgs.
Mustard				
Yellow, Regular	75	130	—	1,252
Brown, Regular	91	130	—	1,307
Yellow, Low Sodium	75	130	10	—
Dijon, Low Sodium	91	130	25	—
Peanut Butter				
Regular	581	670	—	601
Low Sodium	630	N/A	7	—
Salad Dressings****				
French, Regular	410	Trace	—	1,370
French, Dietetic	10	Trace	—	787
French, Low Sodium	10	Trace	10	—
Italian, Regular	552	Trace	—	2,092
Italian, Dietetic	50	Trace	—	787
Italian, Low Sodium	50	Trace	10	—
Tomato Ketchup				
Regular	106	363	—	1,042
Low Sodium	42	N/A	20	—
Tomato Chili Ketchup				
Regular	104	370	—	1,388
Low Sodium	56	N/A	30	—
Tomato Paste				
Regular	19	227	—	200
Low Sodium	19	227	10	—
Tomato Puree				
Regular	39	426	—	399
Low Sodium	39	426	10	—
Tomato Sauce				
Regular	30	325	—	300
Low Sodium	30	325	10	—

*Avoid all candies except those marked low sodium. Commercial varieties usually contain salt.

**Most commercial brands contain salt. Opt for low sodium.

***Do not buy if sodium or pectin are listed as ingredients.

****Beware of salad dressings labelled "dietetic." These are not necessarily low sodium and, while low calorically, generally contain more than 600 mgs. sodium per 3½ ozs.

Table Of Nutritional Values
Per 100 Grams (3½ Ozs.)
Dairy

Food Item	Calories	Potassium Mgs.	Unsalted Sodium Mgs.	Salted Sodium Mgs.
Butter	716	23	10	987
Buttermilk	36	140	130	N/A
Cheese				
Cheddar	398	82	18	700
Cottage	106	85	18	229
Gouda	345	74	35	250
Monterey Jack	345	74	42	N/A
Munster	350	N/A	40	N/A
Swiss	355	104	240	710
Cream				
Half-and-Half*	134	129	46	—
Light*	211	122	36	—
Heavy	352	89	32	—
Eggs	78	98	55	—
Margarine				
Salted	720	23	—	987
Unsalted	720	10	15	—
Milk				
Cow	65	144	50	—
Goat	67	180	34	—
Yogurt	62	140	132	—

*Often prepared with sodium preservative. If so, buy heavy cream which contains no sodium ingredients.

Table Of Nutritional Values
Per 100 Grams (3½ Ozs.)
Fish and Shellfish

Food Item	Calories	Potassium Mgs.	Unsalted Sodium Mgs.	Salted Sodium Mgs.
Abalone				
Raw	98	N/T	N/T	—
Canned	80	N/A	—	198
Bass				
Sea	93	256	68	—
Striped	105	N/T	N/T	—
White	98	N/T	68	—
Bluefish	117	N/T	74	—
Butterfish	169	N/T	N/T	—
Carp	115	256	50	—
Catfish	103	330	60	—
Chub	145	N/T	N/T	—
Clams				
Raw	80	311	205	—
Canned, Regular	98	311	—	500
Cod	78	382	70	—
Crab				
Raw	93	N/A	N/A	—
Canned, Regular	101	110	—	1,000
Eel	233	N/T	N/T	—
Flounder	79	342	78	—
Frogs Legs	73	N/A	N/A	—
Haddock	79	304	61	—
Halibut	100	1	54	—
Herring	176	N/T	74	500*
Lobster	95	180	210	—
Mackerel				
Raw	191	N/T	N/T	—
Canned, Regular	183	N/T	N/T	500*
Canned, Low Sodium	183	N/T	63	—
Mullet	146	292	81	—
Mussels	95	315	289	—
Octopus	73	N/T	N/T	—

Food Item	Calories	Potassium Mgs.	Unsalted Sodium Mgs.	Salted Sodium Mgs.
Oysters				
Raw	66	121	73	—
Canned, Frozen	76	70	—	380
Perch	91	230	68	—
Pike	93	319	51	—
Pollack	95	350	48	—
Pompano	166	191	47	—
Red Snapper	98	323	67	—
Rockfish	97	388	60	—
Roe**	130	N/T	N/T	—
Salmon				
Raw	217	306	64	—
Canned, Regular	210	126	—	473
Canned, Low Sodium	145	N/A	70	—
Sardines				
Canned, Regular	196	260	—	760
Canned, Low Sodium	62	N/A	56	—
Scallops	112	476	265	—
Shad	170	330	54	—
Shrimp	91	220	140	—
Smelt	98	N/T	N/T	—
Snails	90	N/T	N/T	—
Sole	80	342	78	—
Squid	84	N/T	N/T	—
Swordfish	118	781	N/T	—
Tilefish	79	N/T	N/T	—
Tripe	100	9	72	—
Trout	195	300	50	—
Tuna				
Raw	145	N/T	37	—
Canned, Regular, in Oil	288	301	—	800
Canned, Low Sodium	108	N/T	51	—
Weakfish	121	317	75	—
Whitefish	155	299	52	—

*May exceed 500 mgs. per 3½ ounces depending on manufacturer.
**Does not apply to caviar which contains 2,200 mgs. sodium per 3½ ozs.

Table Of Nutritional Values
Per 100 Grams (3½ Ozs.)
Fruit

Food Item	Calories	Potassium Mgs.	Unsalted Sodium Mgs.	Salted Sodium Mgs.
Apples				
Raw with Skin	58	110	1	—
Dried	275	569	5	—
Apricots				
Raw	51	281	1	—
Canned, in Heavy Syrup	86	239	1	—
Canned, Dietetic	38	246	1	—
Dried	260	979	26	—
Bananas				
Raw	85	370	1	—
Powdered	340	1,477	4	—
Blueberries				
Raw	62	81	1	—
Frozen, Sweetened	105	66	1	—
Cantaloupe	30	251	12	—
Cherries				
Raw	70	191	2	—
Canned, in Heavy Syrup	81	126	1	—
Canned, Dietetic	48	130	1	—
Chestnuts	377	875	12	—
Coconut				
Fresh	346	256	N/T	—
Dried, Unsweetened	662	588	N/T	—
Dried, Sweetened	548	353	N/T	—
Cranberries				
Raw	46	82	2	—
Canned	146	30	1	—
Currants	54	372	3	—
Dates	274	648	1	—
Figs				
Raw	80	194	2	—
Canned, in Heavy Syrup	84	149	2	—
Canned, Dietetic	48	155	2	—
Dried	274	640	34	—

Food Item	Calories	Potassium Mgs.	Unsalted Sodium Mgs.	Salted Sodium Mgs.
Fruit Cocktail	92	159	5	—
Grapefruit				
Raw	44	135	1	—
Canned, Sweetened	53	162	1	—
Canned, Unsweetened	41	162	1	—
Grapes				
Raw	69	158	3	—
Canned, in Syrup	77	105	4	—
Canned, Dietetic	51	110	4	—
Honeydew Melon	33	251	12	—
Kumquats	65	236	7	—
Lemons	27	138	5	—
Limes	28	102	2	—
Loquats	48	348	N/T	—
Lychee Nuts, Canned, in Syrup	94	170	3	—
Mandarin Oranges	46	126	2	—
Mangos	66	189	7	—
Oranges				
Raw	49	200	1	—
Canned, Sweetened	52	199	1	—
Canned, Unsweetened	48	199	1	—
Papayas	39	234	3	—
Peaches				
Raw	38	202	1	—
Canned, in Heavy Syrup	78	128	2	—
Canned, Dietetic	31	137	2	—
Dried	262	950	16	—
Pears				
Raw	62	130	2	—
Canned, in Heavy Syrup	76	84	1	—
Canned, Dietetic	32	88	1	—
Dried	268	573	7	—
Persimmons	127	310	1	—
Pineapple				
Raw	52	146	1	—
Canned, in Heavy Syrup	74	96	1	—
Canned, in Water	39	99	1	—

Food Item	Calories	Potassium Mgs.	Unsalted Sodium Mgs.	Salted Sodium Mgs.
Plums				
Raw	66	299	2	—
Canned, in Heavy Syrup	83	142	1	—
Canned, in Water	46	148	2	—
Prunes				
Uncooked	255	694	8	—
Cooked	119	327	4	—
Pumpkin				
Raw	26	340	1	—
Canned	33	240	2	236
Raisins	289	763	27	—
Raspberries				
Raw, Black	73	196	1	—
Raw, Red	57	168	1	—
Canned, Black, in Water	51	135	1	—
Canned, Red, in Water	35	114	1	—
Frozen, Red, Sweetened	98	114	1	—
Rhubarb, Cooked	141	203	2	—
Tangerines	46	126	2	—
Watermelon	26	100	1	—

Table Of Nutritional Values
Per 100 Grams (3½ Ozs.)
Meat

Food Item	Calories	Potassium Mgs.	Unsalted Sodium Mgs.	Salted Sodium Mgs.
Beef, Fat Trimmed				
Hamburger	286	450	47	—
Chuck	377	370	65*	—
Arm	253	"	"	—
Flank	191	"	"	—
Shank	307	"	"	—
Porterhouse	446	"	"	—
T-Bone	442	"	"	—
Club	398	"	"	—
Sirloin	353	"	"	—
Short Rib	432	"	"	—

Food Item	Calories	Potassium Mgs.	Unsalted Sodium Mgs.	Salted Sodium Mgs.
Rib	440	370	65*	—
Round	261	"	"	—
Rump	317	"	"	—
Kidneys				
Beef	130	225	176	—
Calf	113	225	176	—
Lamb	105	250	83	—
Lamb				
Leg	192	290	75†	—
Loin	197	290	75‡	—
Rib	224	"	"	—
Shoulder	215	"	"	—
Liver				
Beef	140	281	136	—
Calf	140	281	136	—
Chicken	129	172	70	—
Goose	182	230	140	—
Turkey	174	141	55	—
Lungs				
Beef	96	N/T	N/T	—
Calf	106	N/T	N/T	—
Lamb	103	N/T	N/T	—
Pork, Fresh Only§				
Ham	217	390	70//	—
Loin	254	"	"	
Boston Butt	244	"	"	
Spareribs	440	"	"	
Veal				
Breast (Flank)	390	500	90 #	—
Chuck	235	"	"	—
Loin	234	"	"	—
Rib	269	"	"	—
Round	216	"	"	—

*For raw meat. Cooked meat contains 60 mgs. sodium per 3½ ozs.
†For raw meat. Cooked meat contains 70 mgs. sodium per 3½ ozs.
‡For raw meat. Cooked meat contains 70 mgs. sodium per 3½ ozs.
§Salted or cured pork, including bacon and smoked ham, generally exceeds 900 mgs. sodium per 3½ ozs.
//For raw meat. Cooked meat contains 65 mgs. sodium per 3½ ozs.
#For raw meat. Cooked meat contains 80 mgs. sodium per 3½ ozs.

Table Of Nutritional Values
Per 100 Grams (3½ Ozs.)
Nuts

Food Item	Calories	Potassium Mgs.	Unsalted Sodium Mgs.	Salted Sodium Mgs.
Almonds	598	773	4	198
Butternuts	629	N/T	N/T	N/A
Cashews	561	464	15	200
Filberts (Hazelnuts)	634	704	2	N/A
Macadamia	691	264	N/T	N/A
Peanuts				
Unsalted	582	701	5	—
Salted	582	674	—	418
Pecans	687	603	N/T	N/A
Pine Nuts (Pignolas)	552	N/T	N/T	N/A
Pistachio	51	N/T	N/T	N/A
Pumpkin Seeds	553	N/T	N/T	N/A
Sesame Seeds	582	N/T	N/T	N/A
Sunflower Seeds	560	920	30	N/A
Walnuts				
Black	628	460	3	N/A
English	651	450	2	N/A

Note: All nuts have salted varieties. Some, including macadamia and pistachio, are readily available only in salted state. Any and all nuts containing salt should not be eaten.

Table Of Nutritional Values
Per 100 Grams (3½ Ozs.)
Poultry

Food Item	Calories	Potassium Mgs.	Unsalted Sodium Mgs.	Salted Sodium Mgs.
Chicken				
Fryers				
Flesh and Skin	126	285	58	—
Flesh only	107	381	78	—
Giblets	103	N/T	N/T	—
Back	157	250	67	—
Breast	110	320	50	—
Drumstick	115	250	67	—
Thigh	128	250	67	—
Wing	146	320	50	—
Roasters				
Flesh and Skin	197	285	58	—
Flesh only	131	285	58	—
Giblets	135	N/T	N/T	—
Dark Meat, without Skin	132	320	50	—
Light Meat, without Skin	128	250	67	—
Duck				
Flesh only	165	285	74	—
Goose				
Flesh and Skin	371	420	86	—
Flesh only	159	420	86	—
Squab				
Flesh and Skin	294	N/T	N/T	—
Flesh only	142	N/T	N/T	—
Giblets	154	N/T	N/T	—

Table Of Nutritional Values
Per 100 Grams (3½ Ozs.)
Soups

(Canned Unless Otherwise Noted)

Food Item	Calories	Potassium Mgs.	Unsalted Sodium Mgs.	Salted Sodium Mgs.
Bouillon Cubes, Bottled				
Beef, Regular	120	100	—	24,000
Chicken, Regular	120	100	—	24,000
Beef, Low Sodium	336	11,824	280	—
Chicken, Low Sodium	336	11,824	140	—
Chicken (Turkey) Noodle				
Regular	23	23	—	408
Low Sodium	29	N/A	19	—
Clam Chowder				
Regular, New England, Frozen, with Water	54	92	—	435
Low Sodium, New England	N/A	N/A	185	—
Mushroom, Cream of				
Regular, with Water	56	41	—	398
Low Sodium	68	N/A	12	—
Pea, Green				
Regular, with Water	53	80	—	367
Low Sodium	21	N/T	10	—
Tomato				
Regular, with Water	36	94	—	396
Low Sodium	63	N/T	15	—

Table Of Nutritional Values
Per 100 Grams (3½ Ozs.)
Vegetables

Food Item	Calories	Potassium Mgs.	Unsalted Sodium Mgs.	Salted Sodium Mgs.
Artichokes, Cooked	44	301	30	—
Asparagus				
Raw	26	278	2	—
Cooked	20	183	1	—
Canned, Regular	21	166	—	236
Canned, Low Sodium	20	166	3	—
Frozen Spears	24	259	2	—
Avocados, Raw	167	604	4	—
Bamboo Shoots, Raw	27	533	N/T	—
Barley, Cooked	349	160	3	—
Beans				
White, Cooked	118	416	7	—
Red, Cooked	118	340	3	—
Pinto, Calico,				
Red, Black,				
Brown, Cooked	118	1,038	8	—
Canned, without Pork	120	268	—	338
Bean Sprouts				
Mung, Raw Sprouts	35	223	5	—
Mung, Cooked	28	156	4	—
Soy, Raw Sprouts	403	1,677	5	—
Soy, Cooked	130	540	2	—
Soy, Canned	103	N/T	—	236
Beets				
Cooked	32	208	43	—
Canned, Regular	37	167	—	236
Canned, Low Sodium	37	167	46	—
Broccoli				
Raw	32	382	15	—
Cooked	26	267	10	—
Frozen	26	212	15	—

Food Item	Calories	Potassium Mgs.	Unsalted Sodium Mgs.	Salted Sodium Mgs.
Brussels Sprouts				
Cooked	36	328	16	—
Frozen	33	295	14	—
Bulgur, Dry	359	262	N/T	—
Cabbage				
Raw	24	233	20	—
Cooked	20	163	14	—
Carrots				
Raw	42	331	43	—
Cooked	31	222	33	—
Canned, Regular	30	120	—	236
Canned, Low Sodium	25	120	39	—
Cauliflower				
Raw	27	295	13	—
Cooked	22	206	9	—
Frozen	18	207	10	—
Celery				
Raw	17	341	126	—
Cooked	14	239	88	—
Chick Peas, Cooked	120	797	26	—
Collards, Raw	29	234	25	—
Corn				
Cooked	96	280	5	—
Canned, Regular	84	97	—	236
Canned, Low Sodium	76	97	2	—
Frozen	96	N/A	5	—
Cucumbers, Raw	14	160	6	—
Eggplant, Cooked	19	150	1	—
Endive, Raw	20	294	14	—
Escarole, Raw	20	294	14	—
Garlic Cloves, Raw	137	529	19	—
Green Beans				
Cooked	25	151	4	—
Canned, Regular	24	95	—	236
Canned, Low Sodium	22	95	2	—
Frozen	25	152	1	—
Horseradish				
Raw	87	564	8	—
Prepared	38	290	—	96

Jerusalem Artichokes, Cooked	75	N/A	1	—
Kale, Raw	28	221	43	—
Leeks, Raw	52	347	5	—
Lettuce (Boston, Bibb, Romaine), Raw	18	264	9	—
Lima Beans				
Cooked	111	422	1	—
Canned, Regular	96	222	—	236
Canned, Low Sodium	95	222	4	
Macaroni, Cooked*	148	79	2	—
Mushrooms				
Raw	28	414	15	—
Canned, Regular	17	197	—	400
Canned, Low Sodium	28	200	10	—
Mustard Greens, Raw	23	220	18	—
Noodles, Egg, Cooked*	125	44	2	—
Oats, Cooked	150	61	2	—
Okra, Cooked	29	174	2	—
Olives	129	34	—	813
Onions				
Raw	38	157	10	—
Cooked	29	110	7	—
Dehydrated	350	110	88	—
Parsnips, Cooked	66	379	8	—
Peas				
Cooked	71	196	1	—
Canned, Regular	88	96	—	236
Canned, Low Sodium	78	96	3	—
Frozen, Cooked	68	135	—	115
Peppers				
Chili, Green	37	564	25	—
Chili, Red	65	564	25	—
Green, Raw	22	213	13	—
Green, Cooked	18	149	9	—
Red, Raw	31	213	25	—
Red, Cooked	25	149	12	—
Potatoes				
Baked	93	503	4	—
Boiled, in Skin	76	407	3	—

Boiled, Pared	65	285	2	—
French Fried	274	853	6	—
Mashed, with Milk	65	261	301	—
Dehydrated	93	286	231	—
Radishes, Raw	17	322	18	—
Rice				
Brown, Cooked	119	70	5	—
White, Cooked	109	28	5	—
Sauerkraut				
Bottled, Regular	18	140	—	747
Bottled, Low Sodium	25	N/A	3.4	—
Scallions (Green Onions),				
Raw	36	231	5	—
Snow Pea Pods	43	119	3	—
Spaghetti, Cooked*	148	79	2	—
Spinach				
Raw	26	470	71	—
Cooked	23	324	50	—
Canned, Regular	24	250	—	236
Canned, Low Sodium	26	250	32	—
Squash				
Summer, Cooked				
Scallop	16	141	1	—
Yellow	15	141	1	—
Zucchini	12	141	1	—
Winter, Cooked				
Acorn, Baked†	55	480†	1	—
Butternut, Baked†	68	487†	1	—
Hubbard, Baked†	50	271†	1	—
Sweet Potatoes	141	300	12	—
Tofu	72	42	7	—
Tomatoes				
Raw	22	244	3	—
Cooked	26	287	4	—
Canned, Regular	21	217	—	130
Canned, Low Sodium	20	217	3	—
Turnips, Cooked‡	23	188	34	—
Water Chestnuts	79	500	20	—
Watercress, Raw	19	282	52	—
Yams	101	600	12	—

Yellow Beans				
Cooked	22	151	3	—
Canned, Regular	24	95	—	236
Canned, Low Sodium	21	95	2	—
Frozen	27	164	1	—

*Use only brands which list the sodium content or which say "No salt added."
†Approximately 20 calories less when boiled.
‡Approximately half the value when boiled.
§Use yellow only. White turnips contain too much sodium.

Table Of Nutritional Values
Per 100 Grams (3½ Ozs.)
Miscellaneous

Food Item	Calories	Potassium Mgs.	Unsalted Sodium Mgs.	Salted Sodium Mgs.
Baking Powder*				
Regular	129	150	—	10,953
Dietetic	83	9,500	40	—
Cornmeal	364	120	1	—
Cornstarch	362	N/T	N/T	—
Flour				
Corn	368	340	N/T	—
Rye	350	203	1	—
Soya	421	1,660	1	—
Wheat	365	95	2	—
Gelatin, Unflavored	335	N/T	N/T	—
Oils	884	N/T	N/T	—
Popcorn				
Salted	456	N/T	—	1,940
Unsalted	456	N/T	3	0
Soy Sauce	68	366	3,569*	7,325
Sugar	385	3	1	—
Vinegar				
White	12	15	1	—
Other	14	100	1	—

*This is not an unsalted product but is among the milder selections available, translating to approximately 600 sodium mgs. per tablespoon.

METRIC CONVERSION

In cooking, we deal with volume and weight. Volume is a liquid measurement, including ounces, pints, gallons, teaspoons, tablespoons, and cups. Weight refers to dry measurement, such as the dry ounce or pound found in meat or produce, and also any teaspoons, tablespoons, and cups found in flour or sugar.

The following conversion charts will enable you to translate American and British units to Continental and vice-versa.

Metric Conversion Chart
Liquid Measures

Some of the most common liquid measures are listed below. These measurements are rounded off to the nearest equivalent.

U.S. Spoon And Liquid Ounces Cups And Quarts	*Metric Equivalent*
1 teaspoon	5 milliliters
1 tablespoon or 3 teaspoons or ½ liquid ounce	15 milliliters
¼ cup or 4 tablespoons or 2 liquid ounces	60 milliliters
⅓ cup or 5 tablespoons plus 1 teaspoon	80 milliliters
½ cup or 4 liquid ounces or 8 tablespoons	120 milliliters
⅔ cup or 10 tablespoons plus 2 teaspoons	160 milliliters
¾ cup or 6 liquid ounces	180 milliliters
⅞ cup or 7 liquid ounces	200 milliliters
1 cup or 8 liquid ounces	240 milliliters
4⅓ cups plus 1 tablespoon	1 liter or 1,000 milliliters

American To Metric

American/British	Multiply By	Continental
teaspoons	5	milliliters
tablespoons	15	milliliters
fluid ounces	29.57	milliliters
fluid cups	0.24	liters
pints	0.47	liters
quarts	0.95	liters*
gallons	3.78	liters

Metric To American

Continental	Multiply By	American/British
milliliters	0.2	teaspoons
milliliters	0.6	tablespoons
milliliters	0.03	fluid ounces
milliliters	0.004	fluid cups
liters	0.42	fluid cups
liters	2.11	pints
liters	1.06	quarts**
liters	0.26	gallons

*To convert U.S. quarts to British quarts, multiply the former by 0.80. Then multiply British quarts by 1.14 to get liters.

**To convert to British quarts, multiply by 0.88.

Metric Conversion Chart
Dry Measures

Some of the most common dry measures are listed below.

U.S. Weight Ounces And Pounds	Metric Equivalent
⅓ ounce	10 grams
½ ounce	15 grams
1 ounce	28⅓ grams
1¾ ounces	50 grams
2⅔ ounces	75 grams
4 ounces or ¼ pound	114 grams
1 pound or 16 ounces	464 grams

American To Metric

American/British	Multiply By	Continental
ounces	28.35	grams
pounds	.45	kilograms

Metric To American

Continental	Multiply By	American/British
grams	.035	ounces
kilograms	2.20	pounds

EQUIVALENTS OF COMMON MEASUREMENTS

3 teaspoons	= 1 tablespoon
2 tablespoons	= ⅛ cup (1 ounce)
4 tablespoons	= ¼ cup (2 ounces)
5⅓ tablespoons	= ⅓ cup
8 tablespoons	= ½ cup
10⅔ tablespoons	= ⅔ cup
12 tablespoons	= ¾ cup
16 tablespoons	= 1 cup
2 cups	= 1 pint
4 cups	= 1 quart
¼ lb. butter	= ½ cup (8 tablespoons)
½ lb. butter	= 1 cup (16 tablespoons)
¼ lb. flour	= 1 cup
½ lb. flour	= 2 cups
1 lb. flour	= 4 cups
7 oz. white sugar	= 1 cup
7 oz. brown sugar (packed firm)	= 1 cup
4 oz. confectioners sugar	= 1 cup

LOW SODIUM FOOD MANUFACTURERS AND PRODUCTS

Manufacturer	Products
Adolph's, Ltd. 1800 W. Magnolia Blvd. Burbank, California 91503	Sugar and salt substitutes, low sodium salad dressing
Amurol Products Company 1100 E. Chicago Ave. Naperville, Illinois 60540	Low sodium candies, cookies, gum
Anderson Clayton Foods P.O. Box 35 Dallas, Texas	Chiffon margarine, unsalted
Arcadia Sherman Foods, Inc. 276 Jackson Ave. Bronx, New York 10454	Low sodium salad dressings, fish
Balanced® Foods, Inc., Dist. 700 Grand Ave. Ridgefield, New Jersey 07657	Low sodium mayonnaise, peanut butter, tomato paste; fruits, vegetables, meat, fish, juices
Barton's Candy Corporation Dietetic Division 80 DeKalb Avenue Brooklyn, New York 11201	Low sodium candies, chocolates
Best Foods Division of CPC International, Inc. International Plaza Englewood Cliffs, New Jersey 07632	Unsalted margarine

Bornibus*
58 Boulevard de la Villette
Paris, France

Dijon mustard, salt free

Bread For Life Bakery
3555 Carlota Blvd.
Los Angeles, California 90031

Low sodium breads

Campbell Soup Company
Campbell Place
Camden, New Jersey 08101

Campbell's low sodium soups; V-8 juice

California Peanut Company
Division of Los Angeles Nut House, Inc.
Box 157, Point Station
Richmond, California 94804

Cameo carob chocolates

Caracoa by El Molino Mills
A Division of ACG Company
345 N. Baldwin Pk. Blvd., Box 2250
City of Industry, California 91746

Carob baking powder, powdered drink

Cellu®
Chicago Dietetic Supply, Inc.
405 East Shawmut Ave.
La Grange, Illinois 60525

Low sodium beef and chicken bouillon,
mayonnaise, baking powder

Chicago Dietetic Supply, Inc.
405 East Shawmut Ave.
La Grange, Illinois 60525

Low sodium beef and chicken bouillons,
mayonnaise, baking powder, pickles, ketchup,
juices, vegetables (Cellu and Featherweight)

Devonsheer Melba Corporation
99 Amor Ave.
Carlstadt, New Jersey 07072

Low sodium juices, vegetables

Dia-Mel
Greenwich, Connecticut 06830

Salt substitutes

Diet Delight
Dist. by California Canners and Growers
3100 Ferry Bldg.
San Francisco, California 94106

Low sodium juices, vegetables

Elam Mills Division
National Bakers Services, Inc.
2625 Gardiner Rd.
Broadview, Illinois 60153

Bread and cake flours, cake mixes

Erewhon, Inc.
3 East Street
Cambridge, Massachusetts 02141

Low sodium cheeses, potato chips

Estee Corporation 169 Lackawanna Ave. Parsippany, New Jersey 07054	Low sodium cookies, candies, snack foods
Featherweight Chicago Dietetic Supply, Inc. 405 East Shawmut Ave. La Grange, Illinois 60525	Low sodium pickles, ketchup, juices, vegetables
Flavor Tree Foods, Inc. Franklin Park, Illinois 60131	Low sodium snack foods
General Foods, Inc. 250 North Street White Plains, New York 10600	Low sodium dessert products (D-Zerta)
Hain Pure Food Company 13660 South Figueroa Street Los Angeles, California 90061	Low sodium mayonnaise, unsalted margarine
Health Valley Natural Foods 700 Union Montebello, California 90640	Salt-free cheeses, fish, tomato sauce, chili, low-sodium crackers, potato chips, soups
Holland Honey Cake Company 420 W. 17th St. Holland, Michigan 49422	Low sodium cakes
Keebler Company One Hollow Tree Lane Elmhurst, Illinois 60126	Low sodium crackers
Kellogg Company 235 Porter Street Battle Creek, Michigan 49016	Low sodium cereals
Knox Gelatin 800 Sylvan Ave. Englewood Cliffs, New Jersey 07636	Low sodium gelatin desserts
Kraft, Inc. Kraft Court Glenview, Illinois 60035	Parkay margarine, unsalted
Manna Milling Company, Inc. 827 N.W. 49th Street Seattle, Washington 98107	Salt-free baking mixes
McCormick & Co., Inc. Baltimore, Maryland 21202	Salt substitutes

Metz Baking Company General Office 1014 Nebraska St., P.O. Box 448 Sioux City, Iowa 51102	Master® low sodium crackers
Mother's Food Products, Inc. A Division of Vita Food Products, Inc. 411 W. Putnam Ave. Greenwich, Connecticut 06830	Salt-free borscht, gefilte fish, margarine
Mrs. Wood's Farms Pikle-Rite Company, Inc. Polka Lane Pulaski, Wisconsin 54162	Salt-free pickles, sauerkraut
National Biscuit Company 425 Park Avenue New York, New York 10022	Low sodium cereal, crackers
Norcliff Thayer, Inc. Tuckahoe, New York 10707	Salt substitutes
Ocean Spray Cranberries, Inc. Plymouth, MA 02360	Juices, cranberry sauces
Reine de Dijon* Velars, France 21370	Salt-free mustard
Rokeach & Sons Inc. 560 Sylvan Ave. Englewood Cliffs, New Jersey 07632	Salt-free borscht
Roland American Roland Food Corporation 46 W. 24th St. New York, New York 10010	Low sodium mackerel, sardines
S and W Fine Foods, Inc. 1730 S. El Camino Real San Mateo, California 94402	Low sodium fruits, vegetables
Saucy Susan Products, Inc. 104 Woodside Ave. Briarcliff Manor, New York 10510	Low sodium barbecue sauce
Season Season Products Corporation 34 Loretta St. Irvington, New Jersey 07111	Low sodium mackerel, sardines
Shiloh Farms, Inc. Rte. 59, P.O. Box 97 Sulphur Springs, AR 72768	Salt-free cheeses

Standard Brands, Inc. 625 Madison Avenue New York, New York 10022	Fleischmann's margarine, unsalted
Sunshine Farms Portage, Wisconsin 53901	Salt-free cheeses
Tillie Lewis Foods, Inc. A Subsidiary of Ogden Corporation Drawer J Stockton, California 95201	Low sodium fruits, vegetables, juices, ketchup
Van Brode Milling Company 20 Cameron St. Clinton, Massachusetts 01510	Low sodium cereals
Van Camp Sea Food Company Division of Ralston Purina Company 11555 Sorrento Valley Rd. San Diego, California 92121	Chicken of the Sea unsalted tuna
Venus Wafers, Inc. 144 Penn St. Quincy, Massachusetts 02169	Low sodium wafers, crackers
Wilbur Chocolate Company, Inc. Subsidiary of MacAndrews & Forbes, Co. 48 N. Broad Lititz, Pennsylvania 17543	Low sodium chocolate
Wyler Foods Borden, Inc. 2301 Shermer Rd. Northbrook, Illinois 60062	Low sodium beef and chicken bouillon mixes

*Available in U.S. health food stores.

BIBLIOGRAPHY

Abel, Ronald M., M.D., Abbott, William M., M.D. and Fischer, Josef E., M.D. "Acute Renal Failure." *Arch. Surg.,* Vol. 103 (1971) pp. 513, 514.

American Heart Association. Booklets: *Your 500 Milligrams Sodium Diet. Your 1000 Milligrams Sodium Diet. Your Mild Sodium-Restricted Diet.*

American Spice Trade Association. Booklets: *A Glossary of Spices.* 76 Beaver Street, New York, New York 10005. *A Guide To Spices. A History of Spices. Low Calorie Spice Tips. Low Sodium Spice Tips.* 580 Sylvan Avenue, Englewood Cliffs, New Jersey 07632.

Bagg, Elma W. *Cooking Without A Grain Of Salt.* New York: Doubleday & Company, Inc., 1964.

Bayrd, Edwin. *The Thin Game.* New York: Avon Books, 1978.

Bircher-Benner. *Nutrition Plan For High-Blood Pressure Problems.* Los Angeles: Nash Publishing Corporation, 1973.

———. *Salt-Free Nutrition Plan.* New York: Jove Publishing, Inc., 1978.

Burton, Benjamin T., Ph.D. and Sheridan, Patricia. "What You Should Know About Nutrition." *Pharmacy Times* (December, 1977).

Charback, Elaine. *The Complete Calorie Counter.* New York: Dell Publishing Company, Inc., 1979.

Conason, Emil G., M.D. and Metz, Ella, Dietitian. *The Salt-Free Diet Cookbook.* New York: Grosset & Dunlap, Inc., 1969.

Hills, Charles E., Franke, Ann H., Schuman, Marian, Jacobson, Michael F., Ph.D. and Liebman, Bonnie. *Petition For A Rule To Label The Sodium Content of Foods.* The Center for Science In The Public Interest, 1755 S Street, N.W., Washington, D.C. 20009, 1978.

Jolliffe, Norman, M.D. *The Prudent Diet.* New York: Simon & Schuster, Inc., 1963.

Kassirer, Jerome P., M.D. *Diet Treatment of Chronic Renal Failure.* Abstract and References.

Labuza, T.P. "Defining Research and Development Priorities for Foods to Match Needs of Renal Deficient Consumers." *Food Product Development* (February, 1977) pp. 64–68.

Margie, Joyce Daly, M.S. and Hunt, James C., M.D. *Living with High Blood Pressure.* HLS Press, Inc. 1455 Broad Street, Bloomfield, New Jersey 07003, 1978.

Morrison, Lester, M.D. *The Low-Fat Way to Health & Longer Life.* New York: Arc Books, Inc., 1971.

Moser, Marvin, M.D. Booklet: *A Sensible Low-Salt, Low-Fat Diet.* Reprinted from *Primary Cardiology,* 515 Madison Avenue, New York, New York 10022, 1980.

National Center for Health Statistics—Vital and Health Statistics—Data from the National Health Survey. Series 10, Numbers 83, 84, 92, 94, 99, 109, 121, 123, 124. Hyattsville, Md.

Payne, Alma, M.A. Booklet: *When The Doctor Says: "Limit Sodium"* (Written for Sunkist Growers, Inc.) Box 7888, Van Nuys, California 91409. Adapted from *The Fat And Sodium Control Cookbook.* Boston: Little, Brown & Company, 1975.

Penwalt Prescription Products. *Are You Really Serious About Losing Weight?* 1978.

Pitts, Robert F. *Physiology of the Kidney and Body Fluids.* Chicago: Yearbook Medical Publishers, Inc., 1963.

St. Elizabeth's Hospital of Boston. *To Your Good Health.*

United States Department of Agriculture. Handbook No. 8. U.S. Government Printing Office. Washington, D.C. 20402, 1963.

Whitney, Eleanor Noss and Hamilton, Eva May Nunnelley. *Understanding Nutrition.* St. Paul: West Publishing Company, 1977.

U.S. Department of Agriculture and U.S. Department of Health, Education and Welfare. Booklet: *Nutrition and Your Health.* Washington, D.C. 20402, 1980.

U.S. Department of Health, Education and Welfare. *Fact Sheet: Arteriosclerosis.* Washington, D.C. 20402, 1978.

U.S. Department of Health, Education and Welfare. *Healthy People. The Surgeon General's Report on Health Promotion and Disease Prevention.* Washington, D.C. 20402, 1979.

Whittlesey, Marietta. *Killer Salt.* New York: Avon Books, 1978.

SUBJECT INDEX

RECIPE INDEX

713